The People's War

OTHER BOOKS BY JOHN WILLIS

Churchill's Few

Secret Letters: A Battle of Britain Love Story

Nagasaki: The Forgotten Prisoners

Fighter Boy

The People's War

*Unheard Stories:
Life on the Battlefront and at
Home in World War II*

JOHN WILLIS

BBC BOOKS

UK | USA | Canada | Ireland | Australia
India | New Zealand | South Africa

BBC Books is part of the Penguin Random House group of companies
whose addresses can be found at global.penguinrandomhouse.com

Penguin Random House UK
One Embassy Gardens, 8 Viaduct Gardens, London SW11 7BW

penguin.co.uk
global.penguinrandomhouse.com

First published by BBC Books in 2025

1

Copyright © John Willis 2025
The moral right of the author has been asserted.

Penguin Random House values and supports copyright. Copyright fuels creativity, encourages diverse voices, promotes freedom of expression and supports a vibrant culture. Thank you for purchasing an authorised edition of this book and for respecting intellectual property laws by not reproducing, scanning or distributing any part of it by any means without permission. You are supporting authors and enabling Penguin Random House to continue to publish books for everyone. No part of this book may be used or reproduced in any manner for the purpose of training artificial intelligence technologies or systems. In accordance with Article 4(3) of the DSM Directive 2019/790, Penguin Random House expressly reserves this work from the text and data mining exception.

Typeset in 11.7/16pt Calluna by Jouve (UK), Milton Keynes
Printed and bound in Great Britain by Clays Ltd, Elcograf S.p.A.

The authorised representative in the EEA is Penguin Random House Ireland,
Morrison Chambers, 32 Nassau Street, Dublin D02 YH68

A CIP catalogue record for this book is available from the British Library

ISBN 9781785949005

Penguin Random House is committed to a sustainable future
for our business, our readers and our planet. This book is made
from Forest Stewardship Council® certified paper.

*To Janet, Tom and Vicki, Beth and Jonny,
Teddy and Rose, Lily and Ida.*

Contents

Author's Note	xi
Principal Characters	xv

PART ONE

1.	War, 1939	3
2.	The Phoney War, 1939–40	11
3.	Evacuation, 1939–40	20
4.	The Battle of France, 1940	26
5.	Homefront, 1939–40	36
6.	Dunkirk, 1940	42
7.	Left Behind, 1940	58
8.	Battle of Britain, 1940	64
9.	The Blitz, 1940–41	73
10.	North Africa, 1940–43	85
11.	Tobruk, 1941–42	95
12.	Wartime Women, 1940–44	102
13.	El Alamein, Egypt, 1942–43	117
14.	Enemy Aliens, 1940–43	129
15.	Children, Teenagers and War, 1940–43	133

PART TWO

16.	The Far East, 1941	143
17.	Singapore, 1942	149
18.	Surrender, 1942	159
19.	Escape, 1942	165
20.	Home Guard, 1940–43	171
21.	Prisoners of the Japanese, 1942	179

PART THREE

22.	Britain at Sea, 1940–42	187
23.	Survival, 1942	198
24.	John Gardiner's War, 1940–43	203
25.	Bomber Command, 1942–44	208
26.	Home Life, 1942–43	218
27.	Burma, 1942	225
28.	River Kwai Railway, 1942	231
29.	Douglas and Jean's War, 1942–44	239
30.	Phyllis, 1943–44	247

PART FOUR

31.	Sicily, 1943	253
32.	Monte Cassino, 1944	262
33.	Home, 1944	273
34.	Anzio, 1944	285
35.	Rome, 1944	290

PART FIVE

36.	Resistance, 1943–44	299
37.	D-Day, 1944	312
38.	Normandy, 1944	327
39.	Ron Homes's War, 1944	344
40.	Intelligence and SOE	355
41.	The Yanks Are Coming, 1942–44	362
42.	Burma Advance, 1944–45	375
43.	Prisoners of Japan, 1944	381

PART SIX

44.	Arnhem, 1944	391
45.	Crossing the River Rhine, 1945	409

CONTENTS

46.	Belsen, 1945	415
47.	Germany, 1945	424
48.	VE Day, 1945	433
49.	The Far East, 1945	439
50.	Japan, 1945	444
51.	Homecoming, 1945	454
	Epilogue: Remembrance	461

Bibliography   469
References   471
Acknowledgements   474
Image Credits   476

Author's Note

In 2005, the BBC marked the 60th anniversary of the end of the Second World War by creating a huge oral history project, called 'WW2 People's War', which captured an astonishing 47,000 memories and experiences. This was not a history told by politicians or generals, diplomats or historians, but by ordinary British citizens, a street-level history in their own words.

The BBC engaged with a multiplicity of partners to collect testimonies, including local libraries, charities, museums, and their own local radio stations. Special collection events were held, and a People's War bus toured the country. Over 2,000 volunteers taught older contributors sufficient computer skills to access the People's War website, and 2,000 school lesson plans were developed. When the initiative closed in 2006, over 657,000 people had participated in the project.

I was the BBC's Director of Factual and Learning at the time, and The People's War sat within my department. I claim absolutely no credit for its invention or success, but I had huge admiration for the ambition of the project, which closed just as I left the BBC. This was a public service broadcaster serving the public. As we now mark the 80th anniversary of the Second World War, it is all the more important that, rather than sitting in the British Library, primarily for use by historical researchers, these memories should live again for a wider public, here, in book form.

This is a special archive, not just because of its size and six-year timeline, but because it positively overflows with courage, passion and humour in a way that no other collection can match. These testimonies reflect the lives of ordinary people who experienced extraordinary events – corporals and privates, cooks and nurses, merchant seaman and air gunners, Home Guard and factory workers, Land Girls and schoolchildren.

The People's War conveys a strong sense that many contributors waited years to have their stories heard; there's a feeling of a logjam of memories suddenly released. The book's direction has been dictated by the archive. So, if the strengths of the archive take us from Dunkirk to Singapore, from the Home Front to Monte Cassino, that is where I have followed. In addition, I have included a few short chapters exploring some individual stories that are representative of thousands of other contributors. These include an English schoolboy, a Bomber Command pilot, and a young couple in love.

Of course, a British-based oral history cannot truly reflect other crucial theatres of the war, such as Stalingrad or Okinawa, but the testimonies are still surprisingly international. Americans and Germans, Canadians and West Indians, Poles and Italians sit alongside men and women from every corner of the United Kingdom. Without the sacrifice of troops from Australia and New Zealand, India and Africa, Britain might well not have prevailed.

The testimonies also reflect the freedom unlocked by war. Men and women who had never left their home area, and who had grown up in the drab 1930s, now explored new horizons in places like Egypt or Burma. The incompetence of some of their officers also made them question their existing position in Britain's rigid social hierarchy.

Men and women now in their seventies remembering a wartime childhood have had time to understand and reflect, and these mature reflections add depth to the testimonies. But, after so many years, memories can be hazy, facts can be slippery, and the language potentially inappropriate for today. Human recall is not always perfect. As Canadian Private Stan Scislowski wrote, 'You could talk to five men who were in a certain battle

AUTHOR'S NOTE

and invariably you would hear five different versions of what happened.'

Scislowski, however, checked his stories against other sources as best he could. Not all contributors will have been as diligent. Some testimonies are based on diaries, notes or letters written at the time, but others are told indirectly, often through their children. Dates and places, military affiliations, and the order of events may not always be clear, but what is inescapable are the powerful, visceral experiences that make this such an astonishing overall testimony. Whether they were driving a tank or navigating a bomber or cooking Spam fritters or plotting D-Day, these men and women fought the war twice, first from 1939 to 1945, and then again in their memories.

In this book I have curated a diverse chorus of vivid voices, giving a unique *people*'s account of their war. The selection is mine, but the words belong to the many thousands of people who were part of WW2 People's War. It is time their voices were fully heard once more, and their extraordinary bravery, determination and thoughtfulness celebrated.

John Willis, November 2024

Principal Characters

Douglas Capes, Army dental technician, North Africa and Europe
Jean Clarkson, teacher, Doncaster
Jim Palmer, tank regiment, North Africa, Burma and Europe
Jock Walker, Army cameraman, North Africa, Europe
John Gardiner, schoolboy, England
Len Baynes, prisoner-of-war, Far East
Phyllis Briggs, British nurse, Malaya, Sumatra
Ron Goldstein, British soldier, North Africa, Italy, Germany
Ron Homes, RAF Pilot, Bomber Command
Stan Scislowski, Canadian soldier, Italy
Tim Hardy, paratrooper, Normandy, Malaya
William Nelson, American soldier, D-Day, Normandy
Zygmunt and Marushka Skarbek-Kruszewski, Polish civilians

PART ONE

The gutters and pavements are full of writhing hoses like giant snakes, and above . . . the sky. To the south it is a deep, beautiful blue, but to the north a vision of hell. It is red, it is orange, it is luminous yellow.

Child's view of the Blitz, London, 1940

CHAPTER ONE

War, 1939

It was a time of innocence. It was a time of uncertainty. Young women were fearful for the future and young men just could not imagine the full horror of war, because it was so unimaginable. Their fathers, who had lived through the mud and mustard gas, the slaughter and the sadness of the Great War only twenty years before understood only too well the shattering impact a world war would have on their children. But life had to go on. Children demanded to be clothed and fed, harvests gathered in, schools and hospitals needed to remain open, trains and buses to run on time, and factories kept busy making Spitfires and Bren guns as well as catering to a nation's daily needs.

In Salisbury, Wiltshire, Reverend Samuel Dabill wrote in his diary on 1 September, two days before the declaration of war:

> A day of terror. Unforgettable. Rose this morning to hear that the Germans had invaded Poland and were attacking on all fronts. This made war absolutely certain. Grave looks on all faces . . . vast crowds of children from Portsmouth, which place they are evacuating. They were being marshalled at the Memorial Hall, and they looked a pitiable sight . . . I have always been a pacifist. I have laboured incessantly for peace but there does not seem to be an alternative . . . there is not room in this world for our way and the Nazi way. One or other has to go.

Eighteen-year-old Post Office clerk George York, from Kilburn, North London, had a new girlfriend.

We arranged to meet for our first date on the following Sunday morning for a walk across Hampstead Heath. Our pleasures were simple then! We knew Mr Chamberlain was going to speak on the radio at 11 a.m. and our walk was interrupted by the wail of air raid sirens. We quite literally did not know what to do next.

We stayed holding hands and gazed towards London waiting for the sky to blacken with hundreds of German bombers coming to obliterate London, and probably us with it. We hardly spoke and just occasionally squeezed hands. There were no words of undying love – we had not known each other long enough for that – there was no kissing and cuddling – you did not really do that sort of thing in public in those days. We just sat there and waited for what we thought was inevitable, but nothing happened. After a while the 'all clear' sounded and we knew we were safe, at least until next time.

The next day George's girlfriend joined up.

On our second date there was a surprise. My girl met me kitted out in the blue uniform of the Women's Royal Air Force – hair in a bun, flat shoes, peaked cap, etc . . . we exchanged a letter or two, but she was posted out of London, and we were never able to meet again, and as a result our love withered on the wartime vine.*

Joan Stokoe reflected on that morning as a seven-year-old in Northumberland.

What was so important about 11 o'clock? My parents were talking in undertones . . . I had heard words like Chamberlain, peace, war, Hitler, gas, wet blankets, and Germans – I knew

---

* George served in the Royal Signals in North Africa, Sicily and Italy. He was married in 1947 – not to the girl on Hampstead Heath – and had three children.

they were what you washed off your hands – but nothing else seemed to make sense. What was a Chamberlain?

This morning it seemed to emerge that Chamberlain was a man (nothing to do with a chamber pot)... Mr Chamberlain said in a very grave voice something about the nation being at war. What did that mean? Something horrific because my father said, 'Oh, my God.' 'Oh God help us,' said my mother.

They were talking about the Germans – no, they had nothing to do with dirty hands. They were men from across the sea and would come to kill us. They would also come in aeroplanes and drop gas... *What was gas?* I wondered.

Panic broke out! No one had noticed that my sister had disappeared. Everyone started to look for her. I broke into tears because I knew what had happened. When nobody was looking the Germans had sneaked up and stolen her and would kill her. We would never see her again.

Thomas Russell was a Yorkshire coal miner.

The German Panzers and Stukas were ripping the heart out of Poland, and, as we gathered round the wireless to listen to the radio, knew that only a miracle would make the Germans give up their invasion... Immediately the announcement was made, I looked out and saw the barrage balloons ascending in a huge circle round Sheffield, all silver in the sun.

'That's it then,' my dad said, as we sat down to dinner, 'Bloody Jerries again. So, now you'll have a chance to see what war is about.'

Fifteen-year-old Joan Quibell lived in Birmingham.

My parents sat, solemn and stunned for a few moments. Pop could hardly believe that 20 years of fragile peace since the last conflict was now over, and we were to plunge into fighting again. Mother began to cry, saying it was the end of life as we knew it... I went out and called for Audrey, my best friend. We carried our gas masks, as instructed, in little cardboard boxes suspended by cord on our shoulders and walked in the warm September sunshine. I am ashamed to say that we had no thoughts of the death and destruction which would lie ahead, of the heartache that had already started for many.

Douglas Higgins was aged five at the beginning of the war, living in Hayes, Middlesex.

My memories of WW2 are like a series of photographs... the Sunday morning of 3rd September is fossilised for ever in my memory and is the first faded photograph of WW2... I was halfway up the stairs looking on, sensing that something momentous was about to happen but too young to understand. But I could see Mum had tears in her eyes.

Eleven o'clock struck on Big Ben and a man's voice, Mr Chamberlain, the Prime Minister, filtered into the silence of the hall. I had never known a silence like this before or seen such worry etched on my family's faces – what did it all mean? Apparently, we were at war with Germany. What was war and who were Germany? Whatever it was, my family were unhappy and sad. I rushed down the stairs and clung to my mother, who was gently sobbing. I had never seen her cry before, and I hated the man on the wireless for making her cry. When the man had finished talking, my brother opened the front door and said he was going to 'join up'. My mother attempted to stop him, but the front door slammed.

In Sidcup, Kent, 12-year-old Pauline Edmondson's family readied themselves for war.

We were told how to protect ourselves in the event of a gas attack. Our front room was turned into a 'safe room' – the chimney and every crack were stuffed with paper and the windows sealed. A bowl of water and a blanket were kept in

> there so we could hang a wet blanket over the door in the event of a gas attack, and we had tinned food, containers of water and a primus stove. Nothing was done about sanitary arrangements, so I presume we were meant to hold our breath while we crept out to the loo ... sand and sandbags were delivered to all the houses, and we spent all day filling the bags. They were then stacked round the front of the house, so the windows were barricaded about halfway up. I don't remember that any were put round the back, so I presume we must have expected Hitler to come in the front door if he came calling.

Sixteen-year-old Ken Rawlinson worked in a Buckinghamshire garage.

> On the Monday morning, I went to work as usual to find that the 'guvnor', who was on Army Volunteer Reserve, had gone. He had been called during the night. That left me, and his aged father, in sole charge of his small garage, which changed dramatically overnight.
> Petrol was immediately rationed, cars were requisitioned ... those lovely gleaming cars, their owner's pride and joy, were all sprayed or painted in rough-texture camouflage paint – quite heart-breaking to see.

Dianna Dobinson, aged 19, was upset when her fiancé was dispatched by the Territorial Army to Cornwall.

> I had made all the plans for my wedding in September ... it had to be cancelled ... now barrage balloons, like great silver elephants on wire cables, appeared all over London.

Her wedding plans rudely cancelled because of Hitler's territorial ambitions, Dianna's salvation arrived courtesy of a sympathetic officer at her fiancé's Cornish base. He arranged for Frank to return to London in an Army lorry to pick up supplies.

If Frank could arrange to get married and return with the lorry the next day, it was up to him. The vicar was brilliant, and, with just two witnesses, we were finally married at our lovely local church.

Next morning, we had to make a very early start as the army lorry was coming to pick my new husband up. It arrived, with much hooting, and all the lads jumped out and insisted on kissing the bride. I waved them off, wondering when I would see Frank again.

Just before the declaration of war, 19-year-old Len Baynes, 1st Battalion, Cambridgeshire Regiment, was posted to RAF Duxford, near Cambridge, to guard their precious array of Spitfire fighter aircraft. Len was startlingly badly equipped.

We arrived on station with only the clothes we stood up in and our 1914-dated Short Enfield rifles. My ammo, as I recall, was stamped 1917. Before fighting the Luftwaffe, we had to find somewhere to doss down, as the RAF quartermaster, it seemed, was disinclined to share the airmen's accommodation with common soldiers. In the end it was the padre who provided the solution. Following the Barnardo dictum, 'No one turned away', he allowed us to sleep on the floor of the church. The next day further research revealed a First World War weapons store somewhere or other. We were introduced to half-a-dozen grease-encased Lewis guns, and one tattered manual.

Seventeen-year-old Tim Hardy (christened Stanley), from a large coal-mining family in Sutton-in-Ashfield, Nottinghamshire, knew war was close.

Even in Sutton's soot-laden atmosphere you could smell cordite: a great war was in the air . . . on one hand the flag-waving and tub-thumping offended my pacifism, on the other some of the things being done in the world were enough to provoke saints to reach for guns ... Europeans were being killed by jack-booted sadists simply because they believed in the equality of all men or because they were short on foreskins or read the wrong books.

Ronald Smith, Somerset, was a devout Christian and conscientious objector.

> How could a Christian go out killing people? That was murder, I could not do that. I believed in peace not war ... one of the sidesmen told me how he was a conscientious objector in the First World War and how some conscientious objectors were shot, not officially, of course, but you know how there are 'accidents' in war. The vicar was preaching peace the week before it started and then preaching war two weeks later. How could that be? Had GOD suddenly changed HIS mind?
>
> Glastonbury was a small town, and reports of a conscientious objector were reported in a local paper. I was refused chocolate in the local sweet shop although I had the necessary coupons and money. Families were split up over the issue, for the war and against the war. It was extra hard for me because my father, Major Frank Smith OBE, fought in the First World War, 1914–18. He wrote me a letter saying he could get me a nice safe job with the Pay Corps in Exeter, with him. I resented this.

Britain's declaration of war was celebrated with renewed hope in Poland. Zygmunt Skarbek-Kruszewski:

> I heard the paperboy's 'Extra! Extra! Britain and France declare war against Germany!' The boys were running through the streets, the trams, and the cafes. Within seconds they were surrounded, and the edition was hurriedly grabbed ... a new spirit, full of hope, came over Warsaw and all of Poland. Although it had been expected, the established fact had a

tremendous uplifting power. All Warsaw spoke about it. Everyone was cheering everyone else, even scoffing at the German danger.

As I was hungry, I went into a pub. 'Hallo Karol, to Britain's health,' called someone, lifting his glass. 'Yes, sure, Britain is a power, sir, the Queen of the Seas. When she takes the business in hand, she will make mincemeat of them.'

CHAPTER TWO

The Phoney War, 1939–40

Despite the confidence expressed in the pub in Poland, within a month of the declaration of war Zygmunt's home city, Warsaw, had been taken by the Nazis. In Africa, Germany's Italian partners had already conquered Ethiopia, and Mussolini was contemplating further expansion. In the east a territorially ambitious Japan was at war with China, which it had invaded on 7 July 1937, signalling what some regard as the alternative starting date of the Second World War.

But in Britain the eight months after Chamberlain's speech were confusingly peaceful. Gas masks mouldered unused; bomb shelters echoed with silence; after a short pause, cinemas, dance halls and theatres burst with noise. This was soon nicknamed The Phoney War, and everyone hoped it would last.

But, underneath the apparent normality, Britain was filled with fear. By the end of 1939 over 1.5 million men had been conscripted into the forces and, although not yet facing enemy fire, their world had shifted from factory and office to parade ground.

The apparent calm of the Phoney War was rudely disturbed on the night of 13/14 October 1939. British battleship HMS *Royal Oak* was at rest in the safe harbour of Scapa Flow in the Orkneys when it was torpedoed by the German submarine U-47, with the catastrophic loss of 833 lives in just one night. If Scapa Flow could be penetrated by the enemy just six weeks after the start of the war, then nowhere was safe, an anxious nation thought.

In Nottinghamshire, Tim Hardy was desperate to escape his tedious job at the hosiery company he had joined aged 14. So, he signed up for the Territorial Army, Sherwood Foresters.

> H. and C. H. Blinkhorn, Hosiery Manufacturers, were bound by law to release me when the army so ordered, and to welcome me back as an heroic defender of the realm... by trebling my annual seven days holiday entitlement I was giving the finger to Blinckhorns, who didn't hold with holidays, and given a chance to see distant places for free and, as a bonus, I was to be taught to kill people like Hitler, which I badly wanted to do. Anyway, the upshot was I shamefacedly took part in one of the many childish rites that makes up the ridiculous mummery by which the British establishment binds its masses to their vassal status – I took the 'King's Shilling.'

While Tim Hardy dreamt of war, the British Expeditionary Force (BEF), a defensive contingent of the British Army, began more serious preparations. The day after war was declared the BEF started moving to Northern France and, by May 1940, it comprised 390,000 men. Reg Gill, a radiographer at Leeds General Infirmary, was deployed to Etaples on the coast in a freezing train. He noticed a large sign proclaiming: KEEP YOUR MOUTHS SHUT AND BOWELS OPEN.

> It was 2 a.m. and bitterly cold. We were hungry enough for cannibalism but no one in my compartment looked edible... boots were frozen to the floor. To get them off the following morning you had to borrow a mallet and actually hammer them from the floor... the only standpipe on the site was frozen solid and was just one enormous icicle. We were told that this site, this icy wilderness, was to be the 18th General Hospital and that marquees had to be erected, roads built and electricity laid on.

THE PHONEY WAR, 1939-40

But Reg Gill was soon enjoying the Phoney War.

> We reached a high state of civilisation. Every morning the local patisserie would send a van round full of goodies – cream things, chocolate eclairs, beautiful bread and cakes.

Near the champagne heartland of Reims, the RAF requisitioned a chateau to house 80 officers and their support staff. Beer tankards overflowed with champagne. One officer wrote to his grandson after the war that 'we went on consuming hundreds of bottles of champagne, popping off corks in the garden for target practice'.

Arriving in Brest, Ken Potter, 98th Field Regiment, was soon out on the town.

> A group of 'young gentlemen' of the Regimental Headquarters Mess, of which I was now a member, invited me to join them for champagne cocktails in a local *estaminet*. Never having savoured champagne cocktails or been in an *estaminet*, I accepted with pleasure ... the plan of action would be to have champagne cocktails followed by oysters ... followed by trout, *pomme frites*, and straight champagne.

In 1934 publican's son, 18-year-old Sergeant Gordon 'Jock' Walker, spurred on by the lack of civilian jobs in depressed 1930s Glasgow, enlisted as a regular soldier, a despatch rider with the Royal Signals.

Sgt Gordon 'Jock' Walker

His remarkable war included service at Dunkirk, North Africa, Sicily, Normandy, Arnhem, Germany and Belsen Concentration Camp. Toughened by five years as a regular soldier, Jock was relaxed when war beckoned.

> Quite truthfully, I was quite happy about it; a small war to round off a few years of soldiering would be 'just the job', in my opinion, and, after a week or so, we embarked for France with the British Expeditionary Force without a care, and, thank goodness, without the foreboding of what was to come in the next six years.

Landing at Cherbourg, Jock was underwhelmed.

> My first impression of it was gloomy. French soldiers on guard at the docks were unshaven, leaning against walls with their hands in their pockets and, horror of horrors, their rifles leaning negligently against the aforesaid walls. There was a general air of 'laissez-faire' about the whole place and it stank with an unwholesome, fishy smell.

Inactivity meant Walker's unit soon descended into what he called 'a semblance of barrack life', with regular trips into the nearby towns, Douai and Lille.

> For us Douai was the most popular. I don't know why, perhaps the cafes were more pleasant... in Douai the girls were knickerless, but with tops, and in Lille they were topless but fully knickered. Strange people, the French, but likeable.

To Geoff Nickolds, St Nazaire was less welcoming.

> A warning was given to us not to go into town and especially to the red-light district. Some idiots ignored this advice. One was found in the dock with a knife in his back.

In Nottinghamshire, 17-year-old Sherwood Forester Tim Hardy was eager to chase Hitler, but his age was against him.

Early in 1940 my rag-tag, ruffianly regiment was ordered to France, a deployment which if noted by his intelligence people would have done Hitler's morale a world of good. Not for me, however, the delights of the *filles de joie* or the culinary marvels of Gaul; not being 18 I couldn't be sent to the frontline.

Disguised in an ill-fitting uniform, I stood guard over our sacred realm – in reality a piddling little airstrip at Hucknall Torkard ... I'd been given a 1914–18 rifle and bayonet ... a ridiculous tent-shaped cap that wouldn't stay on my head, a pair of second-hand hobnailed boots with puttees I never could fasten properly ... and a cap badge saying 'Sherwood Foresters'. Robin Hood would have been disgusted.

Decked out thus, throughout the first winter of the war I stood guard over crappy little outposts that Hitler in his craziest, carpet-chewing moments couldn't have possibly wanted to seize.

Jim Palmer, from a 'less salubrious district of Manchester', was called up to the 3rd Tank Regiment at Warminster, Wiltshire, on his 21st birthday. He bid an emotional railway-station farewell to his girlfriend, Muriel, and his widowed father.

Muriel was in tears and clung to my arm. And Dad turned away when she kissed me. It was all so dramatic and a lump

Jim Palmer

in my throat prevented me from saying much . . . It was with some relief that I scrambled into the carriage and watched the platform fall away behind me. Dad was stood with his arm round Muriel, who was sobbing, and I watched until the bend in the line cut off my view of the platform. I was on my way to God knows what.

In Warsaw, Zygmunt Skarbek-Kruszewski had already experienced the relentless air raids that Britain was anxiously anticipating.

> One could hear the grim wail of the alarm siren – at first the one farther away not so loud, more subdued, then the nearer ones louder and more piercing, and lastly, the nearest one, which shook the house with the piercing sound of maddening fright. The house was teeming like an anthill disturbed by a kick. On the staircases people were running with bundles and suitcases, women with children were carefully descending to the basement. Banging doors, fragments of unfinished sentences, calling and yelling.
>
> Above our part of the city an air battle was in progress. The planes in the sky were like a disturbed flock of crows, flying haphazardly above the city, turning, zigzagging. The whole sky was covered with tiny clouds, some were pursuing the planes as if trying to catch them . . .

This air battle was successful for the Polish pilots, who shot down an enemy aircraft.

> The charred bodies of two young German fliers under the debris of the plane gave off an odour of burnt, singed flesh . . . from a nearby florists, ladies brought flowers and started throwing them over the young Polish officer who was saluting to all sides. His eyes were shining excitedly, and he was very proud. He was the hero of the day. On his chest was a cross of valour and on his conscience were two more human lives.

As a Ministry of Foreign Affairs employee, Zygmunt was ordered to head immediately to the station for evacuation. His overwhelming concern was for his Lithuanian wife, Marushka, who should now be back in her neutral homeland with her mother. How could Zygmunt let her know about his evacuation into uncertainty? He tried to telephone her from the single kiosk at the station.

> The queue for the telephone was long. Many were waiting to contact their nearest before going into the unknown. When I was only a couple of people away from the front of the queue, the alert sounded. The lady from the kiosk locked her door and I ran to the trenches.

This rude interruption happened several times. Zygmunt and the restless queue were growing desperate. He joined the long line once more.

> I turned round ... and stood rooted to the spot, unable to believe my eyes. In the queue, right behind me, was my wife. She was standing with her hand in the pockets of her brown coat, from under her beret masses of red-brown curls tumbled onto her collar. She saw me and her eyes filled with tears.
>
> We fell into each other's arms. Without speaking, Marushka started to cry soundlessly on my shoulder. Her wordless weeping told me more than the most elaborate phrases could have done. A chance of perhaps one in a million for a truly miraculous meeting. Had we missed each other, our fate would have been totally different for the rest of our lives.
>
> We did not need the telephone anymore. We left, holding hands and, without words, knew that from then on, we would not be separated.

But for Jews in Germany there had never been a Phoney War. Eight-year-old Rolf Heymann was one of 133 Jews in a village of 2,000 outside Munich. In November 1938 he witnessed the horrors of Kristallnacht, 'the night of the breaking glass', the savage Nazi pogrom targeting the Jews.

> I was hiding in the cellar with my mum and aunty. We heard this terrible noise of the shattering of wood and the smashing of glass. Even though we had put shutters over the windows an axe came smashing through each shutter, and the noise was just terrible... I was so frightened, I thought they would come into our house and kill us.

Rolf's mother sent her young son to England, one of around 10,000 mainly Jewish children on the Kindertransport, which was authorised by the British government but usually arranged by charities and individuals. Rolf was met at Harwich by his cousin from Sheffield, whose family had wisely escaped Nazi Germany even earlier.

> I arrived in Sheffield with my little suitcase, about one foot high and one foot wide, which contained my underclothes... I went to Park School, which was then a very rough school. The kids were so tough that if they did not have a football, they would head a house brick... I did not get the beatings because I was Jewish like the ones I got in Germany.
>
> Just under 40 of my relatives perished... I had two cousins, twins Inger and Ludwig. They were sent to Auschwitz Concentration Camp. There Dr Josef Mengele had a special interest in twins... he destroyed Inger's ovaries and sterilised Ludwig. They were only a year older than me... they survived because Mengele was experimenting on them.

After the war Rolf stayed in Sheffield, working in the scrap-metal business there, married a local girl, and raised a family.

Trude Feige's sons also arrived in Sheffield, on the Kindertransport from Czechoslovakia. Trude wrote a goodbye letter to them.

> We want to say farewell to you, who were our dearest possession in the world and only for a short time were we able to keep you... Grandmother Betty [was taken]... Aunt Marion, Uncle Will and Paul... your Steiner grandparents... your 90-year-old grandmother... [soon] it will be our turn. We are going on to the unknown; not a word is to be heard from those already taken.
>
> Thank those who have kept you from a similar fate. You took a piece of your poor parents' hearts with you when we decided to give you away.

Their father, Curt, added:

> Your dear mother has told you about the hard fate of all our loved ones. We too will not be spared and will go bravely into the unknown, with the hope that we shall yet see you again when God wills. Don't forget us and be good.

Trude and Curt Feige never saw their sons again. They both died in Auschwitz.

CHAPTER THREE

Evacuation, 1939–40

The evacuation of children from British cities into the safety of the countryside rapidly began. Ultimately, over three million children and adults were shifted to rural locations in the biggest movement of humans in British history. John Pavis was evacuated to a farm in Launceston, Cornwall.

> I suppose these days if someone were to suggest that you pack a few clothes in a small suitcase, pin an address label on your six-year-old child, take him to the station to be handed over to complete strangers, where he would be put on a train to travel hundreds of miles, not knowing when you would see him again, you would be horrified, and rightly so. But that is exactly what happened to me, and thousands like me.

Soon after arrival, John's mother died, leaving him with his kindly host couple for five more years.

> I became a proper 'farmer's boy' doing many jobs around the farm. Fetching cows and helping with the milking, all by hand, of course! Feeding the fowls and collecting eggs. Helping at harvest and with the threshing.

Iris Clark was only six.

> We all had a brown label with our name and age on it. I remember a lot of the children and mothers crying. I had tears

in my eyes saying goodbye to my mother and brother. I said I would write to my mother when I got there, so she would know where I was, as no one knew where we were going.

We were told to gather our things together and to hold hands and walk in twos. We got off the train and walked into a building where everything was pitch black except for some torch lights. We went into this building, and we were blinded for a second by the lights. We were told to stand in a row... names were called out and children went away with different persons.

The place I was staying in was called Brereton, near Rugely, Staffordshire. About Mr and Mrs Haycock, whom I soon called Mum and Dad number two, I class myself very lucky to stay with them. I was treated as one of the family. I knew other evacuees who were not so lucky.

Ivor Ball was equally fortunate. He was evacuated from Folkestone, home to several frontline RAF bases, to Tintern, Wales.

We were greeted by our foster mum, who soon made us welcome. Little did I know I was going to spend some of the happiest days of my life in my short stay in her home.

I awoke the next morning and looked out of the window to a very peaceful scene. The River Wye was drifting silently by, glistening in the sunshine, a slight mist lifting from the waters... the scene was in complete contrast to the sound of heavy gunfire across the Channel [from Folkestone].

In the Yorkshire fishing village of Staithes, evacuees were the answer to Ken Verrill's teenage dreams.

The townies, as we called them, had lived an entirely different life from us... And we spent a great deal of time holding hands and touching each other under the desks... walking back to school we used to pair off and dodge behind the hedge for a cuddle. We learned a lot about nature behind the hedge.

At 98, Ron Jervis is one of a tiny number of evacuees still alive. He departed from Stratford in East London, completely responsible for his five-year-old brother.

> Women all around were crying, kids were crying, it was chaos... there were no toilets on the train, so the boys peed out of the window. I don't know what the girls did.

Ron returned to his evacuee home on a chicken farm at Ardleigh in Essex to work after the war.

> Being an evacuee changed my life for ever.

But not all evacuees were as happy. East Londoner Donald Wharf's experience was rather less cheerful.

> We arrived about lunchtime in Shrivenham, Berkshire... we all had to strip and stand in a line to see an elderly nurse; mainly, I think, to ensure we were clean and free from the dreaded head lice.

Two little girls arrived wearing headscarves.

> Both, it turned out, were in total disgrace; they had nits – the eggs of the head lice – and, according to someone who knew the two girls, the nurse had just shaved all their hair off... I felt sorry for them.

Londoner Audrey Jones was just five when she was shipped to Bletchington (also known as Bletchingdon), near Oxford, with her six-year-old sister, Edna.

> In retrospect we were treated in a similar fashion to cattle, as the villagers came and looked us over and selected and rejected... Edna and myself were the last to be selected. Many people had chosen Edna, as she was a very sweet-looking six-year-old with lovely blonde hair and blue eyes, whereas yours truly was a plain redhead with

protruding red cheeks who sat all the time under a table wetting herself.

Audrey and Edna missed their mother so much they tried an unusual postal experiment.

> Edna tried to roll me into a brown paper parcel and find a letter box big enough to post me home to London.
>
> The bedwetting continued every night, and I now realise how very difficult it was for them . . . we went to bed every night and prayed to God not to let us wet the bed. One morning we awoke to find the bed drenched as usual and Mrs Taylor was even more angry than usual. It was a sheer icicle day, and she shoved me first into the backyard – naked – and threw a pail of freezing water over me, then proceeded to break the ice in the water butt to throw at me. It was like shards of glass hitting my body and, of course, drew blood. The next-door neighbour banged on his/her kitchen window, so I was unceremoniously dragged indoors and thrown on the kitchen floor, where I cut my head on the flagstones, and still sport the scar 60 years on.

Val Shoulder was evacuated to rural Herefordshire.

> At the tender age of six I was expected to help with the housework, which included black-leading the kitchen range and scrubbing the stone-floored passage . . . water was obtained from the river which ran about fifty yards from the back door. It was usually my job to fetch the bucket which would sometimes be full to overflowing and too heavy for me.
>
> Yet when the war ended, I found myself very homesick for this Spartan village life . . . It did not help that I returned to a very unhappy home where my father would knock my mother about, often resulting in her ending up in hospital.

Brian Proctor from York was among 2,600 children evacuated to the other side of the world.

Mum and Dad latched on to the idea of joining the CORB scheme (Children's Overseas Reception Board) to send us away to safety briefly (or so they thought) . . . my parents asked me which I preferred, cowboys or kangaroos, and so I chose Canada. I was nearly eight years old, and I wouldn't see my mother and father again for five years.

An anonymous 14-year-old girl wrote about her own evacuation to Canada:

Two girls, one aged 14, the other nearly 11, stand at the entrance to the pier in Liverpool. Somewhere in the background, a ship. There is a wooden barrier. They stand on one side, their parents on the other. The older child looks with anguish and embarrassment at her mother's face streaming tears, her father's face twitching . . . an adult leads all the children away into an almost empty warehouse, where they are told to sit on whatever is handy. They sit, numb, hardly noticing each other. Eventually, an uneasy adult makes them all sing. Sing what? No idea, all that is left is the grotesque memory of singing, of myself watching us singing as though watching a movie, of being outside it all.*

Eight-year-old Trevor Sawtell lived in Ebbw Vale, South Wales.

Local mountain ponies and sheep roamed everywhere about the town with an air of being our equals. The evacuees thought this was very peculiar . . . ponies and sheep urinating and defecating about the town made their amazement complete.

The evacuees offered Trevor glimpses into a different world.

Of all the evacuees, none attracted more attention than the family who came to us from London. The father was black,

---

* One evacuation ship to North America, *City of Benares*, was sunk in September 1940 with 248 dead, including 77 children.

the children coffee-coloured, and the mother white. Most of the people in Ebbw Vale had never seen a black person in the flesh, let alone a multi-coloured family. They were therefore considered to be very strange, rarities which must be observed at every opportunity; they were stared at in the street . . . we children used to wait outside their house in the hope of seeing a member of this most peculiar family.

Many women considered the white mother 'a fallen woman' for having broken what was then the taboo of marrying a black man. The family must have been aware of our offensive reaction to them. It was, in a sense, a kind of racism based on hurtful curiosity and the ignorance of living in a quiet backwater.

Once people got used to the family, they became part of our community. They did not return to London at the end of the war but remained in Ebbw Vale, where their children married and raised children of their own. This fact is a salve to my conscience, and perhaps the consciences of others too.

CHAPTER FOUR

The Battle of France, 1940

On 10 May 1940, the Phoney War ended abruptly when Germany invaded France, as well as neutral Luxembourg, Belgium and the Netherlands; an unpleasant welcome present for Britain's new Prime Minister, Winston Churchill, appointed that same day. Three days later Churchill famously told the nation: 'I have nothing to offer you but blood, toil, sweat and tears.'

In the military hospital in Etaples, Sgt Reg Gill from Leeds was still relaxed.

> We weren't unduly worried. The French were confident that the Maginot Line would hold, and the papers told us that the British Army was the finest to have ever set foot on foreign soil.

Sixty miles to the east in Arras, Geoff Myers had also been reassured.

Geoff had been a British journalist with the *Morning Post*, reporting from 1930s Berlin. As a Jew, he saw close up how dangerous the Nazis were. Now he was attached to RAF Photographic Intelligence in Arras, where he was billeted with a family who were certain the French would hold their defensive line.

> The Maginot Line ... have you seen it, monsieur? We saw bits of it on the films. Wonderful!

Geoff Myers wrote letters to his French wife, who was living with their two tiny children in what was soon to be German-occupied

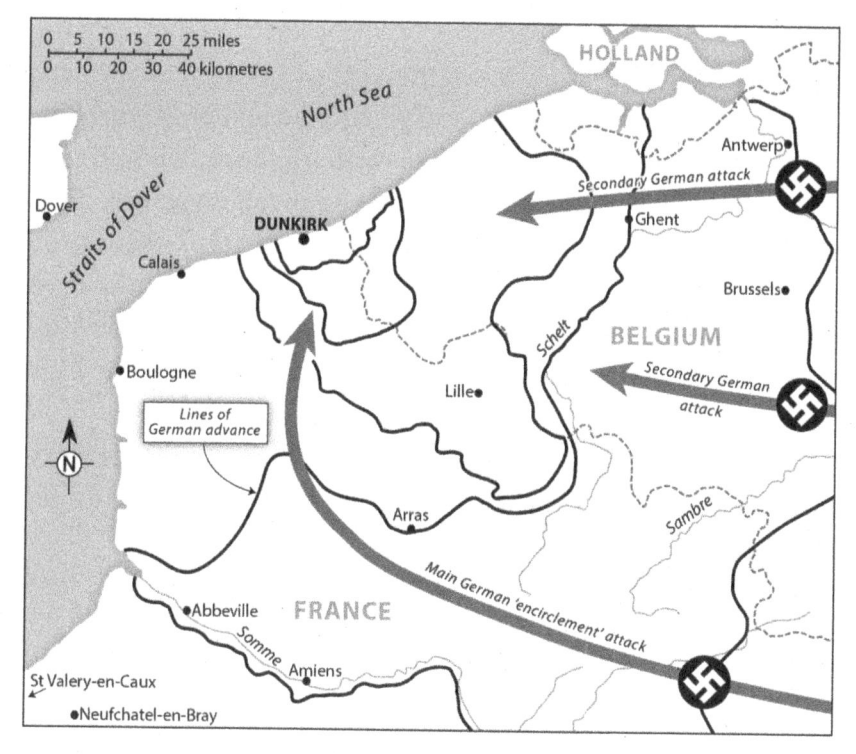

Maginot Line, 1940

France. Myers never sent his letters, because it was far too dangerous; he was a Jewish RAF officer, and his family were living under the noses of the Germans. The letters were to be read after the war – if they were both lucky enough to survive.

> It looked peaceful enough here. In the cafes of Arras, British soldiers were drinking beer, playing their mouth organs, and singing ... officers were in the Café de l'Univers, passing their time over gins and champagne ... I saw the signpost of the Imperial War Graves Commission. Hundreds of British soldiers had been buried here in a common grave. As I walked on, the orange sunlight splashed over the clay-filled sand and gave a touch of richness to the barren uplands. I came across a trench which was overgrown and dated from the last war. And now we were at war again.

Confidence in French defences was misplaced. The Germans sidestepped the best-fortified section of the Maginot Line where over 400,000 French troops were positioned and broke through the wooded area of the Ardennes, which France believed was an impossible terrain for tanks, and swept rapidly south. This was Hitler's *blitzkreig*, or 'lightning war', a rapid tank-led assault supported by bombs and bullets from screeching Stuka dive bombers. Just ten days later, the Nazis had reached Abbeville, near the Channel coast, and British troops were threatened with being cut off.

The hospital in Etaples, 16 miles south of Boulogne, was rapidly evacuated, and medic Reg Gill, well fed on French cuisine, marched north.

> Life was very good ... and then it happened ... The roads were completely choked with refugees ... poor Belgian peasants in carts with women, children, animals and bikes. Overhead were swarms of German bombers, German fighters machine-gunning the roads, anything that moved ...

Edwin Parsons was a tank driver with the 9th Queen's Royal Lancers.

> The poor state of readiness of the regiment can be realised when one considers that it had one tank with a turret made of plywood and another was fitted with a howitzer but had no ammunition, and the regiment had been issued with a new Besa machine gun, but no one had been trained in its use.

Edwin spotted British soldiers by the roadside sitting on tanks.

> The exterior storage boxes of the tanks were open and full of wine and cheese. Edwin helped himself and climbed up on the tank ... as he went to open a turret hatch an old soldier stopped him, 'You don't want to look in there.' These tanks

had been recovered from the battlefield and the remains of the crews were still inside.

Jim Palmer's baptism into the madness of war made his tearful farewell to his girlfriend, Muriel, in Manchester seem like a distant memory. On 19 May 1940, the 3rd Tank Regiment arrived to pick up their tanks at Neufchatel-en-Bray station, 35 miles south of Abbeville, when his train was attacked.

> Out of the sun came a group of small planes and with a sickening shriek, the bombs began to fall. A mad dash ensued. Some of us dived under the train and others threw themselves flat on their faces. Some ran and didn't stop, and others were too petrified to move but just looked up at the sky and watched the little black 'blobs' falling in a gentle curve to the ground. You could feel the earth around you lift as they exploded. As a farewell gesture, the planes circled slowly and came along the length of the train with their machine guns chattering.

Having survived the train attack, Jim Palmer and a friend were deployed towards Abbeville in a regimental Scout Car. They drove through a deserted farmyard and heard cows frantically mooing.

> Three cows gazed at us with big, brown, watery eyes. I had never thought about cows' eyes before, but now I was moved. Never had I seen such pleading for help, and although I was city-bred, I knew at once what the trouble was ... milking cows was not part of my brief, but this was an emergency.

Ironically for a boy from inner-city Manchester, his regiment's nickname was the 'Armoured Farmers'. But that didn't bless Jim with cow-milking experience. After an hour of pain for the cows and limited success for the soldiers, Jim wearily stood back to have a cup of tea with what little milk they had liberated.

> Then it happened! All bloody hell broke loose, and we were flung about like chips of wood ... the crash and crump

knocked us both flat amongst the straw, and flames sprung up all over the place. Another crump and a wall crashed down, followed by another, and it seemed like the whole world was full of flying bricks . . . the roof of the farm was burning, and the barn was belching smoke. The cows would groan no more. One was on its side with its entrails spilled amongst the straw. They were a deep red and rosy-pink, with long ribbons of violet-coloured stuff dangling like worms between its legs.

Our faces were black, and our hands could not stop trembling . . . I felt sick, and my legs seemed heavy and not part of me. A cold sweat ran down my face and back. I couldn't think of anything but the scream of shells as they hit the farm . . . my eyes were stinging and I realised I was crying, but I did not feel shame for my tears.

Attacked on his army train, shelled in a French farmyard, Jim Palmer was no safer when reunited with his tank squadron.*

As we topped the rise, anti-tank guns hit us from the right flank and four tanks were ablaze before we had gone ten yards. We were sitting ducks, and it was sheer murder . . . all around was the smell of cordite and burning and the dust rose in clouds. The noise was unbelievable and through the noise could be heard the screams and cries of dying men . . . Beside the tanks men were huddled, holding torn arms and screaming for help, and some were running among the trees with clothes burning like torches. Shells were whining and clumping, and the air was full of smoke and shrapnel. Men were dragging their pals through the mud, away from the burning tanks, and the smell of burnt flesh was catching my throat . . . our casualties that day were over 20 killed and 23 injured.

* Troops usually consisted of four tanks each, and four troops made a tank squadron.

Sergeant Jock Walker, Royal Signals, from Glasgow, was forced to give up his jaunty visits to the bars of Lille and Douai and was pushed south by the superior Nazi forces.

> We did not know what was happening and the thought of the enemy getting the upper hand did not occur to any of us, that is until we received our first blast of the hot breath of Mars in the shape of a Ju 87, the German dive bomber.
>
> How our little convoy ever got through unscathed will always be a mystery to me. Our collective guardian angels must have spread their wings over us because the death and destruction around us was fearful; buildings crashing down, people wounded, and dead horses screaming, and above it all the hellish whine of the dive bombers as they carried out their tactics of mass execution and disruption.

Nineteen-year-old Laurie Dorins, Royal Engineers, travelled in an army lorry. His war was over before it started.

> There was a sudden crash, and a tank burst through the hedge, hit a telegraph pole which broke and fell across the back of the lorry, covering it with wires. To add to our alarm the tank began to fire bursts of tracer bullets over our heads.
>
> A British Major who spoke some German shouted for us to put our hands up and climb down from the lorry.
>
> Facing us was a machine gun on a tripod and beside us a couple of large carthorses. It looked like a choice of being shot or trampled to death. The Major told us that, according to the Germans, the British were firing on them further down the road and they were going to shoot us... I thought of my mother and home and that this was to be the end of my short life... I don't know why our lives were spared.

Britain was in a dilemma about how much aerial support could be spared in the Battle of France. Prime Minister Winston Churchill did not want to let his French allies down, but Air Chief Marshal Dowding, leading Fighter Command, believed that the rationing of modern fighter aircraft was essential for Britain to survive a likely German onslaught. Dowding wrote to the Air Council on 16 May bluntly expressing his concerns: 'The Hurricane Squadrons remaining in this country are seriously depleted, and the more Squadrons that are sent to France the higher will be the wastage... If the Home Defence Force is drained away in desperate attempts to remedy the situation in France, defeat in France will involve the final, complete, irremediable, defeat of this country.'

The RAF defended France largely with outdated aircraft like the Battle bomber, and the Blenheim fighter/bomber. They were flown heroically but were no match for the Messerschmitt 109, which could fly almost twice as fast as a Battle. Ted Cowling was a Battle wireless operator/gunner.

> I could see the German fighter in the spider's web of my gunsights... I squeezed the trigger with all my might, and I saw tracer bullets rip into his fuselage, peppering the black cross painted below the cockpit. At the same time the German pilot started firing at us, and I could see the flashes from his wing-mounted cannons spitting certain death straight at me. Time seemed to slow for those few seconds; there was no sound, no feeling. I was transfixed by the machine rushing towards me, waiting for the searing pain as the hot metal entered my body. But the impact of my own bullets had been enough to spoil his aim, and the shells flew over our heads.
>
> I am not sure whether I shot down that Me 109, or just riddled it with bullets, and I don't know what happened to the pilot... I didn't know and I didn't care. Had I not fired my guns first the German pilot would have shot us down and killed us... it was war.

> When we landed, we were one of only eight planes to return from the 25 that had taken off. Another 51 airmen had been lost that day. Another 51 husbands, sons, boyfriends...

On 14 May, 19-year-old Blenheim Air-Gunner Jack Bartley, 21 Squadron, flew from RAF Watton, Norfolk, to attack German armoured columns moving south from Belgium.

> I fought down that feeling of over-excitement mixed with not a little fear that seems to bring your heart into your mouth and keep it there... I watched the chalk cliffs slowly grow indistinct in the summer haze, never before had I felt quite so wistful towards them or realised fully how much they really meant to me on that warm afternoon in May.

The night before, Bartley was teased that it was his 'turn'. All the other gunners with surnames beginning with B – Birch, Ball, Burgess – had been killed. Even Charlton, a C, was dead, so Bartley must be next. As he spotted an Me 109 heading his way, Jack thought that might be the case.

> At 200 yards he started firing, giving the appearance of blowing smoke rings from his leading edges... I gave him all I had as he neared the 50 yards range, keeping my trigger depressed and seeing my tracers going firstly into his port wing and then into his fuselage.
>
> I felt a terrible pain in my back as if a red-hot poker had been thrust into it, and turned to see a second 109... he closed in until his machine guns sounded like a much accentuated typewriter... my heart missed a beat or two when I found my turret would no longer respond to pressure – the hydraulics were evidently severed... I was, in effect, disarmed.
>
> Placing my hand to my aching back, I brought it away covered with blood, and a feeling of nausea swept over me. Blood was also streaming from a wound in my thigh... more

jagged rips appeared in the already riddled fuselage, bullets whipped inside the machine clanging against metal . . . I had not much longer to live.

But Jack's determined pilot, Sergeant Johnny Outhwaite, found a relatively flat stretch of grassland.

I saw the ground approaching through the rips in the metal fuselage, heard the swish of air as the flaps lowered and a crash that shook every bone of my body as I was thrown from my grip, dashed against the ceiling of the fuselage and down again two or three times, until, with a scraping and a rendering, the battered machine came to a halt and all was curiously quiet.

I fell to the ground, weak, sick and exhausted, but with that triumphant feeling of exhilaration that only those who have passed through the Valley of Death and survived can ever know.

Four weeks after this brilliant and brave landing, Jack's pilot, Sgt Johnny Outhwaite, was killed over France.

In London, Churchill was eventually persuaded by Dowding to preserve the nation's remaining Hurricanes and Spitfires for the next crucial battle.

Back in Arras, Geoff Myers and his Photographic Intelligence Unit were more concerned about surviving this one, as the Germans swiftly advanced. In an unsent letter to his wife in France, he wrote:

Like ripples of the incoming tide approaching a child's sandcastle the Germans came. Little by little, nearer to Arras. The signals from our missions grew more desperate.

The unit at Arras burned any documents that might help the enemy. Geoff Myers volunteered to dash back to Intelligence Headquarters to retrieve more secret documents they had left behind. He asked his superior officer, Major Chase, if he got caught should he shoot himself?

> 'I can't really advise you about that, Geoff,' he said. I replied, 'I am wondering what to do because I am a Jew and don't know how things are.' Major Chase said, 'Oh, that makes things different', and he gave me such a look of kindness that I thanked him inwardly.
>
> I wrote down your name [Myers's wife] on a slip of paper and handed it to him in case he got out and anything happened to me. At the time, I did not expect to get out of Arras, and nor did he.

Geoff Myers

CHAPTER FIVE

Homefront, 1939–40

At home, food was rationed, beaches were festooned with barbed wire, and churches robbed of metal railings for more essential purposes. Local councils provided 1.5 million Anderson air raid shelters by September 1939. Ray Evans lived in Birmingham at the time.

> These shelters were sections of corrugated iron shapes bolted together, and the idea was for each household to dig a deep trench in their garden, and the shelter was dropped into place. I remember waiting for Dad to come home from work so we could help him dig this enormous hole. We dug every evening and all weekends until our shelter was a regulation depth in the ground ... we could now begin to furnish it with stools, blankets, spare clothing and torches.

In seaside Brighton, schoolboy James Franks was propelled into a new world.

> The beaches were all mined, anti-landing craft spikes dug in ... engineers blew up girders and formed gaps in the Palace and West Piers, intended to prevent invaders from running along the piers ... Blackout ... we moved from living room to first floor in the dark ... we were trained to grope almost everywhere ... outside after dark ... we walked off curbs and into closed iron gates and fell on our faces.

Travelling by railway could be hazardous. Stations were unlit and all station names had been removed to confuse visiting German spies.

Food rationing began in January 1940. Sugar, dairy products, meat and other items were on the list. For Anne Addison, this meant rethinking standard recipes.

Grated carrots replaced fruit in a birthday or Christmas cake ... dried egg powder was used as a raising agent, and this same dried egg could be reconstituted and fried, yielding a dull yellow rubbery-like apology for the light, fluffy real thing – but there was nothing else, so we ate it.

Horse meat was not rationed but you had to queue for it and, sure enough, eventually it appeared on our table. It had to be cooked for a long time and, even then, it was still tough, but it wasn't thrown out.

One highlight was the coming of Spam from America. It was an oasis in our desert of mediocrity, an elixir in our sea of austerity. It seems to me that it was meatier, juicier and much tastier than it is now. (Tricks of memory again, no doubt.) We ate it in sandwiches; we ate it fried with chips; cold with salad; chopped in Spam-and-egg pie ... I never tired of it.

In Birmingham, Joan Quibbell wrote in her diary.

The Ministry of Food churned out their propaganda, assuring us that we would all be healthier for eating less, and producing recipes for strange and unfamiliar items with which they were attempting to supplement our diet, like snook* and whale meat.

Bertha Warren, York:

We'd go to the butcher for bones and stewed these for hours. This was strained and left to stand all night ... The stock

---

* Edible game fish found mainly in Florida and Central America.

was then made into soup. A large tin of minced pork would be opened, and the surrounding fat used to make pastry. The meat was then mashed up with a thick slice of bread, soaked in water and squeezed. This was then mixed to make six saucermeat pies. They were lovely. I often used liquid paraffin to make pastry, and no one was ill.

Eunice Edwards was a short-hand typist in Birmingham.

Potatoes were not rationed, nor root vegetables. We were encouraged to dig for victory . . . people bottled, jammed and dried all the fruit they could.

I used pipe cleaners for curlers. Paper was in short supply. String was another problem. We hoarded every piece of string and paper.

Women took on jobs previously done by men. In Teesside, Frank Mee's mother now worked as an RAF station electrician.

She would often be found high in the hangar roofs on the tower ladders, fitting lights and helping the male electricians. Mum was a bit of a daredevil, and often went where the males refused to go.

Nineteen-year-old Helen Ritchie worked in a Scottish munitions factory.

Our job was to blend sticks of cordite . . . the fumes and the peppery smell of the cordite made you very drowsy . . . we were a mixed bunch – 23 women from different parts of the country, war was a great leveller . . . the toilets were very primitive, a pail inside a little hut. A rumour went round that a girl had been attacked by a weasel and that it had clung onto her bare bottom with its wee sharp teeth until it had drawn blood.

In Grantham, Dolly Garbally built guns for Spitfires.

> They gave me hours of instruction on how to use the huge milling machine ... we worked long hours and one night, as we were finishing, Alf asked me if I would go to the pictures with him. I didn't think I would sleep but I did so I wasn't tired for our date. The film was *One Hundred Men and a Girl* with Deanna Durbin in her first film, and she was lovely!
>
> One morning going home from work at 7 a.m. after my nightshift Alf proposed to me and, of course, I said yes! The following Saturday we went to Leicester, and he bought me an engagement ring. I was 19, and unaware of the problems ahead.

In Horley, Surrey, 16-year-old Joy Hird was attracted to the Women's Voluntary Service (WVS) by the uniform.

> The WVS uniform had been designed by Norman Hartnell, the Queen's couturier, it was a bottle-green Harris tweed suit, a maroon blouse or jersey and a 'pork pie' hat.

Joy's mother set up a canteen for troops, but Joy was unimpressed with some of her workmates.

> Mrs Dennis, who smoked like a chimney, used to let her ash drop into the fried eggs.

Men and women were thrown together in unusual circumstances. Kath Howes's father-to-be was 18 and in the RAF. He was burned and unconscious following a crash and rushed to hospital in Aberystwyth. His nurse, later Kath's mother, was slightly older at 19.

> As he gained consciousness, he said he thought he had died and was in Heaven and mum was an angel sent to look after him. A good chat-up line ... they fell in love and certainly broke hospital rules by meeting in the linen cupboard.

Her father was killed later in the war. Kath was just six weeks old.

Nineteen-year-old Olive Swift volunteered for the Women's Royal Naval Service and was posted to HMS *Midge* in Great Yarmouth, where she worked on motor gun and torpedo boats.

> We were taken aboard and down the hatch into the engine room... the engines were hot having just returned from sea, and the sailors were stripped to the waist. Daphne, a general's daughter, who had led a sheltered life, took one look, and beat it back up the ladder.

Clearly Olive was less shocked by semi-naked men than her friend.

> I never regretted my decision to stick with it. We were taught to change plugs, strip down gearboxes and distributor heads, and anything else needed to keep three Hall Scott or Packard American engines ready for action. We went to sea on trials when the job was finished, and stood on the deck, side by side with the men, as we sailed out of the harbour... we worked, danced, partied and laughed together. We also experienced great sorrow when any of the boats were missing or damaged. I remember one, No. 313, which limped home with a great hole where the engine room had been. The entire engine room crew had been killed.
>
> The bombing [of Great Yarmouth] was devastating, a lot of the service quarters were razed to the ground, including our own. I was sleeping in a top bunk, but found myself blasted from my bed, lying on the floor at the far end of the room amongst a lot of rubble and glass... seven Wrens and our Officer were killed.*

---

* Twenty-six servicewomen were killed. Apart from Wrens, the others were mainly in the Auxiliary Territorial Service (ATS) working as signallers.

Barbara Vanderstock's family life in Croydon was disrupted in a different way. Her father was away at war for almost six years.

> I couldn't remember my father, so he was a semi-heroic figure like the war heroes in my brother's comics and in the films, who would one day return, and we would all live happily ever after.

Young Barbara had an innate understanding of loss.

> My job in the holidays was to wait in the front room watching for the early morning postman. It was important that the telegraph boy rode past the house because he was the one who brought bad news . . . even I realised how worried mother was when a letter [from Dad] finally arrived. I rushed upstairs where she was still on the bed waving the letter, she burst into tears and laughter at the same time.

The telegraph boy did not always cycle past. Michael Wessler, an evacuee from London to Carlisle, was celebrating his birthday at his uncle's house.

> There was a knock on the front door. After it was opened there was a lot of activity and commotion in the entrance hall and within a few seconds the guests were asked to leave. The grim reaper in the form of the telegraph boy had delivered a message from the War Department informing [my cousin] Una that Barney, her husband, had been shot down and killed.

CHAPTER SIX

Dunkirk, 1940

In Northern France, retreating Allied troops were trapped in a small pocket of land between German tanks and the sea. The German Army, the Wehrmacht, had closed escape routes from Boulogne and Calais, so Dunkirk was now the only possible port for a large-scale evacuation. But as his tanks were about to thrust into Dunkirk, Hitler paused the advance. Perhaps he believed Göring's assurances that the Luftwaffe's air power alone was sufficient to destroy British troops on the beaches, or maybe Hitler thought Britain's plight was so desperate she would accept peace terms?

In any event, the halt gave the British precious time to create a defensive perimeter around the town as they prepared for a desperate last-minute evacuation. In late May 1940, Bren Gunner James Bradley was one of thousands of troops retreating towards Dunkirk. He was hiding in a farmyard on his own.

> We had to get back to Dunkirk. If they'd told us to get back to New York I couldn't have been more surprised because I didn't know where Dunkirk was. I began to think to myself, I've got to survive – I must survive to fight on in this war.
>
> It was a really hot day and, looking behind me, I could see a house. The door opened and a woman came out dressed in black, an old woman with grey hair. I was dying of thirst, so I said '*Aqua*.' ... she brought out a tray carrying a glass and a jug of water. She walked across the farmyard, and there

were bullets going over and a few mortars crashing. I thought she was mad! She walked straight back and halfway there she stopped and turned to spit, waving her fist, and said something like *'Salle bosch'* [dirty Germans]. I thought, she's some woman! I wouldn't cross her!

In the chaos of retreat, Sergeant Jock Walker, Royal Signals, was equally alone, happy times in the bars of Lille and Douai long forgotten. When he arrived at his HQ it was empty; in their desperation to escape no one had waited for him.

> I could hear a clanking sound and thereupon ran into one of the outbuildings to hide. The noise grew louder, and peering out through a grimy window, I saw an enemy tank coming along the road. I was petrified with fear and nearly shit myself, but that angel, bless him, was still with me and the tank clanked on and disappeared.

Jock hurriedly rode off on a handy motorbike looking for someone, anyone. He eventually located 1st Corps HQ, where he did not know a soul. A Sergeant Major gave him battle instructions.

> He took me to the perimeter, placed me behind a wall, opened a box of hand grenades and told me that if any Germans came along, to throw them at the motherless sons of so-and-so.
> Never in my six years of soldiering had I seen a grenade, never mind known what to do with it, other than biting it first and then throwing it at the enemy (this being the whole of my war-like knowledge, gleaned entirely from the movies).
> Infantry were for fighting. Signals were for signalling and never the twain would swap jobs. This was our pre-war training – an extension of the 1914–18 style of war.

Jock Walker then headed for Ostend on his trusty motorbike with a second straggler riding pillion.

> The pillion passenger was doubly welcome as he could watch for hostile aircraft ... that period of time was like a mad Big Game Hunt, where everything that moved was shot up, and, of course, this included the endless columns of refugees who were a sitting duck for the Master Race ... the mayhem these planes caused to the poor refugees was frightful and sick-making; with bodies, legs, arms and blood everywhere.

On the way they encountered an officer who ordered Jock to hand over the motorbike. He said he would return with other soldiers.

> Like hell he came back, and it slowly dawned on us we had been conned – he had no intention of coming back, all he wanted was transport, but we noted the direction he had taken.

Ahead Dunkirk was alight, but Ostend looked quiet. It had already been captured by the Nazis.

> Doesn't Fate work in a peculiar fashion? If we hadn't given up our transport to that (unmentionable) officer we would have gone to Ostend and possible death, or at best capture ... we set off in the other direction, towards poor, ill-fated Dunkirk.

Nineteen-year-old Bill Towey was serving in a Casualty Clearing Station on grounds of conscience at La Panne, 10 miles up the coast. A Major drew lots to decide who could try to get to Dunkirk and who would remain to tend the wounded, and inevitably be taken prisoner.

> He put 25 pieces of paper in his hat, eight of them were numbered, if we drew a number we would have to stay and be taken prisoner ... shakily, I put my hand into the hat and found I had drawn a blank and with the others we set off along the beach, littered with bodies and equipment.
>
> As we neared Dunkirk it looked and sounded like an outpost of Hell. A thick cloud of black smoke from burning oil

tanks hung like a heavy shroud over the whole of the western sky, blotting out the sun, fires were burning everywhere out of control, shell bursts hit the beach which was littered with bodies, cast-off equipment, and wrecks of vehicles and boats. Out to sea and just off the eastern Mole, which was a jetty about 500 yards long built of timber, ships were under attack from Stuka dive bombers emitting their unnerving, wailing screams. Some ships had suffered direct hits and were sinking. Enemy fighter aircraft were making low-level strafing runs against the soldiers dug into the sand ... Dante's inferno would have seemed like a Sunday afternoon picnic in comparison, and our hearts sank as we tried to rate our chances of getting away.

In this bleak scenario Bill wrestled with his beliefs as a conscientious objector.

We joined the queue. I saw lying below me, alongside the canal, a number of British dead, oddly enough all with the same type of injury. The tops of their skulls had been taken off as if with a can opener.

There was time for me to resolve my problem of conscience. During our retreat I'd been greatly disturbed by seeing the merciless strafing of the pitiful columns of refugees and now, under relentless attack, all I wanted to do was to hit back and to do so as hard as I could. Scarcely without appreciating it, I had become convinced that the use of arms was fully justified.

An extraordinary rescue was being attempted by about 860 ships, from Royal Navy destroyers to small pleasure boats. On the crowded beaches survival was sometimes just a matter of luck.

The officer shouted, 'Right, Thirteen, take cover in the town.' We ran like the wind and took cover down a side street of the town, rounded the corner and hid, shaking like leaves, under some collapsed railings. There was a sickening roar and thunderous bang, and stones and bricks came hurtling through the air where the bomb had struck a nearby house. The noise was deafening, and the next sight was among the most sickening we had encountered. Three injured horses came stampeding just a foot or so away from us, one poor creature's intestines were hanging from his gashed guts, and he was stamping on his own insides.

We got to our feet, dazed and sick and started to trudge our way back to our place on the beach. Weary from lack of food and shaking from shock we almost tumbled the last few yards onto the beach . . . to find that our places that we had guarded and defended for so long had been stolen. But at what a cost! Everywhere we had stood only minutes before were dead men. There were bodies everywhere. Exactly where I had stood only a short time before, lay a man of approximately the same age – DEAD!

Military Policeman Lance-Corporal Arthur Turner marshalled men queueing for evacuation.

The noise was really terrifying . . . as soon as the Stukas had passed over, everything came together again – there was no jumping the queue. It always amazed me that a lance-corporal in the military police could control fifty men . . .

Arthur eventually boarded a wooden steam-packet ship, *The Fenella*.

It was an elaborate ship, a pleasure steamer with gold braiding on all the curtains, beautiful tables – but they bombed it . . . the galley caught fire and was burning.

Arthur managed to jump onto the Thames paddle steamer *Crested Eagle* instead, and it inched away from Dunkirk.

We sailed about half a mile, and then we were bombed again. The bomb went straight into the engine room and there were spuds, carrots and meat everywhere – evidently the bomb hit the provision store as well.

A motor mechanic was on fire. He was screaming, screaming... we rushed to get a bucket of water and threw it over him. He put his arms in the water, but all his skin came off. The whole place was on fire...

So, I dived in the water and started to swim... I swam for the shore, and gradually got rid of my trousers, even my boots... I swam and swam. Then I managed to stand upright and walk to the shore – I was in vest and pants and nothing else except socks.

Royal Navy Nurse Bob Bloom was badly burnt.

The skin was hanging off my hands like plastic gloves. I tried to pull it back again, and then I just went bump, bump over the wires surrounding the ship and into the water. When I came up the oil was on fire and had caught my legs.

Like Arthur Turner, Bob attempted to escape on the *Crested Eagle* nearby. Despite his burns, he somehow clambered up the wooden ladder. No sooner had he settled in a bunk, shivering and in agony, than his new ship was also hit.

The ammunition aboard the *Crested Eagle* was going off and it sounded to me like naked electricity, splitter and splattering. I saw a chap swimming towards the beach and thought, 'Good, I'll go with him'. He got there first and crawled up the sand and just laid there. I was watching him all the time, and somebody came along – I don't know whether it was a beachmaster or who it was – and looked at him. Whether they shot him to put him out of his misery or whether they did something else to him, I don't know... [but] he didn't stir anymore.*

---

* Of the 600 men on board the *Crested Eagle* only around 200 survived.

Gunner Doug Dawes was ordered to La Panne up the coast. Nothing happened for hours, so Doug made his own way home.

> I decided to desert. I wandered down to the water's edge. The sea was very calm.

Doug stripped off.

> I was starkers... I waded through two beached destroyers in the mucky water, avoiding floating debris...

After a long swim, he struck out towards a paddle steamer.

> [There were] shouts of encouragement from those on board... arms grabbed me, and I was hoisted on board... my appearance livened things up considerably. There were cheers and jeers and laughter and some unrepeatable remarks about my matrimonial prospects... the ship's engineer obtained a sack and cut two bottom corners off and told me to make myself decent. So, I put one leg in each hole.

Private Robert Stateman was a nurse responsible for an ambulance full of patients.

> The scene around us was of utter devastation, lines of burning trucks, bodies, dumps of all kinds being blown up and never-ending air raids. It was hell... the roar of bombs was deafening, my patients were screaming and crying, poor souls. The ambulance shook about like a marionette.

On the beach Robert carried loaded stretchers out to waiting ships, but the shelling restarted.

> A stinging burst of cordite and sand struck me... around me I could hear the sounds of pain, agony and despair as people ministered to the wounded. I ran back to help, dragging stretchers of wounded along the causeway... running to the ships became an act survival as more and more bursts of

shells shot over me. I had to drop flat on the ground and the patients were jarred and screaming in pain.

Ambulance driver Arthur Davey's hospital ship was full. So, he and his patients spent a precarious night and day in Dunkirk. They had no food, so they broke into an abandoned truck. He told the story in a letter home.

> We found biscuits, several tins of milk, corned beef, boiled bacon and some tea ... an officer arrived out of the blue and accused us of looting. After a pretty heated argument, he left us, and we proceeded to make breakfast.
>
> The raids continued, and seemed to increase in ferocity, if possible, and the second day was a ghastly experience ... Jerry [Germany] was systematically blitzing Dunkirk and not missing much. Along the canal bank, both days and nights, soldiers were marching, dirty, bandaged, worn-looking, towards the docks.
>
> The roads were strewn with debris, bricks, masonry, girders, full of carts, here a dead horse, there an overturned ambulance, a couple of lorries blazing fiercely. Houses were blazing, walls tottering, a small band of men doing impossibilities with fire hoses, and, drowning all, the roar of the blazing oil depot, whose smoke and flames could be seen at night from the English coast.

Arthur queued up on the quayside in his ambulance until 8.30 p.m. that night when a Royal Navy destroyer appeared, guns blazing.

> The feeling of confidence that the appearance of the Navy created, I cannot explain – everyone cheered up so visibly and when a hospital ship pulled up alongside, we felt really safe. The ambulances were driven, pushed, towed to the gangways and the neatest, swiftest handling of stretchers that I have yet seen, followed.

Having been conned out of his motorbike, Sergeant Jock Walker, Royal Signals, joined up with some infantrymen and headed towards the blazing fires of Dunkirk. Then the inevitable happened.

> We were shot up by an enemy fighter and that decimated the group quite a bit . . . there was four of us that got away, the rest were cut to pieces, caught fair and square in the open . . . three weeks before we were living the life of Old Reilly and now [we were in] a dirty, hungry state and this was regarded as normal.

Jock Walker's next encounter was more positive.

> Miracle of Miracles! My unit has been found; we had reached a sort of collecting point, and there they were, nobody missing, and nobody hurt. Was I glad to see them! And they, on their part, had either thought I was in the bag* or dead, but they were disabused of that thought by my appearance: dirty, hungry, footsore and weary. Lord, how weary.

Jock was briefed on his perilous position.

> Our only way out was by the Channel. It now depended on the Navy to get us away. We were stunned! Our Army beaten? Surely not, but it was true and that night we got a truck, put all our blokes in it, and I drove it to the dunes at Dunkirk . . . we trudged through the dunes, soft, dry shifting sand . . . there were thousands of soldiers all heading for the beach, like a mass of lemmings, heading to their doom.

Jock arrived at Dunkirk on 29 May but waited nervously until 1 June to escape.

> It was like sitting in a cinema watching a war movie; all the action was taking place in front of us. To the left was the Mole,

---

* Soldiers' slang for being captured.

where the destroyers and larger ships were coming in to get off, in the main, stretcher cases and the walking wounded was a never-ending stream as the Mole was subject to intense bombardment, both by shell and bomb; aircraft constantly harried the ships tied up there and they fired back in retaliation, the noise was unbelievable, and terrible casualties were suffered.

Jock had to survive in Dunkirk for four days without supplies. So, he foraged for food.

The town was like nothing on earth; fires everywhere, bombs and shells banging off, masonry tumbling down, dead and wounded all over the place. We were frightened out of our wits, but hunger and thirst are a great provider and, having come this far, we were determined to find something . . . food seemed non-existent . . . so there was only one thing left – the dustbins.

We searched them and found pieces of this and bits of that, most of it green [and] mouldy but we collected everything that looked remotely edible and took it back to our mates . . . we found new hope. It is indeed wonderful what a bit of food will do for a hungry man.

Finally, Jock Walker's turn came.

The Navy was conducting the evacuation, and I will take my hat off to the officers standing in the water up to their waists, ordering the men forward to the boats, telling the rest to stay, a sight as firm as the Rock of Gibraltar; exhorting, cajoling, encouraging – and not a thought for their own personal safety; they were magnificent.

By the time June 1st had arrived I was at the head of the queue and the boat out there was hit and sunk. My heart also sank but out of nowhere came a lifeboat and some of us got aboard it and were ferried to a Dutch coal barge . . . the panorama was fantastic; scores of little, medium and large boats waiting for the troops to be ferried out; it was a brilliant morning.

Not that discipline was always maintained by exhortation, as Albert Powell, Royal Signals, witnessed during the evacuation at La Panne.

> At dawn the next day we were marshalled in groups of 50 and marched down to the water's edge. A beachmaster, who called each group in turn, maintained discipline there. I saw one group run out of line and the person in charge was promptly shot by the beachmaster.

As screeching Stuka dive bombers strafed and bombed the beach, it was no wonder that the soldiers felt like sitting ducks and wondered where the RAF were. In fact, they were inland attempting to prevent the Luftwaffe from ever reaching their targets on the beaches. The RAF flew well over 2,700 fighter sorties during the Dunkirk phase but the Luftwaffe's numerical superiority, the RAF's limited flying time because of fuel capacity, and some tactical errors, meant that the protection offered to the troops was limited.

The anger of the soldiers could turn ugly. One pilot who was shot down at Dunkirk tried to jump on three different destroyers only to be turned away, 'The Navy said that all accommodation was reserved for the army, and that the air force could go fuck themselves...'

On 1 June, Pilot Officer George Spiers, 254 Squadron, was two miles from Dunkirk flying as an Observer in a Blenheim, when the aircraft was attacked by eleven Messerschmitt 109s. Even without such overwhelming odds, the outdated Blenheim was no match for the modern Me 109. Spiers felt as much a target as the soldiers huddled on the beach.

> The cockpit suddenly filled with acrid smoke and flying fragments, as the dashboard and instruments disintegrated in

front of me under a series of violent crashes and flashes... the fuselage down to the turret was a mass of bullet holes which were accentuated by the sunbeams that shone through the smoke. All I could see of the gunner was a bloody green flying suit slumped over the gun controls.

Turning to the pilot I immediately realised he had been hit, although he still held the controls. His head was slumped forward on his chest and blood ran down his cheek from a wound in the temple that showed through the side of his helmet. Another wound in his neck had covered him with blood and it had gushed all over my left shoulder. He looked very peaceful with his eyes shut; I was sure he was dead. It was miraculous that I had survived that burst of gunfire into the cockpit.

George Spiers was the only crew member alive. He was not a pilot, but his only chance of survival was to fly the Blenheim himself.

I viciously hit the pilot's arms off the controls. Leaning over I pulled back the throttle as the engines were still at full power and vibrating excessively. Yellow flames from the port engine were beating against the front and side windows... when suddenly the windscreen shattered. I felt a searing hot wind on my face, I felt my cheeks, nose, throat and mouth shrivelling under the heat.

George steadied the wounded Blenheim and spotted an armed trawler in the distance. It was time to ditch.

The ripples on the calm sea closed nearer and nearer until there was suddenly a most violent jolt. Although the impact only took a fraction of a second it seemed like a slow-motion cine-film to me.

I can still visualise the water bursting in through the nose like a dam that had burst... the silent cockpit was now full of blood-coloured sea, and I struggled to reach the normal entry sliding hatch above the pilot's head.

I realised I would not escape. I had never prayed to God with such agony or earnestness. I tried to suck water into my lungs to hasten the end, but I was unsuccessful and only swallowed it. My lungs were bursting, and my pulse pounded in my eardrums, brilliant flashes, and yellow spots appeared in front of my eyes. I thought of the seabed, its creatures, and crabs.

George thought he would die in the sinking aircraft but suddenly realised there was a hole in the plane deeper down in the water and found an escape route. When he finally reached the surface, he was amazed by what he saw.

The stub end of the fuselage was pointing upwards at 80 degrees with a jagged scar from which the turret and tail had been torn of.

The trawlermen hauled George aboard.

They sat me in front of a hot stove, but the cheery warmth of the fire was agony to my face ... after dressing my face with ointment they took off my wet clothes. My legs had several lacerations, and they found there were small particles of shrapnel and metal in my skin. These they quickly removed and bound up the small wounds ... the skipper came down clutching a half-pint glass filled with rum. I remember downing the rum in virtually one gulp.

George was then transferred to a tug with about 50 exhausted Moroccan troops on board and landed at Ramsgate.

The injured from other vessels were a terrible sight, particularly one Frenchman who had a large chunk of shrapnel protruding from his forehead. There were troops of various nationalities who looked unkempt, filthy and completely exhausted.

> An attractive young auxiliary nurse came across and looked at my face. She immediately burst into tears when she saw me and said how terrible it was that the sailors had put grease on my face. She then started to clear the grease away with wadding and this was a most painful operation as all the skin was coming off leaving me in red raw patches. She then put a cooling salve on my face, and I felt much more comfortable.*

Military Policeman Arthur Davey landed at Dover.

> We were met by those wonderful ladies of the Women's Royal Voluntary Service (WRVS). They plied us with hot tea, sandwiches and pork pies. They also gave us each a Field Post Card to fill in and hand back to let our families know we were safe. We looked a dishevelled lot.

Some survivors were angry. Sapper Dick Reynolds said:

> We returned beaten in every sense of the word... the sands were blood-red from where our boys were buried, they had given their lives for this so-called 'Victory', someone had blundered and badly, the youth of England paid with their lives for other people's mistakes... England across the water, but many men would never see her green fields again.

Sergeant Jock Walker was delighted to arrive safely in Ramsgate after so many near misses.

> The thing that struck me most was the silence. Nobody spoke above a whisper, and it was as if our reception committee were shocked at what they were seeing. My clothes were only a pair of trousers and a complete coating of stinking brown fuel oil from the sea.

---

* George Spiers became a Squadron Leader. The body of the pilot, John Baird, was recovered from the sea but not the body of the gunner, Sgt Richard. Roskrow. aged 21.

> The people of Ramsgate were kindness itself and probably full of pity for the tattered remnants of the keen young men who had left these shores ... but the spirit wasn't broken, just a feeling of sullen resentfulness with our leaders who had failed to let us know how powerful the Wehrmacht were ... don't they ever learn. I was informed that a recommendation for a Military medal had been made on my behalf. I am still waiting to receive it.

Bill Towey was not warmly welcomed on landing.

> At Dover we were welcomed by a drill sergeant from the Guards in khaki, adorned with a red sash, pace stick under arm, boots shined so you could see your face in them, who bawled at us to pull ourselves together and did we think we had been on a Sunday afternoon outing!
>
> A great feeling of rage swept over me – I wanted to go and punch his smug face in. But then, within seconds, I realised that his was the right touch, even if couched too provocatively, and I felt a strange pride that I was part of an army that could take such a thrashing and yet react in this way.
>
> As the train ferried us northwards there were folk all along the way cheering us to the echo, as if we were heroes, and my first feeling was one of acute embarrassment – what had we done to justify such a welcome. We'd been beaten to a pulp and run away like a dog with his tail between his legs, and it took some time to enter into the spirit of our reception.

Some Dunkirk troop trains stopped at Acton, London, before further onward movement. Frances Reed was a Girl Guide.

> Local people brought tea and sandwiches and cigarettes to the troops while the train was stopped ... some wore tattered uniforms, others had arms in slings, head bandages or crutches. All had days of beard growth. All looked exhausted and dishevelled, yet they managed cheery grins and showed

typical cockney wit and grit as they gratefully accepted the sustenance on offer.

Jewish RAF Photographic Intelligence Officer Geoff Myers, last seen in Arras, where he thought he would be killed or captured, escaped on the last destroyer out of Dunkirk.

> On arrival at Dover, all on board were seen off the destroyer by a policeman whose routine had not changed since the cross-channel services had been stopped. People were enjoying a warm spell. Some were sauntering along the jetty after a bathe. The only soldiers about were those who had already returned from France. Not far away, people were playing tennis. We had come from another world.

CHAPTER SEVEN

Left Behind, 1940

By 4 June, 338,000 Allied troops had been evacuated from Dunkirk: a miraculous escape, victory in defeat. Of the 860 craft deployed at Dunkirk, 243 were sunk, including six destroyers. More than 60,000 men died. Although 64,000 military vehicles, plus equipment, petrol and ammunition had been left behind, there were now 338,000 more troops available to fight in defence of Britain when Hitler invaded.

But the British were still in a desperate position, and they had around 41,000 troops marooned in France. Many had just not reached Dunkirk before the last boat departed. Others had fought tenaciously to keep open an escape corridor for other retreating troops. The fate of those left behind differed.

Attendees at a People's War event in Kent were shown a photograph of a survivor of a massacre by the 'Death's Head Division' of the SS. Of 99 soldiers from the 2nd Battalion, Royal Norfolk Regiment captured after Dunkirk, 97 were murdered at Le Paradis.

> They were lined up in the meadow beside the barn wall. When the 99 prisoners were in position, two machine guns opened fire, killing 97 of them. The bodies were then buried in a mass grave on the farm property.
>
> The two wounded survivors hid in a pigsty for three days before being sheltered by a local woman. They were eventually captured by a different German unit and became POWs for the rest of the war.

LEFT BEHIND, 1940

The largest unit left behind was the 51st Highland Infantry Division, composed predominantly of Scottish regiments. The 51st Highland had fought tenaciously to hold back the enemy, but eventually their only possible escape route was from the small fishing town of St Valery-en-Caux. But the port was just too small for the larger ships that carried thousands to safety from Dunkirk.

On 10 and 11 June the 51st Highland soldiers hoping to escape came under savage enemy fire. The Germans relentlessly shelled them from the cliffs overshadowing the port and Stukas strafed the troops on the ground. Sgt Hubert Tuck, from Hunstanton, Norfolk, was one of them.

> You never forget the sound of lead striking bone. It was a sound I was to carry with me for the rest of my life. It was indeed Hell. You had to be there to realise the madness that was happening around you. Arranging burial for the fallen, and there was a great many of them, was very harrowing for me. I instructed burial details to wrap the bodies in ground sheets as I felt covering an unprotected body with earth was too heathen and barbaric. They were heroes and deserved to be buried as such. With the greatest respect.

Peter Scott Janes kept a diary.

> We went through a town the like of which I could never imagine in my wildest dreams. The place had been blown to hell. Not one single house or building was complete. The roads were littered with debris feet deep, in which lay dead men and horses, discarded guns and other equipment. The whole place stank of a horrendous mix of powder and smoke, blood and burnt wood.*

---

* He was captured by the Germans but, with the help of two French women, hid for a year near Calais. Peter then made it south on the famous Pat O'Leary escape line into Spain.

The 51st Highland was soon almost out of heavy ammunition. Despite the presence offshore of scores of British ships, a combination of bad weather and the massive enemy bombardment into the little fishing port spelt doom. The evacuation, later called The Other Dunkirk, proved impossible. Derek Lang, an Adjutant in the army, awaited rescue.

> We were still hoping to be evacuated into the wide-open arms of the Royal Navy. But things went wrong. The weather was against us. The tide was against us. They simply couldn't get in to take us off.

Lance-Corporal Henry Lund watched enviously as some soldiers escaped in local boats.

> Two boats got away with about 30 men. They were hailed from the top of the cliff by the Germans to come back. They gave the appropriate signs one would expect, and Gerry put a burst of machine gun fire through them and killed the lot.

On the third day of brutal bombardment, French troops fighting alongside the 51st Highland capitulated. Soon after the British also accepted the inevitable and surrendered. Over 1,000 men were dead or wounded and around 8,000 soldiers condemned to spend five years in Nazi prisoner-of-war camps.

These captured prisoners now faced a gruelling march to camps in Poland. Sgt Hubert Tuck:

> The villages we passed through were filled with German troops who delighted in jeering at us and those who spoke English shouted, 'We will look after your women for you when we get to England.' . . . ahead of me four men dashed into a potato patch. There was no warning just shots from a single overenthusiastic guard. Ducking in an attempt to return to the line three of them made it, but a young lad was

hit and spun round with the force of it. Two more shots were fired into his jerking body, and he lay still.

Corporal Ted Wilkins was also marooned in France, hidden from the Nazis by the Urruty family. Wilkins wrote letters home to his wife and son, Arthur, which Madame Urruty agreed to post to England. It was not until 1945, five years later, that his wife eventually received them.

> Whatever happens, dearest, remember that I love you, and you alone. I always did ... darling, carry on for Arthur's sake and if I should die remember it is my wish that you should please yourself about marrying again. Dearest, should you think about this please make sure you make a good choice. You were always too good for me, and I know what rotters men are ... please carry on in your sweet, good-natured way.

Ted feared Monsieur and Madame Urruty would be executed if he was discovered. So, Ted and two other soldiers left their French hiding place. They planned to tie together three inflatable air beds and pieces of wood with wire stolen from a telegraph pole and sail their homemade raft across the Channel.

> I spotted Germans on the cliff top about half a mile away. One was focusing his field glasses upon us ... then I spotted out of the corner of my eye two Germans with rifles covering us about twenty yards away. They approached us, and we gave ourselves up.

He was carted to the German homeland in a railway cattle truck.

> I was to squat there for five days, 40-odd men to a truck, many suffering from dysentery – the truck was like the inside of a cesspool for the floor was just one mass of diarrhoea, excreta and urine. The stench was terrible ... the German public shouted and jeered at us in no complimentary way.

Edward Jouault from Jersey had a strange encounter as a left-behind in France. Riding his motorbike, Edward was hit by machine-gun fire from a tank belonging to Feldmarschall Erwin Rommel's 7th Panzer Division.

> Looking down at my leg, I saw my trousers were torn and soaked in blood ... there was nothing I could do except wait for the end ... I remember shutting my eyes, expecting to be shot at any minute. When I opened them, it was to see three German soldiers standing in front of me grinning ...
>
> One of the officers asked me, in French, if my leg was alright. I said I would like a drink. At a signal from him I was handed a water bottle ... the general then said, 'The war is over for you. France is finished and England will very soon want peace.' This man was Rommel himself, who I shall always remember as kind and chivalrous.*

Mancunian Jim Palmer, 3rd Tank Regiment, was also left behind miles from Dunkirk. His troop train had been strafed, the cows he was milking bombed, and his tank squadron attacked.

> Our position was hopeless, and we were ordered to move south and get the hell out of it ... no more troops could be got out of France, and we were abandoned to our fate. We were all numb and bewildered, but at least we knew where we stood. It was just a case of spending the rest of the war in a prisoner-of-war camp. At least it was all over for us, and we were in one piece.

Palmer saw enemy planes strafing refugees.

> Even from a distance, we could hear the moans and screams of the wounded ... bundles of personal belongings soaked in blood and small groups of civilians digging shallow graves

---

* Edward escaped from German medical care by hitting an orderly over the head with a wine bottle. He was reunited with British forces.

for their families killed in the bombing and strafing. Dante's inferno could be no more horrific than this.

Our horror turned to hate. This wasn't war, it was bloody murder.

Jim Palmer headed to the port of Brest.

> The streets were deserted but, in the harbour, we could see a small steamer chugging away. Another boat was against the jetty, and we jogged down the road shouting and laughing and shouting deliriously, 'Oh God! Don't go without us! Hang on!' ... we scrambled up the gangplank just as they were pulling it up and collapsed in a heap ... fate had been friendly and I lay laughing hysterically, while tears dribbled down my grimy cheeks.

The rescue ship was *The Lady of Mann* – the Liverpool ferry[*] – and unlike the troops captured at St Valery and condemned to be prisoners-of-war, Jim Palmer lived to fight another day. It was 21 June, over a fortnight since the mass escape from Dunkirk.

The next day, 22 June, an armistice was signed, and France was split into two zones. A new French government was formed, led by Marshal Philippe Petain, a military hero of the First World War. The North was occupied by Germany and the South run by Petain's Vichy Government. But no one was fooled. The government in Vichy was little more than a puppet regime.

In Bellingham, South London, typist Gladys Allvey wrote in her diary:

> At lunchtime came the news that the French had stopped fighting. Morale effect of this pronouncement is very bad, but Churchill says we go on fighting. This evening, I planted more cabbages as a contribution towards victory.[†]

---

[*] *The Lady of Mann* was credited with rescuing over 5,000 men in the evacuations.
[†] Her husband, Arthur, was killed in Germany six weeks before the end of the war.

CHAPTER EIGHT

Battle of Britain, 1940

Prime Minister Winston Churchill set the scene for the next phase of the war in stark terms: 'I look forward confidently to the exploits of our fighter pilots – these splendid men, this brilliant youth – who will have the glory of saving their native land, their island home and all they love, from the most deadly of all attacks... What General Weygand has called the Battle of France is over; the Battle of Britain is about to begin.'

As Churchill appreciated, Britain's fate was now largely in the hands of squadrons of 19- or 20-year-olds who, a year before, had been in a civilian job, at university, or even at school. Pilot Officer Geoffrey Page, aged 20, was excited.

> It was absolute paradise because I was young, I was given a lovely fast aeroplane to fly for nothing and paid the glorious sum of £5 a week to do it... it was tremendous.*

Pilot Officer Alan Henderson was more measured.

> Anyone who says they were not frightened in the Battle of Britain is either a liar or an idiot. One of the best reasons for choosing to be a fighter pilot was that you were only shit-scared for forty minutes at a time.

---

* Page was shot down in flames in the Battle of Britain. He spent two years having skin grafts, under the care of Archibald McIndoe, before flying again.

Buoyed by their rapid victories, the Nazis were very confident. Göring assured Hitler that his Luftwaffe could smash the RAF in a month. The Nazis planned that, when the third wave of their invasion was over, 260,000 troops would be ashore in Britain, with more to follow.

In face of this threat, on 13 June a government booklet instructed citizens in the case of invasion: 'Do not give the German anything. Do not tell him anything. Hide your food and your bicycles. See that the enemy gets no petrol.'

Politicians could not imagine another conflict so soon after the Great War, and so the RAF had been shredded into irrelevance. In 1918 the RAF could field 22,000 aircraft. Just two years later they were down to just 371.

Fortunately, at this moment of British vulnerability in 1940, the Nazis hesitated. Surely, the Führer reasoned, Churchill, having seen his army humiliated at Dunkirk, would want to avoid the fate that had befallen France? Germany was brilliant at waging a *blitzkreig* on land, but the English Channel presented a formidable obstacle – essentially a giant moat – and they lacked experience in the use of amphibious craft on such an ambitious scale. Destroying the RAF was an essential prerequisite for a successful invasion.

Nazi hesitation gave Britain precious extra weeks to increase military production. The amount of money allocated to the war effort rose from £33 million in April 1940 to £55 million in June, with priority given to front-line aircraft. Rolls-Royce increased production of the Merlin engines that powered both the Spitfire and the Hurricane by nearly 70 per cent.

Lord Beaverbrook, Minister of Aircraft Production, urged the British public to support aircraft manufacture by providing it with aluminium: 'We will turn your pots and pans into Spitfires and Hurricanes, Blenheims and Wellingtons.' Accordingly, thousands of saucepans were loyally sacrificed.

In RAF Control Rooms, servicewomen from the WAAF (Women's Auxiliary Air Force) plotted the incoming attacks of the enemy, moving aircraft symbols around on huge boards as warnings came in from radar stations and Observer Corps. Joyce Morley, aged 18:

> Thus began a very exciting and frightening five and a half years... three weeks after leaving school I was plotting the Battle of Britain from the safety of Lincolnshire. The plots came thick and fast.

The Battle of Britain started officially on 10 July 1940. Just a few minutes' flying time from the Kent coast, fields around Calais were transformed into airfields for German Messerschmitts ready to attack the RAF. Many Luftwaffe pilots had already been battle-hardened in the Spanish Civil War. So, in summer 1940, the bright blue skies above southern England were filled with duelling Hurricanes and Spitfires, Messerschmitts and Heinkels. RAF pilots could see villages below dotted with pubs, cricket fields and churches. It was a daily reminder of the country they were fighting for. And if a pilot was forced to bail out, it was comforting to know he would land in the green fields of home.

Sgt Denis Robinson

Sergeant Denis Robinson, 152 Squadron, was shot down by a Messerschmitt 109 near Swanage, Dorset.

> I felt the thud of bullets hitting my aircraft and a long line of tracer bullets streaming out ahead of my Spitfire. In a reflex action I slammed the stick as far as it would go. For a brief second my Spitfire stood on its nose, and I was looking straight down at Mother Earth, thousands of feet below. Thank God my Sutton harness was good and tight. I could feel the straps biting into my flesh as I entered the vertical with airspeed building up alarmingly. I felt fear mounting. Sweating, mouth dry and near panic. No ammo and an attacker right on my tail . . . The dread of being burnt to death was one of the worst fears. It drew heavily on any reserves of courage one had. My eyes were searching wildly, frantically looking for my adversary – but as often happens in air combat, not a single plane was to be seen. You only know what it is like to be given your life back if you have been through that experience.
>
> I decided to crash land the aircraft. As the Spit slithered across the grass there was an almighty crash, and the canopy slammed shut over my head. The cockpit filled with dirt, completely blinding me. The awful fear of burning returned at full strength but, to my surprise, the Spitfire didn't burn. I stood back as locals arrived to convey me to a pub in nearby Wareham and fill me with whisky.
>
> Telling this story helps me deal with my survival syndrome . . . one constantly asks, 'Why did I survive, why did others not?'[*]

---

[*] Denis died in 2015, aged 97.

Photo by Denis Robinson of his crashed aircraft, taken the next morning

15 September was later designated Battle of Britain Day. Douglas Cooper, Barnehurst, Kent:

> There was a German bomber flying right towards us... it was a Dornier, one of their biggest. It was so low we could see the pilot flying it and we could see the gunner in the nose of the bomber pointing his machine gun at us.
>
> My dad pushed me and my mum down into the trench of the shelter... at this point Dad leapt onto the top of the shelter waving his arms at the bomber and shouting 'Turn back, turn back.' Why they never shot at him or any of us

we will never know ... suddenly a Spitfire was on his tail blasting away with his guns shooting right into the back of the bomber, which then took a nosedive and crashed into the golf course. There was a tremendous thud, a massive explosion, and the ground shook ... we could hear the machine gun exploding within the burning [German] bomber.

Everyone was excited, cheering and laughing ... we heard afterwards that there were no survivors ... the Spitfire that had shot it down roared up into the sky and turned over into a beautiful victory roll over the golf course and the bomber.

The Luftwaffe pilot was buried locally.

His grave was looked after by local people and always had fresh flowers on it.

This display of humanity was not unusual. There were exceptions, as civilians who had been bombed out of their homes could be angry, but on the whole downed German pilots were treated fairly.
Kathleen Rainer, Sussex:

A pilot bailed out of his Spitfire, his parachute opening, and we watched him slowly descending to the ground. As we watched we were horrified to see the German fighter pilots trying to shoot him out of the sky while he was totally helpless! We

Commonwealth War Graves, Great Bircham, Norfolk
German aircrew killed in the Battle of Britain buried alongside RAF pilots

were gutted at the Germans, of course we know now that they committed even worse acts, but to us this was just horrible.

We were so proud of our pilots for what they did next, though. The other Spitfires began to circle the parachute, protecting the pilot from the German attack. As the pilot descended the rest of the squadron spiralled down with him, guiding him to the ground and protecting him . . . risking their lives to save that one pilot.

Kathleen's view contrasted with the experience of 14-year-old Geoffrey Martin, Kent.

One [German bomber] was coming towards the village; we all stared at this blazing aircraft coming towards us. Then at about two thousand feet it suddenly veered to the right and three of the crew bailed out. It then turned left and crashed in a field in a large ball of black smoke. We made our way out to where the aircraft had crashed; laying by the wreckage was the pilot's charred body. Of the three that bailed out, two were captured. The other one's parachute failed to open, and he fell like a stone and was killed when he hit the ground.

I have always believed that the German pilot, after letting his crew bale out, flew his aircraft to crash in an open field to save it from crashing on the village. He was a very heroic man.

In Coventry, nine-year-old Peter Cox cycled home furiously when he heard the shriek of sirens.

I had just closed the door when a lone German fighter plane flew low with his guns blazing into the road that I had just left . . . you can imagine the cheer that went up when a Spitfire began to attack him. We watched that dogfight as the two planes swirled and swooped in great loops above us and snarled our cheers when the 109 (we knew our planes!) burst into flames and dropped out of the sky . . . I felt no pity for that pilot. He had tried to kill me so why should I?

Pilot Officer David Hunt's Hurricane was hit and burst into flames.

> A dazzling array of multicoloured lights appeared on the starboard side of the cockpit, accompanied by explosive percussions. Immediately flame came through the instrument panel, filling the cockpit and burning my hands, legs and face. The reserve fuel tank had exploded, and I had neither gloves nor goggles, which I had pushed over my forehead to get a better view ... I managed to pull the hood open, undid my Sutton harness, grabbed my helmet off, and plunged over the starboard side of the plane. I started to survey the damage. My hands were all bloody, like I was feeling, and they were covered with projecting tissues; that was my skin; and all that was left of my sleeve was a charred ribbon of rank.

David was taken to Billericay Hospital, Essex. Terry, his wife of just nine weeks, takes up the story.

> David was lying on the bed. The newness of his accident was the sensation in the room. He himself was something brand new and very real. I saw him just for a moment, his face and arms purple with fresh dye and swollen. I thought he had no eyes; and I thought they had not told me that but had left me to find out quietly on for myself; and curiously, how wise they were. Behind all this was David. I saw then, as I cannot see now, how we should manage his blindness.

David was in 257 squadron based at RAF Debden, Essex. The intelligence officer was Geoff Myers, the journalist who was based at Photographic Intelligence in Arras before he escaped from Dunkirk. The squadron was so poorly led it sustained heavy casualties in the early weeks of the Battle of Britain. As Geoff was Jewish, he kept the letters to his wife, who was still trapped in German-occupied France, as they were too dangerous to send, but hoped they would both be alive to read them after the war. They started in September 1940, during the Battle of Britain.

> Three months now and I have kept silent. I have been hoping to write letters that would reach you. I have been wanting to do something that would help you to escape from Occupied France and to get us all out of this living grave. I haven't had the courage until now to write letters in a notebook, with the knowledge that you might never see them... we've all grown old since the squadron was formed a few weeks ago. We've changed. It's grim.

It was the death of Flight Lieutenant Hugh Beresford at the peak of the Battle of Britain in September 1940 that spurred Geoff Myers into writing his secret letters. Hugh Beresford had been forced to take on the unofficial leadership of 257 Squadron because the Squadron Leader was totally ineffective. Beresford was newly married to 19-year-old Pat.

> Hugh Beresford. Another hero gone. Mrs Beresford rang up last night. She was in tears... she asked if she could fetch his clothes. 'She sounds sweet,' the adjutant said. He was almost in tears himself. He had a double whisky after that.
> Beresford was the real leader of the squadron. The strain under which he was living penetrated my system, and I could do nothing for him. It was tough.

During the Battle of Britain, 544 RAF pilots were killed. Of those lucky enough to survive, nearly 800 went on be killed later in the war. Of the nearly 3,000 men who flew in defence of Britain in the summer of 1940, the chances of being killed by the end of the war was close to one in two. But by resisting invasion, the young pilots had not only protected Britain but encouraged Hitler towards the dangerous grip of Mother Russia and changed the likely course of the war.

CHAPTER NINE

The Blitz, 1940–41

In early September 1940 the Battle of Britain entered a new phase when Germany shifted away from bombing key Fighter Command aerodromes, just as this strategy was bearing fruit, to an all-out Blitz on London. Rather than smashing British resistance, as some Nazis expected, Londoners showed great resilience.

Hermann Göring, commander-in-chief of the Luftwaffe, ignored German doubters who believed that a lack of long-distance bombers would make enduring success in bombing London difficult. On 7 September, a bright, clear day, Göring moved up to the Pas de Calais himself to direct operations from his luxurious train. He promised: 'The sky of London will be black with planes.' From 7 September, London was bombed on all but one of the following 57 days and nights.

Doris Bennett was on duty at the London Fire Brigade Station, Isle of Dogs, East London, on the first day of the Blitz.

> Watching from the window towards Greenwich across the Thames, we suddenly saw aircraft approaching, quite low, their shapes black against the bright sky. We watched, mesmerised, until someone said, uneasily, 'I think we better go downstairs, these blokes look like they mean business.' They did. We closed the window and were walking, unhurriedly down the stairs when suddenly came loud rushing noises and explosions. Bombs! We were being bombed!

Down in the control room training was swiftly put into practice.

> Calls came in thick and fast. Discs were shuffled about on the Mobilising Board and coloured-headed pins denoting fires and appliances attending were put into a map of the Isle of Dogs Appliances were ordered out and any who reported back after fires they had been attending were brought under control, were swiftly ordered out again. It was organised chaos.

Angela Cohen, Poplar, East London, aged seven.

> The noise is horrendous. Every time a bomb falls, everything shakes. Above us is the 'voom, voom, voom' sound of the planes . . . we emerge. The house is still standing and doesn't seem damaged. We go through the front door, to see a scene that, even now, I recall as vividly as when it happened. The entire street is choked with emergency vehicles – ambulances, fire engines – all clanging their bells. The gutters and pavements are full of writhing hoses like giant snakes, and above . . . the sky.
>
> The sky to the south still a deep, beautiful blue, but to the north a vision of hell. It is red, it is orange, it is luminous yellow. It writhes in billows. It is threaded through with wisps and clouds of grey smoke and white steam. All around there are shouts and occasional screams, whistles blow and bells clang . . . the gutters run with water, soot and oily rainbows and the reflections of the fiery sky.

Twenty-year-old Dianna Dobinson was newly married.

> People were just blown to pieces and trees in the garden were stripped of leaves and branches; many bodies, or parts of them, were resting in any remaining trees. I was covered in plaster and my eyes were full of dust. But I was in one piece and thankful to be alive. The whole scene was lit up by a full moon; it was like a battlefield.

> Amidst the rubble I rescued my lovely cutlery, part of which had been a wedding gift. I found it all and still use it today... the worst part was seeing all the body parts being put into bags and carried away by little carts that came round daily on their grisly mission.

Ken Long, schoolboy, London:

> In the docks the warehouses were ablaze, as burning butter, sugar, molasses and oils produced dense smoke and pungent smells everywhere as it oozed across roads and into the water of the docks, even the puddles were hot. There was dust, smoke and raw smells of the explosives, sewage and domestic gas; it was the smell of violent death and destruction.

Frederick Reed, London Fire Service, was on duty when an alcohol warehouse was hit.

> The amazingly brave members of both the AFS (Auxiliary Fire Service) and the regular London Fire Brigade were fighting fires of a scope that neither had ever seen before the attacks started.

Job done, Frederick's crew stuffed their fire hose with a few untouched bottles of spirits for their Christmas party. A piece of rag bunged up the end, so the bottles did not break. But they were suddenly diverted to a large house fire.

> The water had to be drawn from the River Thames... each bottle contained within the hose dropped out with a contented 'Perlopp' as it hit the surface of the Thames and bobbed and floated away on the tide. The fire was put out and some very fed-up firemen returned to their station to look forward to just an ordinary Christmas party.

When the bombing started, 15-year-old John Davey, his father and a neighbour ran to the shelter. But it was too late.

> Everything went grey and I was falling sideways. Eventually I settled on my side, trapped by the rubble of our demolished house... I could see the stars in the sky through what appeared to be a small gap. I was finally rescued after eight hours or so.
>
> Unfortunately, my dad, aged 41, and our neighbour did not survive. They found a pocket watch on my dad, stopped at 8.45 p.m.

For eight-year-old Ray Scott from Welling, the Blitz heralded endless possibilities for mischief.

> My brothers and I were avid collectors of wartime souvenirs, and we also became junior pyrotechnic experts... getting up at 6 a.m. to collect items of shrapnel which littered the local streets after a night of bombing. We got lots of bullets and cannon case, shell nose-caps...

Ray and his brothers hid their scavenged munitions in their father's shed. They extracted the powder from unexploded devices and mixed it with potassium permanganate, which they told the local chemist was for their mother's hair dye.

> We found that we could make a self-igniting bomb by ramming this mixture into lengths of copper piping which we retrieved from bombed buildings... we developed the idea further by wiring up a piece of Dad's fuse wire inside the copper tube. We were then able to bury our 'bomb' in a hole in our garden and with a length of electric cable wire it up to a fuse box in Dad's shed. We waited until it was dark and then turned on the power to the fuse box from the safety of the house. There was a great crump from the bomb exploding under the ground, followed by lots of earth crashing down on the shed roof and against our high garden fence. Immediately neighbours came out of their kitchen to find out what was going on, so we called out with similar enquiries to allay any suspicion.

Teacher Margaret Dury also lived in Welling, but a safe distance from Ray Scott's homemade bombs. Her school was hit.

> There was glass everywhere, plaster from the fractured walls, curtains of the stage ripped. But, standing intact, unmoved, untouched, was a statue of the Virgin Mary attached to the wall. And, on the floor, at her feet, was the empty shell of the bomb. Miraculous, certainly, but I have to admit, uncanny. It was as though the bomb had been afraid to go further...

Hitler's Blitz spread beyond London to other industrial cities. When a bomb destroyed their house in Liverpool, young Frances Beckett and her siblings sheltered in their outside toilet all night.

> We cried and huddled together to keep warm. Then we tried to keep the baby from crying by singing hymns... then we heard a big bang, and we were all sitting on the wooden toilet, but the roof and walls had gone.
>
> I think it was the next morning when a policeman shone his light on us and couldn't believe we had been on our own all night... we were given blankets to put round us and cocoa to drink... we were warm at last but still didn't know what had happened to our mum.

Frances soon found out.

> Vin [aged 14] had helped my mum, but she was badly injured. She was taken to hospital by ambulance... my nana had been killed and my brother George was still trapped. George was helped from the rubble about three days later because someone thought they heard him shouting.
>
> In the [Liverpool] *Echo*, Vin was called 'Boy Hero of the Blitz' and both he and George got a ten shilling note off the Lord Mayor.

Keith Payne, Southampton, home of the Spitfire factory:

> The house suffered a direct hit. My mother and father were both killed along with my mother's sister. I was seriously injured, disfigured for life, and lost my left eye.

About 1.4 million people served as air raid wardens, and, at 17, Elaine Griffiths in Swansea was perhaps one of the youngest in the UK.

> I was the only woman in the warden's group, so I was given the task of telling people if their homes had been destroyed. I hated the job, but I did it, as gently as I could, and always seemed to end up with my arms around them, as people sobbed on my shoulder.
>
> The first wave came over and the searchlights trapped a plane in its beam, and it was like a silver brooch hanging in the sky! The guns all opened up and down came the shrapnel like heavy rain ... the streets were full of glass and debris and miles and miles of hosepipes ... the whole world seemed to be on fire ... somehow people were struggling out of this burning hell, and we gradually gathered up about 20 survivors.

To escape the fires, Elaine needed to hurry survivors over two bridges to safety.

> When we arrived at the Tawe Bridge, some of the older ladies just could not face crossing it ... I tried all things to get them to move ... I could see that we were all going to die there if we didn't get across the bridge. But they decided to say their prayers in the middle of the road ... finally with a lot of swearing and pushing the old people started across the bridge. I trailed after them and paused in the middle of the bridge to look at the burning town. It shimmered in the heat and the river reflected the massive flames ... the glow of the fires

could be seen as far away as Devon. Two hundred and thirty people were killed and 409 people were taken to hospital.

Arthur Holman, 17, from the Bristol Gas Company, was called out when a major gas main was hit.

> The flames were 30 feet high and there were fears of many casualties. Bodies had been lying in the street. Arthur's job was to get to the mains and stop gas escaping.
>
> As Arthur looked at the devastation, he was amazed to see some men holding frying pans over the holes in the road cooking sausages with the aid of escaping gas.

The naval dockyard in Plymouth, Devon, was a prime target for German bombers. Derek Dawes:

> Once the air-raid started my mother would leave the shelter because she was an air-raid warden. I can see her now, wearing overalls, Wellington boots and a steel helmet. She carried a stirrup pump and a bucket of sand.
>
> During one raid my mother came and called me out of the shelter to sit on our garden wall and see the Town Hall burning. She said it was something I should witness, and I am glad she did. It was a sight I will never forget. The flames were hundreds of feet in the air, and the whole area where we lived was as bright as day, but coloured red.

Frank Hiley was a night shift worker at a Birmingham munitions factory. When the siren screeched, the workers rushed down to the shelters.

> Some start to eat, some sing, over in one corner an accordion is playing the latest tunes... then comes a dull thud and bright lights stab the darkness for a second, then a rumbling noise, as though the whole building is being crushed in a pair of pincers... a bomb had hit the outside wall and the whole building had collapsed like a pack of cards. Hundreds of tons

of machinery had descended on us... how long I was unconscious I do not know, but perhaps not long, for I came round to find that my two companions had been killed and crushed beside me.

A girder had come down from above but the curve of it had just cleared me and held up the other debris from crushing me. What an escape, but an escape from what, I wonder, for am I in a living tomb? Fear takes hold of me, and I join my shouts again with those poor wounded and dying but little did we realise the depth of the ruins above us. No one from outside could hear our cries.

Then I can hear rumbling noises above me, and I realise they are moving the wreckage to get at me. I wait. It seems hours. Why don't they hurry? Little did I know the debris they had to move... they start to burn away at metal and machinery until they can see the light from my torch... they burn away more metal and then get a rope down and by holding onto this they pull me up and up until my head is through the hole... then by grabbing my arms I am pulled through the hole to freedom.

Never did freedom and safety seem so sweet... I was told later by the manager of the works that of the 83 souls sheltering in that basement, 81 had died. *

Rushing home, to Frank's horror his house as well as his workplace had been bombed. But his wife, Margaret, was safe.

> We clung to each other, crying with joy and fear. As we clung to each other we could tell each other... two souls with a single thought, thank God you are safe.

Perhaps this was the same night that 17-year-old Joan Quibbell was stationed at a First Aid Post in Birmingham. She wrote in her diary:

---

* BSA Factory, Small Heath: 53 killed, 89 injured.

> At 2.30 a.m. the injured began to pour in ... my first case was a poor old lady with a smashed eye. A loose dressing had been tied round her head by the ambulance driver ... I did not know what I'd find as I undid the bandage. Shall I faint, I wondered. Will it be very bad? Well, it was bad enough, but no, I didn't faint. God was very good to me that night and gave me a courage I didn't really possess ... I noticed my best friend Audrey comforting a girl on a stretcher with appalling head injuries, but who was still conscious and crying pitifully. I marvelled at the tenderness with which Audrey handled her. It was a night of misery, blood and tears. Never to be forgotten.
>
> We left the First Aid Post in the greying streaks of dawn ... I went past the Barsby's house, which had received a direct hit and lay in total ruins ... underneath which, although I did not know it then, lay buried my old friend Nina, Ruth, and their mother. Nina was my age.

Like many 9-year-olds, Peter Cox in Coventry found entertainment, even in war.

> [Playing] Hitler was great fun, and we goose-stepped up and down our street with our left index finger stuck under our noses and our right arms held at the slope in front of us, hooting with laughter as we convinced ourselves that anyone who looked so stupid and made his soldiers march in such a ridiculous fashion could not be a serious threat to anyone.
>
> We started all the boring air-raid practices, only relieved by making farting noises through our gas masks.
>
> Then came the real thing and somewhere in the city was bombed every night ... sometimes I was fascinated by the glow of tracer shells as they pursued their targets in fidgeting curves above the city.

Also in Coventry, Elsie Dawes was unable to use the air raid shelter because her two small children had whooping cough.

I sat in a big chair with a tea cosy on my head that my husband Harold had placed there in fun. Our gas masks were nearby, and Harold was wearing a Home Guard helmet. We quietly waited but not for long!

Multicoloured incendiaries were dropping into gardens like fairy lights, but, much more lethal, of course, the whole city was ringed with leaping flames, bathed in brilliant moonlight and a few searchlights were sweeping the smoke-filled sky.

When we went to the city centre the devastation was heartbreaking; the lovely old black-and-white buildings gone, the beautiful cathedral a smoking ruin, a new store just a gaping hole.

The People's War Archive holds a poignant letter from another victim of the Coventry Blitz.

My name is Bear, Bobby Bear . . . the people in the house where I lived ran out to go to the air raid shelters. My young owner dashed back into the house for me. The house was hit by a bomb. My young owner was killed, and I was left injured.

As Christmas was approaching and toys were scarce, I was given to a new owner, Carol, who cared for me with love . . . I still carry the scars of the Blitz but have had a good life and still live with Carol, who is now an OAP, as I am.

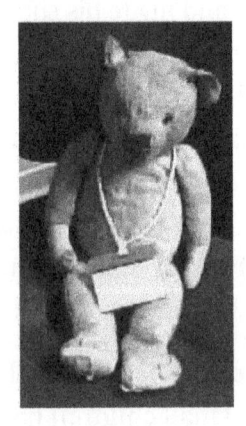

Bobby Bear

In Eccles near Manchester, Betty Hale, and her twin sister, were regulars at the local Air Raid Precautions post. On 22 December Elsie and 16 others were enjoying an early Christmas celebration courtesy of the local grocer, who had gifted a whole ham to the ARP.

> The building received a direct hit from a German bomber, killing 11 people in the building and a family of five next door. My sister and I were sitting on the arms of an easy chair on either side of a young Irish woman. We were buried completely.
>
> Fortunately, a soldier coming home on leave spotted my fingers sticking out of the rubble ... he helped dig me out and I was taken to the local hospital, which was so full I was left on the floor. My sister had survived but the young woman sharing our chair was killed, as was the grocer.

Sixteen-year-old Peter Addis was a paperboy for the family newsagents' shop in the naval city of Portsmouth. Initially, Peter found the Blitz exciting.

> It was one of the most wonderful periods I have ever known. The atmosphere was euphoric. The Germans were regarded as comic figures goose-stepping around wearing coal-scuttle helmets shouting *Achtung*. The fact that they had conquered most of Europe in a few months was ignored.
>
> Then came a time when silly boys stopped praying for air raids ... the bombing started at dusk and the first bombs put out all the lights ... I was not thrilled anymore. I was scared.

Emerging from the air raid shelter one night, Peter was astonished.

> King's Road, which was one of the town's main shopping centres, was burning all down one side ... as I ran a whole side of a building collapsed into the road. I will never know how near it was. I saw a lady lying on the pavement, a couple

of wardens looked at her. One said, 'She's dead', and at that moment she sat up and started screaming.

His parents made Peter promise to meet them at a shelter on Southsea Common if they were separated.

> I can only remember riding as fast as I could, avoiding broken glass and debris and aware of the great noise ... the common was ringed with fire, an incredible scene of destruction. Even the rollercoaster on the side of the blazing pier was on fire.
>
> Then we went home. All that was left was a small square of rubble ... I could not believe that the house I had lived in all my life could only leave a tiny square of rubble. It was a bitter blow to my parents, not only was it their home but also their shop and means of livelihood.

The homeless Addiss family stayed with relatives in Buckinghamshire.

> We were given a great welcome ... they took us to a local pub where there was an impromptu dance. My mum and dad were dancing less than 48 hours after losing everything. My Dad, always good for a quote, said, 'I am dancing with tears in my eyes.'

CHAPTER TEN

North Africa, 1940–43

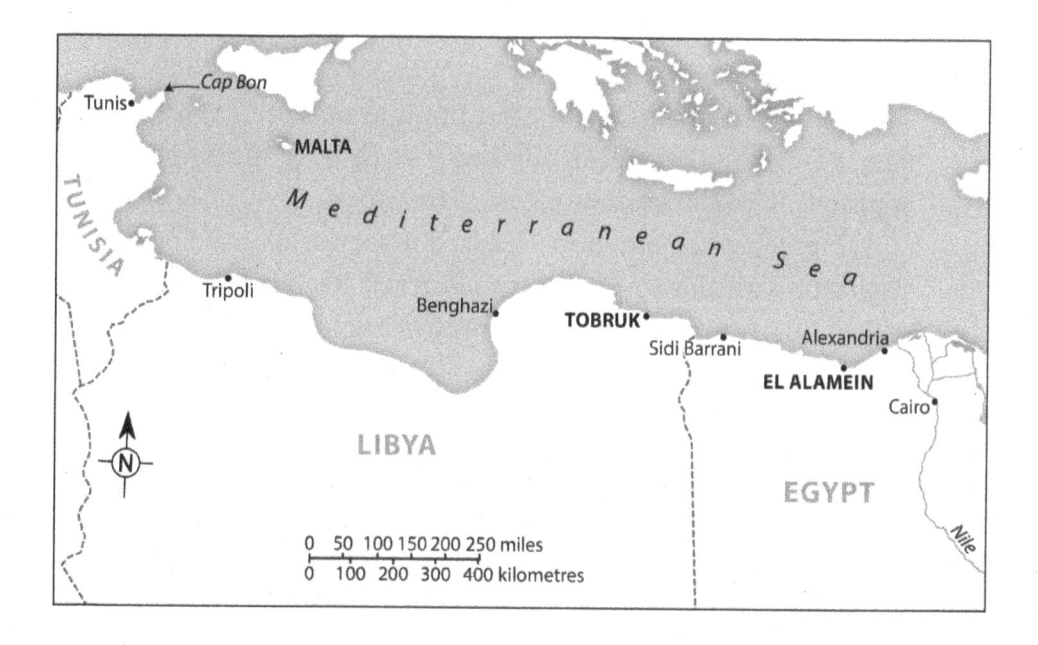

On 10 June 1940, a month before the Battle of Britain started, Italy entered the war on Germany's side. Their Fascist leader, Benito Mussolini, had seen France overrun, and the British narrowly escape from Dunkirk. Opportunistically Mussolini thought he could take Egypt and the Suez Canal while the Allies were on their knees, and, with these conquests, control access to the vital oil supplies in the Persian Gulf. But Mussolini's arrogance led him to underestimate the inadequate weaponry and leadership of his own army.

At home, British families hurriedly reached for maps to locate

Ron Goldstein

Tobruk or El Alamein as they tried to make sense of the challenges faced by their husbands and sons in what hitherto had appeared a distant, irrelevant part of the world.

Nineteen-year-old Ron Goldstein served as a Wireless Operator with the 49th Light Anti-Aircraft Regiment in North Africa. Ron was from a Jewish family of 11 children in Bethnal Green, London.

> The long-awaited buff envelope arrived on our doormat, informing me that I had been called up into His Majesty's Army. The Army had thoughtfully provided a railway ticket (ominously, a single – one way only) and on arrival at Bury St Edmunds we were met at the station by a three-ton lorry, our first acquaintance with this favoured form of military transport. We got to the barrack gates, dismounted, and formed up into ragged ranks against a master roll held on a clipboard by a very important-looking sergeant.
>
> I was the last person to file into the hut, and found my way impeded by what looked like a pair of size ten army boots worn by this imposing sergeant. 'Your name's Goldstein, isn't it?' he demanded. 'Jewish, aren't you?' he continued. Everything I had ever imagined concerning antisemitism immediately came to mind and, with much misgiving, I promptly replied, 'So what!'

'Don't be a bloody idiot,' he replied, 'My name's Kusevitsky' (or some such equally Jewish-sounding name).*

Ron loved the North African desert, so very different from Bethnal Green.

> I personally was in seventh heaven. The brilliant stars in the jet-black sky under which I now lay were the most beautiful sight I had ever seen in my short life. The romance of actually being in the desert was manna from heaven for this particular cockney boy who, until he went in the army, had never been further from home than Brighton. As the war progressed, I was to savour many experiences, and my travels were to take me to Sicily, Italy, Austria, Germany and Egypt. No memory, however, has stayed with me as vividly as that first night in the desert.

Sergeant Len Scott described a North African dawn in a letter to his wife, Minna.

> It is barely light, and the sea lies black and glimmering to the horizon. Far across the bay the mountains are a barely discernible humped mass of darkness against the dark sky. A few Arabs are wandering down the streets, their white robes ghost-like in the dimness. A chill wind blows dust down the seafront, twisting it into little soaring spirals.
>
> Then, suddenly, the mountains become more distinct or is it that the sky has become a little lighter ... a golden scarf of light lies behind the topmost peaks. Now the overhanging mountains take on a rich purple that changes rapidly to red. What a red! It seems as if all the fires in all the hells of men's imagining are burning away on some sulphur-strewn plain behind the mountains and colouring the sky with their glow.

---

* All five Goldstein brothers served in the war. Four survived.

The challenges of desert warfare demanded new skills. Unusually for a woman, Hannah Tilayeff Roberts trained as a driver in Cairo.

> We had to discover how to drive in the dark, over the desert, through quicksand and sandstorms. We had to learn how to maintain and repair the vehicles.
>
> Life in the desert was very hard. Mornings and nights were bitterly cold, while the days were very hot. Often, we had sandstorms, when the sand penetrated everything, even our food. But we were young, full of energy, and working for a cause that made it all worthwhile.

Sand often choked vehicle engines, as Brian Hulse found out.

> [He] lifted the bonnet, poked around the engine for a few minutes and announced, 'the f*****g f*****s f****d.'

After escaping the horrors of Dunkirk, Sergeant Jock Walker from Glasgow was deployed to Cairo.

> We reached the top [of the Pyramid], where there was a flagpole and this too in turn we climbed and, at the top of the pole the view was magnificent. The Nile Delta was laid out like a map, and you could see for miles and miles.

As a devoted member of his unit's drinking school, Cairo provided Jock's last recreational opportunity.

> This was the first time I had seen any ATS [women],* and they were in a barbed-wire compound in the middle of the camp under 24-hour guard. Speculation was rife as to whether the wire and guard were to keep the troops out, or the women in. Personally, I wasn't bothered either way as there was the more important job of tasting the gyppo beer, Pyramid and Stella, which were a kind of chemical lager.

---

* Auxiliary Territorial Service, the only women in the army who were not nurses.

That didn't stop him visiting Cairo's brothel area.

> Each doorway was a separate brothel and was bedecked with the flags of the nation they particularly wanted to attract. An Australian flag, with the legend 'Madame X's', painted on a large board, said 'We served your fathers in the 14-18 war, let our daughters serve your sons.'

When a New Zealander robbed a Scottish soldier of his kilt, a mass brawl broke out.

> The girls were hanging out of the windows of their various houses, exhorting one side or the other to greater effort and heaving the contents of various bedroom utensils down on the assailants ... pouring not boiling oil but hot something else onto the melee.

Jock was posted to the Desert Rats (7th Armoured Division) as a Vehicle Mechanic.

> I loved the life in the desert. It was so open, clean and warm ... but we did have pestilential flies who worried the life out of the troops. Later, the Tunisian fly was a peculiar thing, which had the body of a fly, the nose of a mosquito and used to cause a bit of pain when it settled and drove the nasal spike into the flesh.

Not every soldier was happy in the desert. Fred Smith, also a Desert Rat:

> There were six men in each tent, and it was here on the first night a terrible event occurred. One of the men, who was very quiet and kept himself to himself, was holding his Smith and Wesson revolver in the corner of the tent. No one was paying much attention to what he was doing when he started to point the gun to each man in turn and pulled the trigger. Then he calmly put the gun to his own head and

pulled the trigger. A shot rang out and the man fell dead to the floor.

In August 1940, as the Battle of Britain was raging, and two months after his belated post-Dunkirk rescue from France on a Liverpool ferry. Jim Palmer, 3rd Tank Regiment, was also posted to North Africa. But, first, there was the pressing question of his girlfriend, Muriel, in Manchester.

> Dad lent me some money and I bought a cheap engagement ring for Muriel, and he had our photo taken in a studio on the Oxford Road. Muriel's parents and family were against the engagement. I have never been welcomed at her home, but I wasn't worried. Muriel was the only one I cared about.

There was yet another railway-station goodbye.

> Tears, promises, hugs, kisses and embraces, a final wave of the hand and then deep depression and emptiness.

But Jim was given a surprise 72-hour leave before heading for North Africa.

> I sent a telegram to Muriel simply saying, 'Coming on leave. Will get married when I arrive.'
> No wedding dress, no bridesmaids, no wedding cars and no organ playing or bells ringing. It wasn't the wedding we wanted, but I didn't know how long I was going to be away for or if I would be back at all . . . no member of Muriel's family turned up for the wedding and they completely ignored the event.
> It seemed to me that no one expected me to come back this time and, I must admit, I thought I was pushing it a little to expect to return.

In North Africa Mussolini's Italian Army had pushed 40 miles from the Italian colony of Libya into Egypt and halted at the fishing village of Sidi Barrani.

This was newly married Jim Palmer's first taste of desert warfare.

It was much more open fighting than we had experienced in France. But the dust, the oily petrol smell, the smoke, the cordite fumes and the screech of shells and crump of guns were as before ... actions became quicker and more decisive. A quick thrust forward, a couple of hours of crashing and banging, thumping and clumping, screeching, and thundering.

Tom Barker, Argyll and Sutherland Highlanders, was in the desert near Sidi Barrani.

[We] slept on sand, in sand, under sand, we walked on sand, cleaned our mess tins with sand ... we buried things in the sand.

Churchill tanks in the desert, 1942

Then there were sandstorms.

> The hot wind shrieked and buffeted, and the burning sand stung and was so abrasive it rubbed any exposed skin off... it was a case of move or be barbecued in the hot sand.

The Italian Airforce dropped bombs that looked temptingly like Thermos flasks. Tom's Officer tried to open one.

> The flask suddenly detonated with a roar and a cloud of sand and dust. The Officer's head, shoulder and one arm were gone, the Sergeant was dead, two blokes lay moaning in the hole the flask bomb had made.

Tom Barker and his fellow Argylls dug in for the night and waited to attack Sidi Barrani.

> Dawn began to lighten the night sky, and as the tip of the blood-red sun began to show on the horizon, the long shadows began to creep ever faster across the sand like an army of scurrying beetles.
>
> Suddenly the silence was shattered by a sound like a heavy truck travelling at high speed with flat tyres... then an enormous explosion and the bloke near me was gone. Where he had been was just a huge cloud of dust swirling and rising in the air and a ringing in the ears and a blast of hot air and sound and an acrid smell.
>
> We had suffered for months in the desert. Hands being blown off, disfigurement, blokes killed by imitation flasks of drink, landmines, quicksand, poisoned water, flies, strafed from the air, sickness, and now this final showdown.

The only cheerleader for this military adventure was Mussolini himself. Although he had 236,000 troops in Libya, they were under-equipped, under-motivated and poorly led. Despite superior numbers, the Italians were comprehensively beaten at Sidi Barrani and nearly 40,000 soldiers taken prisoner. Tom Barker:

> Wrecked trucks were littered about, and smoke was ascending from them as they burned to the now clear blue sky above ... black patches in the sand were moving. I discovered they were masses of flies attracted to the blood in the sand.
>
> We took prisoners and they seemed glad it was over.

Jim Palmer rifled through the Italian dugouts.

> There were thousands of packets of cigarettes and small bottles of Vichy water. In some there were bottles of perfume and boxes of contraceptives. Lewd photographs littered the floor.

As the Italians retreated towards Libya, Jim drove miles through the desert to cut them off at Beda Fromm on the Benghazi–Tripoli coast road.

> Deep into the desert we slowly thundered. It was a very lonely place. The tanks had to be coaxed along and so did we, tired and exhausted ... the dirt and dust clings to your skin, your eyes become red and bloodshot, your head aches and your limbs become stiff. The desert is a godforsaken land!

When Jim Palmer peered down on the coast road, he was astonished to see huge numbers of retreating Italians in trucks and tanks.

> They were sitting ducks! Straight alongside the column we crashed, firing as we went and as fast as we could. Trucks burst into flames and within minutes the road was blocked with blazing lorries ... all the gunners were firing as fast as they could load. There was no need to select targets, every shot was a hit!

All the convoy was burning, all their tanks had been hit or abandoned. What was left of the Italian troops were lying down at the side of the road, waving white flags. The wounded were crying, screaming and dying. It was sickening! For two hours we had gone berserk, shooting, killing and burning. Now we were dazed, confused and sickened.

The next day we went to recover what Italian tanks we could. There was a smell of burning flesh amid the smouldering ruins. We find the blackened remains of human beings inside the tanks. It was a sight I shall never forget, and I know that my soul will be damned for having been a part of it!

Graves were being dug by Italian survivors, but no one said much. Tears were trickling down many a face and both sides were mumbling that they were sorry it had happened.

We sat amid the carnage and gave fags to the Italians . . . if that was victory, I didn't want any more of it. I was stunned by the atrocity of war and bloodshed. I had experienced the ultimate degradation of human life.

The Allies captured 138,000 Italian troops. But this was the last rout the Allies would enjoy. The arrival of General Erwin Rommel and his Afrika Corps in February 1941 meant the Allies now faced a much more formidable force than the Italians.

CHAPTER ELEVEN

Tobruk, 1941–42

Rommel swiftly went on the offensive and, just six weeks after landing, he successfully cut off the British 3rd Armoured Brigade in Libya. Four regiments of British artillery, some Indian troops, and around 14,000 Australians retreated to the deep-water port of Tobruk, which, with a flat plain on one side and the sea on the other, was in a good geographical position to withstand German and Italian attacks. On 31 March 1941, a brutal seven-month siege started.

Charles Cooper was an Army baker.

> We had Jerry [the Germans] all around three sides and the sea behind us . . . as the days turned into weeks things got worse . . . I was 21 years old in the desert, up to my neck in flies, fleas, shells, bombs and shit, and surrounded by Jerries . . . but still the bread was baked!

Precious supplies of men, food, materials and even water for the besieged was shipped in from Egypt via a precarious sea link nicknamed the Tobruk Ferry. Reg Copper, Royal Army Ordinance Corps, attached to the 9th Australian Division, arrived by this route after the siege started.

> We were informed that our destination was 'Bomb Alley', otherwise besieged Tobruk! . . . We dug ourselves in . . . literally, keeping back the sand with sand-filled ammo boxes used like bricks until we reached firmer ground. Timbers washed

ashore used in conjunction with lorry tarpaulins enclosed our dugouts, and once covered with sand were invisible.

There were desert rats, like miniature kangaroos with long tails with a brush on the end, and capable of terrific speeds... it was from this little animal we took our title 'Tobruk Rats'.

Jack Hawken, 1st Regiment, Royal Horse Artillery, wrote to his mother in June 1941.

My Dear Mother

Please forgive me for not writing for some time... I hope you have not been unduly worrying yourself about me. I have been in the desert for eight months without a break. We began by pushing the 'Eyeties' out of Cyreneacia [Eastern Libya] but then 'Jerry' took a hand and pushed us back... we rejoined our Regiment at Tobruk where we are holding a garrison with the Aussies. Plenty of bombs, shells, and pamphlets but otherwise everything is OK.

Best love to yourself and keep smiling.
Jack

Tony Walsh's mother was keen to keep her son well-fed.

My mother posted a parcel containing a cooked chicken! Needless to say, by the time this reached me in the searing heat of the desert it was in an advanced state of decomposition.

Jim Palmer, 3rd Tank Regiment, his marriage to Muriel in Manchester already feeling very distant, battled south of Tobruk to relieve the besieged port.

We could see the guns far away to our right and there would be a puff of smoke, a screeching wail, a cracking explosion and whirling, white-hot shrapnel would rain down, as the ground shook... tank crews were scrambling out of burning tanks and tanks were exploding with a thundering crack. Everything was chaos... the Italian tanks panicked and tore straight into a German minefield. Like big, slow, black bugs they swerved left and right through the minefield, but one by one there was a shattering roar and thump and one by one the tanks were blown to eternity.

The German infantry at El Adem* were fanatical, their resistance was unbelievable. The whole area was now a graveyard of burnt-out tanks, vehicles and guns, and black plumes of smoke were rising everywhere from these funeral pyres. We were exhausted but no longer frightened . . . we had experienced the whole gamut of emotions, and our only thought was of our own survival. There were only two kinds of soldier in my mind – the quick and the dead.

The seven-month Tobruk siege was finally lifted in early December 1941 when a breakout from Tobruk linked up with the 1st Army Tank Brigade. But at Tobruk 3,000 Allied men were killed, missing or wounded.

Sergeant Jock Walker was in the relieving force.

We moved west relieving Tobruk, much to their joy. The place was a shambles and once more it made one wonder how men could exist and fight in such surroundings.

The Desert War was a continuous ebb and flow. With only one good road and few towns, this was unlike a European conflict. Advances by either side were soon undermined by stretched desert supply lines. By Christmas the Allies had driven Rommel back almost to where his advance had begun, but joy was shortlived. Rommel regrouped and reinforced. By June 1942 the totemic port of Tobruk was back in German hands.

Jack Merewood, Tank Gunner,† The Queen's Bays:

---

* About 20 miles south of Tobruk.

† Five men in a tank crew: gunner, driver, wireless operator/loader, co-driver/machine-gunner, tank commander.

Soon we could see German vehicles in front of us shimmering in the heat. We shelled them and really wreaked havoc. All hell was let loose as we exchanged fire; the noise was deafening, and the dust rose in clouds. It was an exciting experience but also very frightening.

Jack's tank was hit by a shell.

It came straight through the front of the tank and exploded inside. I looked at Jim; he had taken the full blast in his face and was dead. I had blood on my face and arms but what was hurting most was my leg. It felt as if it had been hit by a sledgehammer.

Jack was evacuated by ambulance and train through the desert to Egypt.

The 'ward' was a big marquee – and to me it looked like heaven. Bright, cheerful, flowers on the table, and the sister was the nearest thing to an angel you could imagine . . . she was one of the most wonderful people I have ever met.

But Tobruk was too important to abandon to the enemy. W. G. Poynor was a mechanic on the light cruiser HMS *Coventry* carrying commandos for a secret landing at Tobruk.

It was about 3 a.m. when we approached Tobruk on a dark, moonless night . . . the boats, which had taken the first lot of marines to the beach, were to return to pick up a second lot. We soon realised on seeing and hearing machine-gun fire from this area, that the Germans had obviously had the guiding lights and drawn the boats onto the rocks, where the marines were mown down.

When Poynor's ship was hit, he needed his tool bag for an urgent repair job.

The most harrowing sight I saw was all the young marines. They were all piled on top of each other in various unnatural positions, all of them obviously dead and horribly burnt, their shorts and shirts practically burnt off and their skin in shreds. The bare skinless flesh of almost the whole body was bright pink... I had to get the bag of tools. I did the only possible thing. I walked on top of them.

Sixty-three Royal Marines on Poynor's ship were killed and, in this disastrous operation, over 700 men were killed, and 576 taken prisoner.

With Tobruk back in Axis hands, Allied fortunes in the desert were at rock bottom, with even Egypt now vulnerable to Rommel's advances. Jock Walker was pushed back towards Alexandria.

We were harried every inch of the way, and even at night bombed and machine-gunned as we tried for a bit of rest, refuelling, and necessary repairs... if a truck was beyond our efforts to get it going, I would have the petrol drain plug removed, the petrol allowed to drain away, and an oily rag set alight and up it would go. It broke our hearts to do this as usually it was a minor fault, but we just didn't have the time as the Afrika Corps were just too close.

We had nearly reached the El Alamein line when my truck was bombed and received a very near miss, which put it and us out of action. The vehicle was a mess with blood and shit everywhere, but nobody desperately hurt.

In the desert Jock Walker was endlessly inventive when it came to food.

In hot conditions you could open a tin of 'bully' [corned beef] and literally pour it on your plate; that, and the flies that went with it, was not at all appetising.

Tins of meat and veg and Irish stew, or dead something or other, would be wired onto the exhaust manifold and at the end of the day's travels a hot meal was ready without the trouble of cooking it.

Every truck carried a chicken or two to provide eggs at breakfast.

> Ours were fed on boiled Army 'hard tack' biscuits and tea leaves. Peculiar diet, but they thrived on it and produced the eggs.

Jock was now a hardened desert soldier.

> Our truck was filthy dirty, the windscreen wiped with oil and sand thrown on so that it didn't reflect the sun, with small areas cleaned off for the driver to see where he was going, covered with tatty camouflage and hung round with pots and pans, vehicle springs, spare tyres and all the paraphernalia of a mobile fitter's wagon, not forgetting, of course, our settee tied on the roof and a German machine gun . . . we were a desert army who had adapted to our environment and maintained a discipline that was based upon respect and comradeship, not spit and polish.

On his safe return to Cairo, Jock received news of his best friend's death.

> I just could not believe it; me, the hard man, felt like crying – and did, a little . . . that night we went out and got tanked up. It is the best way to get malaise out of the system. Never brood, have your moment of sadness, and don't dwell on it.

With the position dire, in August 1942 Churchill put General Bernard Montgomery in command. He immediately tried to rebuild his soldiers' depleted morale. Montgomery told them, 'There will be no more bellyaching and no more retreats.' Jock Walker:

> A new General had appeared on the scene, and he travelled around the various laagers giving pep talks and handing out cigarettes . . . we were assured that this bloke was the one to chuck Rommel out of the Desert.

The Eighth Army under Montgomery became better trained for desert warfare and air cover improved. Montgomery was helped by Bletchley Park's codebreakers deciphering vital enemy messages. At the same time, enemy supply lines grew stretched.

Rommel attempted to turn the left flank of the British Eighth Army at the Battle of Alam el Halfa at the end of August 1942, but the British drove him back. Jock Walker:

> Then the battle opened, with the greatest artillery barrage of all time and it really hammered the enemy . . . for ten days the battle raged and at last the enemy broke and the Master race took off and left the poor, numbed Italians without support and without even a vehicle . . . when my truck eventually got through the minefield, we saw the carnage of that battle. Burnt-out trucks, tanks littered the desert; arms and legs and trunks – with or without heads – were all over the place and the smell was sickening in the extreme, especially the tanks with their incinerated crews. In one we looked in, an Italian tank, there [was] only ashes and a grisly pair of hands still grasping the steering tillers.

But the demands of bureaucracy did not wait for battles to be lost or won. John Hurman, Royal Army Service Corps, received a letter from home.

> It was a summons for parking in Ramsgate (50p). I wrote and told them I didn't have ten shillings, and they could come and get me, 'I'm in the middle of the battle in the desert.' No reply!

John Hurman's fine remined unpaid. To win the Desert War, the Allies still had to triumph at El Alamein, and beyond.

CHAPTER TWELVE

Wartime Women, 1940–44

For a food-stretched nation at war, agricultural self-sufficiency was vital. So, in 1939, the First World War organisation, the Women's Land Army, was reborn. By 1944, 80,000 Land Girls were registered to work on farms while men were fighting.

Mitzi Edeson from Leeds was dispatched to Leominster, Herefordshire, a town she had never heard of.

> Some of the farmers weren't too keen to have us, but we were cheap labour, and it was wartime. I expect their thoughts were mixed when they saw us town girls – most of us were around five feet two inches and about eight stones. They must have thought they'll not last; they were wrong, we tackled all the jobs.
>
> Spud planting and picking was a hated job, especially picking in the rain, struggling to pull our feet out of that mud, sometimes leaving our wellies behind, dragging our buckets along and longing to be rained off. Harvesting was not as lovely as some paintings would have you believe; it was very hard work in the days before combine harvesters.

The wartime shortage of manpower meant that the Women's Land Army was supplemented by enemy prisoners-of-war. Italian troops arrived first in July 1941, followed by 70,000 Germans, who worked in fields and factories.

> Sandwiches, to take out in our Jock tins, were Spam, jam, and cheese, and they were always dry by lunchtime . . . we would

be sitting outside or in a barn or a cowshed when it was cold, and the Italian prisoners would be inside in a warm kitchen eating a good dinner. It wasn't as if they worked hard, they didn't . . . they would be shouting *Bella Bella* and blowing kisses . . . the German POWs, on the other hand, were surly, but they were good workers.

In the fields there were no toilet facilities, so to answer a call of nature, we would go behind a hedge hoping no one would see us, spending a penny was okay after we had undone the belt and the dungaree straps, but to have a two penny one was more of a problem – we rarely had any paper so a good strong dock leaf had to do. There was always the peril of nettles, many a nettled bum was had.

East Londoner Emily Braidwood was sent to Clacton, Essex.

The general opinion was that land girls wore too much in winter and too little in the summer! My uniform consisted of strong brown leather shoes, long woollen socks, fawn cotton aertex T-shirts and . . . a fawn felt hat with a Women's Land Army badge, dark green tie with WLA letters and a dark green woollen jumper.

Reality hit me the first morning when we were told to meet a lorry at 6.30 a.m. in the village. It was dark, very dark. I felt cold and tired. I was convinced the village clocks had been tampered with. I had to break the ice in the water jug before washing.

At the farm we all staggered out of the lorry, slipping in the mud, and somehow stood facing a huge sugar beet field. No one had any work experience, no training.

[But] we all loved the life we had discovered . . . we went dancing in Clacton to great bands. On one occasion the air raid sirens sounded. Lights out, we left the dance hall on the sea front and foolishly watched the dog fights, Spitfires and German planes were caught in the searchlights.

Shrapnel fell at my feet. I realised later that that was a narrow squeak ... these were the happiest days of my life, really, truly.

Sixteen-year-old Grace Jackson was less enamoured with her new life in Wales.

> The lady of the manor took us to a field of about one and a half acres. It was covered in weeds and thistles almost as tall as us. We were told to clear it. We had no gloves to wear, so you can imagine what our hands were like at the end of the day. Even our faces were scratched. If it rained and we went to shelter under a tree she would come round and make us go back. She used to sit in the car at the far end of the field and watch us.

Betty Merritt drove tractors on a Sussex farm.

> It was a wonderful sight to see on a late summer morning, the field of golden corn stretching out before me, and then in late afternoon to see it transformed into neatly lined stooks. It was so rewarding. I loved that job ...

Betty Merritt

> I always had to do my own maintenance, such as point the plugs, clean out the carburettor, grease a dozen or so nipples, empty the dirty engine oil from the sump...
>
> I sometimes worked with a coloured man – his name was Jomo Kenyatta, and he later became President of Kenya. When I knew him, he was working on manure piles, but he always looked so smart in his blue and orange short-sleeved shirts and khaki shorts... I used to talk to him a lot.

The war was never far away, as Patricia Cowen recalled.

> We saw a parachute come down and ran to help the man in it. We couldn't tell what nationality he was because he was so badly burnt. We pulled wooden spikes from the field and made a stretcher, covered him with his parachute and carried him to the farmhouse. We thought he would die. But he survived. He was an American and in 2000 came back to Colchester to thank the Land Girls.

Iris Newbould worked on a North Yorkshire farm, but being left-handed, using a scythe was tricky at first.

> I was ridiculed as a cack-handed townie and sent to the back. After that, I worked twice as hard to prove myself. I loved standing at the edge of the field with the long, curved blade in the air... I developed a powerful swing and a good rhythm.
>
> I remember working in the fields with Italian prisoners-of-war. They used to sing opera as they worked and a few of them fancied themselves as 'Romeos'. They used to write love notes on toilet paper, which they threw at us from their lorries.

Marjorie Webb worked at the Surrey farm owned by Sir Roland Hodge. The hard work had compensations.

> The beginning was horrendous, leaving city life to become farm labourers working manually, long hours in appalling weather. It gradually grew within us a determination, a great

esprit de corps developed by the intense feeling of helping the war effort while many of our loved ones were facing the enemy abroad.

With great kindness he [Sir Roland Hodge] invited us young and awkward girls to dinner and to meet Sonya Hieni* and the handsome Stewart Granger.† I sat there in awe, gazing at my screen hero – me, with my puppy fat in an ill-fitting best Sunday dress sitting in the most elegant dining room being waited upon!

To my great embarrassment I nearly mistook the finger bowl for drinking water. When the time came to part, Stewart Granger smiled softly at me, took my hand, and brushed it with his lips. Back at the hostel I told the girls I would never wash that hand again!

Kay Riddell was dispatched 200 miles south from Yorkshire to Kent.

I panicked when the chap who had taken charge of my suitcase during the train journey refused to hand it back to me unless I agreed to go with him to his flat (all this in the gloom of King's Cross Station). In the end he relented, I'm glad to say – my pleas must have got to him. This was the first time I had travelled on my own and I must have been greener than my Women's Land Army jumpers.

As we cycled to the farm [from our hostel] on that first morning, we were almost overcome by a powerful smell of gas. We later found out that one of the girls had gassed herself because she was having a baby to a married man. She had been one of the hostel elite – a rat catcher.

The work on the farm was divided between a farm labourer, me, and several German POWs. Mr Brightling

---

* Sonja Henie, Norwegian figure skater and film star.
† British-born Hollywood star famous for his romantic and heroic roles.

himself [the owner] was here, there and everywhere. During this time, I became very proficient at milking... I had a lot of fun, mostly with Mr Brightling, who was always teasing me. One night he came into my bedroom, but I pretended to be asleep, and he left.

And then there was Reg, a neighbouring farmer with whom I made love under the moon of that long hot summer. Mmmm... when I left, he said he would never get over it, but I am sure he did.

The female contribution to the war effort was not confined to the fields. Mary Stretch was a 16-year-old clerk/typist in Birmingham who then trained as a nurse working with patients returned from the Desert War.

Most were suffering from severe and complicated leg wounds... the discarded plaster splints and dressings were the most offensive and gave off a smell which none of us working at the time will ever forget! However, they proved to be the salvation of many young men and saved limbs which would surely have required amputation... There was not one case of gangrene, and the particular device became known as the 'Tobruk Splint'.*... we worked non-stop from 4 p.m. to 8 a.m. the next morning. We had the satisfaction of knowing that no amputations had been necessary, but the theatre was a sorry mess. The back lobby was full of discarded and stinking plaster casts and there was blood and plaster on the swing doors of the theatre.

Marjorie Holgate was a Red Cross nurse in the Casualty Clearing Centre, Royal Navy Hospital Hasler, Gosport, Hampshire.

---

* An adaptation of the Thomas Splint, dating from 1875. By using plaster of Paris on the splint and limb, wounded patients were protected from the agony of long, bumpy desert journeys.

The Centre was geared to cope with 300 patients an hour... when the alarm bell rang announcing that wounded men were being landed at the dock and were being transferred by ambulance, we ran to Sister's cabin, put on a runner apron, put a packet of cigarettes and matches in our pockets, and joined our designated team of surgeons and nurses. When permission was given, we would give the wounded men the comfort of a cigarette. This was how I learned to smoke, lighting cigarettes for the lads who could not do it for themselves.

Sometimes there was a party on board a newly commissioned ship and young officers would invite nurses to see a 'special' gold rivet.

If you accepted this dubious offer, you found that the rivet was situated in some out of the way bulkhead. Unfortunately for the amorous sailor, a Red Cross nurse's uniform was so stiffly starched and of such pristine whiteness that even the gentlest hug would have caused most noticeable cracks... a chaste kiss was all that was possible before returning to the party.

In Scotland, Matron warned VAD (Voluntary Aid Detachment) Nurse Elizabeth Hamilton of the dangers ahead.

She said, 'Nubile girls like you [she explained 'nubile' as meaning marriageable] are meeting in work or play with male predators lurking in the undergrowth... it behoves you girls to be on your guard... some of them might be RAF pilots, nightly risking their lives, so don't allow yourselves to be bowled over by them, however sympathetic you might feel.'

I had some experience of a male predator in the guise of an RAF officer (ground staff) whom I met at a dance in the Barracks. He was a Londoner, older than me, handsome, smooth-tongued and knew how to treat a girl... but I never thought of him as a possible boyfriend... he invited me to go to London with him ... I refused and later learned that he was a married man with three children!

Teenager Edna Smith nursed in a large London hospital.

> We nurses did everything we could, but we had so little to work with, little equipment, little technology, little expertise ... many wounds were infected before they reached the hospital and, in some of the worse cases, maggots were crawling over them.
>
> One of our patients was a middle-aged Major who had sustained horrendous facial injuries in a bomb explosion. I had never seen these because he was swathed in bandages, but I knew that even the experienced nurses shuddered when they had to dress these wounds ... the ward sister removed the bandages, and I will make no attempt to describe what I saw. Suffice it to say that I knew that if I turned my eyes away, I would never have the courage to look back. So, I stared, almost without blinking, passing everything [the] sister asked for, and pressing my knees together so that I didn't sway.
>
> I remember so well a young Captain who had won a Military Cross for bravery, second only to the Victoria Cross, and had his leg blown off in the process. The day came when he was to go to Buckingham Palace to receive his decoration.

Edna and other nurses polished and pressed his forgotten dress uniform.

> When morning came, the Captain dressed, the empty trouser leg was carefully folded back ... the hero of the day donned his cap and gloves, and with his head held high went swinging down the ward on his crutches. He looked splendid and we all lined up to see him go, not, as so often, with sadness but with pride. I do not believe there is any glory in war – but, if there is, we glimpsed it that morning.

Edna was transferred to the Queen Victoria Hospital in East Grinstead, where Archibald McIndoe pioneered innovative treatments for badly burned aircrew. McIndoe and his team were dealing with completely new types of injuries; faces and hands fried in burning aircraft.

> These injuries were more devastating than any others because disfigurement is so hard to bear. I have seen tough young men with tears streaming down their faces at the sight of themselves ... I felt more strained after this spell of duty than any other. Families and friends who visited were distressed beyond measure when they visited. Young wives and girlfriends realised that their lives, too, would never be the same again. Many visited regularly and devotedly, but eventually a high proportion could not face a future with a partner who was broken physically or mentally and terminated relationships.

In Liverpool, nurse M. C. Iddon met hospital troop trains.

> In the blackout we had to feel our way through the hundreds of bodies – the stench of blood and death filled the carriages and the cries of the wounded soldiers echoed all around – we only had the tiniest torch around our neck, those who were dead we left and those still alive – some suffering from horrendous injuries – were tended in the dark before being ferried to hospital.

She dealt with the aftermath of bombing raids.

> I remember still today the faces of mothers as they searched frantically for lost children, either on the hospital ward or in the makeshift mortuary. I recall one poor mother claiming a baby boy who wasn't hers – she tearfully returned him a week later saying she had lost her own baby and just wanted a baby to hold.

Anne Curry was a patient in Bristol Children's Hospital during air raids.

> Several nights we were woken and shepherded abruptly to the basement to lie on mattresses under prickly blankets. Above our head the world was exploding, soft rains of dust flew about and never settled. The walls shook. The floor shook. The mattress trembled. Nurses brought warm drinks and held our hands. Somewhere in a dark corner a boy my age died calling for his father, he had briefly been my friend.

Audrey Turner from a Yorkshire village joined the Women's Auxiliary Air Force (WAAF) as a driver in Lincolnshire.

> I was 17 years old, or even 17 years young, dressed in my best with a feeling of adventure coming on . . . the first night was a shock. The girls from towns seemed to come from another planet, they left their make-up on and were seemingly unabashed by having to undress in public. A lot had really fancy underwear, proper bras, we made our own . . .

Assaults on female staff made Audrey concerned about safety when returning from late-night shifts.

> I carried a short tyre iron and fully intended to use it if necessary . . . two drunken, yobbish Poles came out of nowhere and had a go . . . I managed to grab the tyre iron with my left hand, and as the other one rushed forward, I hit him on the side of the head . . . and I took off. I could really run in those days and my anger gave me wings . . . [later] I found out that the one I had hit was dead, he'd choked on his own vomit.
>
> A couple of months later I found a woman in our hut who'd hung a blanket around her bed and was really moaning and groaning. I found out she was giving birth.

Audrey called for the doctor, but the baby didn't wait.

The baby had arrived and neither of us knew what on earth to do... it was a boy, still attached by the cord... the doctor did what was necessary, and an ambulance drew up. The woman's fiancé had been killed eight months earlier and she had not told anyone she was pregnant.

Peggy Cocks was also a WAAF driver.

Douglas Bader flew with two artificial legs, but I think I was the only servicewoman driver with one leg.

Peggy had been hit by part of a bomb near Victoria Station, London.

I nearly died, loss of blood etc. I was taken to Westminster Hospital where I remained for four weeks.

Eventually Peggy was fitted with an artificial limb.

The WAAF offered me an office job, but I wanted to drive again. They took some convincing, but I was reinstated... I drove VIPs all over England until the end of the war.

Justine Dowley-Wise was a 14- or 15-year-old schoolgirl, and Dennis Weston, aged 21, was the first man she had dated. She said goodbye to him at Malvern Link station.

I realised I was going to miss him because our friendship had blossomed, and I had grown very fond of him. He had joined the RAF and was soon to train as a pilot, and as he stood there smiling at me, I thought how stunning he looked in his smart blue-grey uniform... he took me in his arms and hugged me. As we stood there embracing each other, he bent down and kissed me tenderly on my forehead and said, 'Please promise to come back to me after this war is over and marry me because I do love you.' His plea was so sincere I promised I would. I was overcome with emotion and stunned by what he had just said... I waved until he was out of sight and then burst into tears.

We kept in frequent touch by letter... I knew he still loved me... when I returned home from school for the holidays, Mother broke the sad news to me that Dennis had been killed in an air crash... I was heartbroken.*

Tim Hardy's mind was filled with dreams of the opposite sex. At just 17 he had been too young to serve in France and was last seen guarding an irrelevant airfield near Nottingham. Overflowing with boredom, Tim's enthusiasm for the Sherwood Foresters dwindled away.

> Our masters believed that that by their positioning of highly polished mess tins alongside the faultlessly folded blankets and by weekly infusions of the holy gospel, the common soldiery would be turned into efficient manslayers.
>
> [But a]fter Dunkirk the army brass lacked the guts to direct a return to the imbecilities of kit-inspection and church parades. For one thing there wasn't much kit left to inspect, and, for another, back in France God had given the impression of being a Nazi, so they didn't dare risk a mutiny by ordering the rank and file to indulge in such frolics.

His boredom mingled with alienation from many of his comrades.

> As far as they were concerned a touch of Hitler wouldn't have gone amiss at home; they found a lot to their liking in the way the Führer dealt with 'Jew boys', gypsies and the infirm.

Tim and the Sherwood Foresters were dispatched to Scotland.

---

* Dennis was newly qualified, and his Wellington bomber went out of control and crashed in Lincolnshire in darkness. The rest of his crew survived. In 1948 Justine married Bill Towill, who had fought in Burma.

As the days were turned into weeks and weeks into months without as much as an air-raid siren to disturb the peace, old habits were revived. Skiving resurfaced as a way of life; prodigious amounts of army supplies found their way onto the black market; everybody was on the make and sloth became all-pervasive.

When Tim tried to escape compulsory Sunday church services by truthfully claiming he was an atheist, his pleas fell on deaf ears.

> I was accused of 'coming the old soldier' (me an old soldier!) . . . it was an experience that confirmed what I'd already learned – you'd never get the better of the system by protesting against it or by telling the truth, least of all by using common sense; no, to beat it you'd have to use guile.

Tim's desperation increased.

> I had to fiddle my way out of the Sherwood Foresters or go suicidal. In the end it didn't need knavery, just a stroke of luck. Perusing the noticeboard one day I came across a curious announcement inviting 'entertainers' to apply for auditions to work in the 46th Division's concert party . . . to my amazement not only was I auditioned without a question about my qualifications, but I was almost overnight signed up!
>
> Less than a year after joining the army, straining to get at Hitler's throat, I was found to be prancing about acting the fool on town hall stages covering the length and the breadth of the Scottish borders.

To Tim, this was no more a daft way of waging a war than endlessly polishing his mess tin. And, in Ashford, Kent, his life changed unexpectedly once more.

> We faced a half-empty house in Ashford. Across the footlights, however, my gaze came to rest, not on the empty seats, no, my eyes locked as in a trance upon one particular incumbent

of a front-row seat: a well-rounded, long-haired teenage female balancing an open notepad on one of two entrancingly shapely knees.

She was, it turned out, a reporter from the *Kentish Express*.

Doreen Maud Fenner had me in flames the moment she opened her mouth. On the instant her voice was as seductive as the person. She spoke with clear, clean cadenza, diction and articulation, the very tongue I had fantasised about in the ghetto, the voice of good manners, intelligence, education, taste and culture. The lovely sound issuing from its beautifully contoured outer package was irresistible. Of course, like that of all nubile young females, DMF's mouth was made for kissing...

However, Tim Hardy's prospect of encountering those lips looked slim. Doreen's father was an ex-Engineer Commander in the Royal Indian Marine.

What chance had I, a little, sway-backed, semi-literate, unrefined private soldier-cum-alley-lad-cum-amateur player who hadn't even made out with a butcher's daughter, what chance did I have of romancing a daughter of the Raj?

While Tim was prancing around on stage, desperate to impress Doreen Fenner, war's reality was hitting families all over the country. Roy Hails, Northumberland:

Opening the door I was confronted by the telegraph boy. They were nicknamed the angels of death... looking at the telegraph boy's face I knew it as bad news, 'The Air Ministry regrets to announce that LAC William Hails has been killed in action. Letter to follow.' 'No reply,' I said to the boy. The lad mumbled, 'I'm sorry, sorry.'

His mother heard the news that Roy's brother was dead.

Lena and I were still standing, looking at each other, when this most awful howl sounded from the kitchen. It was like the howl of a wolf in the wilderness. It went on for a good five minutes. Lena rushed past me into the kitchen, I ran into the toilet and stuck my fingers in my ears.

The telegram boys were as young as 14. Sometimes they learned that it was their own father or brother who had died. Despite their youth, they had to cope with the reaction when they delivered a devastating plain telegram with a cross. John Vickers delivered to a house where the young woman was expecting good news, not a death notice.

> The poor girl collapsed in front of me and sobbed her heart out. I was then only 14 or 15 years old . . . I felt so helpless and didn't know what to do.

CHAPTER THIRTEEN

El Alamein, Egypt, 1942–43

In early 1942 the Allies were losing the war, and people were desperate for some success. But the news was always bad. Hitler might have failed to invade Britain, but he controlled most of Europe. In the east the Germans had launched Operation Barbarossa, their invasion of Russia, with a massive army of well over 3 million men, supported by thousands of tanks and aircraft. The invasion started well, and the Nazis were besieging Leningrad and were on Moscow's doorstep. Meanwhile, their Japanese partners in the Axis had taken huge swathes of the Far East with astonishing speed, including Singapore, Malaya, Borneo and Burma.

In North Africa, after the arrival of Rommel and his Afrika Corps, ascendancy switched regularly between the two sides. For the sake of morale almost as much as for strategic gain, Britain badly needed a victory in the desert. Maintaining fully functioning supply lines was essential if either side were to win the see-sawing conflict.

Thus, control of the small British Mediterranean island of Malta was critical. Malta was home to several airfields and the only British harbour between Gibraltar and Alexandria, Egypt, and was the vital supply corridor between North Africa and Italy. If Britain held Malta, she could disrupt enemy seaborne supplies between Italian ports and Axis troops in North Africa. But if Germany and Italy took control of Malta, the position would be reversed, and British supply lines would break. So, the Axis tried to bomb Malta into submission in over 3,000 air raids, but its

270,000-strong population held firm despite desperate shortages of food and fuel. Army Radiographer Reg Gill had previously been stationed at Etaples, before the Dunkirk evacuation.

> Malta had taken a terrific battering since Italy came into the war, several hundred raids and lots of fatalities, they said... hungry and apprehensive, it seemed obvious that Malta could not survive long.
>
> If the enemy could capture Crete, with its much larger garrison, then Malta was in desperate straits... we all thought that Malta would follow Crete.*

The Maltese formed long queues for limited food. Fuel for heat and light was almost non-existent. Reg Gill:

> We were swimming off the coast when we saw a large bird flapping about in the water. There had been an air battle, and a griffin vulture had been caught in the slipstream of a fighter and its wing broken. One of the sergeants swam out, wrung its neck, and handed it over to the mess cook, who promptly plucked it and curried it. It wasn't very much. About a mouthful each. It was a scrawny creature, but I don't like to admit to my bird-loving friends that I've actually eaten a vulture.

By August 1942 hopes for relieving besieged Malta largely rested on Operation Pedestal, a rescue convoy that included a fuel tanker, 14 merchant ships, and several cruisers and destroyers. After fierce Axis attacks, just five ships reached the desperate island, but they included the vital US oil tanker *Ohio*, which was so badly damaged it was lashed between two other ships. William Cheetham:

---

* Allied troops were forced to evacuate Crete, where German airpower was decisive. Fifteen thousand troops were killed or injured.

> We steamed through the breakwater into the Grand Harbour at Malta. Two ships, small destroyers, with an oil tanker between them, had safely brought the last ship of the convoy to its destination.
>
> The people lined the harbour to cheer us, and the military band played 'Hearts of Oak' as we entered . . . we did not ask for praise. We had only done what we set out to do.
>
> That night we went ashore, getting gloriously drunk on Ambete, the local wine, but commonly called Stuka juice. Can you blame us? I think we deserved it.

The convoy paid a heavy price in terms of lost ships,* but the arrival of tons of fuel and food helped preserve Allied control of Malta. As military historian Richard Holmes put it, 'The Axis never eliminated the threat from Malta, whose fate rested on a knife-edge throughout and influenced the Desert War to a degree that would be difficult to overstate.'

After so much military see-sawing between the two sides, enduring success in North Africa now rested on the final Battle of El Alamein, two months after the relief of Malta. El Alamein, a town in Egypt, was bounded by the Mediterranean coast and by the Qattara Depression, a long, flat saltmarsh, which was difficult to cross with heavy track vehicles. Despite pressure from Churchill, General Montgomery waited until his soldiers were better trained for desert warfare and until he possessed superior numbers of men and weapons.

There followed a bloody, attritional 12-day battle that started on 23 October 1942.

Tank Gunner Jack Merewood had recovered from his Tobruk injuries and was back in the frontline.

---

* Estimates of the number of dead sailors and merchant seamen vary between 350 and 540.

There's a glorious sunset tonight. What a mad world. Who would think we are on the eve of a great battle – perhaps the fiercest we have been in yet . . . If I have to die, I'm not afraid, but my heart aches for Jessie and my mother and dad. God comfort them.

The air was thick with sand and dust, and although we closely followed each other, it was almost impossible to see the tank in front. The edges of the track had been marked with petrol tins, some of them with dim lights behind, to keep us from straying into mines, for the track was little wider than a tank.

The fighting grew fiercer, and the barrel of our turret machine gun began to glow red, and then become white hot as the bullets passed through it. Ron worked like a demon, and I was firing guns as fast as he could load them. We moved like robots, no time to think.

Alex Clark from Scotland:

On the night before 23rd October we knew it was the big thing. We were ready to do battle . . . I was the Company runner and had to be beside the Sergeant-Major to take messages . . . he was the first man to be killed. It brought me to my senses. I said to myself; this is war and there is no point in being feart [afraid]. I charged forward like a banshee with my bayonet fixed. Men were being killed all around. One man who had been a pal of mine at school was killed. His stomach was blown out.

Cecil Ritson, Natal Mounted Rifles, South Africa:

Shells were bursting all around and shrapnel whistled in all directions . . . there was a blinding explosion next to me. I must have passed out because, when I gathered my wits, I was lying about 15 paces in front of an enemy machine gun pit.

> Our platoon officer was lying on my immediate left. At that moment he raised his head with the intention of charging, and he was shot through the head. I 'froze' in my exposed position, and I could clearly see the gunner pointing in my direction. It was a terrifying moment. Then I was aware of Jimmy Shrimpton closing in from the right and being shot as he jumped in among the Germans. I then rushed at the gun pit as other colleagues converged from the left. The positions were taken, and the prisoners rounded up.
>
> It was now dawn and I was guarding the group of prisoners from a stand-off position. One of the prisoners decided to make a break and with head down he dashed to my left front. I shouted to him to halt, but he continued. My Bren gun was set on single-shot, and I fired from the hip well ahead of him. I was amazed to see him drop like a log, hit in the head by a single bullet. This action seemed to put paid to any further attempts at escaping.

Arthur Ward, Royal Artillery, was loading up with fresh ammunition when he heard the whoosh of a shell.

> I was blown to the side with the blast and, when the smoke cleared, I saw two lads (whom I had just been talking to) laid on the floor. One was Chalky White (from Reading), whom I had known for a few months. I turned him over and he had a hole in his head about 4 inches in diameter. It was obvious he was dead. I turned to Wally Walton (Barnsley) and he was practically the same, a hole in his head and very little blood. I can see to this day his face was ashen white and the sand which was caked to his face was just falling off him, like water running off a boulder.
>
> Seeing two good men lose their lives, which all seemed so unnecessary . . . if only the men who started wars were in the frontline like this they would think twice.

The Axis troops fought tenaciously but their depleted forces were desperately short of fuel. Rommel signalled a retreat. Jack Merewood:

> The desert was a scene of destruction and desolation – burned-out trucks and tanks, dead German and Italian soldiers, guns and equipment strewn everywhere. Then came hundreds of soldiers, mostly Italians, streaming across the desert shouting and waving their arms . . . the German supply lines had been stretched to the limit . . . as they retreated, they just left the Italians behind.

Decisive victory at El Alamein signalled the final chapter in the Desert War. This was the first major defeat for the enemy and was hugely significant for Allied morale. As Winston Churchill later put it, 'Before Alamein we never had a victory. After Alamein we never had a defeat.'

American generals wanted to invade France, but Churchill was more cautious, knowing that a massive increase in weapons production was needed first. Roosevelt agreed, and the Americans joined the fight for North Africa on 8 November 1942. The plan, Operation Torch, was to pincer the enemy between British and American armies in Tunisia. Churchill and Roosevelt's caution was wise; El Alamein was a long way from Iowa or Indiana, and America's greenhorn troops paid a heavy price as they learned

Tom Davies

the grim reality of frontline fighting. But eventually America grew better at war and the German shortage of fuel, food and ammunition increased.

Tom Davies from Neath, South Wales, 1st Parachute Brigade, was deployed to Operation Torch. He was soon raiding an Italian encampment.

> As we moved stealthily through the valley on a beautiful moonlit night, the stillness of the air was broken only by the distant chorus of giant bullfrogs ... as we plodded quietly on, for every mile of the journey my three-inch mortar bomb seemed to double in weight ... rocket flares zoomed into the night sky and for a brief moment seemed to hang in mid-air bathing the camp below in a crimson glow ... The signal to 'Fire!' was given and mortar shells rained down on the huts which housed the unsuspecting Italian troops ... cries and screams of terror rent the sky. Men ran here and there half-dressed, some only in their underwear. As they came out of the huts they ran straight into the stream of machine-gun and rifle fire. More flares added light to the subject, the strange glow giving a theatrical effect to the whole scene of confusion.
>
> After a couple of hours of the long weary trudge back, the first sight of daylight came giving rise to a warm grumbling wind which seemed to be urging us to hurry along. The faces of the lads were pale and drawn in the light of the early morning sky.

Given a chance, Tom and his mates would head to Algiers for relaxation.

> The whole place seemed to shimmer against the background of the clear blue sky, fringed with palm trees in the distance ... Sampling the wines which could be bought cheaply, we would sit sheltering in the shade of the palms in

the big squares adjoining the boulevards which were lined with colourful orange trees . . . there were many brothels in Algiers, kept by some 'Madame Something-or-Other' who paid the girls who worked for her on a commission basis by the number of clients they 'entertained' in their 'labour of love'.

Eric Atkinson performed a very different labour of love in Algiers.

> I pulled my 15-cwt truck sharply when I saw what I thought was the victim of a road accident lying by the roadside . . . two Arabs ran to me and pointed to the figure. The older of the two told me his wife was about to give birth. Would I kindly take them to the nearest hospital.
>
> I knew that giving lifts was contrary to King's Regulations, but I could hardly refuse in this situation . . . we had only gone a little way when the husband shouted for me to stop as the baby was on its way. Fortunately, I happened to have a clean towel in the truck and the husband took off his shirt to lay on the floor of the truck. With much shouting the baby was safely born. With the help of my army clasp knife, we cut the umbilical cord cleanly, and I drove carefully on to the maternity hospital . . . some weeks later I received a wooden plaque bearing a painting of a village scene, which I still cherish.

For other troops, letters to and from home kept their spirits up in the desert. Sergeant Len Scott was posted to the Royal Army Pay Corps rather than a frontline unit because of defective eyesight. From North Africa he wrote passionate letters to his Danish-born wife, Minna, back in Warlingham, Surrey.

> Sometimes, I am wild for longing for your body and then I sit down and relieve my feelings in a letter. What a delicate thing is this relationship. Can we dare examine these fine silken threads that float like summer thistledown between us, gently caressing, but never compelling?

Later he reflected:

> When we desired each other there were no words. A glance, my fingers brushing the nape of her neck, her hands ruffling my hair ... sometimes on long country walks the fragrance of lilac or the intoxicating pungency of pinewoods would bring us together in unworded intimacy.

Minna wrote:

> I find myself over and over again aching for the nearness of you ... I am terribly shy about our life together – I mean talking about it, let alone writing – you can have no doubt whatever that I am passionately in love with you. It sounds childish but I often cry from sheer desire for you ... never let go again, darling, never. I just cannot do without you.

Minna Scott, Warlingham, Surrey

But however good it was to receive letters from home or spend time in the bars of Algiers, the British soldiers still had to win the Desert War.

In early 1943, Tom Davies was caught up in brutal fighting at Djebel Mansour, a peak about 2,000 feet above sea level overlooking the Tunis Road. After several attacks and counterattacks, the Allies finally took control of the summit.

> The bodies of a considerable number of Germans who would take no further interest in the war lay strewn around, some caught in the oddest poses... [one] was suspended like a huge rag doll whose seams had come apart, spewing mangled flesh through his tattered uniform.
>
> Our number-one gunner, Jock Miller, fell backwards into the mortar pit, shot clean through the head. He died in our arms not able to say a word, just a faint rattle coming from his throat as his colour changed from a deep tan to a greyish white in a matter of seconds.

Tom Davies withdrew down the hill.

> It was not easy to distinguish the wounded from the rest of us as we were all covered in blood; a gory sight, stinking of the sweat and dust of the past few days... we took toll of the casualties, which were considerable, about three-quarters of the battalion having been killed or injured.

For Tom, the Desert War tightened the bond with his mates.

> A very strong sense of camaraderie was forged amongst the boys, each of us depending on the others for his existence. We ate, slept, shared the washing water when we were fortunate enough to obtain it and did practically everything one could imagine in each other's company to the extent that our very souls were revealed to each other.

The Allies pushed the retreating enemy through Tunisia, breaking through their final defences before Tunis. Eddie Burke:

> Those of us who had been in North Africa from the start of the campaign savoured the sense of euphoria. We had endured the bitter, cold nights. The persistent rain. Witnessed the death of gallant comrades. Been shocked by the sight of mates agonising in bloodstained battledress from wounds in

legs, arms, and abdomen. The sense of victory was intoxicating. The Royal Inniskillings were the first infantry battalion to enter Tunis. The welcome we received was overwhelming. Young girls threw flowers and blew kisses.

Sergeant Jock Walker swept on for the final liberation of Tunisa at Bizerta and Cap Bon.

At Cape Bon we nailed the enemy once and for all. It was a shockingly bloody battle . . . but the result is history, and many of us had the most wonderful day of our lives, standing up on the cliffs, looking down on the Mediterranean, where the Axis troops were trying to do a mini-Dunkirk.

I suppose it was cruel, really, but having suffered at their hands for so long, it seemed a pleasure to watch the small boats pull away and the RAF would then buzz along and sink them, or the odd 25-pounder would thump them into smithereens. Revenge is very sweet, never mind what the do-gooders say. None of them got away.

On 12 May 1943 the final Axis troops in Tunisia surrendered. Victory at last gave the Allies some good news to cheer the home crowd. Mussolini had been beaten, oil supplies secured, and the Germans had lost two Panzer Divisions. Jock Walker could now enjoy the fleshpots of Tunis.

The scene was indescribable; wine flowed, literally in the streets, and, as near as dammit, everybody was well on the way to getting stoshius [drunk] . . . we were led to a vast wine storage place where the wine was flowing from smashed-open casks . . . we watched in astonishment as a couple of Ghurkhas, kukri in hands, were carving holes in these huge vats to allow the wine to flow freely. Ancient Rome must have been like this, only the women were missing, more's the pity, so no orgy in the fullest sense.

The balance of the war had shifted. The Axis had been vanquished in North Africa, the Seige of Malta had been lifted, and Hitler's dreams in the east were being crushed in the Soviet snow. All-conquering Japan had lost a crucial battle for sea control at Midway and been beaten by the Americans in a bloody fight at Guadalcanal. But finally freeing Western Europe from Hitler's tight grip, and removing Japan from huge swathes of the east, would be a tremendous challenge.

CHAPTER FOURTEEN

Enemy Aliens? 1940–43

British soldiers were engaged in gruelling combat with the Italian Army in the North African desert and, from the outbreak of that conflict onwards, the lives of Italian civilians living peacefully in Britain were rudely shattered. Tony Jaconelli had lived in Britain since the age of eight. On 10 June 1940, Mussolini declared war, and at 2 a.m. that night policemen knocked on his door in Glasgow. Tony was arrested and the family home searched, as his son recalled.

> Next morning, Tony was feeling at his lowest ebb. Locked alone in his cell, unaware of what was going on; of what was happening to him and his family . . . he had lived here for most of his life. He was as British as any other resident. His head pounded as he grappled with the plight he was in. How could it come to this?

Ettore Emanuelli had also been picked up within hours of Italy's declaration of war.

> I was taken to HM Prison Walton, Liverpool, where I was to spend the next seven weeks. We were housed in D Wing, a part of the prison which had not been used since the days of the suffragettes . . . it was in filthy condition with pigeon excrement everywhere.

Racecourses were commonly used as internment camps, and Ettore next spent four months at York.

We were housed under and at the back of the grandstand. My main recollection of York was the boiled rice enlivened by the aroma of chocolate from the nearby Terry's Chocolate factory.

Eventually 4,000 Italians joined 70,000 Germans and Austrians as internees, primarily in camps on the Isle of Man. Around 80 per cent of the internees in one camp were Jewish refugees from Hitler, including distinguished academics and musicians. Before Dunkirk the government set up orderly plans for interning Germans. About 120 tribunals were appointed to sift the 'enemy aliens' into three categories according to the level of risk, but the growing threat of invasion after Dunkirk brought this system to a juddering halt. Spy fever swept the country. Both Germans and Italians were arrested, and some Italian-owned shops were attacked.

When Gaetano Cibelli, who had lived in Britian for decades, was arrested, the police shouted at him to immediately reveal the whereabouts of one of his sons. His godson, actor Tom Conti, recalled:

His response was born of both anger and pride. 'Of course I tell you. He's in the Royal Air Force.'

Pietro Ghiringhelli's father had lived in Leeds since 1919. Like thousands of others, he was arrested by Special Branch the night Italy declared war. A picture of Mussolini on the wall did not help his case.

After three weeks of internment, in what was probably an exchange for Britons living in Italy, Pietro and his family were forced to return to Pietro's birthplace, the small village of Musadino on Lake Maggiore. Ten-year-old Peter Ghiringhelli was now living in a Fascist state at war with the country where he had been born.

I was set upon by a group of lads after school and stoned, the group rapidly growing as more joined in to shouts and yells of 'Inglese'. Having been nearly suffocated in England with smelling salts and called 'Eyetie', I was now being stoned and called English.

As the government ran out of space for internment camps, they shipped their new prisoners overseas. In July 1940, 734 Italians were dispatched to Canada on the *Arandora Star*. West of Ireland the ship was torpedoed by a German U-Boat. Tom Conti's godfather, Gaetano Cibelli, survived.

> My godfather was thrown into the ocean. He survived and spoke to me about it only once, remembering the terrible cold, and the fear that the resulting oil slick would ignite. And his friend, Alfonso Avella, calling across the water, 'Cibelli, Cibelli . . .'

Alfonso Avella and 469 other Italians died, as well as 243 Germans, including some pro-Nazis. The Italian internees had been imprisoned below decks and behind barbed wire.

Paul Crailsheimer was also rescued from the sea around the *Arandora Star*. He had been forcibly separated from his wife, and when Paul was dispatched to Canada, Hanne remained incarcerated on the Isle of Man. Despite the terrible loss of life on the *Arandora Star*, within two weeks Paul was bundled on board a second ship, the *Dunera*, sailing for Australia. The conditions on the eight-week journey were terrible. Guards ill-treated the internees and sometimes threw their possessions overboard. His daughter told the BBC:

> During the two years that Paul stayed in Australia, his wife did not know exactly where he was. When Hanne was finally released from internment in November 1941, she discovered that her mother had died in Auschwitz.

The disaster of the *Arandora Star* prompted more sympathetic public attitudes, and as the threat of invasion receded, the obsession with spies also faded and most of the 70,000 'enemy aliens' were allowed home.

In the German-occupied Channel Islands, the locals, enemy aliens to the Nazis, were not so lucky. In September 1942 the Nazis decreed that anyone not a Jersey native would be deported to Germany. Sylvia Diamond's father was Hampshire-born.

> A German officer and Jersey policeman came to the door, confirming the decree and telling us to be at the harbour next day with one suitcase each.
>
> And so my family were deportees at the harbour next day... crowds watch, some wearing small Union Jacks and shouting defiance, 'One, two, three, four! Who the hell are we for?' And deportees joined in, yelling back 'Churchill! England! Jersey!' But close relatives were distraught, not knowing if they would ever see us again, as the boats took us away.

Sylvia was imprisoned in Southern Germany with over 2,000 other Channel Islanders. She finally returned home to Jersey three years later, in September 1945.

CHAPTER FIFTEEN

Children, Teenagers and War, 1940–43

While fathers had exchanged the factory or office for driving a tank or flying a Spitfire, the lives of their children at home had changed just as significantly. It wasn't only the fear of their fathers not returning home, or of German bombs. The war heralded freedoms unimaginable in peacetime. Fathers were away and mothers preoccupied with scraping enough food together to feed their family while also taking on new challenges, like serving in the forces or working in munitions factories.

So, childhood collided with the adult world prematurely, embracing fear and excitement in equal measure. Seven-year-old Barbara Vanderstock, Croydon:

> I used to go with my brother and friends and play war games in the local woods. We hunted for shrapnel in houses that had been hit by incendiaries and played in the haystacks and a bomb crater in a nearby field. Once when we were alone in the shelter during a daytime air raid, we stood at the shelter entrance to watch a nearby house explode as it was hit by a bomb. We wanted to check that it was a real explosion like the ones in the films.

Schoolboy Henry Forrest in South London was treated to a thrilling experience.

On a bombed site next door to the school was installed, for a short time, a fully operational Spitfire. If you bought a five-shilling National Savings Stamp you were allowed, under RAF supervision, to sit in the cockpit and have the controls explained. What a treat. It was all part of a scheme to raise funds for the war effort.

It was at this school I kissed a girl for the first time. Her name was Doris Haines. I can remember that she had a runny nose, which I took great care to avoid. I didn't really want to do this, but all the boys were intent on the deed. It was considered part of growing up. She was now my 'girl', but I don't think I kissed her again. I was in love with Pat Griffiths, but she was spoken for by a drip called Fletcher who also possessed a snotty nose.

We would watch the pubs 'turn out', there would nearly always be big fights, and we would gaze at the comical antics of these drunks, trying to hit each other. The ladies were worse, and their language was dreadful. My Nan was one of them, she was always fighting with Mrs Wilson her neighbour.

Children crash-landed into a new reality. June Miller's father served on HMS *Glorious.*

The bus stopped in the traffic. I looked out of the window, and there was a newsagent's shop with placards outside – white with big black lettering HMS *GLORIOUS* SUNK – MASSIVE LOSSES. I turned to my aunt and said, 'Look, that's the name of Daddy's ship.' People around us on the bus all seemed to stop talking. Auntie Rene wept and held me close. The war had laid its hand on my childhood, and everything was about to change.

A telegram arrived to advise mother; Daddy was 'missing in action'. Mother was distraught – it could not be true. She waited and waited, hoping that by some miracle he would be safe . . . how do you explain to a child of ten that war means killing one another? Reality was to follow when Mother received a second telegram saying 'MISSING PRESUMED DEAD – KILLED IN ACTION.'*

In the coastal fishing village of Staithes, North Yorkshire, bounty from the stormy sea supplemented the lives of locals. Eleven-year-old Ken Verrill:

> Huge amounts of timber in all shapes and sizes and lengths got washed ashore along with a lot of other things we could find a use for . . . we were not supposed to, but we would go and collect whatever we would find, boxes of tinned food, and bundles of wood usually tied with wire straps . . . we would climb down the cliffs to get at it and if it couldn't be carried up it would be pulled up the cliff face by rope, then, loaded like pack horses, we would carry it home. [As a result] hen houses, garden sheds, pig sties, fences, and outhouses got built as never before.

Even on the remote Yorkshire coast, war was close.

> A plane crashed just outside the village on the edge of the cliff, we rushed to see what we could find before anyone else . . . there were bombs and bodies scattered in the wreckage. One blond-haired young man was the double of a boy who was with us and, on looking at the body this youth, 'Albert' nearly fainted. I saw a parachute hanging on the cliff edge and, thinking mother might make use of it, I went to gather it and found a body hanging from it down the side of the cliff. Unable to pull it up, I had to leave it.
>
> Mines dropped into the sea to sink our ships, and those put there to protect our island sometimes broke from their moorings and washed on to the shore. We got used to the explosions as they hit the rocks.

---

* 1,207 men on HMS *Glorious* died, 8 June 1940.

> One night as I laid in my bed, I heard something solid hitting the sea wall below my window. I was looking at this huge mine bobbing and rolling against the concrete wall. I went downstairs and out of the back door picked up a 20-foot pole I had got off the beach a few days before, laying down under the barbed wire, I pushed at the mine . . . I knew that if one of the horns broke it would explode, I could see one of them was badly bent.

When the tide turned, Ken saw the mine and his pole slip away.

> Next morning, I woke to great excitement and on the lifeboat slipway was a great big black mine, and I could hear people saying if it had gone off, we could all have been killed in our sleep. I dare not say anything but just kept wondering if it was mine . . . I was so frightened I ran home and went to bed telling my mother I did not feel well. I realise now that I should have raised the alarm instead of messing about with my pole . . . my stupidity put the village at risk.

Teenagers, too, were catapulted into an adult world before they were ready. At work they took on early responsibility as adults went off to war, and they also grappled with challenging new ideas.

Sixteen-year-old Dianna Dobinson joined Oswald Mosley's Fascist Blackshirts before the war. She encountered Nazi propagandist William Joyce, later known as Lord Haw-Haw.

> I was completely bowled over by the appearance of the members – girls and boys alike. The immaculate black shirt and tie. The slim trousers tucked into long, shiny boots. Topping it all was the wide leather belt with the large shiny buckle with the Blackshirt emblem . . . under the buckle were several large spikes, which formed an extremely effective weapon . . . as soon as William [Joyce] started speaking the atmosphere changed completely and I was to learn from future meetings that he had the ability to manipulate

a crowd like none I had ever heard before. From then on, I never missed one of his meetings, but, of course, they could be pretty rowdy, and this was when I saw the belts put to good use.

I left the Blackshirts when I met the boy who was to eventually become my husband. War finally came and one evening I turned on my little battery radio and I was astounded to hear a voice I knew only too well saying, 'Germany calling! Germany calling!' ... William Joyce had left this country and joined forces with our enemies and therefore became a traitor.*

This unsettling new world in which horizons stretched beyond their customary domestic confines brought intriguing romantic complications. Pam Cuthbert was a Post Office telephonist.

I met a Marine, Bill, who became my boyfriend. When he went to sea, we corresponded ... meantime I met an American with a stupid name. Chuck, would you believe? He kept me supplied with candy and cigarettes, and sometimes stockings ... a cousin of mine in the Canadian army visited my family and introduced me to a friend. So, now I had three boyfriends!†

Tim Hardy from Nottinghamshire was still a teenager, having been too young to fight in France. He was desperate to bear arms against Hitler but equally desperately in love. Tim had last been encountered gazing with rapture from a concert party stage in Kent upon the shapely features of Doreen Fenner, a reporter for the *Kentish Express* and daughter of a senior officer in the Royal Indian Marines. His hopes of success were encouraged and dashed in the same breath.

---

* Joyce was tried and executed after the war.

† Pam did not marry any of the three. She met and married Spencer after the war and they had two sons.

> In the darkness of the cinema, she allowed me to hold her hand. Our world, however, was too disorderly to allow orderly courtship, and my hopes were short-lived. My sweet reported that she also wanted to take a swipe at Hitler; she joined the Navy and moved clean across the country to Milford Haven, thus adding physical separation to the social divide. So began courtship by letter, not, worse luck, of the French variety but by courtesy of the Royal Mail.

Tim pondered how he could improve his image as a lowly entertainer with a young woman now arming torpedoes against the Nazis.

> The hands that I'd held were now caressing torpedoes – phallic imagery indeed! – in Wales . . . enough was enough, I volunteered for the Parachute Regiment. I was fired by the notion that by displaying a parachutist's wings on my sleeves I'd show proof of my determination to do real battle with Hitler and so persuade Doreen to permit the assuageance of my smouldering lust.

No doubt both Adolf Hitler and Doreen Fenner were quaking in their boots at the thought of Tim Hardy in full paratrooper's gear. But before that Tim needed to be trained.

> I got down at last to some really serious instruction in the brain-splitting, windpipe-slitting art of war . . . I pounded over seven miles of rough track. Then, after scrambling through drainpipes; scaling high, slippery walls, and breeching barbed-wire fences, I'd managed to fire a rifle and hit the target.
> Thrown off high towers we were told, much as public schoolgirls are instructed, to keep our ankles and knees glued together . . . the big day came at the end of a fortnight's hard slog . . . I was told I would be second man out. Number one was the only other aspirant-parachutist who wasn't several inches taller. Together, he and I formed a two-man minority

of 'short-arses'... my diminutive friend swung his legs into the hole alright, but on the bark 'Go' he turned greenish in the gills, opened up his breakfast, crawled into a corner of the basket and whimpered that he'd rather not.

It being up to me to preserve the honour of short people, I swung my own legs into the hold and, imagining myself to be a robot, I waited to be switched on. At 'Go' I straightened up, plunged myself through the hole like a man on the gallows... a hundred feet into the fall I heard a noise as if somebody above me was tearing a sheet of calico; it was the sound of my parachute bursting from its envelope and opening above my head like a fantastic umbrella... I dropped to earth a lot faster than I'd anticipated – in a matter of seconds. Knees together, bending into the fall, I subsided into the grass as gracefully as Nijinsky.

I was to be the consummate parachutist; seated in an aircraft pitching around the sky like corks in a rough sea, I was always close to throwing up and always, therefore, more than ready to jump out. Indeed, I felt so awful at times that I'd have happily leapt without a parachute.

After the seventh aeroplane jump, I was given a red beret, a flashy cap badge, cloth wings to sew on my uniform and two whole shillings a day extra pay. The question was, would all this new frippery and affluence help me to seduce Doreen Maud Fenner?

Tim was pleased with the extra pay and status and was, no doubt, eager to show Doreen Fenner his red beret. But he wouldn't have calculated the dangers that lay ahead or known that he would serve on D-Day. The chances of British and American paratroopers like Tim being killed, wounded or captured on that day or soon after was more than 1 in 3, around 35 per cent.

PART TWO

My legs pressed harder around my father's waist; my arms nearly choked him. His horn-rimmed glasses were steamed up from my breath – or was it from his tears? The humming of Japanese aircraft in the sky was loud enough for everyone to hear now, and panic spread like ink on a blotter.

Leaving her father behind, a child evacuating from
Singapore, February 1942

CHAPTER SIXTEEN

The Far East, 1941

Despite its failure to invade Britain, Germany's European progress continued. Supported by her allies, the Nazis took Yugoslavia and Greece by the early summer of 1941, and Kiev, Rostock and Smolensk in the Soviet Union by November. Meanwhile, in the Far East, despite the military-dominated Japanese government's evermore bellicose rhetoric, life for expatriates was almost unchanged.

Vicar's daughter Phyllis Briggs, from Bexhill, Sussex, trained as a children's nurse, then qualified as a midwife at King's College Hospital, London. Her own parents had met in Odessa, and Phyllis was hungry to also experience the wider world. She joined the Colonial Nursing Service and, by 1941, aged 33, she was a Nursing Sister at Alor Star, Northern Malaya, home to an RAF base.

> We looked after people of numerous races; chiefly Malays, Chinese and Indians, but we had a few Europeans too. The nurses in training were local girls . . . many of the patients had tropical diseases such as malaria, beriberi and yaws. There was a busy maternity ward and some lunatic cells, so we had a variety of work.

For men and women in the colonies, the War was purely a European conflict. Dunkirk or the Blitz felt hugely distant from life in Alor Star, except for families with relatives serving in the British Army or the Royal Air Force.

Phyllis Briggs

Some British Army officers and RAF personnel were stationed near Alor Star, and we had quite a gay time when off duty. They asked us to numerous parties and dances, and we also played golf and badminton. On our days off we sometimes drove down to Butterworth, some 60 miles away, and then over on the ferry to Penang Island. I had many friends there and we used to go to the swimming club, where there was a lovely view of Kedah peak across the water. Sometimes we had picnics on one of the beautiful beaches.

This cosy world of picnics and parties was shattered on 7 December 1941. At 7 a.m. a crescendo of 183 Japanese fighter planes and torpedo bombers attacked the resting US fleet at Pearl Harbour, Hawaii, without warning. American aircraft were smashed, and battleships blown out of the water. That morning 2,400 people were killed, and almost the entire US Pacific Fleet sunk. A once distant European war was now on America's doorstep, and soon engulfed the whole world.

As the fires of Pearl Harbour burned, on the same day Kota Bahru, northeast Malaya, was also invaded by the Japanese. By that afternoon Japan, superior in air power, controlled the precious RAF base at Kota Bahru, and the Allies were in a hasty retreat. The Japanese were already on their way towards their major target: the British strategic naval base in Singapore, at the foot of Malaya. Fortress Singapore was the defensive shield for the entire region, as well as a key distribution point for rubber and oil.

The next day the RAF attempted to regain the initiative by bombing an advance Japanese base just across the Thai border. It was a disaster. Virtually every one of 62 Squadron's Blenheim bombers were hit, but only 28-year-old Squadron Leader Arthur Scarf's aircraft survived. Although completely on his own, Scarf still attacked the enemy but was gravely wounded before crash landing at Alor Star. Phyllis Briggs:

> Suddenly an ambulance arrived. In it was Pongo Scarf, a young RAF officer we knew well. His plane had crash-landed in a nearby field and he was badly wounded. His wife, Sally, was one of our nursing sisters. She offered her blood for transfusion, but it was too late. She left Alor Star before his burial.
>
> I was determined that Pongo would be buried properly. We managed to get a coffin from the jail. Another sister came with me in my Morris 8, and we followed the ambulance bearing his coffin to the local cemetery, where a grave had been dug. Later, when I saw Sally, I could tell her we had done all we could.*

Phyllis and other nurses stayed at their posts for four days after all other European women were instructed to leave.

> We had hardly any sleep with air raids, and casualties being brought in at all hours. The guns firing, shaking the house, joined by the constant noise of trucks rumbling by as the army retreated. Most of our patients were sent home; any remaining being evacuated into lorries and sending south to

---

* For his courage and self-sacrifice, Scarf was awarded the Victoria Cross. Phyllis never saw Scarf's wife again, but she thanked Phyllis for staying behind and ensuring her husband received a proper burial.

other hospitals. One motherless baby I handed to an Indian *amah* as no relatives came to collect it.

Most of the local inhabitants fled from Alor Star. Many of them piled all their belongings into cars and old carts with mattresses on the roof for protection but often planes swooped down and machine-gunned these unfortunate people. Workers in the outlying paddy fields were also shot down... we nursing sisters were told to pack two suitcases and be ready for the password: 'Curtain fallen.' Hearing this over the telephone, we were to drop everything and go.

When the curtain fell, Phyllis headed south in her trusty Morris 8 with two other nurses.

There were burnt-out cars and rickshaws along the way, local buses were crammed with people; others were pushing bicycles along piled high with belongings.

Phyllis arrived safely in Kuala Lumpur before being dispatched to a hospital in Seremban.

The hospital was filled to overflowing with wounded soldiers... we were all working long hours. I had a camp bed in Jenny MacAlister's room. She was engaged to a rubber planter and was getting ready for her wedding. Little did she realise that it would be nearly four years before they could get married.

Romanus Miles was a 12-year-old boy of mixed Asian and European extraction living in Singapore with his father.

It was business as usual in the city and the entertainment centres were packed with soldiers looking for a good time with the many pretty Asian girls... little did I realise what was in store for us in the near future. Neither did Dad, the Governor, and all the Top Brass in charge of our lives. It was sleep before the nightmare.

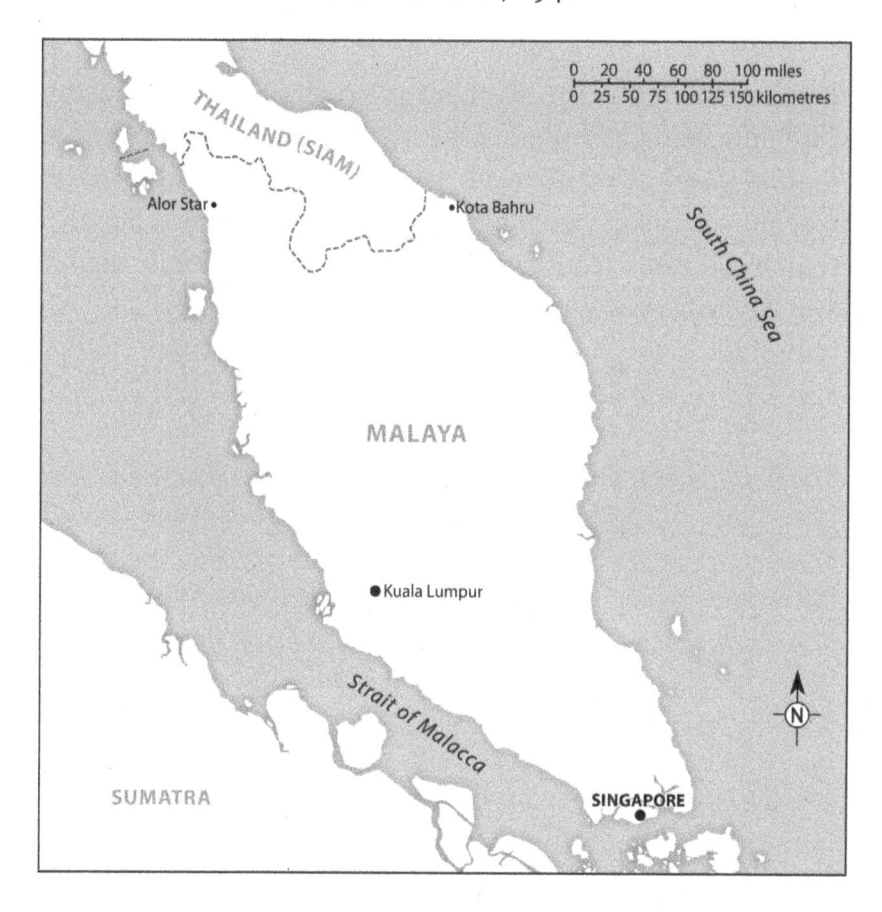

The nightmare was complete when the British battleship HMS *Prince of Wales* and cruiser HMS *Repulse* were sunk by waves of Japanese torpedo bombers on 10 December 1941. The *Prince of Wales* was Britain's most modern battleship, and it was widely believed its enormous firepower made it invincible. American journalist Cedric Brown observed the disaster.

> Japanese bombers are still winging around like vultures, still attacking the *Wales* . . . Men are tossing overboard rafts, life-belts, benches, pieces of wood, anything that will float . . . there are five or six hundred heads in the water. It is impossible to believe that these two, beautiful, powerful ships are going down. But they are.

Japan already had control of the air. Now the enemy also ruled the waves, and 840 British sailors were dead. When Winston Churchill, who had huge confidence in the invincibility of the *Prince of Wales,* heard the news, he was horrified, 'I was thankful to be alone. In all the war, I never received a more direct shock . . . over all this vast expanse of waters, Japan was supreme, and we everywhere were weak and naked.'

CHAPTER SEVENTEEN

Singapore, 1942

From Kuala Lumpur, Phyllis Briggs was ordered to head south once more, to the apparent safety of Singapore.

> Once more I set off in my little car* and took Mary Gentles with me. We drove through Jahore in the pouring rain, and it was difficult to see – the roof leaked, and poor old Gentles put up her purple umbrella in the car! Mary Gentles was one of a several nursing sisters who drowned later when their ships were sunk.

In Singapore, Phyllis nursed air-raid victims.

> This [hospital] was filled with Malays, Chinese and Indians all brought in direct from the streets. Many were already dead, others were dying ... at first, we used to put the patients under their beds during air raids, but it became impossible to do when raids became frequent ... During the raids many Chinese jumped into the monsoon drains by the roadsides. They put their heads down and bottoms up – with the result that many Chinese were brought into the hospital with shrapnel wounds to their buttocks. Some of the patients had infected wounds crawling with maggots. It was the one thing that made me quite sick. One Chinese woman had half her face blown away. I have never forgotten

---

* Her precious Morris 8 was later stolen in Singapore.

her pleading eyes. Large maggots were crawling out of what was left of her nose.

This was the dangerous world that 21-year-old Len Baynes from the 1st Battalion, Cambridgeshire Regiment, known as the Fen Tigers, was thrust straight into. Len had spent the first months of the war guarding Spitfires at RAF Duxford armed with weapons from the Great War. Born in Tottenham, Len's family now lived in Stapleford, Cambridgeshire.

On the long sea voyage from Liverpool, Len was filled with optimism.

> Most of us were pleased and excited at the prospect of seeing the world... At the age of 21, I was leaving England (lovely name) for the first time.

Len's battalion was diverted from North Africa to Singapore. En route, their leaders reassured them that the opposition was weak. Stan Watts:

> We had little to worry about. The Japs were poorly armed, a high percentage wore glasses, and they were also small in stature, so it was not likely they would be good shots. It began to sound very heartening, and our worries diminished.

As Len Baynes and thousands of other East Anglian soldiers approached Singapore, in Europe senior Nazis were meeting in Wannsee on 20 January to plan the implementation of the

Len Baynes

Final Solution, the murder of millions of Jews on an industrial scale.

Ten days later, after two months at sea, Len Baynes finally arrived in Singapore, barely two weeks before the Fortress fell.

> It is the smell of that oriental city that first comes into my mind. It is made up from a mixture of garlic, fish, joss sticks, frying oil, charcoal, and probably much more; I came to like the smell and now think of it with some nostalgia.

On 31 January 1942, the British blew up the causeway linking the mainland to Singapore in order to stop the Japanese entering the city, but, despite that, enemy soldiers successfully crossed over within a week. From then on Len Baynes encountered intense fire.

> It was at this time that our officer and his batman disappeared, and we didn't see him again until just before capitulation. So, I was then responsible for the platoon.

Len and the other NCOs were now responsible for hundreds of soldiers.

> I told Tommy Beatty, our young Company Sergeant Major, that the open space he would need to cross to get to Company HQ was under heavy fire, but he carried on with a cheerful grin. He was only 21 or 22, having obtained rapid promotion through keenness and hard work. When it came to the test, he did his job at least as bravely as the oldest in our ranks. A few hours later we discovered that, when he ran the gauntlet of that open space, he was hit in the abdomen by a burst of fire. He lay where he fell, conscious all day in the blistering sun with his bowels exposed to the heat and flies yet refraining from calling for help lest he cause further casualties... late that night a party of our brave stretcher-bearers crept out and rescued Tommy. Incredibly, he survived.

> Next, we found dear old Simpkin. He was a Gloucester man, slow speaking and thinking but the salt of the earth. Although both his legs were badly smashed, he had managed to drag himself all the way through the scrub until stopped by the barbed wire. He had lost much blood and was in considerable pain; there was unspeakable joy in his eyes as he saw that we had returned to help him.

Singapore Island desperately needed to be reinforced with gun emplacements and other land defences along its 72-mile coastline. But as Singapore was protected by an array of huge guns facing out to sea, this was never seen as a priority. Len Baynes had a clearer grasp of what was necessary to defend Singapore than many military leaders.

> A few thousand pounds of concrete pillboxes, strategically placed, a few mobile guns or tanks, and Singapore could well have proved, like Gibraltar, an impregnable fortress. No plans seem to have been worked out for the deployment of troops, however, should the Japanese do the obvious and attack from dry land instead of sailing into the muzzle of our big guns from seaward.

Stan Watts landed in beleaguered Singapore the day after Len Baynes. He was one of a party of soldiers dispatched to the Naval Dockyard to retrieve some stores.

> It had been evacuated and not a soul was there. We went into what had been the mess hall and found food left on the plates – it was as if they had suddenly disappeared without trace . . . it was beyond comprehension to see the amount of equipment left behind. There were crates lying there just as they had arrived from England, and all the machinery was intact . . . Another building was beyond belief. There in all their array were uniforms for high-ranking officers, complete with swords for ceremonial visits, a great amount

of silverware, a large collection of watches – in fact it looked like something out of Aladdin's cave.

Stan enjoyed a short, contented stint working with the Ghurkhas.

> I did miss the Ghurkhas... as soon as they had a break, there was one mad rush to the post office to send the money home to their families. It was a privilege to meet such soldiers. They suffered badly at the hands of the Japanese, and I wonder how many of those I came to know eventually returned to their homeland.

Chief Petty Officer Robert Curry was Royal Navy Liaison Officer at RAF Seletar, the key British air base just outside Singapore City. A handful of RAF mechanics armed only with rifles had been left to guard the airfield after the last aircraft had attempted to fly off. When they too were ordered to evacuate the base, Curry was the only man left in the entire airfield.

> I found myself alone. I located some bottles of Scotch, had a few drinks, destroyed the remainder, and considered my next move.
> Next morning, I was awakened by explosions, and, peeping out of the window, I could glimpse Japanese soldiers across the Jahore Straight firing mortar shells at our airfield. I could see no future in this for me, so, packing a suitcase, I let myself out of the back door and set off to walk to Singapore City followed by mortar shells.
> I saw a Malayan who was bent on looting stagger and fall, his head had been blown off. I increased my speed.

Over five hours later, Robert Curry reached Singapore City, 15 miles away on foot.

> Hundreds of unburied dead almost blocked the streets, and the smell of putrefied flesh mingling with the bombed

sewerage was appalling. A huge black pall of smoke from the blazing oil tanks hung over the city, and the raindrops were turning black as they reached the ground.

Private Bert Miller, 196th Field Ambulance Company, from Diss, Norfolk, landed the same day as Len Baynes. He was pitched into the middle of the complete devastation witnessed by Robert Curry.

> Buildings folded like decks of cards onto streets festooned with wire that once fed telephones and power. Thousands of refugees crouched in hollow drainpipes and monsoon ditches, seeking protection from shells, bombs, and the machine-gunning from low flying planes ... Smoke darkened the sky and midday became dusk. So high and so vast the great columns seemed to go on for ever.
>
> In the canals and ditches, bloated corpses of air-raid victims and their animals floated on oil from the streaming tanks. Among the ruins, stark and stiffening bodies lay unburied ... it was devastation of devastation.

As a Eurasian, 12-year-old Romanus Miles could not obtain safe passage out of Singapore. Survival depended on his own feral skills.

> Martial law was declared and announced that anyone caught looting would be shot, but this was no deterrent. We also joined in the looting when there was no more food. Abandoned houses with tinned food like condensed milk and butter were targeted ... refugees from all the captured towns and villages poured into the city. They brought tales of savagery which scared us a lot. Friends and relatives turned up on our doorstep asking for refuge, so we took them in, and everyone slept on the floor.

The remaining European civilians never fully grasped the danger that they were in. Despite the obvious lessons from the Blitz, no blackouts were enforced initially, and lights blazed through the first air attacks. Even with the Japanese camped on Singapore's doorstep, couples danced at Raffles Hotel to Dan Hopkins and his band. As late as the eve of surrender, a British officer was told he needed permission from the club committee before mounting guns on the golf course.

Thousands of European women who had left their decision late were desperately seeking escape. Many had been confident that Singapore was indeed a Fortress, the Gibraltar of the East. Now they said hasty goodbyes as they struggled on to overcrowded ships.

Young Donna Farber bid her father farewell at Singapore Harbour in February 1942, before evacuating with her mother to Australia.

> It was a time of crying and a time of dying... I watched the two of them embrace while all around people were screaming and shouting, running to and fro, as if they'd come from a lunatic asylum.
>
> My legs pressed harder around my father's waist; my arms nearly choked him. His horn-rimmed glasses were steamed up from my breath – or was it from his tears? The humming [of Japanese aircraft] in the sky was loud enough for everyone to hear now, and panic spread like ink on a blotter. Some people fell from the quayside into the filthy water as the crowds surged towards the companionway. A Malay porter, watching our own little tragedy, helped my mother disentangle me from my father. Daddy was incapable of it. Together they dragged me towards the companionway, the tops of my shoes scuffling along the ground. Japanese planes screeched by, showering bombs. They missed the ship and hit the sea with dull thumps. People shrieked in terror and Mother crossed herself.
>
> As I climbed up to the top deck [to wave goodbye] I could see the water below through the metal grid. Broken wood and

rotten vegetables swirled in the darkness. Somebody's hat was sucked under the hull but there was no sign of the people who had fallen in . . . gradually the crowds thinned out and my daddy became a spot – still waving. My insides turned cold and heavy.

Her father was Dutch but joined the British Army. He did not survive imprisonment by the Japanese.

Barbara Everard was married to Ray, with one young child, Martin.

I saw the *Duchess of Bedford*, grey painted. And, carrying Martin, picked my way through the hoses and the fires and up the gangway . . . Ray did not stay long on board. He kissed me twice, and also Martin . . . we all crowded on deck, tears running down our faces. There were soldiers cheering and waving as we left. The little island receded, women were crying, women were trying to comfort each other. I looked at Singapore with tears streaming down my face . . . and so we went. And so ended four years in Malaya, so full, so happy, so abruptly ended.

At Naval HQ, Chief Petty Officer Robert Curry, having left RAF Seletar, was drafted onto HMS *Jarak*, a minesweeper tasked with leading escaping ships through the Japanese minefields.

I was horrified to see scores of children and women standing right up to the very edge of Clifford Pier waiting for rescue . . . I looked at those children, dressed mainly in white with ribbons in their hair, waving to us – no shelter at all – dear God . . . I have had the picture of those children in my mind's eye for 34 years.

We heard the drone of planes, there were 27 Jap bombers approaching the docks from the east . . . down below I found an air raid shelter built entirely of tins of corned beef, and as I dived in it was explained that the bomb splinters could slice through the sides of a ship, but it could not penetrate the corned beef. Good old Admiralty ham.

Phyllis Briggs was nursing round the clock. She was offered a chance to leave Singapore but remained at her hospital post. Despite the chaos, Phyllis became engaged to a man she had met in Penang.

> Tony Cochrane reached Singapore and was stationed at the naval base. I saw him briefly a few times and he asked me to marry him as soon as we could meet again in Australia. He made me promise to leave Singapore as soon as I could.

Phyllis was torn between keeping her promise to her new fiancé to leave, and her duty to her patients. But when a doctor was killed by a shell whistling directly through the operating theatre, she headed for the docks.

> There were three ships in the harbour, and we were taken to each in turn and told that they were already overcrowded and could not take us on board. I was quite pleased because I felt dreadful about leaving the hospital.

Finally, one of the ship's captains relented and Phyllis squeezed aboard the *Mata Hari*.

> Despite her romantic name, she was merely a cargo ship with a scratch crew collected from vessels that had been sunk. She had accommodation for nine passengers, but we totalled three hundred and twenty* when we sailed out of Singapore harbour.

It was the early hours, 13 February 1942, Phyllis watched the receding sight of Singapore, illuminated like a giant red bonfire.

---

* There were 483 passengers.

Barbara Everard* and her son, Martin, were safely on an evacuation ship, but her friends Nellie and Jean refused to leave their husbands. Their attempted escape was too late, and their vessel was sunk by the Japanese.

Nellie was drowned. Jean, beautiful, young, golden girl she was, had been incredibly brave, going in and out of the water rescuing people . . . but she was recaptured and taken back to Singapore, and I later heard that she was sent to Japan. She was never heard of again.

---

* Barbara became a well-known botanical painter after the war.

CHAPTER EIGHTEEN

Surrender, 1942

While Phyllis Briggs and thousands of others were trying to escape the inferno of Singapore, it became clear that even nurses would not be spared by the Japanese. On 14 February, around 100 Japanese soldiers burst into the Queen Alexandra Barracks Hospital, Singapore, and slaughtered helpless patients and staff with their bayonets, mowing down those who tried to escape with machine guns and rifles. It was a bloodbath. One patient was stabbed to death on the operating table while under anaesthetic. About 373 people were murdered, including 230 patients.

Elsewhere in Singapore, Len Baynes was in his last two days of freedom, although he didn't know it.

> The enemy began to advance on us, and we gave them all we had . . . We clearly heard for the first time the strange sound of Japanese voices as they shouted their orders; heard for the first time also the screams of their wounded. I recall the satisfaction we derived from killing those enemy fathers, husbands and sons.

His unit was attacked by snipers high up in the trees.

> Cpl Ginn was standing beside me as we searched the trees behind for a glimpse of the snipers, who had by this time killed two of our men and wounded several more. 'I reckon there's one of the bastards up that palm tree,' he said. He took aim with his rifle . . . as his finger squeezed the trigger, he

> gasped and sank to the ground. I quickly knelt down beside him, but he was beyond help.
>
> The next few hours were a nightmare. Men fell to the right and left; the huts all caught fire, and some fell burning into our trenches. Many who were not burned to death died later of their terrible burns, including my old friend Sergeant Wilson, who, in his agony, asked me to shoot him. Dear God, I breathed, as I looked into that awful, burned face, let it all be a dream. I shouted for the stretcher-bearers and, faithful as ever, they ran over and collected him.

Len and his men were ordered to run across open ground to a new position in front of Brigade HQ in the face of a Japanese machine gun.

> I asked for a couple of volunteers to stay behind with our Bren Gun and fire at the Japs while the rest of us broke cover. Utting and Winton instantly claimed the job, although we all knew they were unlikely to survive. As their gun began to chatter, we left our trenches and ran for our lives . . . [on the other side] we lay down and opened fire with our rifles and kept the enemy's heads down long enough for the other two to reach us . . . It is certain that those of us who did get through owed our lives to Utting and Winton. Like most war heroes they received no medal for their valour.

The Queen Alexandra Hospital massacre starkly reminded Lt Gen Arthur Percival, Commanding Officer, Singapore, that civilian losses would be massive at the hands of a merciless enemy. Water supplies were now largely controlled by the Japanese, and food and ammunition were also running out. He wrote to General Wavell, his superior officer, 'There must come a stage when, in the interests of the troops and civilian population, further bloodshed will service no useful purpose.' The Japanese were also extremely short of ammunition and other supplies, but the Allies did not know that. On 15 February, Percival surrendered. Mighty Fortress Singapore had fallen.

Corporal George Brown from Lancashire was ordered to raise a white flag.

> I used a towel on two rifles. Can't put it up myself, feel very upset. I think the silence after all the din is very frightening. I am afraid. Broke down and cried as I have never done in my life before.

The local population was also frightened. Twelve-year-old Romanus Miles:

> This was the beginning of the end for us all and my life changed for ever. The guns stopped firing at eight o'clock that night and the silence was quite deafening.
>
> The enemy had arrived, and they looked fierce with their black beards and dishevelled uniforms. After hoisting the Nippon flag at the flagpole leaving me, Dad, and everyone else petrified. This was the cue for us boys to make a run for it.

Romanus headed for the apparent sanctuary of the convent where he had lived as a young child after his parents divorced.

> The nuns were pleased to see me, and I was soon put to work at the makeshift dressing station. Given a large pot of Vaseline I attended a badly burned boy of my age. His head and arm were burnt so I applied the Vaseline as best I could, and I remember the smell of burnt flesh around the poor chap.

Private Bert Miller, 196th Field Ambulance Company, faced an uncertain future.

> The clouds wept black tears as the rain passed through the oil-laden smoke: there was no escape from the stench of cordite, sewers and rotting flesh . . . we had been blasted

into another world and in this new environment it was silence that screamed at us. Some wept, some cursed and those too exhausted to curse or weep and unable to fight fatigue any longer, fell where they stood and fitfully slept. Then we waited ... we could feel certain only of the past. The present offered nothing but bewilderment and contradiction.

Just before surrender Private Cyril Doy, 6th Norfolk Regiment, was in a small group dispatched into Singapore to fetch rice, but armed Japanese captured them. The unarmed British were rounded up at bayonet point and pushed against a wall. A machine gun clicked into place. A civilian planter in the line next to Cyril collapsed on his knees in desperate prayer. As the Japanese pointed their gun at the line of prisoners, Cyril was surprisingly calm.

> I didn't have a care in hell ... I thought to myself, I wonder if I will feel that bullet going through me. I was so exhausted I was completely relaxed.

The Japanese suddenly started shouting wildly and lowered the machine gun. The executions were halted because seconds before the bullets were to be fired, the British had capitulated. Cyril Doy* had survived only to become a prisoner-of-war and forced to labour for the Japanese building the Bridge on the River Kwai.

Elsewhere in Singapore, Len Baynes was stunned by news of surrender.

> We did not think of throwing in the sponge while any of us remained alive, that was not the British way ... hardly a word was exchanged between us as we silently remained there awaiting further orders.

---

* Cyril died aged 103 in 2023.

SURRENDER, 1942

Private Tanner stood six feet two and had proved himself to be a very brave soldier; when he heard the order, he stood there unashamedly with tears streaming down his cheeks; his were not the only tears that day.

We seemed to wait in our trenches after the arrival of the cease-fire order for a very long time. An hour and a half after we received it, men dug in 50 yards away in the centre of the lawn decided to climb out of their trenches; a machine gun opened fire on them, and they all lay still.

Len Baynes ran to the Regimental [First] Aid Post looking for a Red Cross flag to bring in any wounded from the lawn. He stood by an ambulance.

Bullets whizzed by me and into the ambulance. Although it seemed that I could have touched these bullets, again they all missed me . . . the ambulance burst into flames . . . the fire spread, and the ambulance became an inferno.

Two Japs armed with a light machine gun suddenly appeared from behind a hedge, only four yards away. One yelled something like 'shoot' and the other released a burst of fire from point blank range.

The bullets were so close an officer reported Len Baynes as dead, but the Japanese had missed.

Len was astonished when he finally saw the victors.

I thought for the moment I was dreaming. A wide drive swept round the rear and on it, in full view of both us and his own men, rode the officer in charge of this part of the Imperial Japanese Army. His charger? A captured child's fairy cycle. He pedalled round in circles, knees poking out sideways to miss the handlebars, his long sword dragging along in the dust behind him.

The ordinary Japanese soldiers were our biggest surprise, as they appeared like pieces of jungle, walking. Their uniforms, if such their shabby and mud-coloured clothes could be called, were hung about completely with leaves and twigs. We had done nothing like that.

Len wanted to find out if any men on the lawn were alive. A Japanese NCO shook his head impatiently. But Len took the risk.

> The boys who had been shot on the lawn still lay where they were fallen, there were no survivors around that trench. As I now lowered the head of one of my young lads, lifeless on to the turf, I had difficulty holding back the tears.

Winston Churchill was appalled by Singapore's fall, 'This is a disaster, the worst disaster and largest capitulation in our history.'

CHAPTER NINETEEN

Escape, 1942

While Len Baynes was fighting his last stand in Singapore, Sister Phyllis Briggs was crammed into her escape vessel from Singapore on 13 February 1942. She was lucky. The *Mata Hari* was one of only four ships in the evacuation flotilla of 44 not sunk by the enemy.

> It was a hair-raising journey, as we had to cross a live minefield and the buoy marking the end of it was never sighted ... the sky was red with fire – it looked as if the whole city was burning, with leaping flames lighting the blackness of the sky.
>
> After we got into the open sea I tried to sleep. At 3 a.m. we heard shouts for help; the ship stopped, and we picked six men out of the water. One of them, a young Volunteer Naval Reserve, I had played badminton with in Penang.

At night the escapees were disturbed by an eerie green light.

> As dawn broke a Jap destroyer was seen quite close to us ... the *Mata Hari's* maximum speed was 13 knots, and her sole means of defence was an obsolete gun, so the captain had no option but to surrender ...
>
> The Jap officer came aboard with two sailors carrying swords. The Jap flag was run up, now we were under The Rising Sun.

Like Phyllis, 130,000 troops captured in Singapore were now prisoners. They had no idea how long the war would last; theirs was a sentence without end. Thousands were crammed onto a tennis court without food or water. Len Baynes:

There was no shade, and as the sun rose in the sky our position rapidly became untenable for Europeans; many became unconscious from heatstroke . . . with most of us having diarrhoea by now, conditions became bad; with many unable to reach the toilet corner in time, there was now nowhere clean to sit, and we could scarcely see for the flies which had bred in the faeces. That night the stench hung over us like a vile blanket and it was hopeless to think of sleep.

Next day lines of bedraggled prisoners marched for 17 miles in the Singapore sun to their new home, the former British army barracks at Changi. Len Baynes:

Many of those we carried were very ill indeed, with broken limbs, burns, unstitched wounds and internal injuries. It is impossible to carry a man on a stretcher without some jolting and the patients suffer greatly on the long journey ahead.

Twelve-year-old Romanus Miles was free but scared. Moving through the smouldering ruins of Singapore was dangerous.

Every bridge and major road junction became a terrifying experience for travellers. The soldiers manning these posts looked fearsome in their coarse uniforms and those caps with the flaps. They took delight in kicking or slapping us as we queued up to bow to the sentries . . . All watches and jewellery were taken, the owner usually receiving a slap as compensation, and they liked British-made bicycles, especially the Raleigh make . . . bowing the Japanese way was a source of trouble, so there was much shouting and violence. Often a few unfortunate souls would be bound tightly with a rope and left in the hot sun, their fate unknown.*

---

* Romanus survived the war and lived in the UK. He joined the Royal Navy and later British Airways. He married and had three sons.

ESCAPE, 1942

With minesweeping duties finished, Robert Curry on HMS *Jarak* finally attempted his own escape from Singapore, but on the 15th the Japanese attacked.

> A plane appeared and bombed us ... many were wounded including our Captain and, thinking he was going to pass out, he gave the order to Abandon Ship and we lowered the two lifeboats carrying our wounded.
>
> In my boat an army warrant officer had a large bomb splinter through his thigh, which was protruding through the other side of his leg, and with blood pouring from him, he asked me for water. I got him a drink from the lifeboat stores and tried to stem the flow of blood.
>
> At dawn we found a sandy beach and we managed to get our wounded on the sands, and the lifeboat beached. We found coconut trees, and our five Malayan ratings soon climbed them, providing us with food and drink to augment our lifeboat stores of 12 tins of sardines, one tin of biscuits, and a few pints of water. Our gallant captain, whose back and buttocks were riddled with small pieces of shrapnel, was in great pain, so we all took turns sucking out the metal and cleaning him up.

Curry spotted a Japanese plane overhead. This uninhabited beach was not safe, so they returned to their damaged ship and limped to the island of Singkep. Under cover of darkness, they headed to the safety of the jungle. Robert Curry* fell asleep.

> I woke up as something was itching under my left knee, and putting my hand down to scratch, I felt something wriggle, then a sharp pain – it was a snake about 18 inches long, long, black, with white spots on it. I yelped and an army lieutenant immediately kicked the snake away, slashed my leg with a knife, buried his teeth round the bite, drew out the poisoned

---

* Robert Curry later became a Lieutenant Commander in the Royal Navy.

blood, calling for a tourniquet – all in a few seconds. The Malayan ratings told us in horror that the snake was a black mamba, deadly poisonous and I would know in ten minutes whether I was going to live, or die in agony, and indicated that if the gallant officer had a cracked lip, he would die before me.

The Malayans then vanished, having no desire to witness the agony I was about to endure. I wasn't that keen on it either, although I was given a cigarette and a sardine to help me along. The soldiers applied the tourniquet to drain my leg of blood, and the lieutenant wanted me to agree to have my leg cut off with a blunt clasp knife to save my life. As my chances of survival were pretty slim even on two legs, I declined his kind offer.

We both survived. Grand types to be with, these soldiers.

On 14 February Phyllis Briggs was equally uncertain of her future, as she was bundled ashore by her captors at Banka Island, off Sumatra.

We were taken by launch to a narrow wooden jetty, where we were kept through the long hot hours without food or water. When darkness came a cold wind blew up and we huddled close together to try and keep warm. The night seemed very long; we tried to help the wounded but there was little we could do.

Christine Bundy had more than she could carry and offered me a glamourous black satin dressing gown with long sleeves. This garment I treasured for the next three and a half years, as I slept in it, and it was protection against mosquitos.

We had no food for 24 hours and it was the next night before they gave us some rice . . . we lay on the cold concrete slabs trying to sleep – the small children screamed all night and every hour a Jap guard tramped through our block and seemed to take delight in hitting our shins with the butt of his rifle.

ESCAPE, 1942

A few days later Phyllis assisted a surgeon in amputating the foot of an RAF officer.

> The surgeon had to do it in the most primitive manner. The Japs refused to let the patient go to the local hospital or to send in the right instruments, so someone made a saw out of a knife. It was just as well the poor man was too ill to know what was happening. Another man had been bayonetted in the stomach when trying to get a drink of water... the guard came in and ground his heel into the man's wound.

New arrivals flooded in, many needing medical care. They included survivors of another Singapore escape vessel, the *Kuala*.

> The survivors had clung to rafts, and some were burnt black with the sun. One such girl was brought in, the only survivor from a raft full of people. Her eyes were sunk into the back of her head, and it was some minutes before we realised she was English. This was Margot Turner*... she had survived all this time by collecting rainwater in the lid of her powder compact.
>
> Some people who were able to get onto rafts died of exposure and lack of drinking water, others fell off into the sea as they had not the strength to hold on... we were told that 23 allied ships had either been sunk or captured in that area and the survivors were brought into our camp.

Margot Turner was the only survivor of 16 people on her raft, including four children and two babies. Without water none of them survived the fierce sun. She reported:

> I examined each of them with great care before committing their little bodies to the sea... the last one was a very small baby, and it was difficult to know when it was dead.

---

* After the war she became Dame Margot Turner, Matron-in-Chief and Director, Army Nursing Services.

At the end of February, Phyllis was in the camp surgery when two more bedraggled people were brought in.

> One, a tall Australian Army Nursing Sister called Vivian Bulwinkle,* the other a British Army soldier. Both were covered in scratches and septic mosquito bites. Vivian had had a terrible experience.

Vivian Bulwinkel and 21 other Australian nurses had survived the sinking of the hospital ship *Vyner Brooke*.† They landed at Radji Beach on the north coast of Banka Island on two rafts and were joined by survivors from other ships that had been sunk. The nurses started to care for the injured, emblazoning a Red Cross on their makeshift shelter.

> Soon a number of Japanese soldiers appeared. They made the men walk a little distance away beyond the rocks, then proceeded to machine gun and bayonet them to death. The Japs then returned to the Australian girls and made them form a line and walk into the sea, then proceeded to shoot them in the back.

Vivian Bulwinkel was the only surviving nurse from the original 22. She was shot in the side of the back and lay in the water pretending to be dead. When she surfaced, the beach was empty. British Private Patrick Kingsley (or Kinsley) also feigned death and was the only other survivor. Estimates of those massacred at Radji Beach vary between 72 and 83. Despite the medical care from Phyllis and others, Private Kingsley died from his wounds. Recent investigations have claimed that the Australian nurses were raped before they were killed. Phyllis Briggs, Sister Bulwinkel and the other survivors now faced four years of brutal Japanese imprisonment.

* Correct spelling is Bulwinkel.

† One hundred and thirty-five on board were lost.

CHAPTER TWENTY

Home Guard, 1940–43

The Home Guard, the Local Defence Volunteers (LDV), was mainly comprised of Great War veterans and young boys eager to 'do their bit'. They guarded coastal defences and strategically important factories against enemy invasion. Our picture of them has been shaped by the famous BBC comedy series *Dad's Army*. The Home Guard filled vital roles during the war but, as in all good comedies, truth was never far from the humour. Bill Miles was only 15 and lied about his age to join the Home Guard.

> We were given a Home Guard armband and a broom handle ... we marched about with our broom handles, having to withstand the remarks of the watching public.

Eventually, Bill was issued with a rifle with bayonet attached, which he took proudly home to show his father, a Great War veteran.

> Father said this takes me back and, with a cry of 'charge', lunged forward, sticking the bayonet through the back and out of the front of mother's much cherished settee. Mother screeched, 'You fool, you've ruined my settee.' ... the rifle was never allowed in the front room again.

Bill graduated from rifles to sticky bombs.

> It was like a large toffee apple ... full of nitro-glycerine. You pushed a button in the handle then whacked it onto the side of a passing enemy tank, which in our case was an old iron

boiler towed along behind a lorry. One Home Guard 'bomber' got his sticky bomb stuck to his trouser leg and couldn't shift it. A quick-thinking mate whipped his trousers off and got rid of them, and the bomb. After the following explosion, the trousers were a bit of a mess...

The next challenge was a gun that could fire phosphorus bombs. The gun was assembled, but a small washer was left behind in the box.

Our two corporals were to have the privilege of firing the first shots... there was a bang followed by a huge burst of flame. From out of this conflagration staggered the corporals, their eyebrows had gone, and their tunics were smouldering. They had the appearance of having been on a good summer's holiday... the washer left in the box would have prevented this.

George Murphy, Wexford, Republic of Ireland:

Our commander at a public demonstration was showing me how to hold a very powerful fire-service hose. I was standing a few feet away holding the hose when someone switched the water on. He shot in the air, saturated with water in public. I could not stop laughing. I was not promoted.

Jack Taylor's Home Guard uniform included a pair of trousers but no buttons to hold them up.

Panic ensued... our local shop, Millers, was rumoured to have a stock of the correct buttons. As this news circulated there was a mass attack by Home Guard recruits on the shop... a contingent of police were on standby to control the crowd at Millers demanding uniform buttons.

Pam Heath was a child near Bournemouth.

My father, not content with drilling his Home Guard, also trained us. When we heard him shout 'Gas', we had to put our

> gas masks on asap and not expect any help from him ... my father also had a large map on the breakfast room wall and moved little pins on the map to show where the different battlefronts were. We had little rhyming notices on the wall by the light switches and taps. saying 'Switched on switches and turned-on taps, make happy Huns and joyful Japs.'
>
> They heard there was going to be an invasion, and we were only ten miles from the coast. My father and the farmer stood outside the farmhouse in the dark with pitchforks and rabbit guns, and my mother was instructed to drive us three children north in the car, no matter that she didn't know how to drive ...

John Hutchinson was on nightly air-raid duty at Kew Gardens. His daughter, Nora Chivers, told his story.

> Something hard was pressed into his back!! He froze and all he could think was that a German parachutist had landed, the invasion must have begun!! He is going to kill me!! It seemed to be for ever; nobody spoke. At last, he summoned up the courage to turn his head and he could have hugged it – it was a STORK, with its beak pressed into his back!! My father was trespassing on its domain.

As his son reported, Phil Borman in Grimsby had a close shave during a training session with rifles and blank ammunition.

> The Home Guard in the next room heard an explosion. Expecting the worst, they crept into the room to see Dad sitting on a chair, shaking, and looking up at a bullet hole in the ceiling ... the last bullet happened to be a 'live' round. It could have been Dad's eye and the end of him. How a 'live' round found its way amongst the dummies nobody knows.

Ron Tarling's father, an ex-regular soldier from Garston, near Watford, was typical of eager Home Guard recruits.

The fictitious events portrayed in *Dad's Army* bear an uncanny similarity to those of real life in the Garston Platoon of the Home Guard – even to their commanding officer being a bank manager . . . it was accepted wisdom that the Germans were unable to pronounce the letter W and so the password of *Wendell Wilkie* (an American politician of the time) was demanded of anyone challenged by guards.

My dad and a colleague, whilst patrolling in woodland near Garston Church, spotted a suspicious figure and after a good deal of 'halting and who goes thereing', they pinned the hooded figure to the tree and invited him to say Wendell Wilkie. He proved to be quite unable to say these, or indeed any other words, and was in serious danger of being skewered to a tree by bayonet when he pulled off his balaclava to reveal himself as the local vicar (who suffered from a serious stammer).

As the war progressed, the Home Guard became better equipped and trained, enabling them to take on more serious responsibilities. By 1942 they were equipped with hand grenades and plastic explosives. Peter Helsdon manned an anti-aircraft rocket Battery in Chelmsford.

The Battery claimed hits on several occasions, including one Junkers 88 which came down in flames.

Chelmsford was home to the Marconi radio factory, an inevitable bomb target.

The Suet factory in New St caught fire and the melted fat ran across the road making it difficult to get to work in the Marconi factory the next morning . . . the Territorial Drill Hall was set alight by incendiaries and the ammunition stored there exploded all through the night, throwing burning debris over our gun Battery site . . . two Home Guardsmen were awarded certificates for their courageous actions that night.

As the war progressed, the Home Guard was allocated better weapons than broomsticks and, by 1943, women were finally allowed to join. Folkestone on the Kent coast was so close to German airbases in France that Home Guard night-time patrols carried significant responsibility. Eric Hart:

> Moonlight would filter down through the trees and occasionally the silence would be interrupted by the soulful hoot of an owl. On nights like these the moon's silvery wake across the calm sea made the hard reality of war seem far removed... but when it happened, a veritable fireworks display would ensue with bright flashes as the bombs fell and the ground defences sent up a cascade of tracer bullets into the night sky.

When Eric fired the well-worn Lewis machine gun mounted on Sandgate Castle, the result was surprising.

> A German Dornier bomber with a wisp of smoke issuing from its engines came limping quite low over the hill... I considered it to be out of range for the Lewis gun, but my excited compatriots wanted some action, so I opened fire! My intervention was no hindrance to the aircraft because we were too far away, but we did score a ricochet or two off the spire of the nearby school.

Fourteen-year-old Boy Scout Dennis Perry from Croydon was posted to a Croydon hospital.

> We were each issued with steel helmets and heavy-duty gas masks... we were all trained in firefighting and in handling pressure hoses... I was also a messenger. When next of kin were urgently needed to come to serious casualties, the messages were hand delivered. So, we rode our bikes across Croydon, through the blackout and gunfire regardless of an air-raid.
>
> When the sirens sounded, we went into the Maternity Wards to remove newborn babies in wicker baskets and

carry them down to safety into the deep concrete shelters. The mothers were put under their bed and covered with the mattress for protection.

The Royal Observer Corps was a civil defence organisation that, in tandem with radar, played a vital role in spotting enemy aircraft. Aircraft-mad Frank Smith joined the Royal Observer Corps when they started voluntary air spotters' clubs. His flat factory roof in Coventry was a perfect perch.

As the aircraft got nearer, I felt sure I could see diving breaks on the wings and an underslung gun turret, characteristics of a Junkers 88. By this time, it was closing fast and heading towards me. In those few seconds I had to choose. Get the whole workforce out to the shelters or not. I pressed the button and the whole workforce dropped tools and dashed for the air raid shelters . . . I was right – a Junkers 88 clearly carrying a black-and-white cross on its fuselage and the swastika on its tail. I dived to the floor thinking this was it, knowing that their guns could easily wipe us out. I had no rifle, no steel helmet. I said a quick prayer. The aircraft screamed past and headed towards the factories of Wickmans and Standards less than two miles away.

A few days later, one of the workers said to me, 'Frank we want to thank you for your good spotting and getting us down the air raid shelter in time.' There was clapping and he presented me with an inscribed chromium-plated cigarette case.

Joan Holgate, a teenage telephonist at Wolverhampton Post Office, was enrolled as a fire spotter.

The searchlights lit the whole sky; whistles were blowing, people were running to shelters, and artillery guns started to fire . . . on the flat roof over the apparatus room we found, to our horror, two incendiary bombs burning fiercely. It was obvious they would burn through the roof onto the communications equipment below before the fire brigade could arrive. We decided to try to throw them off the roof using long-handled shovels. Fear, adrenaline, and our combined strength helped us throw them off the edge into the vegetable garden where the engineers had been 'Digging for Victory'.

In the morning, we examined the vegetable patch and discovered that one of the bombs had landed in the potatoes and cooked them. We ate them for breakfast, a delicious addition to our meagre wartime diet, thanks to the Luftwaffe.

After bombing raids factories needed to be repaired quickly. Frank Ainsbury worked on the Emergency Repair Squad, War Damage Commission. He was dispatched to the Midlands to wait for the attacks on Coventry the British knew were coming.

We might be war damage repairers, but we were told that we would also be needed as firemen, doctors and undertakers. Well before we reached Coventry, the skies were glowing red and orange with the help of smoke reflecting the shadows of dancing flames . . . most of us had a stretcher shoved into our hands. I have no doubt at all what hell is like: Coventry on that night.

The ARP man, a real old man called Pop, acted like a sergeant major and was as hard as nails. We were at a shelter that had received a fairly direct hit, and we had to dig out the wounded . . . the ARP man, Pop, held their hand and encouraged them through the hole.

The first cracks of dawn broke through the smoke-laden sky, with it daylight, and a view of the carnage around me with the group of people we had evacuated to a park. Blood-caked with dust and smoke. Black eyes and bruises like people had been in the ring with Joe Louis. Women and children with their hair burnt right off. Great blisters on their faces and bodies from burns, and large weeping red flesh.

After about two hours sleep, Pop took us back into the still burning and smouldering ruins, each with a shovel and pickaxe. We were to search for survivors under the rubble, and this spot was a children's home... Nuns knelt praying and crying over sheeted dead bodies. Bricks, stones, timbers and rubble were cleared under Pop's instructions... little kids with injuries that are indescribable. One, a kid about three years old, was placed in my arms and I was told to take him to the nuns. He was alive... he smiled at me... touched me under the chin. As I laid him down, he held my hand. I felt him stiffen then relax. I cried and cried, and old Pop took the little boy's hand from mine, covered him with his jacket, and led me away.

It stays with me to this day. I can still cry without shame for that little boy and do... it shaped my whole life, my thinking towards people. Old Pop showed me the heights that I could reach. The death and destruction, the utter depths.

'Pop' was a popular nickname for older men in the ARP. A second 'Pop', aged nearly 60, showed the same heroic character as the veteran in Coventry. When a heavy bomb fell, he hurried to the scene although it was his day off. Pop saw there was no crater but a strange ring of fire. Charles Mercer:

The first-aid party arrived on the scene to find Pop endeavouring to smother the flames with earth. As they approached, they felt themselves being drawn as if by magnetic forces towards the spot from which Pop was operating. Flinging themselves to the ground, they just managed to evade being sucked into the centre of the flames... moments later the fire had subsided, but Pop and a valiant helper had vanished, without a cry or any indication of distress, into the bowels of the earth. Despite frenzied digging that night and subsequent weeks of endless toil by specialist rescue teams, not a single particle of clothing or clue to their whereabouts was discovered.

CHAPTER TWENTY-ONE

Prisoners of the Japanese, 1942

After the capitulation of Singapore, oil-rich Java (now Indonesia) in the Dutch East Indies was an attractive target for Japan. Its long coastline and patchy defences made it particularly vulnerable and, apart from a few Hurricanes, the defending air force flew a ragbag of outdated aircraft. On 1 March 1942, the Japanese invaded. The defending Dutch forces were supplemented by British and Australian troops, and 500 soldiers from Texas, but they were poorly equipped. One Australian was armed with a rifle designed in 1903. Java's defenders had no chance against a well-armed, fanatical enemy

Nineteen-year-old Nini Rambonnet lived with her Dutch parents in Java, Dutch East Indies, and worked as a translator for the Chartered Bank of Australia and China, despite indifferent English.

> I found out that I had been appointed because of my low golf handicap, as the Bank wanted me to play for them. The Executives of the Bank were all members of the Dutch-Anglo Golf Club.

Her golfing days were extinguished by Pearl Harbour, and, after the Japanese invasion, Nini served as a nurse at the Allied Hospital, Bandoeng, Central Java.

> Many British and Australian wounded soldiers and airmen arrived daily... none of us Red Cross nurses knew how to

wash parts of a man's anatomy . . . so we were all given a lesson by the Australian nurses.

The Dutch-led Allied forces were overrun in a week, and on 8 March 1942 surrendered. Ron Bryer was part of a small RAF unit who tried to escape but were captured by an enemy patrol. The Japanese officer raised his gun and pointed it between Ron's eyes.

> Down the yawning black tunnel big enough to crawl into, I seemed to see the shining nose of a bullet waiting to smash into a brain that no longer cared or was afraid . . . I lifted my eyes from the gun barrel and looked directly into the almond-shaped eyes below the peaked cap. Expressionless eyes, hard and brittle as black marbles in a dead white face. We both knew that at that moment my life lay in the crook of his forefinger.

Ron was unarmed. The officer slowly lowered his gun. On discovering his prisoners were from the RAF he simply said, 'Ah, England. All prisoners Nippon now.'*

Like Ron, Nini Rambonnet's world had changed for ever.

> Anyone passing a Japanese sentry on foot had to stop and bow . . . a girl I knew ignored this and was thrown on the ground . . . and she was trampled on.
>
> Whenever the local people tried to loot, the Japanese chopped off their hands and strung them up in the middle of the city . . . the Japanese were now arresting the Dutch men and went through each street in trucks. They caught my father and took him to the local police station.

When the Dutch director of the radio station where Nini's mother worked played the Dutch National Anthem against orders, the Japanese executed him. Nini's mother was then questioned by

---

* Ron Bryer was transported to work in Nagasaki.

the Kempetai, the Japanese equivalent of the Gestapo. When Nini tried to deliver a small parcel of essentials for her mother,

> The Kempetai soldier threatened me by holding his sword to my throat and told me not to come back. I did not!

After six weeks, Nini's mother was released.

> She had been accused of espionage for the British ... when she denied these accusations, two Japanese soldiers slapped her face. Then she was tied to a rack with pointed nails in a kneeling position and was kept like this for about two hours.
>
> During the interrogation thin strings were tied around her thumbs to which heavy items like a typewriter and a towel rack were suspended. On another occasion they set fire to her hair as well as breaking her nails ... she was further beaten with bamboo sticks, car tyres and other heavy objects. Her face and eyes were beaten until she could not open her eyes.

In Singapore, Changi barracks was soon horribly overcrowded. In the first 48 hours after surrender, more than 52,000 prisoners arrived at the camp. The astonished Japanese now had to house and feed thousands of prisoners they never expected. To make matters worse, they believed that surrender was dishonourable. Len Baynes:

> Those wounded in battle must try to get themselves killed and, finally, rather than be taken prisoner, commit the Hara-Kiri, literally the belly cut.

But when Len was sent on work parties into Singapore City, he saw some good amongst his captors.

> Our work was carrying sand, and as we still had no food with us, at midday the guards shared their meal with us ... rice and bacon, and it tasted like food for the gods. Some of our men made a point of honour to say nothing good of the

Japs... within my experience there were good men among our enemy.

His views were partly shaped by thieving British prisoners.

> We were marching to work as usual; a young Chinese woman stood at the roadside, a large basket of bread on one hip, a young child on her other. As we passed, she called out her wares... a few yards ahead of me two men left the column, one jumped on the woman's back, rolling her and her child over on the ground. The other man grabbed the basket and tipped the loaves out; before I could act, they had all disappeared into haversacks. The woman picked up her child and ran off weeping. I still feel the shame that I felt on that day.
>
> We gradually began to see each other more and more as we really were, as much of the veneer of civilisation fell away. All races seem to have a similar amount of good and bad, often lurking just under the skin whether they be black, white or yellow.

Len Baynes was a natural survivor. He foraged in rubbish dumps for bits and pieces that 'might come in useful'. These items included a wide-brimmed Australian hat and a discarded mosquito net. When he moved to River Valley Road Camp, he escaped through the wire with money from the cooks in search of extra food for the camp, despite the risk of being shot. He bought supplies for the Allied cooks in a friendly local cafe. One day a Chinese woman sat down at his table.

> With a sweet smile she pulled a parcel from under her garments and handed it to me. Thanking her, I made a movement to untie the tape, but she raised a hand to stop me, and without a word, moved out of the room as unobtrusively as she had entered it.
>
> The parcel contained a vest, Chinese dressing gown, safety razor, a tin of *pâté de foie gras*, a tin of bamboo shoots, and one

of unrecognisable Chinese food. I kept the vest and a tin of food and gave the rest away.

The Japanese were particularly brutal to the Chinese.

> Marching home from work, we passed a green space with three trees growing on it. To each tree was tied a Chinaman, and each of them had a caption over their head reading 'Thief', 'Robber', 'Pilferer'. They were covered in blood and bruised beyond recognition; the centre one appeared to be only about 12 years old. As they hung there, they looked like a depiction of the Crucifixion.*

Baynes moved back to Changi for medical treatment on an injured foot. The overcrowded camp distracted itself from malnutrition and tropical diseases with sport, education and entertainment.

> A first-class concert party had been formed and was now able to present shows of a very high standard. Female clothing and make-up had been acquired or made, so the concerts were not without heroines, many of them indistinguishable from the real thing.

Len was resourceful. He bought some ducklings from a local Chinese.

> I scoured the camp for materials with which to build my duck run; wire netting, trodden into the mud of the coconut grove, odd bits of attap and bamboo retrieved from a hut undergoing repair ... how different life seemed now with my little charges. I built my working day round them ... they were my substitute family ... to my friends I must have been behaving in a ridiculous manner, and they continually pulled my leg.

---

* Thousands of Chinese were systematically killed by the Japanese in the Sook Ching massacres.

Len caught frogs and insects to feed the ducks. He agreed to share his run with an officer who also owned some ducks. But Len grew too attached. The officer broke their 50/50 sharing agreement by stealing 12 of the biggest ducks.

> I stalked over to the Officer's Mess with murder in my heart... He was a coward. I told him, in the loudest voice I could muster, the kind of gentleman I now considered him to be.

The officer returned two of the ducks, but Len was powerless to demand more. His remaining ducks grew bigger, and then there was a deluge.

> The rain was so heavy that one could only see for a few yards... there was already an inch or two of water lying on the ground as I rushed through the downpour to find my little family. They had all disappeared. An anti-malarial drain ran near their run, and now I remembered with horror that they had recently taken to swimming in it... I arrived to see the last of my wards washed down the drain. I would never see any of them again. Life seemed empty for the next few days.

But the loss of all his ducks was soon overshadowed by the reality of his incarceration, as the Japanese tightened their grip on their thousands of prisoners. To make clear who was in charge, two Australian and two British prisoners who had escaped were taken down to the nearby beach and shot by a firing squad.

PART THREE

The moon was full, and over Germany the River Rhine showed up like an illuminated winding ribbon. I will always remember experiencing the spectacular view of aircraft exploding and the crowded sky of shell bursts, and searchlights as the great fires burned below. That is a night I shall never forget, and it brings tears to my eyes even now when I talk about it.

Bomber Command pilot over Cologne

CHAPTER TWENTY-TWO

Britain at Sea, 1940–42

The contrast between the experiences of Phyllis Briggs and Len Baynes in the steamy heat of the Far East and the sailors in the icy waters of the Atlantic or the Arctic could not be sharper. But they were all just trying to survive the same war.

On the frontline, the RAF, Army and Navy all needed a secure supply of bombs, ammunition, food, medicines and men. At home, raw materials were essential to build tanks, aircraft and warships. Britain's maritime power, both the Royal Navy and merchant fleet, had to keep these raw materials flowing freely despite the threat of German U-Boats (submarines). The Battle of the Atlantic was to last for much of the war and, together with Arctic convoys to supply Russia, Britain's success in keeping the supply corridors open was a critical factor in winning the war.

Andrew Andrews, HMS *Pink*, escorted Atlantic convoys.

> People don't really understand the number of lives that were lost in the Battle of the Atlantic. At one point there were at least 50 submarines which came up in the middle of one of the convoys. When we arrived at the scene, there were bodies floating everywhere, women and children as well. It would have sickened anybody. We rescued 126 survivors.*

Walter Edney, HMS *Vanoc*, 17 March 1941, 03.18 a.m.:

---

* Over 70,000 were believed to have died in the Battle of the Atlantic, including seamen, merchant mariners and aircrew.

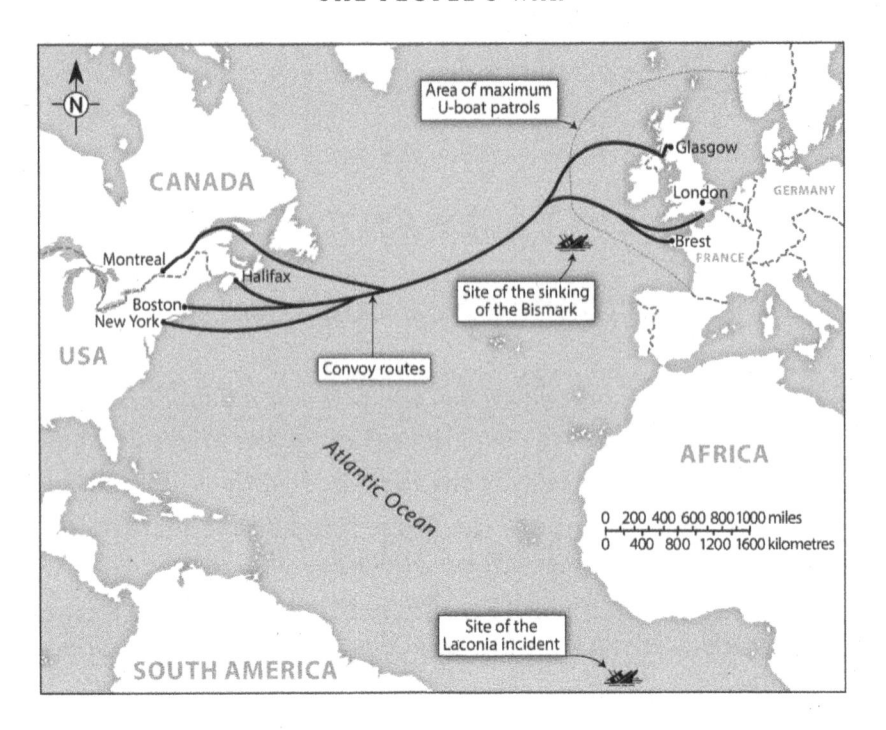

[Map with labels: Area of maximum U-boat patrols; Glasgow; London; GERMANY; CANADA; Brest; FRANCE; Montreal; Halifax; Boston; New York; Site of the sinking of the Bismark; USA; Convoy routes; Atlantic Ocean; AFRICA; 0 200 400 600 800 1000 miles; 0 400 800 1200 1600 kilometres; Site of the Laconia incident; SOUTH AMERICA]

> The silhouette of a U-Boat could be seen on the surface, so without hesitation our Captain gave the order 'Stand by to Ram'. This we did, in no uncertain manner, at full speed, hitting the U-Boat amidships and toppling her over... the U-Boat rose high in the air and sunk, the Captain still on the bridge wearing his white cap but badly injured, went down with her. There were few survivors, just five from a crew of 50.

The *Bismarck* was Germany's most powerful battleship. In May 1941, *Bismarck* vividly demonstrated her enormous threat to Allied shipping when she sank Britain's largest battle cruiser, HMS *Hood*, in just 16 minutes.

Sam Wood was a doctor on board HMS *Prince of Wales*, sailing alongside HMS *Hood* that day.

> There was a terrible explosion and a blinding flash of light... all that remained was a huge pall of smoke where a few moments earlier the pride of the Royal Navy had been.

Only three members of *Hood*'s 1,418 crew survived: the largest single loss of life in the war for the Royal Navy. No wonder Churchill was desperate to 'Sink the Bismarck.'

Three days later *Bismarck* was in the Atlantic, 350 miles west of Brest in German-occupied France, where it had undergone repairs. It was attacked by Swordfish torpedo bombers from HMS *Ark Royal*. The attacks jammed Bismarck's rudders, preventing her escape. Next morning two Navy battleships and two cruisers pounded the wounded Bismarck for nearly two hours before she sank.

Robert Nicklin was on heavy cruiser HMS *Dorsetshire* when she finally dispatched the *Bismarck*.

> I could see ours and the battleship HMS *Rodney*'s shells smashing into her superstructure and, when she was nothing more than a burning wreck, we were ordered to finish her off, and as we closed to fire three torpedoes, I could see scores of men jumping overboard into what was a very rough sea.
>
> The pride of the German Navy was no more, and the Royal Navy had avenged the sinking of HMS *Hood*. We started the dangerous task of picking up survivors ... we were sitting ducks for any U-Boat in the area ... we managed to pick up 84 men of the just over 100* who were saved. We were still hauling men over the side when an officer on the bridge spotted what he thought was a periscope ... our skipper had no alternative but to push off. Men were still trying to get on board as the ship started to move, and the cries and screams of those poor souls as they fell off the ropes, I live with to this day.

British Merchant ships and converted liners ferried huge amounts of men and supplies across the Atlantic. About 185,000

---

* British ships picked up 110 survivors from *Bismarck*'s crew of 2,200 but had to leave the area because of U-Boat threats.

men served in the Merchant Navy, including 40,000 from India, China and elsewhere.

In 1940, SS *Severn Leigh* was steaming between Hull and Canada with a crew of 43 when it was torpedoed. Eighteen-year-old Bill Garvey's family feared the worst when they heard nothing for fourteen days and listened to Lord Haw-Haw boasting on the radio that the *Severn Leigh* had been sunk 'with all hands on deck'. Fifteen days later the local chaplain visited, as reported by Bill's sister, Tricia.

> 'Your son has been found alive in an open boat which drifted into the Isle of Harris.' ... Bill was one of ten survivors ... he had sea boils all over his body and was in a terrible state ... they had been sucking fish's eyes to get moisture.
>
> The captain was rationing the water for each man but, after eating the hard biscuits, some of the poor souls began to drink salt water ... they went off their heads and the poor captain had to shoot some of them.

On Harris, 11-year-old Finlay Macaskill saw the grounded boat.

> The scene was unforgettable – living dead is the only description ... everyone was in a state of dehydration almost to the point of no return. All were helped, some carried to the nearest houses.*

The fishing village of Staithes, North Yorkshire, lost 8 men when the SS *Empire Heath* was torpedoed in the mid-Atlantic when carrying iron ore from Brazil to Scotland. There was only one survivor from the 57 men on board.

When another Staithes man went down with the SS *Beaverford*, their last wireless message was: 'It's our turn now. So long, the captain and crew of SS *Beaverford*.'

All 77 hands were lost.

Private Stan Scislowski of the Perth Regiment was from

---

* These were the only 10 survivors.

Windsor, Ontario. He crossed from Canada on the peacetime luxury liner, *Andes*, now carrying 5,000 troops.

> The magnificent crystal chandeliers that had once hung from the ornately decorated and painted high ceilings had given way to single lamps hanging from long cords . . . the individual berths had been reduced from stately beds to the spartan conditions of hammocks stretched between steel supports in which men slept jammed in against each other like sardines in a can.
>
> No meal had been laid on for that first day . . . by mid-evening I was so hungry I could have eaten the asshole out of a skunk.
>
> Canada had slipped beneath the horizon and was gone. I got to thinking, 'Would I ever see it again?' And I could lay a bet that most of the others on board were thinking the same. For some, it was indeed their last sight of Canada. They lie buried in cemeteries across the face of Europe and Asia. And there had to be some amongst us who would have no known grave. They would be consumed in the flames of their aircraft or, along with men who sailed the angry seas, swallowed up by the ocean deep.
>
> I had assumed we were going across in a large convoy with cruisers, destroyers and corvettes to escort us, so it came as a

Stan Scislowski

> surprise when I saw only two other ships. On the second day we were all alone, no ship ahead of us, no ship behind us . . . I said to myself, 'Oh boy. Now we're in for it!'

Stan was mightily relieved to finally enter the River Mersey to dock in Liverpool.

> On both sides of a buoyed channel, the rusting masts and super structures of sunken freighters protruded [out] of the channel . . . it was literally a cemetery of torpedoed and bombed ships.

Alfred Johnson served on the *Queen Mary*, returning from New York to Scotland with about 15,000 American troops on board. HMS *Curacao* was deputed to lead her into Glasgow from 200 miles offshore on 3 October 1942. The *Curacao* zigzagged closely in front of the *Queen Mary*, the standard technique to confuse enemy submarines.

> I said to my mate, 'You know she's zigzagging all over the place in front of us. I'm sure we're going to hit her.' And, sure enough, the *Queen Mary* sliced the cruiser in two like a piece of butter . . . it was the policy not to pick up survivors even if they were waving at you. It was dangerous as the threat of U-Boats was always present . . . I estimate that about 600 men were aboard the cruiser, and I don't know if there were any survivors or not, as the collision was covered up.*

Ena Stoneman from Plymouth sailed on RMS *Laconia* with her husband, George, an RAF Sergeant, and daughter June. The ship carried over 2,700 passengers, over half of them Italian prisoners-of-war and, over 30 years later, a local newspaper carried Ena Stoneman's dramatic story of what happened 260 miles north of Ascension Island in the Atlantic on 12 September 1942.

---

* The accident was not made public until after the war. The Court of Appeal apportioned 2/3 blame to the *Curacao* and 1/3 to the *Queen Mary*. About 100 men were rescued but at least 337 died.

> A torpedo from a German U-Boat struck the ship below the waterline... water was streaming down the passageway and there were people screaming and shouting... I was half-lifted, half-dragged by George and he was carrying June with the other arm. It was a nightmare.

The Stonemans struggled into a lifeboat with 47 others.

> June was wearing her flower-patterned pyjamas. I was still in my party frock and George was wearing only a heavy coat, underpants and singlet... we were quite alone on the ocean. There were no other lifeboats at all.

The family were adrift at sea for five days.

> The five days were a nightmare of heat during the day and cold at night, with very little to eat or drink... we had no compass and no idea of the nearest land... I was sure we were going to die; I think we all were.
> Then on the fifth day the miracle happened. About mid-morning our submarine – the one we later came to think of as ours – suddenly surfaced with a great gushing of water and a roaring noise. It was huge and painted on the bow were two pigs – one with a head like Winston Churchill and the other like Roosevelt.

This was U-507, captained by German U-Boat Commander Harro Schacht. His orders were to pick up Italian POWs first, and then tow any boats carrying Allied survivors to a rendezvous point. When Schacht saw the terrible condition of the women and children after five days adrift at sea, he disobeyed orders and took them onto his already crowded submarine. Ena Stoneman:

> He shouted, 'Bring the women and children aboard. Drape the gun with a Red Cross... don't listen to any refusals and do it quickly.' U-507 had ceased to be a deadly ship of war. She was now a cross between a hospital ship and a kindergarten.

I was convinced something awful would happen to us...
[but] thick vegetable soup and coffee was passed down to
us... a sailor took June on his knee, and she ate chocolate
and drank a glass of milk. This wasn't anything like the stories
I had been told about the Germans... I think they were
missing their own kids and were spoiling ours.

Meanwhile U-507's sister submarine, U-156, which had fired the fatal torpedo, had also draped a Red Cross on its guns and was towing lifeboats to safety. An American B-24 bombed the submarine but only succeeded in killing many lifeboat survivors.*

Prime Minister Churchill also committed to regular convoys carrying tanks and aircraft to Britain's other major ally, Russia.

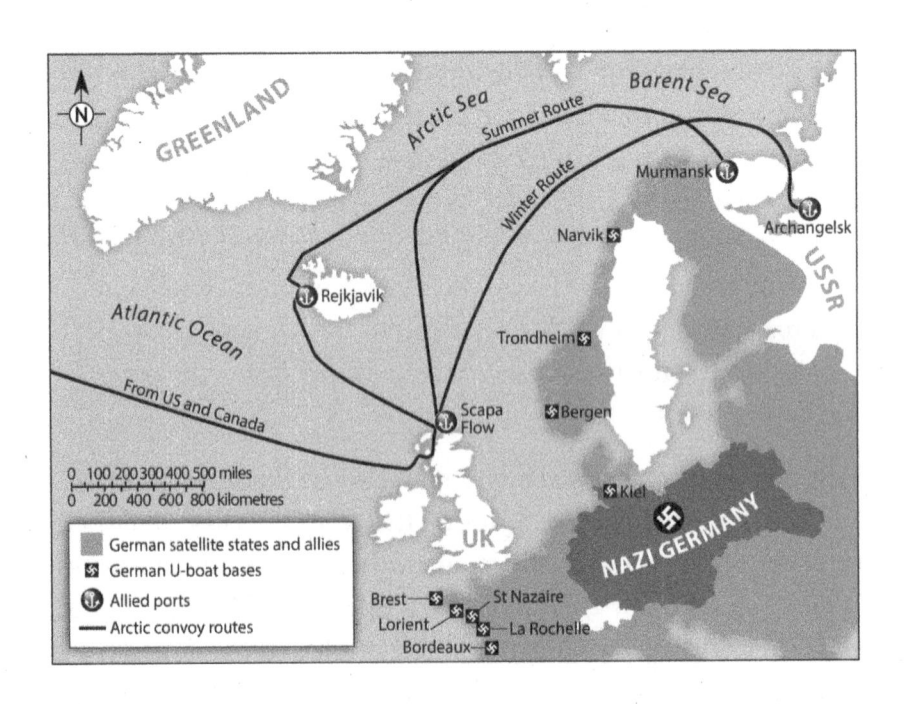

---

* Around 1,700 *Laconia* passengers, many Italian POWs, died. The attacks on their U-Boats led to the banning of German rescue attempts for the rest of the war. The sympathetic U-Boat Commander Harro Schacht was killed later in the war.

Alfred Longbottom from Halifax was on cruiser HMS *Nigeria* on convoy escort to Murmansk in the Arctic Circle.

> Escorting those convoys was sheer murder. We were continually under attack, even after we docked at Murmansk. It was only 50 miles away from German-occupied Norway. Sometimes temperatures fell to minus 40 degrees C... there was no heating on board and ice formed on the inside of the cabins... we couldn't win either way – when it melted, everything got soaked.

Terry Hulbert, HMS *Norfolk,* was fired on.

> An 11-inch shell coming towards you is like standing in the middle of a railway track with an express train thundering towards you at 150 mph. It starts off very faint, gets louder and louder and finishes in a big explosion and shrapnel flying all over the place. The next two shells hit the ship, one exploded on 'X' turret killing an officer and four ratings... the other exploded inside the ship killing two stokers.
>
> The blast from the shells blew me off my feet... on reaching the snow-covered main deck... I heard this terrible screaming; coming towards us was a marine from 'X' turret, a ball of fire from head to toe. He went to the guardrail to throw himself into the sea, which would have been certain death. Chief Petty Officer Ogilvy grabbed hold of the marine, threw him down on the deck, rolled him over and over, and put out the flames... if any man deserved a medal, he did.

The next day Hulbert cleaned up the area where two stokers were killed.

> I was cleaning up bits of skin, bone, fingernail and blood – the disinfectant that was once white was now a milk-chocolate colour.

George Green, HMS *Foresight*, 1942:

> The three German destroyers decided to sink HMS *Forester* first ... In a matter of seconds, she was a blazing hulk. All her superstructure had been blown away and all her officers, and many of the crew, killed ... [then] they hit us with two direct hits. One exploded in the boiler room, killing all who were down there and ripping a hole the size of a bus in our port side. We all felt this was the end of our story. The Chief Stoker, a very brave man, gave his life to save the ship. He went into the wrecked boiler room in scalding steam to turn the main taps off and prevent the ship from blowing up. He died within minutes.
>
> The captain asked us if we would be prepared to save her or go down with her. We gave three cheers – and he placed a barrel of rum on the deck to help ourselves. The ship was now listing 30 degrees, in danger of capsizing. We moved everything to the starboard side. After eight hours she was nearly righted, and the hole was out of the water. We plugged it with hammocks, kitbags, everything we could. Towards midnight we got an auxiliary engine going ... by the grace of God we arrived in Murmansk. All that was left was to bury our dead. There were 35 of them, sewn up in their hammocks. They were committed to the deep a few miles from Kola.

Austin Byrne, SS *Induna*, 30 March 1942:

> The *Induna* was torpedoed in the number five hold right under a load of aviation fuel and the explosion turned the deck into a burning mess ... a few people started to run through the fire, whilst some jumped into the sea and away from the flames.

Byrne jumped in a lifeboat but spotted a burning man nearby.

His hair was burnt off and his face and hands were badly burnt. As his jacket and trousers were also burning, we rolled him into the boat and beat out the flames.

The boat was lowered into the sea and as we rowed away another torpedo smashed into the ship, which then sank with all the men who were still on board. We were in the lifeboat in terrible weather, after all it was winter in the Arctic. The burnt man had few clothes, and he sat in the boat with the seas breaking over him and we covered him with a blanket and a spare coat . . . a coat of ice formed on him which got thicker over time, but never once did he moan.

The survivors were at sea in sub-zero temperatures for four days. In another lifeboat 17 out of the 34 men died.

At dusk on the fourth day we sighted land . . . the burnt man said 'put an oar in my hands and I can rock my body to help.' . . . his hands were twice as thick as they should be, with his fingers drawn and bent with the cold, all black with knuckles burst and covered with scabs. And still he wanted to help.

Then a Soviet minesweeper arrived.

After a few tots of vodka, I was taken to see the burnt man, who put his hand out to me, and said as best he could, 'WE MADE IT, KID', words that I will never forget from a man who was now suffering from both burns and terrible frostbite . . . [later] I was told that the American had died from his injuries. Who was he? I will never know for certain, but there is a grave in Murmansk to an unknown sailor.*

---

* Russell Harrison Bennett, American merchant seaman. Three thousand men died on Arctic convoys, but transported 4 million tons of supplies, including 5,000 tanks.

CHAPTER TWENTY-THREE

Survival, 1942

Far away from the freezing seas around Murmansk, after the arrival of Vivian Bulwinkel, the only woman to survive the Japanese massacre of 22 Australian nurses, conditions for Phyllis Briggs in the steamy heat of Banka Island deteriorated. In March 1942 most of the women in the camp were moved to mainland Sumatra, but Phyllis and five others stayed behind to nurse the sick.

> Twice a day we were given a small bowl of rice with some thin vegetable soup ... once we had a small amount of stewed dried octopus with our rice, which made a change. Dysentery developed and most people had swollen ankles.
> I exchanged a blue handkerchief for two rolls of bread from an Indonesian guard ... every morning there was a great scrabble for the bathroom; the smell of the latrines was dreadful. We bathed by having 'dipper' baths – throwing tins full of water over ourselves from the water tank. At first the Jap guards used to walk in and watch us, but they soon got bored and walked out again ... there were not enough drugs for the sick and wounded. I used a pot of face cream for burns on a man's buttocks.

Phyllis grew friendly with Mary Jenkins, who had been in the Auxiliary Medical Service in Singapore.

She slept beside me on the concrete slab... Mary could have left by ship some weeks before but decided to remain with her husband and help the wounded.

Three-year-old boy Mischa Warman's father had drowned in front of him when their escape ship was hit, and was then orphaned when his mother died of pneumonia in the camp.

Mary Jenkins took charge of Mischa. She made clothes for him and a little mattress out of sacking. Mary and I became good friends.

Twice a day we had to line up on the road outside our houses to be counted by the guards. This roll-call was known as 'Tenko' and we had to bow to the guards as they came by. If we did not bow low enough, we would get a face slap.

Eventually, Phyllis, Mary and Mischa were transported from Muntok to Palembang, Sumatra, to join the other women in another Japanese camp. Having survived a vicious bout of dengue fever, Phyllis fell ill for the second time and nearly died.

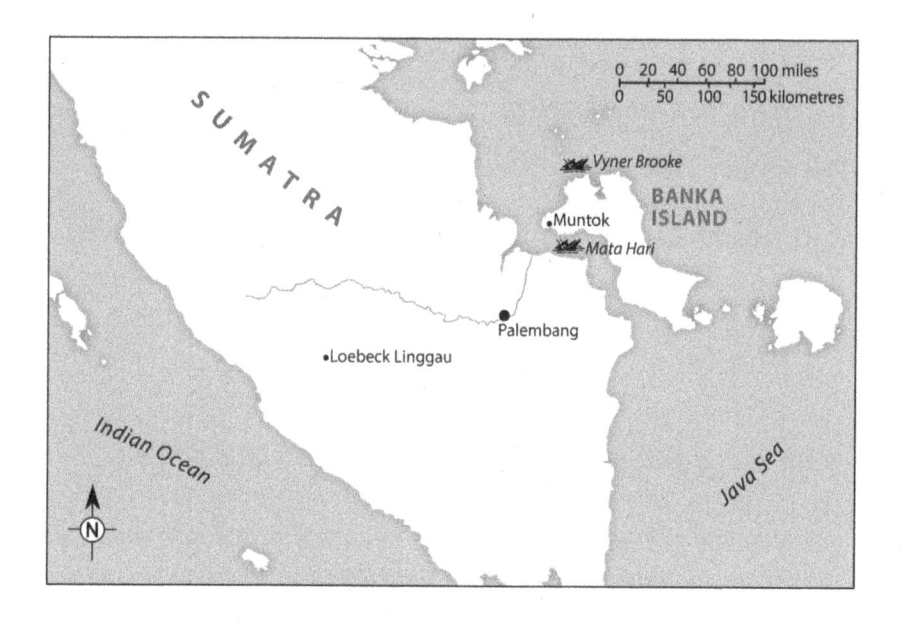

> I became ill again, passing blood . . . fortunately Alice Rossie saved my life; she came to see how I was and found me unconscious.

Sister Rossie massaged her unconscious comrade until Phyllis's circulation started again.

> Many people had swollen legs, rice tummies and mosquito bites. The children were miserable because there was no milk for them, and my hair started coming out in handfuls, but apart from that I felt better. By this time practically all the women had stopped menstruating, which was a blessing as no toilet facilities were provided.

Phyllis lived with 14 others in what was called Garage 9. To keep disease at bay, women used coconut shells to scoop faeces into buckets from the open-drain latrines. By June 1942, rations had deteriorated further.

> Half a rotten cabbage was thrown into the road for us to collect, and some days we only had rice, which was full of weevils. Sometimes there was no water, and, on these days, long queues formed up at the guardroom at the bottom of the hill where there was a tap.

The women developed survival strategies by keeping busy.

> Georgette Gilmore started a French conversation class, and the Australian sisters made some playing cards . . . we had no books to read so most evenings we just sat and talked. Once a week Mamie Colley held country dancing classes . . .

Back in Java's capital, Batavia (now Jakarta), Nini Rambonnet, like Phyllis Briggs, toiled long hours nursing a growing number of sick internees.

> By now patients were dying at the rate of ten a day. We had to lay them out and carry the bodies to a small mortuary. The

> Japanese used to have a ceremony for the dead and coffins made of coconut leaves were placed on trestle tables. Each coffin was given a bunch of bananas, which was rather ironic as the patients had all died of malnutrition.
>
> I tried to communicate with locals living across the river and the Japanese doctor gave me a severe beating and made me stand on gravel, in bare feet, in the midday sun for six hours. Not very pleasant!
>
> When some men patients arrived, I learned that my father had died of dysentery and malnutrition in a concentration camp in Bandoeng.*

While Nini was mourning her father, Phyllis Briggs, her imprisonment stretching into the unknown, made herself more comfortable.

> Mary Jenkins and I got hold of an old mattress, which we divided into two and filled rice sacks with the contents. Then Mary cleverly stitched them so we could roll them up during the day, tied in a neat bundle. Up to then we had slept on a stone floor – it was bliss to have something to lie down on.

Phyllis had wisely hidden what little jewellery she owned in her hair, covered with a scarf. Now it came in useful.

> Those of us with no money sold our jewellery to buy little extras ... I bought some navy shorts and two red-and-white tea towels, which I made into sun tops ... [but] it was not long before the Japs stopped the merchant coming.

Christmas 1942 sparked mixed emotions. Better food was briefly provided, but at the same time their uncertain future weighed

---

* Just after liberation, Nini met Bill Hannaford from the RAF. They married in Scarborough in 1946.

heavily on every prisoner. But the women still made Christmas tolerable for the children.

> Dorothy Moreton made rag dolls and toy animals ... Joan Maddams made and drew 'snap' and 'happy families' cards ... On Christmas Day the food was the best it had been for many months. Each group was given a piece of beef, a few onions, and a piece of *gula malaca* (palm sugar).
>
> We used to catch a glimpse of the men's working party marching back and forth from the jail. As we saw them returning that day, we sang 'O Come All Ye Faithful'. They stopped to listen, and in the distance waved to us.
>
> On Boxing Day morning, they stopped at the same spot and sang the same carol to us in English and Dutch. It was wonderful to hear the men's voices singing, but we all felt very sad.

CHAPTER TWENTY-FOUR

John Gardiner's War, 1940–43

Compared to the children in Phyllis Briggs's Japanese internment camp whose only playthings were rudimentary homemade toys, British children were lucky. War was frightening, but also exciting. They watched dogfights between Spitfires and Messerschmitts, foraged for fragments of bombs and raced bikes through smashed-up streets.

Children who were bombed out or evacuated across the other side of the country were surprisingly resilient. Of course, there was natural anxiety about fathers away fighting, but wartime childhood also ushered in unimaginable freedom.

John Gardiner was a young boy living in Walsall, ten miles from Birmingham. His war was not marked by high drama, but his daily life was representative of the new normality for many children.

> My mother had just returned from queuing at the local greengrocer for at least an hour and a half (not that she knew what she was queuing for). Rumour had it they had some oranges but, as usual, by the time she made it to the head of the queue they had run out anyway. All was not lost, as while they waited the ladies would have a great time with a good old chat about the state of the war, whose sons and whose daughters had gone missing, who had received the dreaded telegram and how many Yanks the floozy down the road had been entertaining that week.

After our evening meal we would all listen to the radio, and the programme would be interrupted by special messages for the secret agents abroad, things like, 'The doves have settled in for the night' and the very ominous Lord Haw-Haw... 'Germany Calling, Germany Calling.' This was meant to scare, and it did! We listened in complete silence, and he would tell of glorious wins. You could see the depression in both Mom and Dad's faces.

The dreaded fear of an air raid was all too often realised when the awful screaming of the siren began to howl over the rooftops. Mom and Dad would take us down to the Anderson Shelter at the bottom of the garden. It was pitch dark and inside the musty smell of damp earth greeted you at the door.

Rumours were flying around the butcher's shop queue that German paratroopers had already landed in Britain.

This particular night was beautifully clear, and the stars shone like jewels in the sky, complemented by a full moon. As children, we could feel the fear and tension our parents were suffering. Mom said, 'I hope this raid isn't German paratroopers.' Dad replied, 'You women and your rumours.' After an hour or so we heard the unmistakeable step of army boots coming nearer. Mom, who by now was scared to death, said, 'Bill, I think it's them.' My dad picked up the garden fork, leapt out of the shelter, held the fork in front of him and in a menacing manner shouted, 'Who is it? Speak or you will get four holes all at once.'... a man dressed in an army overcoat and huge boots shouted at the top of his voice, 'Hey Bill. It's only me.'

Uncle Jack had been on the night shift at the local copper works and had just popped home during his break to collect his snap [meal]... and had popped in to see if we were all safe. My dad collapsed with relief on the turf outside the shelter and Mom was physically sick!... had the garden fork been a gun, poor Uncle Jack may now be dead!

I hated Saturdays... the day would actually start well with a slice of bread toasted on the coal fire and covered in beef dripping (lovely and hot with a salt and pepper dressing). But every Saturday was the day of the dreaded coke fuel run... [our] mission was to take our wheelbarrow to collect our ration of 1cwt of precious coke... as you turned the corner you were confronted with a daunting vison of a two-abreast queue... hundreds (it appeared like hundreds) in the queue, the hated queue... me and our Billy were going to be here for HOURS! How the Gas Board treated us scarred me for life. There was only ever one man serving and one man taking the money, and they had the manners of pigs (no, that's unfair to pigs!).

We heard one solitary aircraft flying low and fast. We could see it was a German... our garden was next to the school, and I could clearly see the pilot's face grinning at me... Mom was screaming at him, 'Please, not the school, God, not the school!' The bombs fell crazily from the plane's open doors. We watched helplessly as they fell, and we saw a flash. Something suddenly picked us both up and flung us at the back door. It really hurt... amazingly, not one person was lost. Several houses were demolished... the Gasometer was gone, but the Gas Board deserved it... Billy and I both thought: great, no more queues.

Like many families, the Gardiners kept chickens. Sundays, when local food inspectors were not working, was unofficial slaughter day. It was a family affair.

Plucking was a terrible job. All the feathers would get up your nose, especially Mom's and mine, as we had the biggest 'hooters', but gutting was worse and oh, the smell! Dad would kill about twenty birds in a session over the drain in the yard using a sharp knife. Sometimes the head came right off, and the poor bird would do a lap of honour around the yard with its head in the drain singing, 'I ain't got no body!'

By nine o'clock we would go to bed (and what an ordeal that was!)... My brother and I slept together for warmth with old blankets and an old army greatcoat. Mom would put a house brick in the oven for a couple of hours, wrap it in an old towel, and place it in the sheets at the bottom of the bed – it worked a treat.

I hated Mondays too. This day was dedicated to the chore of all chores – washing!... only near death could get you excused from wash duties... the boiler was made of a cast-iron pot about 18 inches in diameter and about 18 inches deep... there was a hive of activity of stoking, prodding with the boiling stick, stirring, lifting, tossing sheets, shirts, pillows, socks, nighties and knickers... Mom would demonstrate with great vigour how to beat the living daylights out of our laundry. There was no sanctuary from the pain, nor peace... On a nice day the sheets would be cascading down the garden like the sails of a regatta, but on a bad day, slung across from corner to corner of the living room, with the rest of the evening like being on board a tea clipper with the full rigging above your head.

There would sometimes be treats for the family.

Occasionally we would dine out. Freddie's Oyster Bar did beautiful fish and chips with a round of bread and butter served on a plate with a cup of tea. It was fantastic – to our family this was the Ritz!

Cigarettes were another comfort.

Everyone smoked; when you visited the cinema the air would be thick, the projector would cut huge beams through the dense smoke blankets... on the upstairs of the first morning bus, the poor conductor would almost be consumptive. You would see some old chaps nearly bursting blood vessels in their throats, but who still refused to put their fags out. On foggy days the smog would drop like a stone, stick to your eyelids, and your mouth would look as if you had been eating liquorice.

John's Uncle Jack owned a motorcycle combination. On Sundays Jack would disconnect the sidecar from the chassis for cleaning. One Sunday he forgot to reconnect it.

> Everything started out very smoothly with Aunt Lill (who was a bit of a snob) sitting like the Queen behind the Perspex screen. It was only when they accelerated and they were approaching the first 'Y' junction that things went horribly wrong... as Jack proceeded towards Kinver Edge, Lill headed off in a different direction, to Dudley... Lill didn't speak to Jack for weeks and the motorbike was never ever used again!*

John was only dimly aware of adult pleasure. Women routinely wore overalls during the week, but at the weekends their attire changed.

> They would 'doll themselves up' with lipstick and Pond's Cream, put on their best dresses and wash their legs with a solution of sand and water to make-believe they were wearing stockings. When their legs had been painted and dried, a girl friend would take a soft lead pencil and, from bum cheek to heel, draw a straight line down the back of each leg. These were 'poor girl's nylons', which sometimes became a bit of a problem if it started raining on the way to the dance...
>
> The exception was the 'floozy' down the road... she never wore overalls only pencil-slim skirts with proper nylons... women hated her, and men dreamed on!... men would open the door for her just to see her walk away, and the butcher always found her a bit extra.

---

* Despite this, Jack became a bombardier on Lancasters and Lill an ambulance driver, although local gossip claimed she 'liked the company of Yanks'.

CHAPTER TWENTY-FIVE

Bomber Command, 1942–44

Views differ as to what was the most dangerous wartime service. Was it more precarious dodging torpedoes in the Atlantic than avoiding German shells in a desert foxhole? But, by any measure, flying with RAF Bomber Command was lethal. Long flights bombing German cities required enormous skill and courage, and the risk from enemy fighters and anti-aircraft guns was high. Bomber Command casualties – killed, injured or captured – were 55,573. According to the Imperial War Museum, only 24 per cent of aircrew survived unscathed, with 51 per cent killed, 13 per cent prisoners-of-war, and 12 per cent wounded.

As Commander-in-Chief of Bomber Command, Air Chief Marshal Arthur 'Bomber' Harris had grown increasingly concerned by the heavy losses sustained by the British on daytime raids over Germany. To avoid more losses, he developed a new strategy involving huge swarms of aircraft bombing at night. The raids were not only aimed at destroying Germany's military machine but also undermining civilian morale.

RAF Gunner Jack Farmer:

> Bomber Command was a very efficient organisation. Bomber Harris would hold his meeting at nine o'clock and, after considering the weather forecast and other factors, would announce the 'target for tonight'... up to a thousand planes could be taking part and the crews had to be briefed. The fact that they would often take off less than ten hours after Harris

had made his decision illustrates how impressive were the mechanics of command and control.

On the night of 30 May 1942, Harris launched his first 1,000-strong bomber raid on Germany's third-largest city, Cologne. It was not only a major industrial hub, but Cologne was a much shorter flight from RAF's airbases in East Anglia than Berlin and many other cities. Geoffrey Porter flew a Wellington bomber that night.

> The moon was full, and over Germany the River Rhine showed up like an illuminated, winding ribbon. I will always remember experiencing the spectacular view of aircraft exploding and the crowded sky of shell bursts, and searchlights as the great fires burned below. That is a night I shall never forget, and it brings tears to my eyes even now when I talk about it.

Sergeant Victor Martin was on the same enormous Cologne raid. At 11.58 p.m. on 30 May, Victor's Halifax Mk2 lifted off from RAF Marston Moor, North Yorkshire.

> In the dim glow of the cockpit all is well, and with everyone in his place silence reigns . . . shortly after crossing the coast we encounter the defensive line of searchlights and anti-aircraft guns set up to protect entry into Germany. The searchlights sweep the sky . . . the first wave have now attacked, and in the distance a red glow is already visible in the sky.
>
> Above the fleecy lining of the clouds hiding the enemy below, all seems peaceful . . . suddenly the heavy anti-aircraft guns open fire, and the exploding shells shatter our world of peace. The aircraft ahead receives a direct hit, and with a blue flash is gone. Taking the immediate evasive action of undulating, and banks to port and starboard, we continue our course.
>
> Closing in on the target the intensity of the fire becomes more apparent . . . the complete area below is ablaze in one large fire. A feeling of sorrow came, but with the ferocious burst of anti-aircraft fire bouncing the aircraft about with explosions,

concentration on the purpose of our mission became uppermost... the navigator lying down over the bombing sight gives instructions for lining up the target – 'left, left, steady, right, steady, bombs away.' As all the bombs are released at once, the aircraft, relieved of its heavy load, rises like a lift.

Course is now set for home and the running of the gauntlet of Ack Ack,* searchlights and night fighters once again... we are suddenly in a ring of searchlights giving a most eerie feeling, a ghostly light filling the darkness of the cockpit. The tracer shells from the guns seem to be still as you look at them, coming up and then flash past the windscreen, a bank to starboard gives the gunners a better view to return fire, the aircraft is filled with the sinister sound of machine guns firing at a rate of several thousand rounds a minute.

Dawn is breaking as we cross the coast and the number of aircraft in the sky is awe inspiring... 915 tons of incendiaries and 540 tons of high explosives were dropped in 90 minutes, causing awful devastation.

That night, according to the RAF, 41 aircraft and their crews were lost. In Cologne, 469 German civilians were killed and 45,000 made homeless.

Three weeks later Victor Martin headed to Bremen on the third 1,000-strong bomber raid. As he crossed the enemy coastline, one engine failed.

Shortly afterwards a second engine dies, throwing us behind our specified time and a secondary target has to be considered. Suddenly the sky was filled with cannon fire, exploding shells and tracers creating lines of light as they tore through and past the aircraft... without full power for evasive action, the aircraft was immobilised within minutes and left us no alternative but to abandon.

* Anti-aircraft.

> I dropped through the escape hatch and hurtled down through the darkness of the night into the pitch blankness of the unknown... strangely my thoughts at this moment were not the usual associated with a dangerous situation but about missing a mess do that evening. Landing in a ditch without injury... I found cover under trees. I sat down to consider the uncertainty of the situation.

Five crew members, including Victor, survived the attack, but the pilot and one aircrew were killed. Victor evaded the Germans for several weeks and progressed well into Holland.

> I was captured while resting in a wheatfield, and surrounded by six men, each pointing a revolver at my head and saying 'stay still'... I found myself interned in Stalag Luft 3 POW Camp.

Nineteen-year-old Wireless Operator/Air Gunner Jack Farley flew Lockheed Hudson bombers with 206 Squadron, Coastal Command, based at Aldergrove, Northern Ireland. Jack was on the same huge Bremen raid.

> I remember the words spoken by the station commander, as clear as if it were yesterday, 'It has been decided to obliterate Bremen.'
>
> We flew at 18,000 feet, the first time ever I, and the rest of the crew, had flown at this height, and it was the first time we had needed to use oxygen... we were above the target, and we released our bomb load. Devastation was immense – the whole target was a mass of flames.

Jack hadn't even crossed the coastline on return when the crew realised there was only 15 minutes of fuel left.

> For the next ten minutes there was silence in our aircraft, and we all held our breath. By the time we landed we only had five minutes of fuel left... we counted ourselves lucky because we lost three aircraft out of 12. ... The total loss for Coastal

Command, Bomber Command and Training Command was 51 aircraft.

Flight Sergeant Bob Pointer was an upper gunner flying from RAF Oakington, Cambridgeshire. On 2 February 1943, there was anxiety in Bob's Stirling bomber because it was his final operation, the 45th, before resting.

> As we flew out over the sea, I wondered how Joan, my wife, was, as she was five months pregnant...
>
> We were flying straight and level, with the target coming up in the bomb sights. Bomb doors open – with a left, steady, right, steady – bombs gone... suddenly there was an almighty explosion as a flak shell burst our starboard side, and at the same time there was the sound of cannon shells ripping through the fuselage and the smell of burnt cordite filled the plane. I felt a sharp pain in my right buttock as if a knife had been stuck into me... the turret went dead, the hydraulic pipes giving me power had been shot through. I tried to speak over the intercom, but this was dead also...
>
> Looking forward I could see several large holes in the starboard side... I found that Eddie, our Wireless Operator, had been badly injured in the hand, a cannon shell had severed the two middle fingers of his right hand... I gave him a shot of morphine and put a tourniquet on it.
>
> Never was I so pleased to see the homing searchlight over Oakington. By word of mouth, we received orders to take up crash positions and a red distress cartridge was fired. The Skipper made a very good landing, and the emergency crews raced up to us as we taxied to a halt. We had our hands behind our heads in case the aircraft crash-landed; mine felt all wet and sticky, having banged my head a few times during the flight. I wondered what on earth had happened... the sticky liquid, although red in colour, turned out to be tomato juice,

which had dripped from the pack above my head when it was punctured by shrapnel.

As soon as we had rolled to a stop and climbed down, the first thing I did was to kiss the ground, the 45th Op was over.

The ground crew told us there were 174 cannon shell hits on the fuselage and wings. One of the rear wheels was punctured and there were large holes from flak . . . a small piece of shrapnel was embedded in my right buttock, but it was left there, and I was told it would work itself out; to this day it has never done so.

Sergeant Leonard Bolke was a wireless operator with 431 Squadron, Royal Canadian Air Force, based at Burn, Yorkshire. In April 1943 his Wellington Mk 10 headed for Frankfurt. Despite very heavy flak they bombed their target and turned for home. Petrol was very low when the engines started to falter over the German-occupied Channel Islands. The pilot decided to ditch in the sea.

I waited for the crash landing, which was perfectly done, using the technique of lifting the nose at the last moment so that the tail hits the water first and then settles with the next bump or so. We hit the water again and I was thrown around the aircraft like a pea in a bucket. The fuselage was burning from midship to tail, and belts of ammunition were on fire and exploding.

The wrecked aircraft sank . . . I started to swim towards the island in view . . . I must have lost consciousness . . . I awoke to see German soldiers round my bed in a hospital ward. One soldier said in English, 'For you, the war is over.'

Bomber Command was an unforgiving environment. In July 1943, Johnny Johnston piloted his bomber to Hamburg. It was heavily hit but made it back to British soil. Next morning Johnston surveyed the aircraft damage. Flight Engineer John Martin, aged 20, who had not been on the previous night's flight, was with him.

> It was riddled. I don't know how it ever got back. The crew escaped injury, but it was riddled. That night it was Hamburg again. Johnny and his crew went out to the aircraft, and the crew said to Johnny, 'We would like a rest tonight.' Johnny said to them, 'If you feel like that, there is nothing I can do about it.'
>
> They were arrested and put into military custody. They were kept in jail overnight . . . they were stripped of their brevets and sergeant stripes . . . they were sent to the airmen's mess and made to peel spuds. That was a demonstration to the others on the base not to 'go LMF' (lack of moral fibre) whatever you do! I felt sorry for the crew, the whole lot of them.

John Martin was soon on another Hamburg bombing raid. Following their fellow aircrew's arrest nothing was going to make this crew turn back.

> We ran into an electric storm in the North Sea, you've never seen anything like it, St Elmer's fire around the props and St Elmer's fire on all the wires. We were really lit up . . . I was scared stiff, scared stiff . . . when we landed back at base the ground crew asked us where we had been. We said, 'We've been to Hamburg.' The ground crew said nobody else went, they all turned back because of the weather . . . I think there were 30,000 people [German civilians] killed in those raids. It was terrible, thirty thousand.*

Paula Kuhl was a 30-year-old woman living in Hamburg at the time of the raids. She experienced the shattering impact of Hamburg's firestorms directly. But like many young women on both sides of the conflict, she tried to have fun despite the war.

> Dancing was prohibited then, but we had a lot of fun just the same, we laughed, and we sang . . . I saw everything in a

---

* About 37,000 people died.

rosy haze. It was often very late, and more than once enemy bombers approached before I reached the safety of home. But did I care? Not in the least! With searchlights illuminating the night sky, and the planes roaring overhead, I just laughed, waved, and shouted, 'Hello, Tommy, how are you?' (The only English words I knew then).

Then suddenly, on July 27th, the terrifying holocaust started, three nights and three days of almost non-stop bombing, as long as I live, I shall never forget it. It is beyond my comprehension how anyone could have survived the inferno of burning, crumbling houses, and come out alive... I jumped on a bike and rode to my mother's house. The roads were riddled with smouldering craters and houses still burning like bonfires.

When I reached mother's place, I was struck rigid with shock. There was no house left, the whole four-storey block of flats had collapsed and was a burning heap of rubble... There I stood, all alone in a smouldering wilderness, it was very eerie, nobody was to be seen, most people who had lived there must be dead, buried under the bricks.

Soldiers dug through the rubble searching for Paula's mother.

I was certain I had lost my beloved mother, that she must be lying dead under the ruins, otherwise she would have surely come out to me. The strangest part is that I did not feel anything at all, no tears came flooding to my eyes. I was too dazed and numb with looking at all the inconceivable horror around me. Although still alive, I seemed to have died inside.

A week later Paula visited her aunt in a small village outside Hamburg.

I could not believe my eyes, and thought I was dreaming, for there in the sitting room I found my mother, whom I thought had perished in the flames. Completely speechless we fell into each other's arms and just cried and cried, all the dried-up tears flowing freely now, washing away all the pent-up emotion. Such feelings have to be experienced to be understood, it is impossible to describe.

That night her mother had wisely not sheltered in her basement but in a well-protected public shelter. She did not imagine her daughter could have survived such an inferno.

During that night of intensive bombing, whole suburbs of Hamburg were wiped out and flattened to the ground ... hundreds of houses were burning fiercely, the smoke obscuring the sun for days. My once beautiful hometown was reduced to a heap of rubble. Uncountable lives were lost, street after street was littered with unrecognisable bodies, the stench of burned flesh was extremely nauseating, and hung over the town for a very long time.

One could not, even with the wildest imagination, anticipate that any sort of civilisation could ever arise out of the ashes. And yet it happened.*

Sheilah Cruickshank, serving with the Women's Auxiliary Air Force, was close to Paula Kuhl's age; two young women, divided by war. The theatrical troop at her bomber station, RAF Waddington, Lincolnshire, toured nearby airbases with productions.

The RAF lorry swayed and rocked through the darkening evening, as we made our way to yet another RAF Bomber Station. Inside, the mixed group of men and women of all ranks laughed and sang together ... the parts were given out on the basis of acting ability and not RAF status. A Flight Sergeant played the male lead, and a Flight Lieutenant swept the stage and cleared up.

* Paula married Cecil Alexander in 1952. They lived in Carlton, Nottinghamshire.

These were sad times for us, for our friends would be eating with us, laughing, going to dances in Lincoln, listening to music and sharing our lives, and four hours later they could be blown to tiny pieces high in the sky. The personnel on the station always went out to the airfield to wave the queues of Lancaster bombers into the air. It was a more subdued group who stood in the dark in the middle of the night, counting the planes back and realising that A for Apple and F for Freddy were not there. There could be as many as nine missing in one night, which meant that 63 men were not there at breakfast. The toll of able, fit, unselfish young men from all over the world was very high.

In Buckinghamshire, WAAF Marie Shelley, aged 17, had known Bill for six months and grown fond of him. She was shocked when she received a letter anticipating his death.

Dearest Marie,

It has taken me some time to compose this letter, as it is not easy to write in anticipation of not returning from a raid . . . first and foremost I must tell you I love you. Why I never said it before I can't quite tell, but now, when brought face to face with the facts, I realise it. I think I must have always loved you and always get a good feeling from the thought that I believe you love me . . . we would have made a good job of facing life together, Marie . . . I hope this is not 'Goodbye' but should it be, please do not take it too much to heart, rather think of the amount of pleasure that you've made possible for me – that is the memory I carry with me. So, rather than say 'Goodbye', I'd like to say, 'til we meet again.'
All my love,
Bill

Marie does not mention that they ever met again.

CHAPTER TWENTY-SIX

Home Life, 1942–43

As the number of war casualties rose and replacements were needed, recruitment into the forces grew ever more eager. Russell Billson:

> When I was in the Sixth Form at school in Nottingham, we were called to hear a lecture about the progress of the war. The man speaking to us was a splendid gent, festooned with gold braid and medals. He turned out to be an Admiral and told us the Fleet Air Arm were losing pilots and needed to replace those lost (I discovered later that the average life expectancy for a Fleet Air Arm pilot was six months).
>
> I was so fascinated and thrilled that I enrolled on the spot, there and then. I didn't say anything to my parents about this, but when a telegram arrived inviting me for a medical... they went into orbit.

Not all recruitment was as glamorous. Twenty-three-year-old Leslie Shiers was a newly qualified doctor. He was keen to join the Royal Navy, but the Admiralty claimed to have no vacancies. So, he queued up at a dingy Recruiting Office.

> The column of men shortened... I peered through the open door and, to my surprise, I saw the man standing next to me and the one who had gone in just before with their trousers round their ankles while an elderly grey-haired man sitting on a stool was closely inspecting their private parts with the aid

of a torch. I began to wonder if the stories I had heard about the Royal Navy were true. I decided I would not have my private parts examined by a stranger, so I stepped out of line.

Despite his caution, Leslie was eventually appointed a Surgeon Lieutenant and dispatched to Rosyth, Scotland, to wait for his ship.

Each day I went down to Rosyth Dockyard to enquire as to the whereabouts of my ship. This lasted for 12 days, during which time I made the acquaintance of a rather agreeable WREN staying in the hotel. On the eleventh day I failed to go to the dockyard because I was a little delayed in my room and, Sod's law being what it was, when I went down the following day, I found that my ship had come into [the dock] to refuel and re-ammunition and was already back at sea . . . so another 12 days passed happily in the company of this charming lady.

Finally on board, Leslie inspected the sick bay.

[It] contained two swinging cots and had an elderly sick birth attendant . . . in the Navy the sick birth attendant was known as the doctor and the doctor was known as the quack.

When it was her turn to be called up, Eunice Edwards, a typist with Birmingham Corporation, was drafted into the Directorate of Emergency Works and Recovery. The unit was responsible for the upkeep of POW camps and military bases and the recovery of scrap metal to be turned, no doubt, into Spitfires and guns. As Eunice put it, her story of daily wartime life 'is not a tale of heroics or great deeds, but of how life went on during the war.'

Twenty-two-year-old Eunice soon realised the war's impact was not the same for everyone.

We noticed an elderly lady in the office in tears. She was Miss Solomons. 'You don't understand,' she said. 'You've no idea what it will be like.' Then it dawned on me that she was a

Jewess . . . we tried to comfort her, but I don't think we did much good.

Eunice Edwards was determined to look good.

> Girls kept a pride in their appearance. We still had our hair 'permed', used Fuller's earth for powder, and painted our legs to save on stockings . . . we also made undies out of any material we could scrounge. How lucky the girl who got hold of some parachute silk.

Freda Hartley, also from Birmingham, was always on the hunt for parachutes.

> Very occasionally when a German plane was shot down the pilot's parachute would be recovered by locals. They were very valuable on the black market because the fine silk that they were made of were ideal for making knickers, which were in short supply.
>
> Barrage balloons were like big sausages with tail fins on them . . . one morning there was a commotion in the local park because one of the balloons had gone missing. I suppose the guards on duty had dozed off during the night and someone had stolen it . . . the barrage balloon had a lot of material in it which was ideal for petticoats and blouses.

But homemade underwear had its perils. Kathleen Godfrey, daughter of a senior intelligence officer:

> I chose to make a pair of white satin pants, called French knickers, with fashionably wide legs. No elastic at the waist. They were kept up with one pearl button . . . the button flew off on the platform at Tottenham Court Road Station, allowing the knickers to slip to the ground round my ankles. Impossible to conceal what was happening from the current boyfriend. Covered with confusion I picked them up and stuffed them into my bag.

Crisis averted, Kathleen enjoyed a lavish 21st birthday party thrown by her grandfather at the Savoy Hotel in London in 1943.

> I wore my first evening dress, sparkling black net with yards of material in the skirt... the band made us forget about the dangers and uncertainties of the real world outside.

The glamourous evening over, Kathleen grew keenly aware of London's gloominess.

> Now it seems hard to imagine or even remember the shabbiness of our lives... we had got used to living in cold, cheerless places and walking along dirty, unlit streets; gloomy, dark, and ugly. No houses had been painted for years, no trees planted, no roads repaired. In cities, where the parks should have been protected by elegant railings there was either barbed wire or nothing at all. The railings and even saucepans had gone to win the war and in London most buildings which had been bombed were still standing in ruins.

Rhoda Woodward worked in a military base's canteen. The dances were a far cry from the Savoy, but to Rhoda they still overflowed with glamour.

> These evenings were very romantic affairs, with aircraft lights in the corners of the room that shone onto a large, mirrored ball in the centre of the ceiling.
>
> We were lucky, we were allowed to wear civvies. We used to make a headband out of the top of an old stocking and roll our hair round the band. This style was known as the 'Victory Roll'.

Brook Hospital, Woolwich, South London, treated wounded servicemen, but twentieth-century diseases also needed care. Nurse Lillian Ewins:

> A child would come in with diphtheria, the type in which the neck swelled, and the child would go blue and be unable to breathe. On the table they would go and in seconds a tiny vertical cut would be made, and small tube passed into the trachea. A woman called Dr Coutts was a wonderful doctor and by far the fastest and neatest at this operation.
> One day we would be on a general ward, another would be delousing children who had been sleeping in shelters or we were looking after babies who had been abandoned. There was a ward full of healthy babies who had been left in churches, on doorsteps, or on Woolwich Common.

Eunice Edwards drew comfort from Britain's leadership.

> I will never forget the occasions when Winston Churchill spoke to us. His 'Blood, Sweat, Toil and Tears' speech rallied everybody. Without him, I do not believe we would have survived.

Eunice became an avid student of the war in Burma.

> I corresponded with my brother's friend, who was fighting in Burma (the Forgotten War). I usually had a letter from him every few weeks. I suddenly realised I had not heard from him for 12 weeks, and wrote to his mother, who I had never met. She wrote back to say that the War Office had told her not to expect to hear from her son for at least three months as he was on a special mission. I learned later he was on the first Chindit operation under Orde Wingate, which was a long-range penetration into the Burma jungle on foot. The chance of survival was low . . .*

As a Birmingham typist, Eunice was distant from the frontline but was certainly not insular.

---

* Cyril Jones. He and Eunice were married in 1947.

> We were so lucky we weren't invaded. Our privations amounted to nothing when compared to what Occupied Europe went through. Winters were cold but we didn't suffer like the people of Leningrad, who starved to death in freezing conditions. We didn't have the Gestapo to deal with and those awful concentration camps . . . we held our breath when we retreated in North Africa . . . the defeat at Singapore . . . [and later] the battles at Arnhem and Stalingrad, the landings at Anzio were all subjects of worry. It was like watching an everlasting newsreel.

Eunice watched on from afar for what became a very real experience for Maria Hay, living on her family farm in Poland.

> I was 17 when the Germans came . . . they began to take the children, some only three to five years old, blond with blue eyes, Hitler's Children. One morning about 10 a.m. the SS arrived with a big van . . . they told mother to pack my bag, and she would not stop crying . . . I was taken to the lorry with my bag and sandwiches my mum had made. Inside were more boys and girls of my age all crying.

Maria was forced by the Germans to work in a spaghetti factory near Hanover. She lived in a fenced camp, working very long hours dragging sacks of flour around. The main diet was cabbage soup.

> When prisoners were sick and coughing and sent to the doctors. I went with them to act as interpreter . . . if they found anything wrong with these people, you never saw them again. We were told they had been sent home but we knew they had been put down like a dog. I wanted to put a knife into the doctor.

In England Tim Hardy, now a fully fledged paratrooper, was still laying siege to Doreen Fenner, lately a *Kentish Express* journalist, who he had spotted as she reported on Tim's concert party performance. As the son of a mining family who had left school aged 14, Tim was acutely aware of the social chasm between the two prospective lovers.

> If the class divide between [butcher's daughter] Joyce Beastall and Tim Hardy had been wide as the River Trent, then that between my exquisite wordsmith and the same me was as wide as the Bay of Bengal.

Days were filled with practice parachute jumps but there were still chances to chase Doreen Fenner, now loading torpedoes in Milford Haven.

> I spent a lot of time laying siege to, but failing to breach the ramparts of, Doreen Maud Fenner, with whom I engaged in overheated skirmishes in all manner of places: Cardiff, Bognor Regis, Portsmouth, Newbury, Littlehampton and, most memorably, Brighton, where Doreen chose a room in the YWCA as a battleground. What girl ever needed to wear a chastity belt in a YWCA.

But at least Tim was now closer to his other ambition, sticking it to Hitler.

> I was a paratrooper in the 6th Airborne Division. The 6th? There certainly weren't five others, the 6th, I suppose, was meant to fool the enemy into shaking in his boots thinking there might have been.

CHAPTER TWENTY-SEVEN

Burma, 1942

While the Germans were consolidating their grip on Europe and taking on the Allies in North Africa, their Japanese partners in the Axis did not stop at conquering Malaya, Hong Kong and Singapore. They protected their flank by invading another British colony, Burma, strategically placed between India and China and with much-coveted natural resources, including oil. But London was pre-occupied with the Western war and British troops were poorly prepared for jungle warfare. Bob Duff:

> An officer said that if you survived the snakes (from 18 inches long to 30ft pythons), crocodiles (25ft long), leeches, mosquitos, flies, red ants, black panthers, jackals and hyenas, you then have to deal with the Japs. You can't see them, but you feel they are watching you all the time, sometimes from in front and sometimes from behind.

A week after the Japanese attacked the American fleet at Pearl Harbour and landed in Malaya, they invaded Burma. On 8 March 1942, the all-conquering Japanese took both the resources-rich island of Java, part of the Dutch East Indies (present-day Indonesia) and Burma's capital, Rangoon. For the British, Burma was to prove the longest land conflict of the war. In Rangoon, Jim Palmer, 3rd Tank Regiment, was ordered to destroy everything valuable to the enemy before leaving the city.

The docks at Rangoon were deserted, the cranes and derricks were sticking up into the sky, motionless, and the warehouses were locked and closed.

> Everything that stood up had to be blown down and all the food and stores we could not carry had to be destroyed. Any surplus vehicles had to be burnt, and artillery shells dumped in the river. The whole of Rangoon was ablaze as we moved out.

Jim had already fought in France and North Africa, and married Muriel in Manchester in between. Now he was in a humiliating British retreat through 1,000 miles of difficult terrain towards the apparent safety of India.

> Most of us were covered in jungle sores caused by thorn scratches festering and bleeding. Dysentery and diarrhoea were rife, and jungle fever hit everyone . . . we were becoming a very sorry sight indeed . . . our daily mileage got less and less.

In the oil fields at Yenangyaung, Jim's situation worsened.

> The oil derricks were burning like tall candles. There were rivers of burning oil all over the place . . . a burning derrick toppled onto the tank . . . we clambered through the blazing debris and the tank driver caught fire just as the fire reached the fuel tank. There was a terrific explosion, and the tank was blown to kingdom come.

Jim found himself surrounded, and doomed.

> The padre came along to give those who wished to take it [their] final communion. It was, in fact, the end.
>
> At first light we were to make our last stand, as the Japs came down from the surrounding hills to finish us off . . . mortar shells hit the vehicles and smoke poured from stricken tanks. Stretcher-bearers scuttled around, dragging the wounded into a first-aid post.

Then a miracle happened.

> The Japs began to clamber back up the hillside, followed by little men dressed just like the Japs. It was the Chinese army! . . . we had a chance to break out of our trap.*

With his tank destroyed, Jim retreated through the jungle on foot. In a small village he saw two Allied tanks.

> The crews were all dead at the side of the tanks, but they had not been killed in action – they had been brutally murdered. Their hands were tied behind their backs, and they had been shot in the back of the head. One of the crew was a corporal named Charlie, who had been born in Liverpool of Chinese parents. They hadn't shot Charlie but had cut his head off and it was lying in a pool of blood beside his body.

Jim was in a desperate race to get to the Chindwin River, and beyond to India, just as the monsoon began.

> That night the rains started, and the lightning flashed, and the thunder roared. Within hours the trails became torrents of water, and we kept moving through the night, wading deep in the rushing deluge. Scrambling through the mud, we crawled through the undergrowth like drowned rats.

They finally reached the Chindwin but crossing the wide river was dangerous in such apocalyptic weather.

> Ropes were strung across the river, and we clung to them and clawed our way through the flooding torrent. Some lads lost their hold on the ropes but managed to reach the opposite bank; some were swept back to where they started from . . . some were lucky to get washed ashore

---

* The Chinese Expeditionary Force were fighting with the Allies and the 38th Division tried to relieve the encircled Allies at Yenangyaung.

downstream... many were out of luck and disappeared into the raging foam.

Jim Palmer had retreated 1,000 miles to reach the river, but now he was safely under the protection of the Naga people and was evacuated from Burma to India in June 1942.

Other retreating soldiers were less lucky. Leslie Spoors was wounded and captured by the Japanese.

> We were all wounded – that's why we were taken so easily and couldn't make a run for it... we were tied together and marched about five miles back down the road. Over 30 died on the way; mostly men who dropped through exhaustion or lack of food or drink. These were just dragged to the side of the road where their backs were broken with a rifle butt. A bayonet was used to finish the job.

A guard asked Les if he wanted a drink.

> He indicated that I should open my mouth, which I did without thinking. He lifted the bottle towards my face and then flicked a lighted cigarette right down my throat.

During the retreat Allied guerillas fought behind enemy lines. Led by Brigadier Orde Wingate, the Chindits, or Long-Range Penetration groups, showed that the Japanese could be taken on, even in the jungle. Sergeant John Moore, Essex Regiment, was one of 3,200 Chindits.

> The Burmese jungle is very dense and hilly, airstrips had been built in the jungle for aeroplanes to land and that was how we landed behind enemy lines. We went in columns of about 300 men, we had many mules to carry heavy equipment, like our wireless sets... our main job was to blow up bridges, railways etc., and ambush Japs in small villages wherever we could find them. We did not take prisoners because we were always on the move... we got our food

and other supplies dropped to us every three days... we had
a Burmese guide who knew the country well, which was a
great help.

The Chindits finally retreated to India, but they had demonstrated that the enemy was not invincible. According to one source, the Chindits had about 27 per cent of their force killed or wounded, 818 men in total.

Twenty-year-old John 'Jack' Capper had joined Irish regiment the Royal Inniskilling Fusiliers (The Skins) as a boy trumpeter five years before. His extraordinary, almost unbelievable story had never been told until an anonymous contribution to BBC's The People's War. The 1st Battalion, The Skins, were dispatched to blow up the Yenanyaung oilfields. They were dropped miles away from their target, but Jack still made it to the oilfields and planted his charges.

> A huge blast consumed the oil and metal, but Jack's eardrums burst. He survived the marauding Japanese troops but crawled away, blood pouring from his ears.

But Jack felt his life was at risk from his own side. The Major in charge continuously placed his men in mortal danger.

> The final straw came when Jack was ordered into a village in broad daylight to scout for Japanese soldiers. To everyone present it was clearly a suicide mission. Jack went ahead into the jungle. He skirted behind his own positions and shot the Major dead. The company of men moved on with a Second Lieutenant for a commanding officer.
>
> Burma was chaos in this period and many civilian stragglers were found on the jungle tracks... it was when a Buddhist priest was in their rag-tag company that they were to suffer from a series of ambush attacks. Suspicion intensified and eventually Jack slit the man's throat. The ambushes subsided.

Later Jack found himself alone in the jungle. He killed snakes for food, before being rescued by the Kayan Bronze Age people whose contact with the modern world was almost non-existent. With their help he was eventually able to move, but soon collapsed again.

> Two Gurkha soldiers found the stricken Englishman. They lifted him up and carried him through another stretch of jungle to the edge of a clearing... in this clearing was a small airfield with a single passenger aircraft remaining, to fly across the border to Assam, India... a rag-tag of stragglers were being hurriedly loaded onto the aircraft. It was a charter aeroplane piloted astonishingly by a 14-year-old Chinese girl... with places on the aircraft running out a padre on board gave his place up to Jack... a Roman Catholic minister also decided to stay on the airfield, allowing the wounded more space. This when the Japanese bullets and mortars were just beginning to fizz around the landing strip.
>
> The remains of the two ministers were later found, crucified upside down.

The 14-year-old girl pilot got the little plane airborne and made it safely to India.

The 1,000-mile fighting retreat from one end of Burma to the other had been humiliating for the British and Indian troops. General William Slim later said, 'I have been kicked by this enemy in the place where it hurts, and all the way from Rangoon to India, where I had to dust off my pants.'

The Allies needed to regroup and learn lessons before fulfilling Slim's wishes to kick the Japanese back out of Burma and extinguish the bitter memory of their retreat.

CHAPTER TWENTY-EIGHT

River Kwai Railway, 1942–43

In 1942, as British troops were desperately retreating through Burma, Sergeant Len Baynes, Cambridgeshire Regiment, and keeper of ducks, left the security of Changi Camp, Singapore. His destination was unknown, but the Japanese assured departing Allied POWs that the climate, medicine and food would be better in their new location. Instead, for the next three years, Len faced 'a world of chaos, filth, blows, pain, disease, and death'.

The Japanese badly needed a secure supply line from Thailand to arm and feed its forces in Burma. The sea journey was slow, and increasingly vulnerable to Allied attacks. Building a railway was the alternative, even though it involved 258 miles of track and 10 miles of bridges across treacherous terrain, including thick jungles and huge mountain passes. Luckily for the Japanese, they had a disposable labour force of prisoners-of-war on hand. Ultimately 61,000 POWs, including Len Baynes, built the railway without mechanised machinery, just with rudimentary hand tools.

Before leaving Singapore Len loaded himself up with so many 'useful' things, including old hacksaw blades, wire, rope and sacks, that he looked like 'a Christmas tree'. With more than 30 other men, he was shoved into a railway cattle truck with the doors padlocked.

The temperature must have been about 120 degrees F (48 degrees C) in there with the doors open, who would survive now with them closed? . . . we needed a dozen times the water we got.

Twenty-year-old Alistair Urquhart, Gordon Highlanders:

> Animals would not be transported like this . . . it was like being buried alive . . . several were very ill with malaria, dysentery and diarrhoea. People vomited and fainted.

After nearly six days, Len Baynes finally arrived at the southern railhead of Ban Pong, Thailand.

> Ban Pong initiated us into the state of things that prevailed in many places where we were to live from now on . . . our hut was absolutely filthy, littered by rubbish, scraps of food, and even excreta . . . everywhere was ankle-deep in mud.

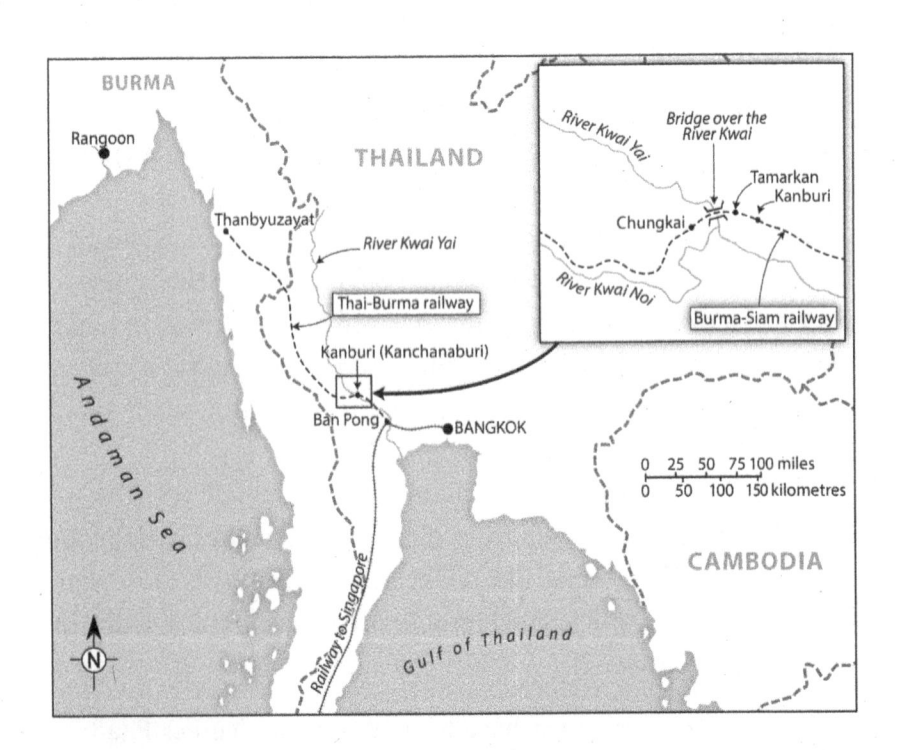

From Ban Pong thousands of prisoners were marched north along the planned line of the Thai (then Siam)–Burma railway. Alistair Urquhart:

> We were told we would walk 50 kilometres per day until we reached the work camp. We had to hack our way through impenetrable jungle. If you fell by the wayside, unless someone carried you, you were left to die. We lost quite a few that way. Five days later we came to what was to be our camp.
>
> We had to go out with pick and shovel to where our part of the railway was to be. Dense jungle had to be cut through. Worse still, we had to blast our way through solid rock. Then the rocks had to be broken by sledgehammers. All we got to eat was a handful of rice and to drink – boiled water with leaves.

On his first night Len Baynes worked by floodlight building an embankment in blinding rain.

> By the time we reached our hut, we were wading through two feet of swirling water ... some of the men's belongings, including their bedding, had already floated away ... lighting my improvised lamp I saw faeces floating along the passage from the flooded latrines ... at 4 a.m. the filthy water began to overlap our end of the hut; the time had come to move. Our thoughts, as we waded off not knowing where we were in the dark, perhaps going uphill, perhaps down dale, are not difficult to imagine.
>
> Nothing was said, blank despair flooded our hearts ... with the water up to our chests we met some more men passing through the waters and they knew where they were, slowly but surely the waters receded as we climbed the only hill in the camp.

Conditions deteriorated further when the Japanese sped up the railway's construction. 2nd Lieutenant Louis Baume:

> The working conditions are almost unbearable – hacking away at the rock in the full gaze of the midday sun or digging up the thick red clay in teeming mud; bare-footed with feet cut and bleeding from broken rock or sharp bamboo thorns, hatless and naked except for a brief Jap happy* ... and all the time the bloody blasted Nips screaming and shouting ... bellowing, beating, bashing ... forcing and bullying us to work faster, faster, faster.

Len Baynes:

> Many of us fell ill with dysentery, due to the flooding of the latrines. I spent all night sitting on the latrine pole, and nearly dropped off to sleep on it. That night our Quartermaster Sergeant, Bill Wilby, did drop off and dropped in; he was saved from drowning by his friends.
>
> Those of us with dysentery were given a dose of Epsom salts by the medics, but we still had to go out to work in order to fulfil the quota ordained by our captors. This was the last time I saw any medicine of this kind, and no more was ever obtainable.

Food was merely rice and watery soup. So, Len supplemented his diet as best he could.

> Shouts brought me quickly outside the hut, just in time to take part in a snake hunt. I managed to kill the unfortunate creature, and so skinned, cut up, and cooked it for my midday meal. As it had been about three feet long there was just enough for one, which was as well as no one else fancied trying it.

Christmas Day was bittersweet. Work stopped, but thoughts of home flooded into everyone's mind.

---

* A loincloth.

> The cooks, who had been putting rations on one side for several weeks, excelled themselves with our first Christmas dinner as POWs; and in the evening there was a concert accompanied by a band of home-made instruments. It was a very good effort. I remember finding it hard to believe that it really was Christmas and wondered if my folk had heard that I was alive and a prisoner, since I had heard nothing from home. As later I was to learn, they had heard nothing, nor were they to hear for another year or so.

One Japanese guard, Yoshio Suzuki, was sympathetic.

> He came over to our hut, this was most unusual ... sitting beside me he produced a large piece of cake and a handful of cigarettes. Shyly, he handed them to me and waved his hand round in a gesture for me to share what he had brought.
>
> I would like to know if my friend survived the war, it would be good to write to him after all this time with some little token of affection and gratitude.

Len Baynes moved to Tamarkan to build the bridge over the River Kwai,* made famous by David Lean's Oscar-winning film. Survival often depended upon the skills of Australian doctor Arthur Moon.

> The most terrifying and hideous of all our diseases were the ghastly tropical ulcers. Once started, they would enlarge at an amazing speed, and the foul stench of putrefying flesh kept away all but the Good Samaritans and our ever-faithful medical orderlies ... an active ulcer looked much like a lunar crater ... as a last resort to avoid amputation the wound would be scraped out with a sharpened tablespoon, the patient held down the while by three or four orderlies.

---

* There were, in fact, two bridges: one made of wood, the second of steel and concrete. The bridges were over the Maekhlaung (Big Kwai) River.

> The screams coming from the ulcer hut each day told us that the orderlies were trying to squeeze out the pus between muscle and sinew.
>
> Finally, the last option; I watched Major Moon cut through a man's thighbone with what looked like a carpenter's saw ... bamboo 'peg legs' were made in the camp for the limbless, and eventually we had dozens of men strolling about very effectively on these legs.

Len was not portrayed in the famous film but had enormous respect for Tamarkan's Commanding Officer, Colonel Philip Toosey, who was very different from the compliant Colonel acted by Alec Guinness in David Lean's movie.

> Col Toosey turned out to be the best officer I was ever to find running a camp ... [he] had stamped out all the rackets and the atmosphere was very pleasant compared to most other camps.

When Len was caught trading with locals, he felt the full force of Japanese punishment.

> A scream of rage filled the air as the Jap came rushing over. A teak two-handled practice sword was raised over his head and, in his fury, he sounded like a madman ... the heavy weapon came crashing down on my skull. Again and again, it landed ... as each blow landed, it felt as though my brain were soft and was being gently pressed in while everything became momentarily dark ... blood was by this time everywhere, over my mate, over the Jap and beginning to form a pool on the ground.

Len survived but then suffered from a terrible attack of malaria. Luckily for him, this prevented him from being marched further up the line. His healthier colleagues were less fortunate.

> That most dreaded disease of all, cholera, appeared among them. Cholera untreated will dissolve away half a strong

man's body in less than a day; it is so contagious that contacts are almost sure to contract it.

Hundreds of our friends died, until there were hardly sufficient men left to perform the essential task of burning the bodies. Thus, on the only occasion of my POW life when I fell out of a march, it was to save me from making the acquaintance of the arch-enemy Cholera, whose touch meant death.

Captain Harry Silman, a doctor from Leeds, recalled a makeshift cholera ward:

Over a hundred thin skeleton-like beings, writhing on the long platform, vomiting, and passing motions where they lie. Groans and cries are the only noises to break the silence ... about nine corpses lay outside covered with blankets and, a little distance away, the smoke of the pyre where the corpses are burning could be seen.

Len encountered Tamil labourers from Burma and elsewhere, called *romushas*. Thousands of them had been forced into building the railway but their conditions were even worse than those endured by Allied POWs.

We were aware of dozens of furtive figures appearing from the nearby huts. Some were staggering on fleshless legs, most were crawling on hands and knees, too weak to stand. We were soon surrounded by these poor Tamils, whose shrunken lips, but still-white teeth gave them an appearance of walking dead. Eyes and cheeks were sunken, bodies fleshless. Belsen could not have looked worse; I shall never forget them.

On completion of the River Kwai railway in October 1943, Len received six letters from home.

The letters were all over a year old ... I spent every spare moment reading them over and over. Difficult to understand now perhaps, but that first evening all my friends, and even a

> dozen strangers came to me with a whispered request to read my precious letters. Many of our men, some with wives and children, received no mail during the whole time in captivity.

On the final day at the bridge on the River Kwai, a farewell concert was held.

> One of the Japanese sang a plaintive song on very few notes, in strange rhythm, and to graceful hand and foot movements, the like of which we had never before seen. His sad expression as he sang told us without need of word understanding, of the nostalgia in his Japanese heart for his homeland.

More than 12,000 prisoners died building the railway, about half of them British, a death rate of around 20 per cent. In F Force, 7,000 British and Australian prisoners marched 185 miles to their remote camp high up the line, with a death rate of 44 per cent. The death rate of native labourers (*romushas*) on the railway is unknown, but at least 150,000 died.

CHAPTER TWENTY-NINE

Douglas and Jean's War, 1942–44

Twenty-five-year-old Douglas Capes was a dental technician in North Africa, attached to the 7th Armoured Division, the Desert Rats. For a man with such a humble status, Douglas's contribution to the war was extraordinary, including El Alamein, D-Day and Belsen.

He also oversaw Army stores in their desert camp and Douglas noted that many handmade socks had been donated by a Mrs Clarkson in Northeast England, who he had once met. Douglas wrote a thank-you letter, which Mrs Clarkson showed to her student-teacher granddaughter and a friend. They were impressed by Douglas's politeness. The students drew lots as to who would write to him. Eighteen-year-old Jean Clarkson, studying at St Hilda's College, Durham, won.

In March 1942, Douglas received Jean's first letter out of the blue.

> Dear Douglas,
>
> I'd better begin by telling you who I am. I'm Mrs Clarkson's granddaughter. You will be surprised to hear from me, no doubt... I hope you don't think I am awful, but I do like writing letters... I am 18 and half, have brown hair cut in an Eaton Crop,* blue eyes and am very tall – and lively – any idea of a picture of me? Not very adequate, but never mind. You

---

* The Eaton Crop was a short hairstyle, fashionable from the 1920s.

needn't reply if you don't want to. But I'd be rather pleased if you did.

My best wishes, either way

Douglas replied:

It was jolly decent of you to write . . . I certainly don't think you were (to use your own expression) 'awful' in writing to me, on the contrary, you sound rather nice.

Douglas described the desert wildness to Jean:

It's a rough night, so dark outside the blackness is more like that of a closed and sealed room than just mere darkness. For a while there is dead calm and then for ten minutes or so the wind blows with gale velocity, threatening to tear down the theatre tent. The paraffin lamp is swinging now at such an angle that at the end of its arc it almost touches the canvas roof. Outside four-gallon petrol cans are hurtling through the air like cardboard cartons.

Jean graduated from Durham and taught deaf children in Doncaster. Douglas reassured her about the value of her job.

Our job is to destroy the old world – yours is to build the new. Our job is perhaps the more dramatic but yours is the nobler task.

A combination of military censorship and natural modesty prevented Douglas from telling his new pen pal exactly what he was up to. His lowly status as a Private masked a highly skilled craftsman whose work was devoted to repairing the smashed faces of men in the frontline. Short of materials, he invented a cannula* made from the windscreen-wiper pump of an American aircraft. He created emergency blood transfusion kits out of battlefield

---

* Thin tube inserted into the body for medication or to drain fluids.

debris, and an improvised jaw splint enabled soldiers with facial injuries to feed themselves. His letters to Jean revealed a romantic side to a very practical man.

> I climbed onto a hillock in the middle of the clearing, partly to get a bearing before it was dark, partly to watch the sunset ... the glowing hue, honoured for a moment over the horizon, reluctant to leave, then down! Down! ... as yet the moon was pale and wan, but already she was gaining strength. Soon she would discover her fleecy clouds, diverted by her stronger rival. The loss of their gold and rose would be compensated by a silver radiance, and the pale Queen of the Night would reign, calm, serene, unconscious of the war beneath ...

By later that year, the letters grew more intimate.

> I'm just dog-tired, Jean – but I always feel lighter when I have written to you ... I've read your letters with such a warm glow of loneliness dispelled. I write with the same feeling – you have so much more than filled the need. Dear, my only fear is that you may get tired of writing, or that I might become boring or, Heaven forbid, that some nice fellow might carry you off before I meet you!

Jean:

> I don't think you're silly when you say the things you do because right from the start our friendship seems to have been so right and natural – almost as if it were pre-arranged ... I can't explain it, but sometimes I feel as if I have been put in cold storage to wait until you come home. There – I've said it all at last ...

Douglas:

> The reason for me liking your letters so much, is that you just tell me all sorts of things ... I just love reading them. I love

writing to you too – I don't think at all, my pen just seems to write.

Jean:

> I only wish I could describe things the way you do – you seem to notice everything and then be able to put them into words . . . but I can never find the words to express my feelings.

For a dental technician, Douglas's war was dramatic. When a refugee boat sank (or was sabotaged) off Haifa early in the war, he gave a child trapped in the water the only help he could, a morphine injection, and held her hand until she died.

In the desert he was ambushed and taken prisoner. Fortunately, the enemy were ambushed in turn. Douglas hid under the dead bodies and used a magnetised needle and a thread to find his way back to his unit 50 miles away.

At Tobruk, Douglas worked for four days and three nights without sleep, extricating the injured from the carnage. He injected himself with Benzedrine to keep going and was mentioned in Dispatches for 'gallant and distinguished services'.

Eighteen months after her first letter, Jean was calling him My Dear Douglas. She described her job:

Jean Clarkson

Any form of teaching is tiring, because you are giving to the children all the time, and therefore, with small children who are deaf, it is perhaps tiring at times. However, to have them run to you with open arms whenever they see you is worth anything in the world. To know that these little children love me – and I'm sure they must the way they greet me – gives me a tremendous thrill.

Douglas:

We write without restraint, we discuss anything that comes to mind, probably both of us touch the other on the raw sometimes. How could we help it? But we get along Jean! We ought to have either quarrelled or lost interest long ago, all the odds have been against us! But the mail plane still flies both ways! Don't let's worry about us not having met Jean! Let's just take a chance and swap letters and photographs as fast as we can!

Jean wrote about the hazy figure of another man. Douglas was clearly not her only admirer.

He is a friend, and only a friend. He knows all about you and the loyalty I mean to keep . . . I won't let anyone have the slightest opportunity for getting 'serious' before you've come home, and we've had a chance to talk things over. We may find that it's no use going any further – or we may not – but we will have a clear way to decide when we meet, and I feel I must keep the field clear until we have had our chance. <u>Please Douglas, write straight</u> back when you get this . . .

Douglas:

Jean, darling! You asked me to write straight back to tell you I 'understood'. Oh Darling! I'd give anything in the world to be able to tell you how I really feel but I can't! Anything I could say would read like cheap sentimentality alongside what I feel! Let's not worry about what happens when we meet – we came together by a miracle, a very private miracle, which only we two could even understand. I don't think our miracle will fail us, Jean!

He described a dream to her:

> I was driving an open car . . . and you were alongside! . . . the only sound was the crackle of frost on the tires. We both wore thick coats and scarves, and a heavy rug pulled over our knees. I don't think the seats were separated, we sat very close. I can't remember any words between us, but I looked sideways, and you did too, and then you vanished I had one hand on the steering wheel – I put the other one under the rug and you pulled off my glove. Our hands touched and closed.
>
> Jean Darling . . . God grant us the pure happiness that filled that dream! Goodnight, Dearest!

Jean:

> I can't write down my feelings for you – I could perhaps explain if you were here . . . I have, for a while now, had a curious feeling of trust in you – I somehow feel that I know you are worth waiting for. I cannot answer for how we will feel about each other when we meet – but I have my hopes. Gosh, it is awfully hard for me to say these things in writing! PLEASE, DOUGLAS, UNDERSTAND THAT YOU ARE UNDER NO OBLIGATION – NEITHER AM I.

At the bloody battle of El Alamein, Douglas worked in a field hospital, repairing the faces of injured frontline troops, but one day stepped on an anti-personnel mine. Douglas remained firmly on the mine until his colleagues moved away to safety. Then he was pulled off by rope. But his foot was full of shrapnel, and a lifetime of pain lay ahead.

He was shipped back to Britain for surgery. Douglas rang Jean and they heard each other's voice for the first time, but it was an awkward conversation. Finally, almost two years after Jean's introductory letter, the couple met. Based on her mother's diary, their daughter, Ruth, wrote:

> 14 January 1944
>
> She stood waiting for the train to pull into Doncaster Station feeling sick with fear ... The 5.25 train pulled in and even more men arrived wearing uniforms. She stood on tiptoes, and from the last carriage alighted a tall figure who glanced towards the barrier, and their eyes met. Electric recognition was immediate.
>
> Two bright blue eyes looked through her eyes and into her soul. She glowed all over with love for him.
>
> Her heart nearly exploded as she witnessed the struggle, he was forced to make up the platform, in evident desperation from the crowds and pain from his foot wound. In his hurry to be with Jean, Douglas could not get the train ticket out of his glove and so he just gave the glove to the smiling ticket collector. He charged through the barrier, and Jean and Douglas fell into each other's arms. He gave her a big kiss on the mouth and said, 'Hello, Darling. I knew you'd be more beautiful than your picture.'
>
> The explosion of emotion halted part of Doncaster Station for a little minute as everyone close by shared the moment of evident joy and relief with a chorus of 'Ahhhh!' ... the couple walked off the platform arm in arm, speechless ... but as one.
>
> They went for tea, then a YMCA colleague told her of a bed and breakfast place where he could stay. They arrived hand in hand and the landlady showed them a small single room. She nodded at their clutched hands and said, 'But it's only a single bed.' They both stared at their toes and said nothing. She smiled and left them in their room.

Douglas survived the war. On D-Day he drove a landing craft and helped setting up a Field Hospital at Arromanches. Later, he

Douglas and Jean

was in one of the first medical teams to enter the Concentration Camp at Belsen.

Douglas and Jean were married in 1946, even though her father did not approve of Douglas and cut her out of his will. Jean spent 40 years teaching children around Hexham, Northumberland.

The two-year courtship conducted entirely by letter, a relationship between two strangers, worked. Jean and Douglas were happily married with three daughters until Douglas died in 1989. His last words were, 'Jeannie, I love you, love you, love you – you are my reality, Darling.'

Douglas and Jean with their family

CHAPTER THIRTY

Phyllis, 1943-44

Just as with this pen-pal romance between total strangers, Phyllis Briggs's romantic life was filled with uncertainty. At least she had met her fiancé Tony Cochrane in person, but where was he now? Had he escaped safely from Singapore too? Or had he perished in the sea like so many escapees crammed into boats bombed by the Japanese?

Perhaps Tony gave her something to live for, but dreams of the future could also be corrosive. To survive, Phyllis had to live in the moment in her Sumatran camp, and manage the brutal days one by one.

Finding enough food was a daily struggle.

> Nothing was ever wasted – eggshells were crushed and powdered – if we had fish the bones were boiled then pounded into a rather gritty powder after being dried in the sun. We sprinkled this on our rice, hoping it would provide us with some calcium.
>
> A Jap doctor arranged for some tinned milk for the children, and sick people to be sent to the local hospital ... but soon the kind Jap doctor was prevented from visiting us again, so the rations deteriorated.

In September 1943, the men's camp emptied out. Phyllis and the other female internees took their places.

Amongst the articles that had been left behind was a wooden stool made by Mary Jenkins's husband. He had carved his name on it, and she was delighted to have it.

Our conditions in the new camp were depressing, with hard work, much carrying of water and digging and planting ... there was a communal washroom with water tanks, but there was often no water ... the sight of so many naked women of all ages made one feel one never wanted to see another nude body. The women were either very thin and scraggy or else had swollen rice tummies and legs, and most of them had septic sores and mosquito bites.

We took great care of our clothes as there was no hope of getting anything new. Needles were more precious than diamonds.

Phyllis's friend from Garage 9, Shelagh Brown, wrote in 1943:

> Rats, rats, rats. They eat our clothes, bananas etc., and lay their young in our luggage. There are bugs in our dorm ... bugs, rats, the trots – life is not such fun. When we go to the lav, the mossies bite our bottoms. It is all very ghastly.

A few months later, Phyllis's second Christmas in Japanese captivity was even more dispiriting than Christmas 1942. Another miserable year had passed, a prison sentence without a release date.

> Christmas Day came and went without much enthusiasm; we sang carols at a service and the Dutch children did a nativity play. We had tapioca root, vegetables and a little pork given to us by a Chinese contractor, and this was a real treat because we had had no meat since September. On Boxing Day, we gave a concert.

It didn't seem possible, but in 1944 conditions in Palembang worsened further. Sick women were no longer sent to a local hospital but were treated in the guard room, now converted into a rudimentary ward.

> From March 1944 an increasing number of women became ill. Mary Anderson was one of these; I used to wash her and make her comfortable. She was so desperately thin that no one would have recognised her. I had known her in Penang; she had been a large woman with a booming voice and a keen golfer. Now she was frail and pathetically grateful for anything one did for her. She died * during a Jap holiday and her body had to remain in the camp for two days. In the tropical heat this was dreadful. We moved her body to the centre of the compound under an open shed and had an all-night vigil.

Phyllis noted in her diary:

> We are to be handed over to the military . . . all had to go outside to be checked. I am counted amongst the sick so lay down outside. All the others had to stand in the hot sun, most were collapsing when the Japs had finished checking everyone.

At Easter, Phyllis and her fellow prisoners tried to keep their spirits up.

> We got up a concert in spite of having little energy. The Japs gave us a tin of meat which was shared by the eight of us. I was given as a prize for an item in the concert entitled 'A Musical Market' and I sang 'Cockles and Mussels'.

Rations grew evermore meagre, as Phyllis wrote in her diary:

> Getting very short of water as the well is almost dry. A few people allowed outside the camp to go along the road with a guard in search of edible vegetables. Weed soup! For the first

---

* She died 5 May 1944, aged 46.

time the Japs seem really anxious about the food shortage . . . there are now 594 people in the camp.

Sally Oldham* died – she was a middle-aged missionary – very Lancashire . . . very hot and no rain . . . everyone is getting thinner and weaker.

* 19 June 1944, aged 51.

PART FOUR

I sometimes used to picture what peacetime would be like. No more bombings and sudden death, no more partings from loved ones . . . the winds of time would blow away harsh memories and heal our hearts.

A woman in the Auxiliary Territorial Service (ATS)

CHAPTER THIRTY-ONE

Sicily, 1943

In 1943, while the female internees in Phyllis's camp were surviving on weed soup, for many veterans of North Africa the next challenge was the invasion of Sicily, a first foothold in German-occupied Europe. Relatives at home, who had located distant places like Tobruk and El Alamein on maps, now looked up Catania or Messina to find where their loved ones might be.

A previous Allied attempt in 1942 to gain a toehold in Europe – a landing at the French port of Dieppe – had been disastrous.

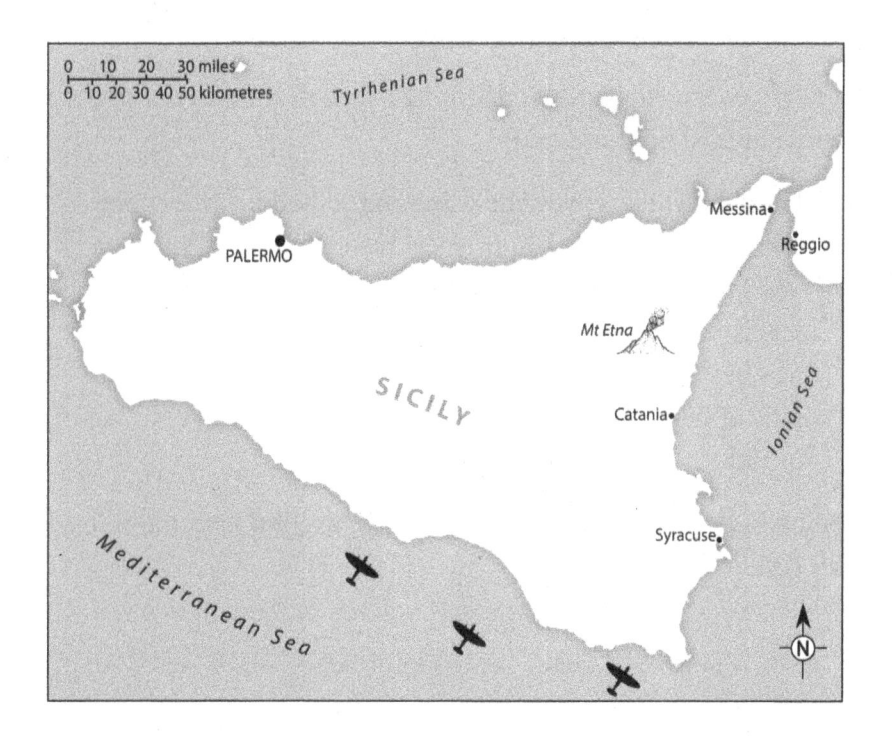

The Allies were forced to retreat ignominiously, and 3,623 men, over half the raiding force, were killed, wounded or captured.* A second defeat in Sicily would throw serious doubts on the ability of the Allies to ever retake Europe from the Nazis.

The Sicily invasion was preceded by Operation Mincemeat, the most famous deception of the Second World War. An elaborate plan involving a floating corpse, and fake documents, helped fool Hitler into believing that Greece and Sardinia were more likely Allied invasion points than Sicily. He therefore moved additional weapons and troops into Sardinia and Greece.

On 10 July 1943, a huge convoy left Egypt for Sicily. Bill Cheall, 6th Green Howards, was among the 150,000 troops landing by sea and air.

> Never before had anyone seen so many ships at one time, over 3,000 craft of all sizes . . . during the early hours, about 4.30 a.m., we climbed down the scrambling nets and into our assault craft, which were bobbing about like corks.

The 6th Green Howards landed at Jig Beach near Avola unopposed and marched up the island.

> I could vividly remember searching a shed for the enemy and what did I find? – four naked men lying on tables, their bodies starting to decompose. They were being eaten by maggots and the bodies also showed evidence of torture. It was beyond my comprehension how anybody could do this kind of thing to another human being – I hope they perished in Hell.

Not all Sicily landings were unopposed, as John Hammond told his son.

---

* Most of them were Canadians, 68 per cent of them were killed, wounded or captured.

As they reached the shore, the soldier next to my father was killed. Despite the heavy fire, my father bent over the dead soldier, undid his tunic, and took his pack of Woodbines [cigarettes].

My father felt guilty about this until his dying day. He wept when he told me the story.

Waves of airborne troops also flew in from Egypt. Tom Davies from Neath, 1st Battalion Parachute Regiment, had already fought in North Africa.

As our aircraft approached the Sicilian coast, we ran into very heavy 'flak' from the shore batteries. The plane bucked and rocked drunkenly, red-hot sparks shooting past the portholes of the Dakota. Then, with a terrific lurch, we plunged recklessly seaward. Every rivet of the machine screamed in protest at the heavy load... we were all thrown on top of each other into an untidy heap on the floor at the front of the aircraft. Panic set in as we tried to untangle ourselves in order to make for the door... the engine noise now rose to a crescendo as we caught a quick flash, by the light of the pale moon, of the mountainous waves of the angry seas below. Then, by some Herculean effort, and the grace of God, the pilot had the plane righted again and flying on an even keel.

Sergeant Jock Walker, a veteran of Dunkirk and North Africa, had moved on from driving his repair truck through the desert and retrained as a paratrooper. Jock had been nervous waiting for his first drop as a Trainee.

A friendly boot in the back saw me on my way. Falling made me frightened but not for long, as a crack was heard above and the parachute opened and I assumed a parachuting position, as taught, and looked round in wonder. To say I felt ten feet tall and the cleverest bloke in the army would be an understatement...

Training complete, Jock headed for Sicily.

> About a hundred aircraft plus a score or so of gliders, with airborne artillery . . . after a while we got close to the Sicilian coast where our troops were still being disembarked, when suddenly the shit hit the fan – we were being fired on by the Navy!
>
> Our Dakota got hit, which put the wind up me, vertical. The dispatcher, a Yank (it was an American crew flying us) came back and said, 'Holy Cow, the Limeys are shooting at us; get hooked up quick and ready to go.'
>
> The aircraft had been crippled and we got the order to bail out. It was pitch dark, the terrain was unknown, we didn't know our height, and, of course, we could have been jumping into a German garrison for all we knew. However, out we went, my position in the stick was fifth and, after the chute opened, adopted an 'about to hit a tree position', and, after what seemed hours, a very frightened parachutist was deposited in a cornfield.
>
> I couldn't believe my luck, truly a parachutist should be a fatalist because if your number is on it, you'll get it. If it isn't, you'll survive. Terrified, I lay still for a moment or two, then my training asserted itself; hit the buckle, get out of the harness quick and see what is around, cautiously. Nothing but corn . . . so I stayed there until first light so that the view would be much better; not that I knew where I was. I didn't even know if this particular terra was Sicily.
>
> I crawled on my hands and knees to a stand of trees on the edge of the field . . . I saw a farmhouse some distance away and decided to take a chance and go to it, as all the area was deserted.

Jock Walker and other paratroopers had missed their drop zones by miles. Now on his own, Jock approached the farmhouse cautiously.

A civilian appeared at the door with his hands up shaking with fright . . . he thought I was a German, coming back to shoot them all, so with the good news under my belt, we shared my rations and his vino, and I waited for the Allied troops to show their faces, which they did later in the afternoon.

Then I was told about the shambles the operation had become, due to the Navy not receiving information about us, and, on our part, not sending a recognition signal. As I understood it, only about a third of our force got to Sicily, the rest went back to Africa with damaged aircraft, or were at the bottom of the Med.

Once more the Gods had smiled on me, or as I later put it – the Devil looks after his own!

Twenty-year-old Liverpudlian W. J. Collings's glider was released too early and crashed into the sea.

As we hit the water I was forced through the top of the glider and as I reached back inside, I caught hold of Pte Arkwright and pulled him onto the wing . . . during the night searchlights from the shore were scanning the sea for gliders. When one was found the others joined in and we could hear machine guns open fire on the unfortunate lads in the water. We were lucky to be too far away for the searchlights to spot us.

I lay on the wing of the glider and held on as best I could as I had no lifebelt, nor could I swim.

At first light a Navy gunboat spotted the men clinging to the smashed glider.

We shouted that one of our lads was in a bad way. Without hesitation a very large rating dived in to rescue him. He seemed to go through the water like a torpedo. By 8 a.m. we were all on the gunboat after ten long hours in the sea.

Bill Williams, Tank Commander, 50th Tank Regiment, progressed smoothly into Sicily at first, but then his Troop was attacked.

> All three tanks of my Troop were hit, and mine started to burn. I knew I had to get out quickly and let out the gunner and the loader, as my seat was in the turret exit ... the Germans started machine-gunning, and the bullets started rattling around the tanks ... then I found my gunner on the ground in a bad state with severe leg wounds and his clothes smouldering. He was calling my name over and over, and without thinking I started to pull away his burning clothes ... To attend to him I had to kneel, and Jerry thought fit to open fire again, and I was hit in the left shoulder and through the body. I only felt the exit wound, like the thump of a hammer – a sledgehammer.
>
> I thought I'd been shot through the lungs and lay for a few seconds expecting blood, when my Troop Officer came along and said he would take over tending to my gunner. I started crawling along with one arm to a bomb crater, where another of my crew was lying. Suddenly the tank blew up, one or two bits scraped along my arm ... But when I looked around my Officer lay flat out and motionless, I presumed dead. I remember thinking that should have been me. I seemed to have a charmed life.

Bill was now a prisoner-of-war.

> We were the only two survivors of the whole Troop. I thought I was fortunate to be taken prisoner by ordinary troops, who in general were quite friendly and no better or worse than the British. [But] soon an SS officer appeared ... and threatened to shoot us if we did not answer his questions. He was waving his automatic about and at the time the barrel looked as big as a cannon.

Harry Hargreaves was serving on the destroyer HMS *Wallace* off the Sicilian coast at night. The ship's wake glowed with phosphorescence in the moonlight, offering a clear target for the enemy.

> The explosions were much nearer and the deadly whistle of shrapnel, accompanied by the dull thud as some of it made its mark on the ship's side . . . it was obvious we were the target for the night, and they would not stop until we had suffered a fatal hit.

As a diversion, the First Lieutenant launched a raft with a smoke float on either end.

> The billowing clouds of smoke interspersed with small bursts of flame gave a convincing imitation of flaming debris . . . the next few minutes were the most tension-racked minutes I think I ever went through.

The ruse worked. The enemy bombed the smoke-filled raft instead of the limping ship.

> Sometimes I look back on this incident and in view of everything that came after I wonder what would have happened to the Royal House of Windsor if Philip had not thought of this ruse and carried it out so successfully.

Philip, then aged 21, later became the Duke of Edinburgh. No doubt his ruse saved lives.

If the Allies were to drive north, controlling the Catania Plain was essential, but the 6th Green Howards were stopped by a brutal battle at Primosole Bridge over the Simeto River. Bill Cheall:

> The encounter with Jerry had been very fierce, bodies were scattered all over the river and on the ground, corpses, parachutes and weapons lay around everywhere.
>
> Once again, we were on foot and walking through the villages which had recently been occupied by the enemy; we

were welcomed by the inhabitants. We walked along this street making sure that no enemy had been left behind to harass us, when I saw a small boy on the street, and he stepped on a mine. He was blown into the air and killed.

After 38 days bitter fighting, the Nazis were driven out of Sicily. About 23,000 Allies had been killed, wounded or were missing. Axis forces had lost more than seven times that number.

The Allies' next challenge was mainland Italy, but an occupying force was still needed in Sicily. Arthur Allvey wrote to his wife, Gladys, in South London.

> We sleep beneath lemon trees arranged neatly in rows like the orchards in Kent; all around us are hills upon the slopes of which are vineyards and many kinds of fruit and vegetables such as figs, dates, pomegranates, tangerines ... the sun is sinking behind the highest hill and very soon it will be dark ... Gracie Fields was here and gave a show but I missed it ... yesterday we had a big parade before General Montgomery, and he issued medals.

Navy Marine Dennis Freeman:

> Through the open windows of a white, square building in Messina, the music of the dance band escaped brazenly into the sunlit evening air. Inside, British sailors and marines danced with Sicilian girls. The girls wore white dresses and had coloured ribbons in their hair. In chairs along the walls sat the mothers of the girls, dressed in black.

Sicilian men were excluded from the dance, but when freshly released Italian prisoners-of-war stormed the door, fighting followed.

> Suddenly the short sharp crack of a pistol rang out. The fighting stopped. All eyes watched a British sailor who had

slumped to his knees. Blood ran from his mouth and formed big red clots on his white tunic.

At the sailor's funeral the sky was blue and cloudless. The padre wore a hip-length surplice. At times a breeze lifted dust in small clouds from the sandy soil, and the surplice billowed and fluttered like a sail. The padre bowed his bald head and placed his hands together. He prayed . . . when he finished his prayer an uneven murmuring of 'Amen' rippled through the ranks.

The Sicily invasion gave the Allies a foothold in Europe for the first time since Dunkirk, but taking mainland Italy would be more challenging. Churchill called Italy 'the soft underbelly' of the Axis, but conquering a well-fortified country where defensive troops enjoyed the advantage of a mountainous terrain would never be easy, even after Italy's fascist dictator, Benito Mussolini, was deposed in July 1943.

CHAPTER THIRTY-TWO

Monte Cassino, 1944

Two months after Mussolini was deposed, the Allies invaded mainland Italy. Montgomery's 8th Army landed at Reggio di Calabria unopposed, but the landing at Salerno, Southern Italy, led by American Mark Clark was a disaster. Clark tried to surprise the enemy by not launching an advanced naval bombardment, but the Germans were on alert and almost retook the landing beach.

When 19-year-old Private Victor (Donald) Delves, 2nd Battalion Hampshire Regiment, landed at Salerno the Germans were ready.

> The enemy opened up and the sand was torn up around us as the beach was raked by enemy machine-gun fire, the landing craft in the second wave were being machine-gunned as soon as their ramps were open, some were burning. Our LST* was blown up by a mine, the explosion blew a hole in the side of the ship which listed badly . . . we secured some of our objectives, but we suffered many casualties, dead, dying, and injured . . . I had some real good friends, we were only young boys.

Donald Delves was pinned down for seven days but, eventually, bombardments from ships in Salerno Bay helped the Allies win through, though only just. Among the soldiers preparing to

---

* Landing Ship, Tank.

invade on 9 September was 1st Lt Harmon Buckley from Holdenville, Oklahoma, serving with the 45th Division. Harmon wrote to his newborn son:

> I am the happiest daddy in all the world to have such a precious baby boy as you, and such a darling wife as your mother . . . your mother and I are very proud of you, and we love you so much . . . Take good care of Mommy for me and tell her not to worry about Daddy because he will be careful, just for you and Mommy.

A month later Major Everett Duell wrote to Harmon's wife, Anita.

> There is nothing I can say or do that will make the loss of Harmon any easier for you to bear and I'll not even attempt to do that . . . I am from Holdenville and have known Harmon for some years. I was deeply attached to him and being over twice his age looked on him much as a father would on his son. His death affects me considerably and I have been completely broken up over it since. He was one of the finest young men I have known.
>
> I want you to know that he never suffered one moment from his wound; he died instantly from a machine-gun bullet that pierced his heart. I was terribly shocked and instantly went to pieces. I remained with Harmon at the Medical Aid Station until we could get transportation for his body.
>
> I hope this letter hasn't made things harder for you. I hardly knew what to write but, you see, I too loved Harmon and felt you would like to have me write this letter with this information. I hope his son grows up to be as fine a man as his father.

Harmon was one of over 10,000 men killed or wounded at Salerno.

From their landing points in the south, Allied troops pushed painfully up through 'the soft underbelly' of Italy. They encountered fierce opposition across mountainous terrain until their slow progress was firmly blocked by the well-fortified Gustav Line stretching across Italy, 87 miles south of Rome.

The Line's hinge was the town of Cassino, dominated by an ancient Benedictine monastery over 500 metres above the valley through which the key route to Rome ran. Built on solid rock and protected by rivers, and with higher ground beyond, the monastery offered Germany the perfect defensive position. For bloodiness, the Battle of Monte Cassino could only be rivalled by Stalingrad. It started on 17 January 1944 and lasted five brutal months.

George Daily served with the Black Watch.

> The Germans had control of the monastery and had a clear field of fire all round. They could see every move by the Allied armies... the battle fought there was one of the hardest, cruellest battles of a hard, cruel war.

Military historian Richard Holmes:

> It was one of the strongest natural defensive positions in military history, with the monastery, like some great all-seeing eye, peering down on everything.

The monks and 70,000 precious manuscripts had been evacuated from the monastery and the Nazis had agreed with the Pope not to use the holy site for gun emplacements. But they had fortified monastery hill, and nearby caves stored ammunition. Whether they were in the monastery itself or close by, the Germans were killing Allied soldiers from their towering vantage point. They needed to be driven out, and on 15 February 1944 the monastery was bombed by the Allies to rubble.

Freed from promises to the Vatican, German troops moved into the monastery ruins, which gave them an improved stronghold. The Allies might have air supremacy and greater numbers, but the Italian mountains and terrible weather were on the Nazis side. Allied soldiers up the mountain had to be supplied at night by mules.

Jim Hughes, Royal Inniskilling Fusiliers, escorted the supply mules.

> This was a place I imagine Hell must be like... we would start off from the Mule Point as it got dark and make our way over the land, hoping that the Royal Engineers had cleared the mines and laid white tapes, and that Jerry didn't catch us with an Artillery 'Stonk'. We had to go over a small bridge over a river. This stretch was called the 'Mad Mile' because

> the enemy knew we had to cross it. From there we started to climb up. The smell of dead men and mules was terrible.

Donald Delves, Hampshire Regiment, had already survived Salerno.

> Suddenly, a shell burst quite near and injured some of us ... I heard someone shouting, and crying quite loudly, I looked round and saw one of the mules with its intestines coming out of his stomach ... I will never forget the mule handler calling out the mule's name and, as it got weaker and could struggle no more, the poor soldier had both his arms round the mule's neck, and kept shouting its name as the tears rolled down his cheeks ... after about three minutes, I heard a rifle shot. The poor mule had been put out of its misery.

Having escaped from Normandy two weeks after Dunkirk, fought in the North African desert, and retreated through the Burmese jungle, Jim Palmer*, 3rd Tank Regiment, was now in the fierce battle for Cassino.

> The mountain trails were littered with dead donkeys, blown to kingdom come by the bombing and shelling ... everywhere was confusion and fear. Men were screaming and dying and being killed by their own fire. Everything was a cauldron of fire-thumps, crashes, crunches, smoke, cordite, dust and moans; there was nowhere you could avoid the mayhem.
>
> Thousands of tons of bombs were dropped, and Cassino became a mass of rubble ... fierce street fighting was taking place, with enemy snipers behind every crumpled wall and in every bomb crater ... the rains came and soon the area of Cassino was a muddy bloodbath. Tanks were stuck, guns could not get up the mountain trails – infantry were fighting

---

* Between the Desert War and Italy, Jim served in Iraq, Palestine and Syria (October 1942–September 1943)

individual battles, face to face with fanatical German youths. The Gurkhas were using their knives, and the Poles were pushing on through the mountain.

Ron Goldstein, from a large Jewish family in Bethnal Green, had fought in the North African desert. Now he was dug in at Monte Cassino in appalling winter conditions reminiscent of the trenches of the First World War.

> Our camp was just below the ridge of a small hill that faced the Monastery . . . it was very menacing right from the word go, and it was fairly obvious that every move that was made below could be seen, plotted, and shelled with relative impunity.
>
> We dug in, literally, each man responsible for his own 6ft x 3ft x 3ft of Italian mud and perched on top of each trench we put up our bivvies (bivouacs) in a vain attempt to keep the rain out. Some of us tried to give our trenches a bit of individuality by making the top of the trench slightly wider, thus making a ledge on which we could stand a lamp or our personal belongings . . . the weather was atrocious, mud was the name of the game.
>
> It was nothing to have wet clothes on for three days at a time . . . it was not unusual to dig a slit trench to sleep in and to wake up and find yourself floating in a foot of water. But it was the cold that we all hated the most . . . it was a vicious, life-sickening cycle that sapped our energy and turned us into morons.

Fred Beacham, Devon Regiment:

> I saw two Fusiliers lying out in the open. I went to them and recoiled in sheer horror. One was dead, lying face down, and he was still clutching his rifle . . . a burst of machine-gun fire had hit him on the side of the head. The side of his brain had slipped out onto the grass. A swarm of flies arose from the body. I turned my attention to the other long-serving soldier.

I could see he had severe wounds to his legs, one of which was practically hanging off. He had lost a tremendous amount of blood and looked up at me and whispered, 'Give me a drink, mate.'

I knelt and cradled his head in my arms as gently as I could. He made no sound and looked at me as I placed the water bottle to his lips to moisten them. He took the smallest of sips and said, 'Thanks a lot, mate,' and died.

Sergeant Brian May was shot in the hip and became a prisoner-of-war.

I was transported away from the front on a horse-drawn cart, with another horse tethered behind the cart. My head rested on hay at the back. The horse there fancied the hay and chomped at it busily. Each mouthful flicked my right ear, and I was unable to move. I have since composed the official demise of Sgt B May to grieving parents: 'Eaten on Active Service.' Fortunately, the horse preferred hay to my head.

An anonymous contributor told The People's War:

The enemy used the dreadful six-barrelled mortar. The noise of it being fired sounded like the screaming of all the tortured souls in hell. Wrecked tanks, ambulances and transports of kinds lay at all angles, the ground on both sides of the road being a huge area of murdered earth. During the hours of darkness, smoke shells were fired into the town, to cover any movement. The men scrambled over heaps of rubble, house timbers, and shell and bomb craters. The smoke gave them a ghostly appearance as the leading figures in their file disappeared into it . . . dawn revealed the precarious position they had to hold. For five days and nights they sat there enduring all the enemy could sling at them. To each of them every minute seemed like an hour, every hour seemed like a day, and every day seemed like a week.

To add to the drama, Mt Vesuvius erupted. Eric Griffin was a medic, handling casualties from Cassino.

> After much rumbling under foot and the skies filling with ash, torrents of lava burst forth and for the next few days troops massing for the 3rd Battle of Monte Cassino had a front seat for one of the world's greatest events. The stream of molten lava, visible for miles lightened the night sky.
>
> The heat was blistering and every so often large burning pieces of red molten rock would fall ever closer... looking down the main street of San Sebastiano was a large, red, glowing coke fire that towered over the building with the defused, bright light of the distant moving lava stream coming out of the volcano.

Dealing with the wounded in mountainous terrain was challenging for the medics. Bill Quirk:

> We had a stretcher chain reaching over three mountains with about 1,000 men... they were spread out four to a stretcher with varying distances between each, team according to the difficulty of the terrain. Each group brought a loaded stretcher, anything from 50 to 400 yards each, and handed it over to the next group and took an empty one back with them... the chain worked well into the darkness in pouring rain and even snow and ice on the higher reaches.

George Groom had met a girl working at Woolworth's in Birmingham. When she heard nothing for months, she presumed George was dead.

> I received a letter from a hospital close to Monte Cassino. It said he had been wounded trying to capture the mountains from the Germans... after some time he was found and tied to a mule. All the wounded were taken down the mountain this way. The mules struggled down the mountain, down

a narrow track. Many of the men fell to their deaths as the mules tumbled off the mountain when they lost their footing. George was in hospital for six months. He came home in 1946, when we got married.

Soldiers from many nations fought bravely to take Monastery Hill – British and American, French and Indian, Canadian and New Zealand. One company of Punjabis entered the line with 180 men and left with just 37. Finally, the sheer weight of Allied numbers told with Allied forces, now nearly twice as big as the first attempt, allowed them to take Cassino in January. Despite heavy bombardment, the 2nd Polish Corps took Monte Cassino in May. John Cory, 8th Survey Regiment, Royal Artillery:

> They went in to finish the job, together with their General who had torn off his badges of rank and grabbed a gun. They took the surrounding area giving no quarter, no prisoners taken. Then it was the turn of the Monastery itself. Working along the ridge they stormed the ruins. The remaining Germans left alive were mostly wounded and the Commander and 30 survivors surrendered. They were spared.

Although later Allied leadership was criticised for choosing to pierce the German defences at their strongest point, the Gustav Line was now broken and route 6 to Central Italy lay ahead, The Polish flag was hoisted over the Monastery at 10.20 a.m. on 18 May. Nearly 1,000 Poles had died.

Karol Jastrzebski led a Polish medical team at Monte Cassino. Karol's son:

> Early morning the fire died down a bit to allow his medical team to pick up the casualties. There were hundreds of them. My father had tears in his eyes remembering badly injured soldiers, some with limbs blown off, being overjoyed by the victory. They were dying not being able to see their loved ones, yet the victory was sweeter than death.

Jim Palmer was relieved when the brutal battle ended.

> A dreadful silence descended. The crackle of machine guns ceased; the shells stopped falling and the smoke swirled away. Men lay hidden in holes in the rocks, their faces blackened, and eyes glazed, staring and twitching. We climbed from our tanks and slumped to the ground, red-eyed and dazed. Men were sick and moaning; some were crying, some were sobbing; some were just cowering behind heaps of bricks, staring and motionless. Mules stopped braying and lay down as if dead, and the wounded men began to crawl towards the first-aid posts and stretcher-bearers.

John Cory, a veteran of North Africa, was in the village.

> On Cassino liberation day, the villagers declared a fiesta, at midday there was another religious procession, the blessing of houses . . . the villagers somehow found some wine, and, in the evening, we joined them.

Romuald Lipinski, 2nd Polish Corps, surveyed the aftermath of months of brutal fighting.

> The area was a living testimony to what war was all about. There was not one tree that had its branches green with leaves. There were only naked limbs, stumps sticking out here and there. Grass has disappeared also. There was the testimony of what was there in the past – dead bodies. Some were half-decomposed, some were half-covered with dust or whatever dirt could be scraped from the surface, in most cases they were covered with lime. They were the reminders of the ferocious fighting that was going on there for four months . . . the entire history of the battle could be read from these corpses. There were the corpses of the Americans, Germans, Ghurkhas, British soldiers, some with their face half-eaten by insects, mice, or other animals, darkened by time, empty

eyes, with only teeth shining. They were all quiet now, resting in their eternal sleep, after the dance of death a few months ago. I looked at these dead men, who at one time were young, vigorous, full of life and hopes for the future. And look at them now.

And flies. They were big, fat, gorging themselves on the decomposing bodies. Stink of death was everywhere. Down below was a beautiful valley of red poppies. I thought, how can these two worlds coexist side by side? But that was how it was.

CHAPTER THIRTY-THREE

Home, 1944

In 1944, a month after the final victory at Monte Cassino, London's citizens endured a further unwelcome threat when Germany fired its first V1 rocket at the British capital. V1s (and later V2) rockets were dubbed 'Doodlebugs' or 'Buzzbombs' because of the frightening sound they made in flight. The V1 was a primitive ancestor of the cruise missile with an 1,800-pound warhead and a top speed of up to 400 mph. On reaching its predetermined flight time, a V1 engine would stop, and the rocket crash. To the Londoners below, this suddenness and the disturbing noise were a terrifying combination. The Nazis called them 'wonder' or 'revenge' weapons and hoped that they might shift the balance of the war back in Germany's favour. An 18-year-old anonymous contributor witnessed the first V1 on London on 13 June 1944, a week after D-Day.

> The air raid sirens sounded in Woolwich just before the first light of dawn flecked the eastern horizon ... the darkness of night not really dark at all ... we saw searchlight beams crossing under the low cloudy sky ... the strange-sounding plane was over Blackheath, and less than two miles away from us, flying low with its tail ablaze and leaving a short trail of brilliant flame ... it was over the Greenwich Observatory and hurtling headlong towards St Paul's Cathedral ... the reverberating throb was to haunt us for the rest of our lives.

Three nights later the same 18-year-old was on fire duty at Woolwich Barracks when Hitler launched a fusillade of over 200 V1s from launch sites on the Pas de Calais.

> Yet another Buzzbomb headed directly towards us, out of sight above the scudding clouds. Almost directly overhead the engine stopped . . . we stood rooted to the ground watching the missile spearing out of the clouds and diving diagonally towards the earth, straight towards the frontage of the Royal Artillery Barracks overlooking the vast parade ground . . . the mental image of the sight still haunts me, many of my pals would be lined up for breakfast in the mess hall the missile was about to blow to smithereens. Seconds later the flying bomb was lost to our sight behind the barrack frontage, then the flash of the explosion and the sighting of ornamental masonry shooting skywards, then the boom of the explosion split the silence of the early morning.

Victor Spink, aged six:

> If the deafening pulse engine cut out there was a heart-stopping 7-to-12-second silence followed by a huge bang as it exploded . . . we heard the racket of a V1 coming from the direction of Mitcham . . . it just passed over our heads when Mother came running down the pavement like mums do on a school sports day parents' race. She had her skirt lifted up showing her knees and thighs, which I had not seen before. She swept us under the Morrison shelter as the bomb stopped. Her head was under the table, but her rear poked out as there was not enough room for her because our Alsatian dog had got under first.

Pat and Bill Baughan's experience in Cricklewood, London, was recounted by their daughter:

> In the kitchen they heard the unmistakeable drone of a V1 doodlebug and held their breath hoping it would pass by.

HOME, 1944

> Suddenly the engine cut out ... afterwards they recalled the whistling sound getting louder and louder ... there was a tremendous explosion, and the window blew in.

Amidst the wreckage, thoughts turned to Aunt Doll, ill upstairs in bed.

> Doll appeared from the bedroom looking very pale-faced and saying, 'I think they got me', and then started to hobble slowly down the hall ... [they] were relieved to find no blood. 'I can't walk properly,' said Doll, and sat down heavily ... in her panic to get up, Doll had put both legs down one side of her knickers and could barely move. The laughter which followed soon turned to tears when they found out that two neighbours had been killed by the rocket.*

Later, long-range V2 rockets were added to Hitler's armoury. Teenager Edward Siggins was part of a large family in Stratford, London, whose house was hit.

> I could not move ... as soon as I opened my mouth it filled with dust and grit, and I started coughing ... it had been silent until now but then I started to hear people crying and it could have only been [my younger brothers] Les and Peter lying against my legs. They were struggling and crying, and I began to realise we were trapped underneath rubble ... I told them not to cry as someone would come and get us out.
>
> It must have been in an air pocket, and I could breathe, but tasted dust as I opened my mouth ... I continued to talk to them and after a while I could feel their struggles getting weaker and then cease altogether. I continued to talk to them, but they were silent. I remember thinking perhaps they were dead and, if so, it would be my turn next ... I heard muffled

---

* Figures vary with sources, but more than 10,000 V1s were launched against Britain, killing over 5,400 people.

voices coming from above, and pressure on me as if someone was walking over me, so I started calling out again. Then I heard a voice say 'here's one', a couple of minutes silence, then 'he's gone', then 'here's another' then 'he's gone'.

I then felt the bricks and rubble being pulled away from my head and saw the dark night and how bright the stars were. As I took in great gulps of cold, sweet, fresh air I was lifted out and onto a stretcher ... what had been my home was now a big pile of grey dusty rubble. There were people in dark boilersuit clothing and tin hats, kneeling and moving about the debris. There were searchlights and spotlights and other handheld lamps.

Thirty people died that night, including six of Edward's close family.

James (father) aged 40; Les, 11; Peter, 7; Betty, 3; James,1; Stanley, 7 weeks; plus two cousins, Ivy, 20, and Doreen, 9.

I was taken to see Mum in another hospital. When I saw her, I burst into tears, I was so relieved to see her ... there was no counselling in those days. You just had to get on with it.*

Hitler's 'wonder weapons' were frightening but they also distracted the Germans from the efficient waging of war. The Nazis were so entranced by symbolism and propaganda that they wasted precious resources developing new, often larger weapons when more of their good existing tanks or aircraft would probably have been more effective.

Children evacuated into the countryside were unlikely to encounter doodlebugs, but they had to manage living away from their parents. Many were happy as the war progressed, but sisters Audrey and Edna Jones in Bletchington, Oxfordshire, were not

---

* Attempts were made to shoot down flying bombs, and eventually their launch sites were captured when Allied forces controlled Northern France.

in that category. They were now on their third host family in the village. Audrey's regular bed-wetting had been an issue in her first two billets, and the two young girls still desperately missed home in London.

> The six years of evacuation were ones of waiting and longing. I'm sure I gained many things from my years at Bletchington, but the overall feeling is one of loss.

One of the 'gains' for Audrey was encountering adults from overseas.

> We awoke one morning to the sight of hundreds of men camped in the field. They were Canadian soldiers on manoeuvres. We went among them to explore, and it was great for us because they gave us chocolate and tinned fruit. I was sorry when they left as we often stole bread because we were hungry.
>
> Summertime was fun because we helped the prisoners-of-war in making the haystacks. The prisoners all had circle patches on their clothing. These patches were the 'shoot spots' in case they tried to escape. The Italians were given more leeway, but the German prisoners always had a guard nearby with a gun. They were very nice to Edna and me and were among the few men we had any contact with.

One highlight was a visit from their father. The two girls excitedly headed to the local station.

> We saw this man walking towards us – we had dawdled and were late or the train was early – it was DADDY. I don't know how long it had been since we had last seen him, but I felt shy and hung onto Edna's hand. She said, 'Let's just walk past him and say "Good morning, Mr Jones."' He replied, 'Do I know you two young ladies?' and we both cried, 'Daddy, Daddy, it's us', as if he didn't know. I was walking absolutely ten feet tall, as was Edna.

Such moments of pleasure were rare for Audrey.

> We were always getting thrashed and 'told off' and, although never rude, I had a habit of giving a LOOK which I expect was insolent.
>
> When I was approximately nine years old, I told Edna I was going to run away. As there was nowhere to run to, we found a big bush for me to hide behind ... when it started to get dark, I came out of my hiding place and let them find me, thinking that Mrs Harris would be so upset and yet pleased to see me. Ha ha, that was all wrong.
>
> She beat the calves on the back of my legs so hard with a copper stick that Edna had to help me walk to school on the Monday.

Fifteen-year-old Tad Podhorodenski escaped from Poland, and caught a boat from St Jean de Luz, Southwest France, to England.

> We went to Scotland and stayed with a lovely, kindly family. They took us to church ... the minister started the sermon ... he was addressing us in phonetic Polish, welcoming us to Scotland and expressing his sorrow and sympathy with our predicament. We were very touched by the man's compassion.*

In Dorset, Gavin Kirkpatrick's father taught German and French, and employed German POWs in the garden. The family grew fond of a German called Heinz.

> There were those my father liked, like Heinz, and those he didn't care for, particularly the ardent Nazis ... Heinz was different from the other German POWs ... it was evident my parents regarded him with much affection ... in some ways he seemed to become almost an extra member of our family.

---

* Tad moved to the Isle of Bute and went to Rothesay Academy and Glasgow University.

> During the Christmas of 1944, Heinz and another prisoner spent whole days of the holiday with the family. They were given presents from around the tree. They joined in the carol singing... the war was forgotten.
>
> My last memories recall Heinz playing the piano at a concert for the local children... a few days later he was gone. Sixty years later, I often wonder what became of Heinz.

The small village of Hesketh Bank near Preston, Lancashire, kept its citizens informed via the parish newsletter.

> Already a good deal of the harvest is safely gathered in and, so far, the rain has not harmed it. We may well look forward to an excellent ingathering, for which we thank God.
>
> Stan Johnson writes from North Africa that the scenery here takes a lot of beating but that, in spite of its beauty, he still prefers the view out of his bedroom window in Hesketh Bank.
>
> Joan Binns of the WRNS tells us her unit has recently been inspected by the Duchess of Kent who is WRNS Commander-in-Chief. She was very charming, has a most fascinating voice.
>
> Ronald Whiteside says he has not seen rain since May (unlike us!) so we can guess what colour he will be when he gets home. He has heard George Formby and also a very fine Egyptian Military band.
>
> We deeply regret to inform you that Harold Wignall (The Green) has been killed in action in Italy.

All over Britain communities steeled themselves for tragedy and dislocation, none more so than West Tofts near Thetford, Norfolk. In 1942, 1,000 people were compulsorily evacuated from 17,500 acres of land to make way for an army training area. Vera Tolman, headteacher at the school in West Tofts, was appalled, as journalist Conal O'Donnell reported:

The war had taken our husbands, and now our homes and way of life was to go.

Local landowner Lord Walsingham noted:

> They had about a month to get out. No arrangements were made, no nothing. It was a tremendous upheaval.

Lord Walsingham himself was also forced to move.

> Lord Walsingham was no exception to the general discomfort... the family seat, Merton Hall, had already been requisitioned and he had to live in a Boulton and Paul prefab.

Headteacher Vera Tolman recalled her last day:

> I locked the school door and gave a last glance across the park. There stood a great antlered deer. He just gave me one stare from his gentle brown eyes, then we turned our backs on each other, and I left West Tofts for ever.

The average compensation was £12. The thousand evacuees were promised their homes back at war's end. It never happened.*

Young women grew used to loss, intertwined with excitement. Scottish WAAF Sheilah Cruickshank from RAF Waddington, Lincolnshire, was co-organiser of a first birthday party for the Royal Australian Air Force 463 Squadron.

> The Group Captain was so delighted with everything that he promised I would be taken home by Lancaster bomber on my next leave ... it was strictly a court-martial offence for a WAAF to fly ... [but] it was exciting to don a parachute over my battledress, have it fastened on my back and between the legs and clamber up into the dark, hard, strong-smelling interior of the Lancaster ... [there was] an exciting void in my

---

* The Stanford Training Area, as it is now called, is still sealed off and used for military training for recent conflicts, including Afghanistan and Ukraine.

stomach, as we left the earth and soared into the air. It was a beautiful sunny, cloudless May day ... after two short hours we landed at Prestwick, near Glasgow.

The last I saw of the Lancaster bomber, as it taxied away from me, was the smiling face of the Group Captain, as he waved goodbye from the cockpit. Sadly, I never saw him again. He was killed shortly after.*

Audrey Turner (later St John-Brown) was a Women's Auxiliary Air Force (WAAF) driver in Lincolnshire and Yorkshire.

I drove coke-fuel lorries, ration lorries, ambulances, crew buses, tractors with bomb loads, vans, cars and motorbikes.

I had no real interest in close relationships, the world seemed such a fragile place, so many people were dead or still to die ... driving crews to their planes and never seeing them again was an all too familiar pattern. I grieved for them, we drank to them, and accepted this was going to recur time and again.

Life was an ever-changing black-and-white film, it was intense, sometimes funny, extremely busy ... our nights were tense and utterly draining ... when the planes returned, I always had a flask-coffee, tea and seven cups – I'd drive them to debriefing and saw which planes had not returned.

I met one South African ... he did propose, and I did say yes, but I had no intention of marrying anyone until this was over. It ended when he was killed, of course.†

Chris Saunders did not agree with killing, but like many conscientious objectors still faced danger.

---

* 463 sustained the highest loss rate of any Australian squadron: 563 crew in 17 months.

† Soon after, Audrey met F/O Vic Brown, and eventually married him.

> I was a conscientious objector (no religion or faith), simple humanitarianism, my conscience directed me against killing – thrusting a bayonet into some man's belly just because he was born in a different country... I volunteered for RE (Royal Engineers) Bomb Disposal Squads [dealing with] the threat of unexploded bombs in London for two years.*

Another conscientious objector, 27-year-old Donald Barkshire, refused to attend his medical examination and was sentenced to 12 months imprisonment in Wormwood Scrubs.

> For the first six months I was in Solitary Confinement. The only time I was out of the cell was when I was released in the morning to clear the pot and wash... after my stint in prison I went back to the Volunteer Unit... working as a nursing orderly for terminally injured ex-servicemen of the First World War at a residential nursing home.

Joan Quibbell from Birmingham was one of 190,000 women who joined the Auxiliary Territorial Service (ATS), the women's branch of the British Army. Joan kept a diary.

> I sometimes used to picture what peacetime would be like. No more bombings and sudden death, no more partings from those we love. No shortages. Streetlamps would shine and shops would be full of good things to eat and lovely clothes to wear. Rubble and ruins would be swept away, new houses would be built, and gaping holes would be grassed over. The winds of time would blow away harsh memories and heal our hearts.

Nineteen-year-old Joan was deployed to Uxbridge, London, by the ATS. She spent a day off with her friend Ruby in London.

> We made our way to the Services Club to have lunch and play some table tennis. After our meal we went over to the Games

---

* Later Chris served at the Battle of the Bulge in Germany, and Palestine.

Room and sat down to wait our turn. A sailor and an Air Force chap were using the table at the time, playing a cracking game, which we watched with interest. Suddenly the ball ricocheted off the sailor's bat across the room, to land fairly and squarely in my lap. The sailor, grinning broadly, came over to retrieve it. 'Sorry about that,' he said, as I handed him the ball and liked the way his brown eyes twinkled.

His boat had been sunk in action two days before . . . I took to him enormously and readily agreed to come to London to meet him again.

For that second meeting with Les Sprigg, Joan escaped her ATS camp without a pass, praying that she wouldn't be caught by the military police. She repeated her escape for a third date.

He had such an honest face, such a dependable air about him, I instinctively knew I could put my whole life in his hands . . . he then declared that he had fallen in love with me, and I said I felt exactly the same. I returned to Uxbridge on wings.

In war, love moved fast. It had to. Les was due to return to his ship. Twelve days after their first meeting, according to Joan's diary, they met for the fourth time.

He asked me to marry him and, with a heart full of love and joy, I said yes. We knew it wouldn't be for quite a time, but we made the promise to each other that one day our dreams would come true. [The next day] he returned to Dover.

Unfortunately, Joan's parents would not give permission for their daughter to marry before the age of 21. Les was suddenly granted six days leave.

I dashed happily to see him, but how awful was his news. His ship had been very badly smashed up, the bridge had received a direct hit, killing or injuring all the officers. One had died in his arms. He brought the poor vessel back, stern-first, through a minefield. His terrible experiences showed in his tired, sad face.

Joan and Les finally married January 1945

Paratrooper Tim Hardy was still dreaming of life and (unrequited) love with Doreen Fenner, now across the country in Wales. Tim's unit received a VIP visit.

> We couldn't believe our eyes; the unremarkable-looking fellow who was pushed in front of the rest of the red-tabs couldn't possibly be anyone but a warm-up comedian, but to our astonishment he was introduced as 'General Montgomery'.
>
> From this bank-clerkish figure there issued forth a bank-clerkish voice; a piping snooty squeak in which we were informed that we were the world's finest (a statement I considered to be lacking in empirical evidence), that we were led by the world's finest (which had been vividly demonstrated to be untrue), that God was on our side (ditto as things stood) and, in peroration, that he, Montgomery, conqueror of Alamein, was 'looking for an ocean he could push the Nazis into'. For a battle cry it was hardly *Henry V*, but then Montgomery wasn't Olivier, more like Stan Laurel.

CHAPTER THIRTY-FOUR

Anzio, 1944

With the slow Allied advance towards Rome, and with the Germans holding the prime defensive position at Monte Cassino, the Allies attempted a second breakthrough to circumvent the Gustav Line. On 22 January 1944, a few days after the Battle of Monte Cassino began, they launched an ambitious seaborne invasion at the small port of Anzio, south of Rome. Hitler was determined to drive the Allies back into the sea and proclaimed that the invasion needed to be crushed 'in the blood of British soldiers'. He nearly got his wish.

The Allies had one eye on D-Day and deployed fewer amphibious craft than desirable for such an ambitious assault. So, American General John Lucas cautiously waited for nine days on the Anzio beachhead to be certain he had enough men and firepower for success. But, by then, 100,000 Germans were holding the high ground around the Allied perimeter.

Sergeant William Heard, 7th Battalion, Oxfordshire and Buckinghamshire Light Infantry:

> We were vastly outnumbered ... we were continuously shelled and mortared, and under these tragic and trying conditions had to prepare for the next attack. Many of the wounded had to bandage their own wounds as best they could ... things were not looking good. Our ammunition was low, and every round had to be used to its greatest advantage. Rations were desperately needed, and we resorted to

collecting up any crusts and scraps that we had thrown away during previous days.

When the enemy finally withdrew, their casualties had been heavy, with dead and wounded lying everywhere. However, they quickly regrouped and continued to batter our position.

1st Infantry Division, Anzio

Robert Warren, Duke of Wellington's Regiment, was cut off from his battalion.

> With the coming of daylight, the Germans apparently realised they had not mopped everyone up, because we were subjected to a sheet of machine-gun fire and a bombardment. All we could do was crouch in our trenches; to have put our heads up would have been suicide. One bullet went right through my knapsack resting on the parapet of my slit trench. I thought

my end had come ... it was quite clear we were the last survivors and that we were well and truly behind enemy lines.

We were no suicide squad ... we put up our hands and shouted *'Camarade'* in time-honoured fashion.

His 25th birthday ended with Robert Warren as a prisoner.

Gordon Bingham-Hall, 46th Royal Tank Regiment, appeared to have nine lives.

At about 7 a.m. I was at the rear of the building 'abluting', trousers down, froglike position. The sun was at a low angle, but something was creating a vague shadow ... yes, it was a plane, an Me 109 gliding in and heading for me ... he spat a few bullets at me before aiming his bomb which missed, just!

His next close shave came when his much-decorated Captain halted their Sherman tank because a surrendering German soldier was ahead.

Unbeknown to Captain Roberts, who was letting his thoughts run to further medals, a German soldier had climbed on the back of our tank and, after a short struggle, he dropped a potato masher, our word for a German hand grenade, into the turret ... I knew nothing of this ... regaining consciousness I found that my co-driver, Bill Taggart, was laying across my lap and the turret was full of smoke. The turret crew had got out, miraculously uninjured except that Captain Roberts's foot was hanging off; he saved us, but, of course, he caused it.*

How many times I lost consciousness I don't know, but each time a shell came through they hit our shells, splitting the cases and causing the cordite to burn; the instrument panel was well alight. With enough heat the whole thing

---

* Capt Edward Roberts, MC, was killed later in the Anzio campaign on 1 June 1944.

> blows up like a fireball! I realised that Bill was no longer on me, so I assumed he had got out. I should have known better, because his body juices were all over me . . . I hope he died instantly.

Gordon escaped from the tank just before it blew up. He had never seen a woman at Anzio and so was amazed to soon come across a brothel full of Americans and laughing women. He warned them of the danger but to no avail.

> I was flat in a deep ditch as the first shell screamed in just behind the truck! At 50 yards I was safe but looked round to see bodies and parts of same scattered. Screams and panic from the house [brothel] and out came more nutters . . . everyone jumped on the truck which sped away; my final vision was of a stump of leg hanging out of the back of the truck pumping blood.

The sea was as dangerous as the land. Bob Burns served on the destroyer HMS *Laforey* at Anzio when she was hit by a German torpedo.

> I was conscious, between bouts of blackness and pain, that the *Laforey* was breaking up in her death throws . . . I clung to the rigging as she started her final plunge. Frantically, I tore myself free and, with arms working like pistons, propelled myself as far from the inevitable whirlpool of suction as possible. Suddenly, like a cork, I was whirled round and round and drawn towards the vortex where our beloved ship had finally disappeared beneath the waves. Fortunately, my half-inflated life belt kept me on the surface. Gradually, the black silence was broken by the cries of shipmates, dotted around the ocean . . . 179 men lost their lives.

Grenadier Guardsman Sydney Wright was sent to search for the Company Commander, Captain Christopher Ford.

As we went forward with our Red Cross truck, we passed a field on our left. Here lay dozens of Irish Guardsmen, dead. They were face-down, as if asleep (as indeed they were, with God), complete with all their equipment. They couldn't have stood a chance, nor did the Company Commander.

Eventually I found him, 250 yards back, where he had crawled with a row of bullets across his chest, till he finally died. He was 6ft 8ins tall and I couldn't help thinking that if only he'd been 6ft, he could have still been alive.

By grim coincidence, Captain Ford's brother, George, was also in the search party. Sydney Wright asked if he wanted anything from the body.

His brother said, 'Yes, his cufflinks and tiepin, they were a Christmas present from our mother.'

The attritional stalemate at both Anzio and Monte Cassino lasted for months. It was not until just before D-Day, on 23 May 1944, that constant shelling had weakened enemy artillery enough for the Allies to finally break out of the Anzio beachhead.

Bloody victories in Italy finally opened the door for the Allies to reach Rome. But American General Mark Clark failed to destroy the retreating German 10th Army as ordered. Instead, in his showy desire to enter Rome first, Clark left the German Army to fight another day.

CHAPTER THIRTY-FIVE

Rome, 1944

On 4 June 1944, General Clark fulfilled his ambition when the US 5th Army entered Rome. Across the Channel from Normandy, the Allies were making the final preparations for the D-Day landings just two days later. Conservative MP Lady Astor called British soldiers in Italy 'D-Day Dodgers'. Her tasteless comment angered veterans of the brutal Italian campaign for decades to come.

Sergeant Len Scott, Royal Army Pay Corps, followed the Army up through Italy to Rome's doorstep.

> There, far away, was sunlight and something which looked like a golden bubble: St Peter's dome, riding high over all. We were seeing Rome as many a conqueror had seen her, a great city, far-off, flame-coloured under the setting sun.

Survivors of the Italian campaign were probably less struck by Rome's beauty than relieved to be alive. Among them was Ron Goldstein, 49th Light Anti-Aircraft Regt, who had survived Monte Cassino's carnage. While his mates visited local bars, Ron searched for something more meaningful.

> I saw the synagogue on my left. It was huge. Moorish in design with a large domed roof. I walked completely round the outside until I found a small side door that looked as if it was in use. After knocking a few times an elderly man, obviously a caretaker, let me in, and when I explained I was Jewish, he let me wander round unescorted.

I saw a small, whitewashed garage facing the synagogue. What drew my attention to it was a large Magen David [Star of David] that someone had painted on its walls in black paint. More than 50 years later I can still feel the mental blow to the pit of my stomach on seeing this crudely painted sign with all its obvious connotations.

I made my way into its dark interior and, once my eyes had adjusted to the dark, I saw a young man working on a car engine. *'Sono ebrei qi?'* ('Are there any Jews here?'), I called into the darkness. There was a pause and then back in Italian came, 'Why do you want to know?' This, in the most unfriendly of tones.

'Because I am a Jew,' I replied and gestured, as if for confirmation, to the Star of David that was now dangling from my breast pocket. He came close, studied my face carefully, then the Star of David, and then, all restraint aside, bearhugged me as though we were brothers.

Eric Atkinson had already delivered a baby in his truck in Tunis, using his army clasp knife to cut the cord. Rome was equally eventful.

We heard a plaintive cry of *'Kadro, kadro'* (Thief, thief). We turned and saw a girl in her late teens clad only in a cardboard box, which came to just below her knees. The girl pulled gently on my sleeve murmuring, *'Camica, camica, bene.'* I guessed she was begging for my shirt. I peeled off my khaki drill shirt, which was quite long, and gave it to her. Tom and I discreetly looked away whilst she slipped the shirt over her head and stepped out of the cardboard box. She took hold of both of our hands, saying *'casa, casa'* ... we walked through several narrow streets before reaching Maria's home. Her mother immediately guessed what had happened and rewarded us with warm hugs. Maria returned a little later in a pretty white dress. Mother insisted on pressing my shirt ...

General Clark's unseemly rush to Rome ensured that the Nazis were not totally defeated. Another heavily fortified Line, the Gothic, ran north of Florence between Pisa and Pesaro and presented a formidable barrier, blocking Allied access to Northern Italy. The enemy had to be cleared out one valley at a time.

Having survived Normandy, North Africa, Burma and Monte Cassino, Jim Palmer, 3rd Tank Regiment, found himself near Urbino, inland from Rimini in the Marche, where the hilly terrain meant Jim's tank was of little value. The retreating Germans had dug themselves in at the local cemetery, erecting their machine guns behind the large, box-like gravestones above ground.

> Tombs were bursting open when hit, and human bodies and skeletons were flying through the air. Men were wounded and lying among long-dead human skeletons, and we were just watching it all, frozen and unbelieving at what was happening ... for over four years I had been part of the destruction of mankind, but each day had shown me deeper depths of human madness. Would it never end, or would it end with me being a victim of this frenzied desire for the extinction of the human race? I felt sick of it all and despaired at the madness of the world that had lost all belief in the sanctity of human life.

At 19, Donald Delves, Hampshire Regiment, was already a veteran of Sicily, Salerno and Monte Cassino. His experiences had already ranged from seeing soldiers incapable of fighting...

> A soldier, who had deserted for a short while, was made to stand on a wooden box, and we had to gather round for a few minutes and were told that this would happen to us if we deserted. The soldier had all his hair cut off and was shaking. He had previously fought in the North Africa campaign. He was suffering from shell shock. He was ill and did not deserve this!

... to burying the dead.

> It was very late in the day; the sun was going down and the sky was an orange-red. We were on a mountainside and had two young soldiers to bury. One was quite a bit bigger than me and was hard to drag to the shallow grave I had dug. I eventually laid him to rest but noted that his eyes were still open and, while Padre Brown prayed over him, I could not help thinking what his last thoughts had been. Was it for his family back home or could he have possibly seen Angels in the sky? After putting the second soldier in the shallow grave, which was only the temporary burial, I put their steel helmets over their faces to shield them from earth and stones . . . the sun was setting behind the mountains and even the land seemed to reflect the red sky. It was so peaceful at that time, even though we could still hear some shelling in the distance.

Some of Donald's Italian experiences were headed WARNING: NOT FOR THE FAINT HEARTED. The exact location is unknown, just 'a garden by a river in Italy'.

> We noticed something white in the garden of a house that had been badly damaged, most likely by shellfire. As we got closer, we were shocked to see it was a very pretty little Italian girl in a white nightdress, she must have been about nine years old and looked as though she was asleep. We were used to seeing dead soldiers around us, both German and British. But this was very different! . . . it very much upset us to see the trail of blood from the house to this dear little girl. We stood there spellbound, thinking what harm had this little girl done in her short life to have this happen to her.
> To this very day, this little girl keeps coming back to me, and yet over 60 years have gone by.

Canadian troops were also caught in terrible battles as they pushed northwards from Ortona, south of Pescara, up the Adriatic coast. Twenty-one-year-old Private Stan Scislowski from

Windsor, Ontario, served with the Perth Regiment. They stopped for a church service on the frontline just before a major attack.

> Services weren't held within the sanctity of a place of worship beneath soaring vaults and surrounded by the icons of Roman Catholicism. They were, through circumstances and necessity, held behind the bomb-shattered and bullet-scarred walls of any building that would serve the purpose. At times, whenever possible and prudent, they were held in an open ravine or valley out of sight of the malevolent eyes of the enemy artillery who would have soon unleashed their hate on us ... never had a hymn meant so much to us as it did in those unlikely places of worship. We sang with uncommon reverence ... then the Service came to that part where we sang 'Abide with me'. I found myself inserting my own feelings between the lines, feelings that harboured the fear that I might not be coming back at battle's end ... I couldn't help but let my mind take me back home, wondering how my mother and family would take it when the telegram came saying I had been killed in action.

Stan particularly remembered one young soldier fighting at Fosso Munio near Ravenna.

> The night was black as pitch, no moon, no stars, no flash of artillery fire to light the way for the Canadian Infantry Division moving forward to the start line of the next attack. The only sound came from the scuffle of the infantrymen's boots on gravel as they worked their way forward ... the enemy was very much awake and alert.
>
> In the lead platoon of the Perth Regiment from Stratford, Ontario, was a 17-year-old Windsor lad. Lance-Corporal Freddie Lytwyn who had to have lied about his age to get in the army. But he was a veteran now, a veteran of several hard-fought battles as he marched on towards yet another.

The immediate danger was not in the open fields to their left, nor was it in the impenetrable darkness to their right. It was straight ahead along the line of the ditch. An enemy machine-gun crew hidden behind a stone culvert waiting for them, their weapon pointing down the centre of the ditch ... at 25 yards range the enemy Fusilier squeezed the trigger, the gun ripping off a long burst. Four hundred steel-jacketed slugs slammed into the bodies of the two lead sections. Twelve men died instantly, their bodies literally torn apart in the slash of bullets ... somewhere in that pile of torn bodies was that of the 17-year-old Windsor lad. He was too young to die in battle, too young to die at any time.

I've taken the liberty of describing the last moments in the life of one young Canadian who represents the hundred thousand and more other Canadians who laid down their lives. In remembering one ... you remember all.

The brutal Italian campaign has been overshadowed by the success of D-Day, but it cost 312,000 Allied casualties, 65,000 of them killed. The campaign was littered with leadership mistakes but did succeed in keeping a huge number of German troops fully occupied in Italy when they could have been better deployed elsewhere.

Stan Scislowski finally made it to the supply port of Bari on a short leave. He saw a production for Allied servicemen of *The Merry Widow* at Bari Opera House.

Most of the occupants [of the boxes] were British and American officers, none below the rank of Major. And most were in the company of strikingly attractive and fur-bedecked signorinas. These stunning ladies had to be the daughters, even wives, of some of the Italian tycoons of industry, or else they were simply the most expensive prostitutes in town.

In the interval, far to the rear of the staid old Opera House, an uncouth officer pulled off a stunt more likely to happen at a high school basketball game. Whoever the culprit was, took a condom out of his pocket and without a trace of inhibition proceeded to blow it up to a grand and obscene four feet length. He then released it out into the smoky air where it began a slow descent toward the audience below... on the whims of air currents the unspeakable object floated first in one direction, changed course, and floated off in another.

When it came down to audience level it was propelled upwards by a hundred upraised poking hands and down it went all over the Opera House like the bouncing ball on the screen at a movie sing-along. And then it disappeared with a bang at the touch of someone's cigarette end.

A minute or two later there must have been five hundred blown-up condoms floating up and down in that smoky hall of culture... I can't recall what the rest of the play was about.

PART FIVE

'God, buddy,' spoke an unshaven man next to me. 'We came very close to hell.' I looked at him, 'Close to hell. My friend, we are in hell.'

American soldier soon after D-Day, 1944

CHAPTER THIRTY-SIX

Resistance, 1943–44

Every corner of Europe, including Italy, harboured resistance movements and, through the Special Operations Executive (SOE), the British supported local defiance wherever possible.

George Evans, a cook in the 4th (Durham Survey) Regiment, Royal Artillery, was captured at Tobruk and transported to Italy as a POW. When the Italians capitulated in September 1943, leaving the Germans to fight the Allies, he was working in the rice fields of the Po Valley, Northern Italy. George was faced with a dilemma. Should he remain in the safety of the camp where, even though the guards had disappeared, the Italian commandant was still in charge, or should he escape and risk being recaptured, this time by the more ruthless Germans? George and three other POWs took the risk.

> Life was rather difficult, but we always managed to find a barn or some form of shelter to spend the night. If offered I would never accept the hospitality of the civilians' houses as anyone found sheltering POWs had their house burned to the ground ... I knew in my own mind that this way of life could not continue ... we made contact with a party of Jews who had suffered at the hands of the Fascist regime and were now attempting to form a resistance movement (partisans). They were very good and not only fed us but explained what they were attempting to do ... I agreed we would help because it offered us a stable existence

George soon understood the reality of partisan life in Piedmont, north of Turin. When reports were received that a local official was collaborating with the Fascists, the embryonic partisan group, ten Italians and four British, paid him a visit.

> He was fetched to appear before a 'kangaroo court'. My knowledge of Italian was not too brilliant; he protested his innocence but to no avail; he was found guilty and shot.
>
> The following day a detachment of Germans arrived in the valley below. They mounted a small artillery force in the valley opposite and proceeded to blast our house to pieces.

One POW was captured but the remaining three escaped to a small village further north.

> Information came through that a build-up of German troops and Fascist militia was gathering ... this meant only one thing; we were about to be sorted out.
>
> The partisans had acquired a machine gun (which looked very effective), the road came round the mountainside and as you approached the village there was a high ground with a promontory, which allowed you to look directly down onto the road. This is where we mounted the machine gun.
>
> I had a young lad assist me in feeding the ammunition into the machine gun, and as they came into view round the corner, I counted one officer and 22 troops. I opened fire and one can imagine the surprise effect.

George knew he was certain to be caught eventually, so with two others tried to cross into Switzerland. Unfortunately, his two comrades ran into a German patrol.

> They were asked to surrender. One realised he could not escape but the other made a run for it and was shot dead ...
> I rejoined the partisans.

Contact was made with Britain and a parachute drop of Sten guns and other equipment was received. Then Major Alistair Macdonald of the Special Operations Executive (SOE) arrived from Britain in October 1944, followed by a team of three. The addition of George Evans and two other POWs to the SOE team created an effective unit.

> Major Macdonald's first task was to organise and distribute the largest arms drop in Italy; this kept our unit very busy because everything would arrive under cover of darkness when we felt the tension waiting for the codeword on the radio. It was bedlam trying to get everything away because we only had a mule or two.

In December 1944, partisans, supported by the British, blew up a vital railway bridge at Ivrea, which for a time halted transportation of steel and torpedo bodies to Germany from a factory in the Aosta valley.

> The partisans followed this up by ambushing a patrol of Germans and killing some of them. This really infuriated them, and they began house-to-house searches. Major Macdonald* was caught but was taken in for interrogation rather than being shot on the spot by the Gestapo. He managed to escape from the prison camp and make his way to the safety of Switzerland.

For the rest of the war George Evans and the partisans destroyed bridges, locomotives and electricity pylons before the Americans finally liberated them.

> I would like to pay tribute to the many Italian civilians who helped me... the Germans offered a reward for information and capture of any POW, but I never heard of anyone in our area being betrayed.

---

* Macdonald was awarded the Military Cross.

The Axis powers had declared war on Greece on 28 October 1940 and resistance was dealt with brutally. If a German soldier was killed, reprisals meant whole communities being wiped out. Doctor Athanasius Kapranos lived in an Athens suburb. One summer day all the men were rounded up.

> German soldiers, and local hooded collaborators, walked about the square and picked up various men, mostly with communist affiliations, who disappeared inside the Civic Centre building.

When it was Athanasius's turn, he was lucky to be recognised as the local doctor and put in the back of an army truck parked by the high wall of the Civic Centre's courtyard. His son, Plato:

> After some time had elapsed, he heard a muffled popping sound followed by restrained applause. This continued every so often that my father's curiosity took the best of him, and he climbed on top of the roof of the truck . . . he could see that chairs had been arranged as when attending an outside function and at the front was an oversized German officer with a handgun. Every so often soldiers would walk forward with a detainee who they would hand over to the officer. He would grab hold of them by the scruff of the neck with his left arm and he would place the muzzle of the gun on the side of their heads. He would then pull the trigger (the popping sound) and he would dispatch the body to the pile of bodies already gathering at the front. That would be followed by the reserved clapping of his appreciative public.

Captain Conal O'Donnell, a 28-year-old Irishman with SOE Middle East, was parachuted into Occupied Greece to build isolated mountain airstrips for delivering arms to the resistance in the Peloponnese. But he found himself in a situation beyond his control when the Greek communist partisans executed 78

German soldiers near the village of Kalavryta. The Nazi reprisals were even more brutal.

> All males aged 12 and over were marched out of Kalavryta to a large hollow-shaped area ... the German machine guns opened up, murdering at least 463* men and boys ... the town was then set on fire. The town's church clock still stands at 2.34 p.m., marking the time ...

O'Donnell was one of the first on the scene after the massacre. His son, also called Conal:

> He never really talked about the massacre apart from remarking that the wailing of the women was 'unbearable'.

In Poland, Warsaw's huge Jewish ghetto was systematically starved by the Nazis. Locals helped with food when they could. Danuta Juszkiewicz's mother lived next to the Ghetto.

> Non-Jewish Poles would walk along the walls and occasionally throw food over the wall ... when the Germans saw this, they would gun down the people trying to help the Jews ... the Germans had signposts saying that anyone helping Jews would be executed. Many Poles helped them regardless ... she would often hear machine guns on the other side of the Ghetto wall. From drainage openings at the bottom of the wall the gutters would fill not with water but blood.
>
> After the extermination camps were built, transport trains full of Jews would leave the Ghetto. My mother would toss food and water into the open tops of cattle-cars crammed full of people. German guards would shoot anyone trying to help ... mother was with a friend when this woman was shot

---

* Estimates of the dead vary, but the memorials in and around Kalavryta contain nearly 700 names.

by a German guard in the head. All she could do was watch her die as the train went by.

Maksymilian Jarosz lived in Piaski, near Lubin, Eastern Poland. He was 14 when war started but grew up fast.

> All of us except for our older sister, who was married with small children, joined the Polish resistance . . . Piaski had a large Jewish population, and we lived in peace side by side for many years. With the arrival of the Nazis things began to change rapidly.

The Jarosz family smuggled food and medicine into the ghetto and delivered false identity documents to help Jews escape. They also hid Jews on their farm. There were 11 children and, in February 1941, when Maxsymilian was 16, two of his elder brothers were informed on and arrested by the Gestapo. They were both murdered in Auschwitz.

Two years later in 1943, tired of hiding from the Nazis in surrounding villages, Maksymilian returned home for a night and stepped outside for some fresh air with his brother, Czesiek.

> We heard a voice calling in German, 'What's your name?' . . . when the figure moved closer, I could recognise the local SS man, Schulz. He ordered my brother to march in front of him. After a few minutes, which seemed like hours, I heard four shots and then it was very quiet. At that moment my heart stopped beating . . . I ran towards my brother. I could see by the look on his face that he was in a lot of pain. He held his right forearm with his left hand, and I could see a stream of blood.

Czesiek was rushed to the local doctor.

> When my mother returned home with my injured brother, the Gestapo were already waiting for them. They ordered that Czesiek, and my father, walk to their quarters. From the

window in the attic where I hid for the night, I saw my father walking his son to a certain death. Czesiek was murdered the same night. The next day I was on the run again.

Two days after Czesiek was murdered, my other brother, Stasiek, came out of hiding to organise provisions for his colleagues in the resistance. He went to a safe local shop in the village. He saw through the window Gestapo cars approaching. Concerned about the shopkeeper's safety he ran towards the outbuildings, unfortunately he was spotted and shot at by the SS-man. He was killed with a single shot through his heart.

When the war started, I was a teenager, when it was over, I was a broken man.*

In Yugoslavia, Captain Cornelius Turner led the first daylight glider raid of the war, codenamed Operation Bunghole. The task was to fly 36 Russian officers in three gliders to a mountainside 100 kms inland from Split to meet with partisans.

My tow-ship pilot, Wendell C. Little of Indianapolis (he wrote it down on the back fly leaf of my Bible), wished me luck just before take-off, 'You'll need it,' he said.

As we approached the peaks Droop [the pilot] had all his work cut out to hold the rocking, bucketing glider. I reckoned we were drifting east of the track by several miles; as we staggered over the divide the tow ships and gliders, leaping all over the sky. We tumbled over the icy teeth of the ridge with a hundred feet to spare . . . The interior opened up before us, a great white valley, timbered on the high slopes, and beyond gentle hills losing themselves in the northern mists . . . we'd got to 3,000 feet and could hit the landing zone easily. 'I'll take her Droop! Hit the tit! We're going down.' He held up his hands and then hit the release lever without a word . . . there was a wide white shelf on the hillside and a fire surely.

---

* Maxsymilian lived into his nineties.

> Yes, a fire, two fires, little black dots against the snow ... the others were off by now drifting gently down beside us and we flopped down onto three feet of snow. Three perfect landings.
>
> Everybody embraced everyone else; the partisans armed to the teeth, rifles, crossed bandoliers, knives and grenades, bearded and stinking they swarmed over us. Anchoring the gliders down with fallen timber, we climbed on to the sleds and set off for town, the ponies up to their bellies in the track. It was a heavy night in the little town hall, as from six to near midnight we sat and drank toasts to the whole free world.

For five weeks Turner organised Allied arms drops.

> Night after night we would lie out in the hillside, curled up in holes we had dug to get out of the bitter winds, our straw fires laid out beside us, the signallers trying to make their homing beacons work ... a couple of times there were men on a parachute. They stayed a day, collecting a guide and pack animal, then disappeared into the forest bound for Greece, Romania, Hungary or Austria to live out a hazardous and lonely war in some outpost of resistance.

Belgian 16-year-old, Andre Mommen, moved to France and lied about his age to join the Resistance, as his daughter Josiane told The People's War. At first, he helped the downed Allied aircrew escape into Spain but was eventually promoted into a group of saboteurs.

> This cell of men was great, they did everything to interfere with the German War machine, blowing up bridges or railways was one of their favourites.
>
> My assignment this day was to blow up a train which was carrying German soldiers. Our boss had a girlfriend and unknown to us he had had a fight with her the night before and told her they were finished. The next day we had prepared everything, secreted dynamite round the rail, and waited for the right moment to finish the job. Then we were ambushed.

There were Germans everywhere, we got shot at, several of our men died. One of them even fell over me. To my dying day I know he saved my life. We were told much later that the girlfriend had betrayed us, just to get back at her so-called boyfriend.

I was sent to Buchenwald,* a prison camp in the middle of West Germany where I spent the rest of my childhood, doing hard labour, and being experimented upon. I was strong and that helped me survive the brutality and starvation of this war.

Andre died in 1966, aged 40. He was awarded several medals for his resistance work.

Barry Wilson-Law was flying with 419 Squadron, Royal Canadian Air Force, when his Lancaster bomber was shot down. Five fellow crew members were all shot by the Germans as they parachuted down into France. But Barry escaped and was hidden by Pierre Gillootes.

> When it was dark, Pierre took me into his farmhouse and gave me a substantial meal and a bed for the night. The next morning, I had breakfast with him, and he gave me a suit of his clothes, having burnt my uniform in the night... whilst I was having breakfast there was a knock on the door and Pierre answered it. When he came back to the table, he told me it was the Germans looking for me. He assured them he had no knowledge of my whereabouts. If I had been found, Pierre and everyone on the farm would have been shot.

Barry was helped by one French farmer after another until he reached a Maquis (Resistance) safe house, where he met two American airmen. They resolved to escape through France into Spain.

---

* More than 56,000 people died at Buchenwald.

At one safe house we were introduced to the local resistance leader, a 'Monsieur Chocolate' ... an 'insurance agent' had been found to be a collaborator ... after a brief conversation between the two Frenchmen, Monsieur Chocolate drew a revolver from his pocket and made the agent captive ... we did not know what happened but I don't think he was left alive.

After one incident the SS hunted the band we were with, and the Germans captured two of the Maquis. They were hung by a rope over the branch of a tree and from the end of the rope a butcher's hook was attached. It was forced into the lower part of their jaws and up through the roof of their mouths and they were left to die. Neither side took any prisoners.

It was a case of walking, sometimes cycling, towards Spain ... alternating between day and night movement, we progressed, but capture was never far from our minds. Finally, we had sight of the Pyrenees and in a safe house we met a Spanish Basque man. It had taken nearly three months so far.

I will be eternally grateful to all the brave people who helped us on our way to safety. Had any been with us if we had been caught, they would have faced torture and death, along with their families.*

Albert Falla from Guernsey was an ideal candidate to be dropped behind enemy lines. He was fluent in French and had bomb experience as a Sapper. His son:

> His first job was blowing up some railway lines and a bridge. Unfortunately, the railway bridge was guarded because a train carrying tanks was due to pass through.
>
> My dad found himself in the unenviable position of having to creep up behind a sentry (as did several of his comrades)

---

* Barry returned to France with his wife in 2000. He visited the graves of his crew members and found the family of Pierre, the farmer who first helped him.

armed with a commando knife and kill him. He told me, 'It is an awful experience, to have to kill another man in such a manner, but it was him or us... war is a messy business and it was quick, so he was lucky I suppose... the next day we found out that the German train had been nearly at the bridge when the charge went off... he hadn't managed to stop in time and crashed. Only one tank was serviceable enough to drive off... the others were wrecked.'

Treachery, accidents or bad luck were commonplace for men dropped behind enemy lines. Captain Victor Gough, once of the Somerset Light Infantry, was dropped into the Vosges area of France with a wireless operator and a French officer to arm several thousand resistance fighters. His nephew, Colin Burbidge, told his story:

> The drop did not go well... within three days the French officer was killed, and the wireless operator captured after a German ambush... 100 Maquis killed, 100 captured in the same battle.

Several days later Gough was also picked up by the Nazis and taken to Strasbourg for brutal interrogation. He was shoved into trucks with 13 other men, including two French priests.

> Near the cemetery at Gaggenau was the Erlich forest. It was here that the trucks stopped and the prisoners, including Captain Gough, all his comrades, and the two French priests were taken to a bomb crater and murdered.

Before D-Day, student André Heintz in Normandy provided information on German military movements and created new identities.

> I was responsible for passing on all the information we collected to our leader, whom I met regularly in a church in Caen... we would kneel together in a quiet corner of the

André Heintz, Bayeux, Normandy

church, and he would pass the prayer book to me, containing the questionnaire for the next week. I would pass my prayer book back containing all the answers I had been able to gather that week. We were asked things like where headquarters were positioned, where weapons were hidden, how many vehicles were at each place, and what the names of the officers were.

The Germans knew that the BBC was transmitting coded messages, so they ordered everyone to hand in their radio sets. Many people had their sets around the house but for Resistance members this was too risky. I had a crystal set so small I could hide it in a bean can, with dried beans on top. I knew about Heinz 57 varieties, and I called this my Heinz 58 variety. When my friends needed me to listen to a coded message they would say, 'Use the 58 variety.'

Another of my jobs was to provide new identities to people who were in trouble. They were often Jews and people who had escaped prison, but sometimes also British soldiers ... there was a space on the French identity cards for 'a special mention' and in the case of British and American airmen who could not speak French, we used this space to fill in 'deaf and dumb'. But, of course, it was not too easy to be able to feign being deaf and dumb! ... the escape line was always divided into small parts so that the whole system wouldn't collapse if one person was caught. It took about 18 different people to help one person escape.

In 1943 André's leader was arrested.

I couldn't swallow my soup after I heard the news. I kept thinking of him in jail, possibly already being tortured, giving them the names of the people involved in the Resistance. He was eventually shot on D-Day, 6 June 1944 . . . they were taken out in groups of six and shot . . . it was a horrendous crime, and the poor families were extremely distressed because these men's bodies were never found.*

---

* Eighty-seven prisoners were executed and later buried by the Nazis at an unknown site.

CHAPTER THIRTY-SEVEN

D-Day, 1944

D-Day was the largest combined operations invasion in history. First, paratroopers were dropped behind the coast to secure strategically important bridges over the Caen Canal and Orne River to protect the Allied flank from enemy attack. Soon after, a vast armada landed waves of soldiers and their weapons onto the Normandy beaches. Near Arromanches, the British landed at Sword and Gold Beaches, the Canadians at Juno, and further west the Americans took Utah and Omaha. The invasion had to succeed at all costs because, if the Germans drove the Allies back into the sea, a second chance of recapturing continental Europe would be years away.

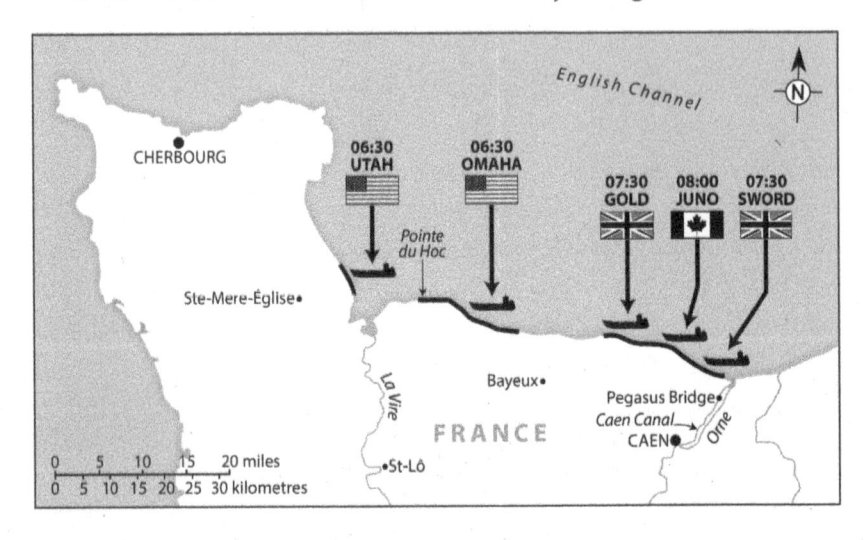

Ginger Thomas was a shorthand typist in the Town Clerk's Office in Swansea. Within a few weeks of joining the Wrens, she was working for Lieutenant-General Frederick Morgan, Chief of Staff to the Supreme Allied Commander. Morgan was responsible for planning D-Day while the appointment of American General Eisenhower as Supreme Allied Commander was waiting to be made. For young Ginger, this was a giant step from Swansea Town Hall.

> We realised it was all very hush-hush and very important . . . it was also a little bit frightening because I never thought I would be involved in anything so important. Whether the invasion plans would be successful was a big worry in my little mind.
>
> On the night of 5 June 1944, we didn't go to bed . . . we went out to watch the gliders being towed over to the continent. I vividly remember the sound of the aircraft. We all knew where they were going, but we didn't know what would happen when they got there.

Margaret Boothroyd and Laura Mountney had been Wrens for less than three months when they began working as teleprinter operators in the D-Day War Room. Margaret:

> The War Room was the nerve centre of the invasion plans; the King and Winston Churchill came often, and there were regular meetings between General Eisenhower, General Montgomery and Admiral Ramsey. Secrecy was of the essence, and it still amazes me the tremendous responsibility we were given . . . we were both on night watch that fateful night and before morning arrived messages were coming through to us from the beaches of Normandy.

Invasion planning started in 1942, but a rehearsal at Slapton Sands, Devon, on 28 April 1944, was a disaster for American troops. Poor communication and intelligence led to German E-Boat attacks, resulting in about 749 deaths. Some soldiers were also killed by friendly fire. Many died in the sea waiting to be rescued. Stoker/Driver Arthur Hill, London:

As the bodies of the victims were washed ashore after dawn, the full scale of the disaster became known. Most were wearing Mae West life jackets but had never been instructed how to use them. It was a training exercise that lasted 40 minutes and cost 800 lives.* The Commander's first concern was to suppress the news, which was successful for 40 years . . . the bodies were temporarily buried in a mass grave on the exercise site.

Much more successful was an elaborate British bluff. On the eve of D-Day, Special Duties 138 Squadron, attached to the Special Operations Executive (SOE), flew their Stirling bombers across the Channel to the Pas de Calais. The plan was to fool the Germans into thinking the invasion would happen near Calais, rather than miles further west in Normandy. Geoff Rothwell was the Squadron Leader.

> The Stirling dropped a phantom army of parachutists known as 'gingerbread men', with packages simulating gunfire. These dummy parachutists were made of hessian stuffed with straw. They were about two feet six inches in height and looked like pygmy scarecrows.

The 'gingerbread men' were one part of an ambitious deception involving inflatable rubber tanks and false agents, creating a ghost army poised to land at Calais. This was underpinned when the charismatic American general George Patton inspected his imaginary forces. As many as 150,000 German troops were stuck on alert near Calais when the invasion was taking place in Normandy.

While the dummy parachutists were dropped near Calais, the real paratroopers were readying themselves for a massive

---

* The figure of 749 deaths is widely recognised but some estimates put the number higher.

invasion in Normandy. Nineteen-year-old Signalman Danny Lyons from London was with the Royal Signals Regiment, 6th Airborne Division. His story was written by a third party.

> The thunderous roar of engines and the buffeting of the wind filled Danny's ears as the aircraft bounced its way through the windy night! . . . His head was spinning, his stomach churned, there was so much to be remembered, so little time left before he had to put it into practice.
>
> As the pilot slowed the aircraft, the order was given to stand, and the aperture door opened . . . all around the aircraft two hundred fingers and thumbs moved in the semi-darkness acting out ingrained routines. Checking buckles, checking straps. Tugging and tweaking . . . then someone in front stumbled and this rippled domino-like back down the line . . . until Danny had little option but to dive out of the aircraft into the swirling night sky!
>
> It was H-Hour plus 50 minutes, ten minutes before 1 a.m., the morning of 6 June 1944. Somewhere in that black night, 800 feet below on the green fields of Normandy, D-Day awaited the men of the 6th Airborne Division.
>
> Danny fell for a five-second eternity, whilst his last connection with England and safety, his static line, snatched, setting into motion the series of events that would pull his parachute clear. One second. Two seconds. Three seconds. Four seconds. Five seconds. Then his harness grabbed him like an iron fist and the silken canopy tautened as it swallowed the rushing air. For a few seconds he just hung there as he tried to get his bearings. But he saw nothing in the pitch-black night, and only heard the quickening beat of the Stirling's Hercules engines as the aircraft climbed away

Danny landed two miles from his scheduled landing site near the village of Le Bas de Ranville. As the dawn light bled into the dark sky he took stock.

His blood froze. He saw his rolled-up chute, the empty kit bag, his tell-tale boot prints in the soft earth and a wooden sign bearing skull and crossbones accompanied by the chilling words *'Gefahr Miner!'* He had landed slap-bang in the middle of a minefield.

Further down the road they came across the remains of a fire fight. Slumped against the wall was a young German soldier... he was in a poorly state. A British officer lay dead on the other side of the wall. He had been someone they both knew. They disabled the officer's body, taking his dog tags, paybook, cigarettes and revolver. They gave the smokes to the wounded German... it was not yet 6 a.m.

The 6th Airborne had to hold the line until troops landed on the beaches. Four years after the humiliation of Dunkirk, Danny dug a trench and sent his first signal from France.

Private Tim Hardy from Nottinghamshire was also a trained paratrooper with the 6th Airborne. He had enjoyed an uneventful military career since joining the Territorial Army aged 17, but now he was ready to finally leap into action.

Over four years had gone by since I'd burst into the Drill Hall on Alfreton Road straining to get my hands on a gun with which to shoot Hitler. Four years and I had not seen a Nazi, let alone fired a shot at one. Four years and I was still a lowly private soldier. Four years and I was 22, and still a virgin... [but] at long last something was about to happen.

I was told we would be spearheading an assault on the Germans in Normandy with the aim of taking and holding a vital bridge over the River Orne... [the plan] looked foolproof and, to make us feel even better about it, we were shown photographs of our bridge, and we actually built a scale model of it. We grew so fond of it we didn't want to blow it up.

D-DAY, 1944

Twenty paratroopers, including Tim, were crammed into a Douglas DC3.

> We had to be pushed up the landing steps by loaders as if we'd been Japanese commuters being sardined into bullet trains... it didn't help to be told that our Canadian pilot had never dropped parachutists before... we flew bumpily across to France. I wasn't the only one sick enough to hope we'd be shot down and so have done with it and who greeted the order to jump with glee. I stepped through the door, turned left, and, like a ton of bricks, I dropped into the dark French sky. It was an unusual mode of immigration I suppose but there I was, overseas at last.

Tim landed far from the bridge and was immediately dazzled by flashing lights.

> It was as if I'd landed on Blackpool promenade at illumination time. For another stomach-churning thing, the only other living creature I could see was a white horse I'd nearly fallen on; what's more, judging by the sound of gunfire blazing away there were plenty of angry soldiers about, a good many of them, presumably German.

Tim hid in a roadside ditch until daybreak with five colleagues.

> We six forlorn creatures viewed our situation with alarm... the platoon signaller was humping a thundering great wireless set that he couldn't get a spark out of... poor sod, he became the first and nearly the only man I saw die during the war. He perished, not by bullet or bomb but, unbelievably, by sinking in a split second into the mire at the bottom of the ditch. He and his wireless disappeared with a sort of 'whoosh' – Roger and out.
>
> Abandoning him to his watery grave, the remaining five of us fled to higher wooded ground where dawn found us

hugging the earth while shells from our own ships at sea screamed over our heads.

They were rescued by a 13-year-old French boy called Daniel, who bravely led them through woods to reconnect with other stragglers.

> God knows what Daniel thought of his first sight of the cream of the British army; we looked more like cut-throats on the run than liberators . . . nobody knew exactly where we were, where the sea-borne soldiers were or what was best for us to do?
>
> What happened to Daniel? Since we were unable to take him back safely home, he was sent to help in the field kitchens; a stray shell (possibly one of ours) landed on the cookhouse and killed him. *C'est la guerre.*

Brigadier James Hill was also in the 6th Airborne Division, commanding the 3rd Parachute Brigade. Like Tim Hardy, he landed distant from the planned drop zone. Brigadier Hill headed through a valley veined with irrigation ditches, when enemy aircraft attacked.

> I knew I'd been hit. I saw a leg lying in the middle of the path and I thought, God that's mine. Then I noticed it had a brown boot on. I didn't allow brown boots in my brigade, and the only person who broke that rule was my friend Lt Peters. I was lying on top of him. He was dead, I wasn't, but I'd been hit, and a large chunk of my left backside was gone.
>
> The dead and injured were all around us. I was faced with a choice; did I stay and look after the injured, or do I press on? I had a great responsibility, so I had to press on . . . we set off and the injured chaps gave us a cheer . . . we started off with 2,200 men and ended up with about 700 at most.

Back in England, WAAF Audrey Hirst was on control tower duty at RAF Tangmere near Chichester, watching D-Day glider forces overhead.

> The door flung open and Grenadier Guards in battle gear rushed in with Bren guns and demanded that the airfield be surrendered in the name of the King. They thought they were capturing a German airfield in France.
>
> Their glider had slipped too soon and landed in an English cornfield that they thought was French. The commanding officer was overcome with emotion at what they had done and burst into tears ... they could have easily opened fire.

Eighteen-year-old Frederick Glover, 9th Parachute Battalion:

> Everything that could go wrong did go wrong ... I was wounded in one leg first and then the other ... and the navigators mistook the River Dives for the River Orne. We lost, regretfully, a very large number of men who were drowned in the flooded area by the Dives ... it was decided I should stay behind with two wounded Germans to wait for our troops advancing from the beach. I administered morphine to the German with the worst wounds, an act that later saved my life.

Frederick was captured by an enemy patrol.

> I feared for my life, but the young German suddenly spoke up and pointed to his comrade, who I had given morphine to. The atmosphere changed immediately, and I was taken to a field hospital.*

Despite the inaccuracy of many parachute drops, enough gliders landed close to what became known as Pegasus Bridge that the

---

* Frederick escaped from a Paris hospital, helped by the French Resistance

first objective of securing the bridge was achieved by soldiers from the Oxfordshire and Buckinghamshire Light Infantry and British commandos. This capture would protect the Allied flank when the beach landings began. Louis Gray's small motor launch acted as a guiding beacon for the troop-carrying ships to follow.

> Dawn revealed the astonishing sight of serried ranks of ships heaving over the horizon and passing in wave after wave, packed to capacity with soldiers and weaponry . . . [and] endless flights of aircraft passing overhead to saturate the countryside behind the beaches . . . my overwhelming impression was the almost incredible degree of imagination and ingenuity that had been planned into the whole operation . . . perhaps the first sign of it was the slow-moving arrival of the Mulberry harbour* . . . my second impression of detailed planning was the sight of landing craft fitted out with floating bakeries and kitchens.

British Gunner Edward Wightman served on HMS *Ramillies*, supporting the invasion by pounding enemy defensive positions with its guns. He wrote in his diary just before action stations:

> Let's hope the boys have it all their own way with the opposition blasted to hell and back. E-Boats and submarines and minefields are expected. Should be quite a party . . . we are to enter harbour with full ceremony, and a band playing. All this is to buck up the morale of the pongos (soldiers) on shore . . . action stations in ten minutes time. All that we have trained for etc. is going into this effort. Pray God it shall not fail.
>
> Just as we were preparing to leave, hundreds and hundreds of gliders came in, in great masses . . . we estimated over a

---

* Two portable, concrete harbours which enabled the Allies to unload materials onto the beaches safely.

thousand... what a sight! Just like a Wellsian dream of the future.

As the first British paratroopers were airborne, at Chateau de Tracy, a mile from the British landing site at Gold Beach, German officers were heading for bed in the chateau they had semi-requisitioned. They had relaxed with a grand dinner and a concert.

The officers from Chateau de Tracy commanded over seven miles of fortifications, including four huge long-range 150 mm guns close by at Longues-sur-Mer. The Wehrmacht was also protected by a well-fortified coastline, part of Hitler's Atlantic Wall stretching from Norway to Portugal. The coast was studded with concrete gun emplacements and bunkers bristling with machine and mortar guns. Beaches were festooned with barbed wire and peppered with mines. Behind the beaches waited German tanks and artillery.

The enemy were heavily outnumbered on D-Day but enjoyed positional advantage. Omaha and Utah were backed by bluffs, perfect perches for German machine-gunners. Attempts to destroy enemy bunkers by shelling from air and sea were ineffective. So, as the first heavily laden Allied troops struggled out of the sea and across wide-open beaches, they were cut down by gunners in their machine-gun nests.

In the first wave 150,000 men and hundreds of military vehicles landed in over 5,000 ships.

Lance Corporal Reg Clarke, Royal Engineers, served with the 3rd Canadian Infantry Division that morning. His ship was crammed with French Canadians heading for Juno Beach.

> Our landing craft was now speeding through the black cloud of acrid smoke. Plumes of waterspouts were shooting up left, right and centre as the mortars and shells came down... The stench of spilled diesel oil and cordite stung my nose and made my eyes water.

A Beachmaster Major was standing right out on the open beach and the water's edge bellowing instructions through a megaphone. He was a very brave man ignoring his dangerous surroundings.

No time to think now. Out at the double into about four feet of water, just about up to my chest. I touched the bottom and forced myself forward. The water seemed to be holding me back, but at last I was on the beach and running like hell for cover.

An assault craft, broadside onto the beach, lay on its side next to us . . . It was a bloody mess, two bodies were hanging from the side, where they had been blown by the force of the explosion. The clothing on the lower parts of their bodies, which were badly mutilated, was missing, and large streaks of red ran down the side of the assault craft to the sea.

I was out of breath and my heart was thumping. There was an enormous crash behind us as I felt the blast in my back. The assault craft which had brought us in had caught a packet . . . peering through the black smoke I could see that only some of the crew had survived . . . there were a number of dead bodies floating at the water's edge and they were being pushed out of the way by the swimmers coming in . . . the beach was carnage with the dead soaking the sand red with fine Canadian blood.

Reg pushed through a breach in the sea wall.

We saw our first French civilian shortly after this. He was standing on the Western Wall, out in the open ignoring all the missiles whizzing around . . . the Frenchman looked typical in his black beret and light blue overalls. He was gesticulating and shouting, I presumed greetings to all of us, and we waved back. He certainly looked elated – I wish we felt the same.

C. R. Wampach stormed a German pill box with the Canadians.

Some 100 yards away they spotted a group of civilians standing together at the side of the road. When asked what the hell they were doing there, they replied that they were waiting for a bus!

A few miles up the coast, 23-year-old Philippe de Bourgoing, having put out the chairs for the German officers' concert at Chateau Tracy the night before, cycled up to the cliffs when he heard bombing. The sea was so full of ships Philippe could scarcely see the water. He pedalled furiously home and told his family.

It's the liberation, we have not long to wait.

One image stuck with J. E. Davies, 3rd Battalion Scots Guards, after he dashed inland from Gold Beach.

> I came to a pasture on a small hill on whose flank lay a dead Coldstream Guardsman. Near him was a more mature Coldstreamer digging a grave. I recognised his type, a long-serving soldier with no promotional prospects nor home or family other than the army, performing his 'dug in' job of Dan Dan the sanitary man. He dug his unit's latrine pits when in harbour and graves for those killed in action. Every battalion had a Dan.
>
> I looked at the dead Coldie; he was sprawled on his back with arms flung out and knees slightly bent, his webbing straps biting into him as his corpse distended under the hot sun. His chin was missing, and a beard of blowflies buzzed there instead, his upper teeth startling white against the busy dark background. Dan the sanitary man paused in his labours to watch me go by, removing his steel helmet to wipe sweat off his brow.

The absurdity of war was never far away, as John Emrys Williams, HMS *Diadem*, noted in his diary just after D-Day.

> This morning the Commander gave us the daftest talk on the loudspeakers. He complained about us wearing overalls and overcoats during the day and gave us an order that all men must be in the rig of the day and look as smart as possible... fancy worrying about dress when there are hundreds of young fellows losing their lives. What is this, an invasion or beauty competition?

Twenty-year-old Private William Hershel Nelson from Camden, Maine, was one of thousands of American troops landing on the five miles of Omaha Beach. The ridges above Omaha gave German machine-gunners elevation for their line of fourteen gun-emplacements. A second string of armed bunkers closer to the beach added to their defensive capability. The mood on the ship carrying William and the 315th Infantry Division was uneasy.

> The sky was overcast but occasionally I could see the odd star shining through the breaks in the mist. The whole ship seemed to reflect an omen of disaster, for everyone on this craft had no doubt that terrible trouble lay ahead... here and there I could hear weeping... 'Get me out of here,' yelled a young private. 'I don't want to die, please would someone help me?'
>
> The mist began to clear, and one was able to see the brightness of the sun just clearing the edge of the horizon. This was when we heard the machine guns. The Germans were shooting at the first wave trying to land on the beach. Two boats to the right of ours were blown completely out of the water, leaving debris and parts of bodies floating on the sea. It would be impossible for me to describe the yells of pain, and the death cries of the wounded.
>
> All at once the front of the landing craft disappeared, breaking in half and also detonating booby traps hanging from the barbed wire, killing nearly everyone at the front... leaving me in the water up to my neck but just able to reach the

bottom of the sands on tiptoes ... the dead were floating all around me and I had to push them away. About a dozen of us survived and at the waterline threw ourselves down amongst the dead bodies being washed up ... In fact, I played dead for it did not take too much working out what the machine-gunners were doing. The Germans were having a picnic ... bodies were floating in the sea as far as I could see ... I would suppose one man in every twenty reached the beach alive.

Plans to bomb craters in the beach for soldiers to shelter in had gone awry, and now the Americans were being killed in such numbers they had to get off the beach, whatever their orders, and take the fight to the enemy.

On this day I knew what it was like to stare a man in the face and kill him, and this stays with me for the rest of my life ... I recall the last man on D-Day whose life I took ... [out of bullets] I did the only thing I could to beat him. I stood the rifle bayonet upwards on the cold hard earth, pulled it from the barrel and threw it at him with all my might. I can remember even today the look on his face as my knife went into his body up to the hilt.

The sheer weight of Allied liberators was eventually too much for the Germans. Even if hundreds of soldiers were cut down on the beaches, there were always more waves to come. The Nazis had plentiful tanks in reserve, but they could not be released to the frontline without Hitler's direct orders, and precious time to summon these reinforcements was lost because the Führer was asleep and could not be disturbed.

D-Day was an astonishing feat of planning and logistics, as well as courage. In all 156,000 men landed or were dropped in Normandy on D-Day. The Mulberry harbours were dragged in prefabricated sections over 100 miles from England and then assembled. Once inside the temporary harbour, floating roadways and bridges enabled ships to unload military vehicles, food, fuel and other essential supplies. It was a remarkable exercise of imagination and engineering. In 100 days, 220,000 soldiers, 530,000 tonnes of supplies and 39,000 vehicles were unloaded at the British Mulberry harbour at Arromanches.

D-Day was the first painful step on the hard road through France, the Low Countries, and into the heart of Germany. An operation of such scale and complexity against a determined enemy came with a high price, with, according to the Commonwealth War Graves Commission, around 10,250 Allied casualties with 4,400 dead and the rest wounded or missing.

Private William Nelson, American 315th Infantry Division, was hit by enemy fire.

> The trickle of blood started to ooze from my leg . . . I also felt sticky around the forehead, reaching above I slipped my helmet off . . . my finger went into a jagged hole that brought blood streaming from my finger.
>
> If it had gone an inch lower, I would not be alive to tell this tale . . . never will I forget the killings I performed nor the hell I went through including details of the blood-stained battles I was engaged in and there are certainly no words to describe the agony I went through. This bloodshed went on for 28 days.

According to the Commonwealth War Graves Commission, there were 3,600 army casualties on Omaha Beach, including 770 killed, plus 539 naval casualties. But there were more to come. D-Day was over, but the Battle of Normandy was only just beginning.

CHAPTER THIRTY-EIGHT

Normandy, 1944

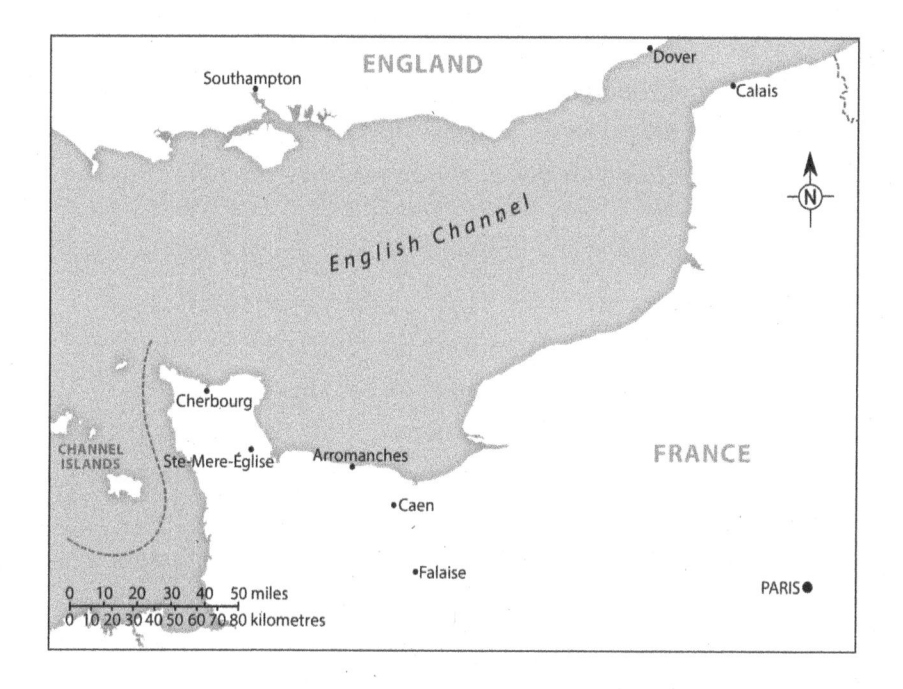

If anyone expected the war to be easy after D-Day, they were wrong. Normandy was to be one of the greatest killing fields on the Western Front. More Allied troops died in the subsequent battles inland than on D-Day itself.

British soldier William Palmer, 11th Hussars, wrote to his parents on 27 June 1944.

> I have had enough excitement out here to last me a lifetime. Shelled from Calais, strafed, mixed up in a two-day tank

battle, shelled, mortared, machine-gunned, sniped, cut off and surrounded, and fought our way out with German infantry within 50 yards of us at times ... and frightened? I have never been so scared in all my life.

Having survived Omaha Beach, Private William Nelson and the remnants of the US Army 315th Infantry Division worked their way inland. They trudged past an ancient farmhouse.

This was where I saw my first dead civilian. The corpse of a woman lay half-in and half-out of a huge puddle ... and as for her age I could only guess, for a tank had run across her head and the smell of death was everywhere. Horses and cows lay bloated, with the dead woman as well, the air made me sick to breathe.

William was soon under enemy fire.

The heavy guns threw everything at us barring the kitchen sink, and bodies of my comrades were floating in the air. I made a dash for a huge hole and jumped in. Another man landed on top of me, and he completely covered my body ... as we both leapt into the hole an 88 shell struck just on the lip of the bank blowing the man on top of me apart ... The place of refuge we had both jumped into was a cesspool and with the stench coming from below and the bloody remains on top of my body I could not move. Then I remember sobbing like a small boy ...

William Nelson dug himself a slit trench. He was soon wakened from sleep by vibrating earth.

To my amazement I saw three Panzer tanks almost upon where I lay ... I lay deadly still and the large, muddy grey tank drove over my hiding place.

A key American objective was liberating the inland town of St Lo, the gateway for American troops to drive into Central France. But the enemy resisted fiercely, using the Norman landscape, the

NORMANDY, 1944

bocage, to their advantage. The small Normandy fields separated by ditches and robust hedgerows around 10-feet tall, led to days of brutal attritional fighting in what was called the Battle of the Hedgerows. This battle was measured field by field, not mile by mile. The thick hedgerows afforded the enemy good cover, and William's friend was killed by a German hiding in a hedge.

> Without thinking I grabbed the German weapon, still smoking, and pulled it towards me... the German fell to the ground just at my feet, but we both had hold of his gun. I released the rifle and as he swung it towards me, I shot him with my own weapon and will always remember his look of surprise as he fell to the ground.

William was then sent ahead to reconnoitre.

> A young man lay against the stump of a tree. A young soldier dressed in a Nazi uniform, but with sightless eyes staring straight ahead... He had been dead for quite a while. I gazed with sadness as I noted, in his outstretched hand, he held a photograph of two little children and a very pretty woman. This was one of the times I felt distressed and bitter with this damn war. I am not ashamed to admit I was sobbing as I trudged away from this scene.
>
> The liberation of St Lo* went beyond expectations, for the inhabitants of this large town acted with a speed that amazed everyone... it became very quiet... 'Thank God for this,' I thought to myself, but I'd no sooner thought it when one of my chums just fell in front of me. As the rifle shot sounded [from the church], I flung myself to the ground just below a gravestone... three German soldiers stood in front of the church door with hands above their head, and the fourth one stood a few yards to the side with smoke coming out of

---

* 18 July 1944 – St Lo was called 'the capital of ruins'.

his rifle. He had already lined his rifle towards me and to my amazement as he pulled the trigger all the weapon did was click. He had a dead shell in the cylinder of his rifle . . . the rifle was dropped, and his hands flung skyward. My friends and myself nearly shot him but I could never shoot an unarmed man.

Joy Taverner (later Trindles) was a Queen Alexandra Nurse in St Lo.

Eventually we landed and were sniped at by the Germans. One of our doctors was killed and an orderly was shot, and we had to amputate his leg at the side of the road. We had to be careful. Everywhere was mined. Lots of dead bodies.

We went to St Lo and put tents up in a field as a frontline hospital. In the operating theatre for three days and nights – only having a few hours off. Polish men, German and Canadians came in, as well as our own troops. I had only the clothes I stood up in so washed my underwear – wrapped them in tissue paper and dried them in the camp oven!

Captain Paul Riley, Royal Army Medical Corps:

I found a 15-year-old French girl in one of the houses who had lost most of her left arm. I bandaged her up. She needed hospital treatment, but the nearest hospital was in Caen, which was still in German hands . . . I said [to her parents] that I thought I could get her to England.

Madeleine, a very brave girl, said she knew the best route to the coast . . . we had probably now crossed into German-held territory . . . I saw a German staff car parked on the road with a German officer sitting in the passenger seat apparently looking at his map. It seemed very odd. He must have heard us but was sitting quite still in the car. We parked the jeep, and I got out and walked up to the car, only to find out he was dead, but sitting quite upright.

How, Paul Riley thought, can we get back across the German lines safely?

> I climbed into the German car next to the dead officer... my driver, with Madeleine in the jeep, led the way, towing the German car. I sat beside the German captain who from a short distance still looked alive, and I steered his car. Shortly before we reached the coast, I met our front line, greatly to the surprise of the British Officer in Command who was wondering what to do with a British jeep towing a German staff car being steered by a British officer with a German officer sitting next to him! The Germans must have been equally confused because they also didn't fire on us.

Madeleine arrived safely in England.

East from St Lo, the strategically important city of Caen was the gateway for British and Canadian troops into Northern France and onwards to Paris. Caen's capture was expected by Montgomery immediately after D-Day, but a month later was still in Nazi hands. It was only on 9 July that Allied troops entered Caen, a ruined city following a brutal Allied air bombardment.

Gunner Ray Dalley witnessed the aftermath of the ferocious battle. He wrote home:

> Caen was big; was prosperous; was peaceful; now, it is a mere skeleton... thousands of Jerry prisoners are coming in, most of them youngsters. The Officers and the SS men are very arrogant indeed and are kept separate from the rest.
>
> Strewn all alongside the roads were burnt-out wreckage of German cars and tanks... on our journey through France everything eatable was thrown at the kiddies. Biscuits, chocolates and sweets, although these were part of our rations. It hurt me deeply to see the pathetic look upon their faces when the last one had gone... the expression of thanks on their faces was reward enough...

Paratrooper Tim Hardy from Nottinghamshire saw Caen's destruction.

> Caen, the city that the military genii had sworn to liberate within a couple of days... a thousand bombers from my own side unloaded God knows how many bombs on Caen because that city was still held by the Germans! Berlin, it seemed, was still an awfully long way away.

Caen was free, but 20,000 civilians had been killed, more than half of those by Allied bombs. Leaflets were dropped on the city urging its inhabitants to leave, but many went unread, blown away in the wind. Normandy had been sacrificed so the rest of France could be freed. Caen's population was relieved to be liberated but too many had died for this to be a liberation without reserve.

L/C Tony King, Tank Driver:

> The suffering caused by Allied operations was severe; in the main, only the ladies of the night in Bayeux and Caen extended the welcome mat every evening.

Resistance member André Heintz had provided vital information for the Allies but did not escape the bombing.

> The city was practically razed to the ground... there are historians today who say that the bombing of Caen was a crime but even under siege the people of the city did not feel resentful about what was happening. We knew it was necessary for the liberation.

André and his sister volunteered at the local hospital, which they hoped would be safe from bombing.

> I got on board an ambulance to find some of the wounded... I could see a bomb leaving a plane and coming straight towards us. I gave a last look at the people around me, and suddenly there was a massive blast. It felt like we were on a

railway track with the train coming straight at us... we were surrounded by smoke, but it was the house behind us that was hit.

Back at the hospital André tried to make a red cross, which was visible to Allied aircraft.

I went looking for paint, but I couldn't find any. My sister had the idea of dipping some sheets in blood in the operating theatre, and we laid them out in the garden. A reconnaissance plane came over and dipped its wings to signal he had seen the cross.

When André saw his first Allied soldier, he was given food.

That was the most beautiful day of my entire life. I could hardly believe that I had survived the German occupation, and the battle [for Caen]... I thanked God for the privilege of being alive and free again.

Equally painful was the fierce battle for control of a gentle rise in a cornfield near the River Odon to the west of Caen, known as Hill 112. This overlooked the plains south of the city, the route for troops to sweep east. But by 9 July when the Allies entered Caen, Hill 112 was still in German hands, well-fortified and with an SS Panzer Division defending the summit. Capturing the Hill was to take almost a month's more brutal fighting.

Signaller Douglas Burdon, 179th Field Regiment, Royal Artillery, on Hill 112:

Two of our men lay dead in the field. They lay on their backs, with their still-faces turned towards the steel-blue sky from which the blazing July sun scattered its powdered gold over the Normandy countryside.

The older man was a sergeant, perhaps in his early thirties, and his bronze complexion told of a healthy outdoor life. His eyes were wide open, as though he did not quite understand what had happened to him ... there was no mark visible to show how he died.

The younger man, a private, appeared to be no more than a teenager ... his eyes were tightly closed, and a happy grin suffused his fresh young face, as though he had been enjoying a particularly pleasant dream or had been struck down while laughing at a joke. He looked so full of life and fun that I half-expected him to leap to his feet at any moment and make some humorous comment; but a shell splinter had sliced a triangular piece of bone from the middle of his forehead and exposed part of the brain. A big, ugly fly was crawling over the wound, its wings spread upwards from its metallic blue body rubbing its legs together as though in gleeful anticipation and jabbing its sucker on to the brain cells with obvious relish.

The British did not finally control Hill 112 until early August. About 7,000 troops died in those gentle Normandy fields before the Allies were ascendant.

The Allied soldiers were well-supported from the air. Normandy wheat fields were transformed into runways for the RAF and constant strafing and bombing of Nazi supply lines kept the enemy short of ammunition and other supplies. Allied reinforcement of men and materials, on the other hand, flowed steadily through the Mulberry harbour at Arromanches.*

This is where Margaret Boothroyd and Laura Mountney,† WREN teleprinter operators in the D-Day War Room, landed in Normandy to work closer to the action. As they were under 21, they needed their parents' permission.

---

* A second American-built Mulberry harbour was not as resilient and was destroyed in a storm.

† After the war, Laura Mountney became Laura Ashley, world-famous designer and businesswoman.

Netting and ladders were thrown over the side and we clambered down from the ship onto the Mulberry harbour at Arromanches.

There were some women in Granville with shaven heads . . . they had fraternised with the Nazis. Now, this does not seem a great crime and for some of those women life must have been very difficult . . . The town was quite desolate. There were still dead bodies and many derelict properties.

With so much brutal fighting it was no wonder Normandy's orchards were dotted with field hospitals. Dorothea Chisholm, a Queen Alexandra's Nurse, even found herself nursing soldiers from Hitler Youth.

Many of them came to us with limbs already amputated by their own doctors. We were told it was German medical policy, if the wound looked nasty, to simply take off the limb in the field. They were really young, 16 or 17 . . . You wanted to feel sorry for them, but they were so unpleasant it was hard.

From field hospitals like Dorothea's, patients were transported to hospital ships waiting off the Normandy coast to ferry the injured to Southampton. Patrick Manning was a galley boy on the SS *Amsterdam*.

There was a muffled explosion, the lights went out, and the ship listed . . . there was a horrible smell of ether in the air . . . it was a nightmare . . . I could hear a lot of screaming and shouting.

Two nurses, Sister Anyta Field and Sister Mollie Evershed, bravely helped carry 75 wounded patients from the swiftly sinking *Amsterdam* to the lifeboats. They tried one final rescue, witnessed by Patrick Manning.

I looked around and could see wounded soldiers jumping over the side, and there were two people stuck in portholes. I was told afterwards they were nurses.

The two nurses had died attempting that last rescue.*

In Normandy Jock Walker's appreciation for the medical staff deepened.

> People just don't realise the horrific wounds that frontline doctors and their staff have to deal with ... these men are amongst the noblest of beings ... people think that wounds and death are caused by neat little bullet holes, all very tidy and noble but that is not so. Can you imagine a man with his jaw shot off? Or his stomach ripped by a jagged piece of mortar and his tripes strewn all over the place?

Back in England, Jean Bowman had good cause to remember the name Caen. Her husband, Albert Rule, 12th King's Royal Rifle Corps, was one of the thousands who clambered ashore onto the D-Day beaches. A few months before Jean herself had given birth to their first child.

> I had one letter from him about a week before D-Day and then no more after. It was in August I got a letter saying he was missing but could be a prisoner-of-war ... a fortnight later I got another letter, and my dad offered to open it, but I opened it myself. The first thing I saw was a death certificate. He had been killed on July 26th, one day after his 27th birthday in Jessel Wood near Caen.†
>
> But his personal belongs they sent me were disgusting. It was writing paper and envelopes that had been in the sea (when they were going ashore in France) and a pullover with the back all bullet holes, that was all.

If there were still significant battles in Normandy for the British and Canadians after the liberation of Caen, progress was not

---

* There are over 22,000 names on the British Normandy Memorial. These are the only two women.

† Ten years later Jean Bowman remarried.

easy for the Americans after the capture of St Lo either. Private William Nelson was caught in a well-planned German ambush but survived.

> 'God, buddy,' spoke an unshaven man next to me. 'We came very close to hell.' I looked at him. 'Close to hell. My friend, we are in hell.'

As medical teams picked up the wounded, William Nelson and Private Jones went ahead to scout out the enemy.

> We were very close to the forest and a very dark mist hung over the tall trees making it difficult to see anything. The two of us approached a very large clump of evergreens and a shot was heard. Looking to my right, my friend was spread-eagled on the ground, with his rifle still clutched to his side... I almost felt the bullet as it passed my head... there was only one thing to do, 'play dead'... fifteen minutes later a German appeared. He walked over to Private Jones, kicked him, then turned him over to look at his face to see if he was dead. He seemed quite satisfied and approached me. He drew his long-booted leg to kick me and then he realised I was only play-acting. He raised his rifle up, but he was too damn slow... I got in first and shot him in the upper leg. I could still see the look of disbelief as he stared at the gun pointed inches from his head. Then out of the trees three Germans ran, brandishing their weapons... keeping my trigger finger as it was, I raised my other arm to make a slicing movement at the Jerries neck. They stopped suddenly, shouting, *'Nein, nein, nein.'* And all the Germans dropped their weapons and raised their arms above their heads.

As darkness fell, some soldiers dug foxholes, but William was so weary he just slept behind a hedge in a field full of cows. It was the right decision.

> The place we were digging in was a death trap, the Germans knew we were in the field and all they had to do was wait for daylight . . . mortar shell and artillery shells were exploding all around our hiding places. The poor cows seemed to be floating in the air and where they once stood, I could only see pools of blood . . . tiny flecks of animal blood were landing on my face . . . men who had taken two or three hours to build their foxholes were literally being blown out of them. God, whoever thought that this was a safe area probably never had brains . . . the sound of the mortally wounded screaming out in agony made me want to get the hell out of this place of death.
>
> I saw a friend of mine lying on his side with a tourniquet around the top of his thigh. The flow of blood had stopped but he needed treatment. I slung my rifle over my shoulder, stooped down and picked him up . . . with my gun over my shoulder and him in my two arms I carried him away from the battle area. I could not help anyone else, but God knows there were plenty of others needing help that day.

The Americans counter-attacked but the battle was not finished.

> The whole day from start to finish had been a catastrophe . . . I felt the bullet enter my right wrist. I immediately dropped my rifle and, as I fell, blood gushed from the wound. I don't believe I've ever been in such pain.

William Nelson's Battle of Normandy was over.

> Later that evening, my whole arm in a cast, I was driven back once again to see the blue waters of the Channel, with large ships moored offshore . . . I felt a hand on my shoulder and a voice saying, 'Is that you, Buddy?' . . . it was a man I had grown up with. He wore the blue of the Navy . . . he held my hand and chatted to me all the way across the Channel.

Nelson went on to fight the Japanese in the Far East. After the war he settled in England, married, and worked as a hospital porter in South London and a delivery driver in Horley, Surrey.

Luckily for him, paratrooper Tim Hardy from Nottinghamshire, encountered little resistance as he chased the Germans through calvados country,

> Newly freed Normans paraded in front of us dozens of haunted-looking shaven-headed females, demented creatures with the eyes of caged animals. They'd been tried by kangaroo courts and convicted of having 'fraternised with the enemy'. Their summary punishment was to have their heads shorn by thugs wielding old-fashioned cut-throat razors; then, bloodied and horribly disfigured, they were put on display... it was a sickening, uncivilised spectacle but one which nevertheless drew loud applause from a large majority of my fellow liberators.

Everywhere liberation had been followed by head-shaving for women accused of fraternisation. In France alone at least 20,000 women had their head shaved. As historian Anthony Beevor pointed out, the *tondeurs* or head-shavers were not always from the resistance and were sometimes petty collaborators themselves, trying to divert attention from their own crimes. Beevor also noted that some women 'were daubed with tar, some stripped half-naked, some marked with swastikas in paint or lipstick.' No doubt some of the women were falsely accused, and to others fraternisation was the only way of putting food on the table. Many were prostitutes selling their wares to whoever had the money, whether they were local men or the enemy.

Not only had Tim Hardy been appalled by mass shavings of women's heads, but desperately keen to get at Hitler's throat, Normandy had also been a disappointment from the killing perspective.

Head-shaving, Marseilles, 1945

I'd flown out of England as one of the nation's military elite – the most macho of its machismo and hyped up to a crazy pitch of blood lust, my company had spearheaded the greatest cross-water military action in history. But back in England I walked away from a DC3 with my ammunition bandoliers unopened and my gun barrel as virginal as my body.

Not everyone was as fortunate. In August the last major battle in Normandy was fought south of Caen in what was known as the Falaise Pocket. About 100,000 Germans were virtually encircled here, and the only escape route for them was through a narrow corridor a few miles wide.

In the fierce fighting in the Falaise Pocket the tanks of the 4th Canadian Armoured Division were heavily hit when some of them took a wrong turn. Stan Scislowski, Perth Regiment:

> It was soon to be a killing ground – a graveyard for the flesh and blood of the British Columbia Regiment. They were about to fight to their finish, powerful elements of the 12th SS Panzer (Hitler Youth), many of them teenagers devoid of

principle and compassion, as ruthless as any soldiers can be. They thought nothing of shooting [prisoners] in cold blood.*

Tank after tank took killing hits. Some became horrific cauldrons in which crews were killed at the moment the armour-piercing shot slammed through their turrets, screamed their way into eternity as their bodies were consumed by flames. The hill shuddered and thundered to the drum-roll bark of tank cannons, the rending crash of mortar bombs, and the non-stop cackle of small arms fire. It was the hell of hells on earth.

Forty soldiers from the British Columbia Regiment were killed, 80 wounded and 34 captured.

Veteran of Dunkirk, North Africa and Sicily, Sergeant Jock Walker's colourful military career took a new twist. He had already been a Despatch Rider, Vehicle Mechanic/Driver and parachutist when he spotted a notice.

> It simply said: *Parachutists required to volunteer as Cameramen.*
>
> Nothing more, no clues to what it meant. So, in my usual fashion for volunteering for anything that took my fancy, I applied ... along with some others; waited awhile, still clueless as to what we were to do, and then six of us received our marching orders, to of all places Pinewood Studios, Iver Heath, Buckinghamshire.
>
> We didn't know an F-stop from a roll of film, that's how ignorant we were, but the instructors were patient and taught us a very high standard.

In this new role Sergeant Gordon 'Jock' Walker of No5 Army Film and Photographic Unit[†] photographed the slaughter at the Falaise

---

* Some were only 15. They shot 11 Canadian prisoners in the back of the head on 7 June at Ardennes Abbey.

† Forty AFPU cameramen were killed in the Second World War.

Pocket. When soldiers discovered that Jock was going into battle armed with a camera, they said:

'Bloody *hell*.'

Of course we were armed, officially with a pistol . . . but I have always maintained that if you were close enough to use a pistol you are too damned close, so I carried an American carbine, very light, very accurate semi-automatic which I had acquired, and a pair of hand grenades, whenever I was going to be at the sharp end . . . and wearing my red beret.

Usually, the paras fought wearing their berets. I am certain when the Germans saw one, they got the wind up [them].

The enemy casualties were very noticeable; heads, arms, trunks, bits of this and that, were strewn everywhere.

Mind you it made some very good pictures, especially if arranged a bit artistically, but that bit was never published. I wonder why? . . . but what is wrong with a bit of visual proof that our boys are helping the Wehrmacht in their wish to die for their country?

Some Wehrmacht soldiers escaped the Falaise Pocket when it was not closed quickly enough, but the rest were fatally trapped, as Jock witnessed.

Killing ground was no exaggeration at all; the enemy were trapped and couldn't get out and our people were knocking seven different kinds of shit out of them. Artillery was literally firing point blank into the area, the tanks were giving them stick, and the RAF were thumping their tanks into scrap metal . . . And so it went on until the Germans surrendered and left the road open to Belgium and Holland.

When the fighting finished I went touring round the killing area to see if there was anything to put on film that hadn't been done already; there was the usual wreckage of war, the hundreds of dead, the burnt-out tanks, some with a driver killed trying to get out of the hatch, the outside half of him more or less whole, the inside bit just a bit of charred nothing – and the smell. Phew!

We saw a sight I had never seen before, it was a young German, stark naked, lying on top of a girl who was also 'starkers' and it was obvious what they had been doing, they were both as dead as doormats but without a sign of injury. We reckoned they had been killed by blast and whether he was a rapist, or they were lovers, we will never know . . .

Tank Driver Tony King was horrified by Falaise's aftermath.

Smelling the decaying human and horse flesh after the massacre of the Falaise Gap . . . mile after mile of dead bodies and abandoned equipment . . . by an odd quirk of human nature we were more saddened by the dead and dying horses than by the mangled human corpses.

King shot a young German sniper who tried to break cover.

The killing I had contributed to seemed impersonal when caused by shells or machine gun bullets, but this was different . . . like me, he was a young man around 20 . . . I had difficulty holding back the tears as I searched his pockets for identification . . . what a stupid, futile business war was.

Estimates are that 10,000–15,000 Germans were killed in the Falaise Pocket, with up to 50,000 taken prisoner. General Dwight Eisenhower described the 'killing fields' where 'it was literally possible to walk for hundreds of yards at a time, stepping on nothing but dead and decaying flesh.'

CHAPTER THIRTY-NINE

Ron Homes's War, 1944

While Allied troopers pushed their way through Normandy after D-Day, British and American bombers continued to pound German cities, destroying their war machine and terrorising civilians at the same time. The People's War archive contains a bomber pilot's diary which describes just one night. His words speak eloquently for all Bomber Command aircrew.

On 12 August 1944, the day the Battle of the Falaise Pocket started in Normandy, Pilot Officer Ron Homes, 101 Squadron, Bomber Command, was preparing to bomb Germany from RAF Ludford Magna in rural Lincolnshire. On arrival at 101, one pilot remembers being told, 'Your expectation of life is six weeks. Go back to your huts and make your wills.' On this night, Ron's normal seven-man crew* is joined by an additional member on 'Special Duties' carrying an 'Airborne Cigar', a secret radio for jamming Luftwaffe radio transmissions. These radios were manned by German-speaking, often Jewish, operators.

> The sun is shining, the weather looks fine, and the morning air is heavy with the scent of new-mown hay and life seems very sweet. With a jolt we wake to reality. Our names are on the Operations Board for tonight! . . . oh hell, our own Lancaster L-Love is still unserviceable. You develop a fondness for your own aircraft, it just feels right . . . the change of

---

* Pilot, navigator, flight engineer, bomb-aimer, mid-gunner, rear-gunner.

Ron Homes with his crew, Ron back right.

aircraft does nothing to settle that nasty sinking feeling, and the thoughts of whether you will see this sunshine tomorrow have to be quickly dismissed. Don't think like that! Think of something else. Anything, but don't show fear.

Ron and his crew cycle out to the aircraft for final checks.

The bowsers, heavy with fuel, are approaching the aircraft to fill up their tanks with thousands of gallons of 100 octane fuel. Following them come the 'trains' of bomb trolleys with the various bombs on board.

Behind all the Nissan huts further up on the hill a tractor is working in one of the fields and its muted engine noise joins in with the birdsong and the warm air is full of the heavy smell of new-mown grass. Life seems so good you wouldn't think there was a bloody war on . . . I wish I didn't have to fly tonight!

Then it is lunch.

The smell of food being cooked is a bit hard to take and I would rather go to the bar for a swift drink, but I need to keep a clear head for tonight. Just take a deep breath and go into the dining room and try to do justice to the steak and kidney pie and boiled cabbage . . . oh dear!! . . . I might be able to manage a little sleep this afternoon. I should really try because it will probably be near dawn tomorrow before I have a chance to sleep again. Oh, dear, I wonder what will happen between now and then? I wonder if there will be a 'then'?

Our proficiency in our respective jobs and the camaraderie between us helps to build confidence. The jokes are a little too loud and are rather forced but they will get worse as the day goes on as the anxiety gnaws away at our insides...

The day hangs heavily for Ron and his crew. There are old magazines to be listlessly flicked through, an hour's sleep to be grabbed, and more food to be eaten. It is a long wait until the 7.30 p.m. briefing.

'Tonight's target is Russelheim between Mainz and Frankfurt... it's the Opel motor works we have to flatten, gentlemen, in order to reduce Hitler's already shortening war supplies even further. There will be 450 aircraft on the raid and as usual this squadron will be timed evenly through the bomber stream... take off at 21.30 p.m.... hit the target hard, and good luck chaps.'

All kitted up and ready to go we file out to the crew buses. Nerves are stretched to breaking point now... we drop off crews at their respective aircraft with loud shouts of 'farewell' and 'good luck' and 'see you in the morning'.

In the cool light of the evening, the aircraft stand there, big, black and menacing against a turquoise sky... Stan, our Flight Engineer, and I go round the aircraft doing the external checks... settling into the pilot's seat on the parachute, buckling it on and doing up the seat belt, my hands are shaking a bit... helmet on, plug into the intercom and connect oxygen, check the instrument panel, switch on the radio.

On the intercom Ron checks his crew's readiness.

'Pilot to Rear Gunner, OK'... 'Right, start-up number one.' The big prop turns slowly with a whining noise, it kicks and with a cloud of exhaust smoke it bursts into life with that deep-throated roar. Number two-three-four. All engines running now, all gauges OK... all the crew are working like clockwork, going through the actions they have been well trained to do... you can feel the confidence building, the butterflies being flushed out.

The light is beginning to fade and other Lancasters are rolling along the perimeter track, big and black with their navigation lights on... the usual group of well-wishers are gathered at the end of the runway. All ranks, Officers, Airmen and WAAFS, all with friends and loved ones taking off into the evening sky, perhaps never to be seen again.

The aircraft is throbbing, the roar from the four engines is deafening. Airspeed is building, '60. 80. 90 mph' is called out by the Flight Engineer... the full, massive weight of 2,000 gallons of fuel and six tons of bombs makes itself felt through the controls and the end of the runway gets nearer and nearer. If one engine fails now, we would run off the end and the whole lot would blow up and leave [a] nasty hole in the ground... all the rumbling and shaking stops, and we are airborne, just in time to see the end of the runway slide away underneath... 'Undercarriage up. Undercarriage up,' responds the Flight Engineer.

The higher we climb the brighter it gets and now the low-setting sun glistens on our Perspex and that of a swarm of Lancasters all gathering around us and going our way. The sky ahead is deep indigo with the oncoming night and the coastline is just visible in the grey mist below. Another crew check and everybody is OK except Smithy the rear-gunner who can't see a thing with the setting sun in his eyes. I tell him not to look at it in case it spoils his night vision. We shall need all the good eyes we can muster to look out for enemy fighters and to avoid collisions with friendly aircraft.

With a steady drone we climb into the darkness as the outside world fades away with the cold, now invisible sea, two and a half miles below. It's warm in this part of the aircraft now and one could begin to feel that the rest of the world does not exist, just this cocoon of metal with the instruments glowing comfortably.

The bomb-aimer spots another Lancaster a shade too close ahead.

I make some adjustments to avoid him. It's not healthy to creep behind another aircraft, a twitchy rear gunner is likely to think you are an enemy fighter and give you the benefit of his four Brownings . . . such a waste to be shot down by a friendly aircraft.

Ron's regular crew checks punctuate the night.

Everybody is fully occupied with their own job and deep in their own thoughts . . . my eyes sweep the green, glowing instruments again and again, then into the inky black sky all OK – just saw another sparkle of exploding anti-aircraft fire ahead. It looks quite pretty from here, but it won't when we get nearer.

Again, another Lancaster in this Armada is too close.

Staring into the black night sky to hold onto a black smudge while you're searching for other black smudges which could turn out to be a lot more sinister is very tiring, but if we can spot them first, we stand a chance of living . . . onwards into the blackness relieved only by the red glow from the port inner engine. They always seem to be uncomfortably bright on these very dark nights, 'Pilot to Navigator, we must be getting close to the turning point now.'

Suddenly a bright orange ball of fire lights up the sky about [a] quarter of a mile on the port beam when a Lancaster and its full fuel and bomb load disintegrates, 'Some poor sods have bought it, Skip.' 'Pilot to Mid-upper, OK, we can see it.'

Onward we drone with the aircraft swinging slightly from side to side as the gunners swing their turrets in endless searching of the blackness. Eyes staring into the night sky... what's that... a faint patch of light. What the? Of course, it's the moon just coming up behind a patch of cloud.

Only ten minutes to the target now! You can feel the tension growing, five pairs of eyes constantly searching the blackness... eight minutes to go and some green target indicators start to go down way out in front... 'Searchlights and a bit of flak coming up now.' Suddenly there is a concentrated load of flak finishing with a bright orange ball as another Lancaster is hit. 'Another one's got the chop, Skipper,' somebody shouts over the intercom.

Ron Homes tunes into the frequency for the Master Bomber, as other Lancasters drop their bombs.

Fires begin to light the night sky over the target and more flak is coming up ahead. Five minutes to run now... we slowly, oh so slowly, advance towards that huge dome of fire. Exploding anti-aircraft shells sparkle in clusters like iron filings dropped in a flame, just at our level but a little ahead. The fires begin to reflect a glow on the underside of the aircraft and other Lancasters come into view like little black toys silhouetted over the fires of the target.

'Roger, bomb-aimer over to you.' 'Roger, bomb doors open skipper'... a slight change of trim as the two massive doors under the aircraft open, fluttering into the slipstream and a tremble comes up through the controls. Everything has to be very steady now... I hold it at 073 degrees, brilliant flashes in the target as bombs burst, sending out concentric ripples in the fires below. The tension mounts, everybody seems to be holding their breath... CRUMP, CRUMP, two shells burst near enough to be heard above the roar of the engines.

Flashes from exploding shells seem to be all around us now. The bomb-aimer instructions become more frequent 'right ... steady ... left-left ... steady ... steady ... s.t.e.a.d.y ... s.t.e.a.d.y ... BOMBS GONE!' Donk, Donk, Donk go the bombs, as they are released from their hooks and the aircraft rears up as its massive six-ton load drops away... keep her steady now for a long, oh so long, two minutes, while the flak bursts seem to be getting closer and closer, until the photo flash goes off and the camera takes a picture of where our bombs would strike. BOMB DOORS CLOSED

You can sense the massive release of tension in the crew as the engine's roar takes on a higher note and the airspeed builds up to get away from the target area and out of the flak as fast as possible.

Homes checks his crew once more.

'Right chaps, everybody's OK, let's go home' ... there is comfort in the steady drone of the engines now and quite an elated feeling at having survived another target, and we are on our way home. Suddenly, the Mid-upper Gunner shouts 'FIGHTER'. I slam on the full-left rudder, control column forward and hard to port, his guns begin to chatter and instantly the plane is shaken by a series of dull thumps. What a strange noise – WE'VE BEEN HIT! A brilliant orange light fills the cockpit. 'Starboard outers on fire,' shouts the Engineer. 'There's a bloody great flame going past the tailplane,' shouts the Mid-upper. We must be a choice target now, lit up in the night sky like a flaming comet and if we don't get this fire out, WE'VE HAD IT!

The flaming engine is shut down and the crew grab fire extinguishers. Two other engines shut down of their own accord.

They need to urgently calculate how much fuel is left and exactly where their Lancaster is in the night sky. The Engineer works out that there is just 90 minutes of fuel remaining.

> 'Navigator, would you take a guess at our ETA for Base.' 'Navigator to pilot, my guess is about one hour fifty.' 'Roger Navigator, that seems a bit tight.' . . . without hydraulics, no flaps, possibly no brakes and a chance of a dodgy undercarriage, an emergency field seems to be the answer.

The crew set course for an emergency landing at RAF Woodbridge, Suffolk, which has a two-mile runway.

> Is it getting darker? . . . I think it is . . . 'The fire's going out, Skip.' . . . we have lost a lot of height, and we are now down to 10,000 feet and won't be able to maintain that just on one engine . . . I become conscious of the sweat on my back and a dryness in my mouth and a growing determination to get this lot back. Please God, I don't want to end up in a prison camp.

Ron must restart engines. If he can.

> The big propeller by my left-hand window slowly begins to turn as it becomes unfeathered, a couple of blue flashes from the exhaust and she winds up to 1,200 revs. I get the thumbs up from the engineer. Another hurdle over!

The Lancaster has lost 300 or 400 gallons of fuel, and all its guns are out of action. And Ron's crew don't know where they are.

> Suddenly a hundred searchlights pierce the night sky, forming an impenetrable fence of light . . . one catches us like a moth in a flame, the whole cockpit is lit up with a brilliant blue-white light. Immediately five or six others join in, and we are coned, a sitting target . . . no German guns fire! Not one! That could only mean that there are fighters in the vicinity and the searchlights are holding us as a sitting target for them. I've got

to get out of these lights. Another heave on the controls into a vicious diving steep turn to port.

The lights continue sweeping and searching as we weave our way through them ... nearly through and out to sea ...

Below they make out the shape of an island: Walcheren, Holland. At least they now know their location. Woodbridge is 44 minutes away.

Onward through the night, the engines keeping up the continuous drone ... we must keep wide awake for we are not home yet. It would be a shame to be shot down on the last leg and the thought of all that cold black sea underneath us sends a chill down my back and a longing for a warm bed. 'Roger, fifteen minutes to run now.' ... ahead all is dark until we see a glimmer of light flashing, yes, the beacon at Woodbridge. 'Woodbridge, NAN Squared, landing instructions please ...' 'What is your damage, over?' ... 'Three engines, no hydraulics, undercarriage suspect, your runway in sight, over.'

The crew can only see one green light. They peer optimistically out of the aircraft with a torch. The starboard leg looks down, but no one can be sure, and even if it's down, will it hold for landing?

As they prepare to land, the control tower scuppers their plan.

'Roger NAN Squared, can you do another circuit and be number two for landing, we have another aircraft in distress.' 'NAN Squared, Wilco.' Blast! I guess they don't want us doing a wheels up landing and blocking the runway. Ease over to starboard to fly upwind with the runway lights looking very inviting down on the port side.' 'Pilot to crew, hang on chaps we are doing a circuit.'

They complete a very tense circuit. Finally, it is their turn.

This is it; will that undercarriage stay down? Round we go again to the left in a gentle turn with the perimeter lights sliding away underneath, reduce power to start a gradual descent. I can sense everybody holding their breath... 'Engineer, I will land slightly port wing low to keep the weight on the port wheel as long as I can. As soon as I feel the starboard leg collapsing, I will shout "Undercarriage up", OK?' 'OK Skip, I'm holding the lever.'

The runway lights slowly come round into line as though the land below is twisting, and we are standing still. 'NAN Squared, Finals.' 'NAN Squared, clear to land.' Glide path indicator showing green, now changing red, GETTING TOO LOW increase power... that's it, airspeed 130, back in green... runway suddenly approaches rapidly... end of runway coming up... 'Pilot to Crew, BRACE, BRACE'. Back gently on the control column, left wing low, ease off power, back, back, power off... with a slight squeal the port wheel touches the ground... rumbling along faster than usual, the starboard wing gently sinks and as the wheel touches, we hold our breath and IT HOLDS!

Silence, everything is still while everybody digests the fact that we have survived and slowly we start to unbuckle our seat belts and parachutes and gather our bits and pieces and start to make our way to the exit door... 'OK, Stan, we made it!' 'Yes, Skip, I'm glad the undercarriage did not fold up'... we should be cheering and shouting but we don't, we just climb into the crew bus which takes us over to a welcome cup of coffee, a tot of rum, and a debriefing... at four o'clock we fall into bed and sleep the sleep of the exhausted.

Next day no aircraft can be spared, so the crew must return to RAF Ludford Magna by train, via London.

We are a motley bunch in our flying boots, Mae-Wests and parachutes etc. as we board the train for London where we found we have missed our connection to Lincoln and have to stay overnight. Who's complaining? I live in London and so do two others, so we make our way through the underground and on buses, six of us to my home where I can be with my wife.

It feels as if we are invisible and nobody knows that a few hours ago we were over Germany in an aircraft in flames, facing oblivion. Oh well, we won't tell them, we will just go on enjoying the fact that it's good to be alive and hope we can survive the next twelve operations.

That wasn't quite the end of the story. Before the war Ron was an art student at Willesden until he joined up aged 18. Ron survived 31 operations over enemy territory and later flew in India, Burma and Japan. He was awarded the DFC (Distinguished Flying Cross). His chance of surviving so many ops without being posted missing was less than 50 per cent. After the war he became a teacher of art and industrial design and used his artistic skills to paint this portrayal of that night. He called it *Against All Odds.* *

Against All Odds by Ron Homes

---

* 101 suffered one of the highest casualty rates of any squadron in Bomber Command.

CHAPTER FORTY

Intelligence and SOE

The contrast between the bloodbath of Normandy, or the claustrophobic intensity of a night-bomber raid, and the quiet Buckinghamshire countryside where Bletchley Park was housed could not be more marked. But winning the Battle of Normandy, smashing the German war factories and successful codebreaking at Bletchley Park to forewarn the Allies of Nazi military plans were all vital to winning the war.

Kathleen Godrey was the daughter of Admiral John Godfrey, Director of Naval Intelligence, one of the early architects of Operation Mincemeat. He may also have been the model for M in the James Bond books, as author Ian Fleming was Godfrey's right-hand man. Kathleen was not considered for university, both because it was wartime, and because she was a woman.

> I don't remember any discussion about my future, and it was decided that the easiest thing was to send me to what was called a Domestic Science School... for a few months I endured this dreadful place.

Then Kathleen joined the RAF as an Aircraftswoman Second Class.

> After six weeks training, I was a radio operator... I was sent to Ventnor, high on the southern cliffs of the Isle of Wight, one of a chain of radar stations looking out over the channel

towards France... we worked underground in shifts, far from any airfield.

After almost a year on radar stations I was moved to Bletchley Park in Buckinghamshire, where a large team of Army, Navy and Air Force personnel as well as civilians had been working on breaking the Enigma code used by Germany for all the operational messages on land and in the U-Boats. Secrecy about our work was of the utmost importance... how such a secret was kept when so many people knew about it, remains one of the war's great mysteries and triumphs.

Cambridge University graduate Joy Higgins (later Russell) also worked at Bletchley Park.

Bletchley Park, BP, Station X, Ultra, Enigma, they were names that meant nothing to the world at large then, or for 30 years to come. National security and the Official Secrets Act saw to that.

The servicemen were greatly outnumbered by the civilians, who were mainly women. They came – service and civilian – from many walks of life. Authors – I remember Charles Morgan and Angus Wilson – diplomats, bankers, journalists, university professors, teachers.

I signed the Official Secrets Act, was issued with a pass, and told where the cafeteria was. I was told that my pay would be £3.15s per week, plus a 'war bonus' of ten shillings.

In theory, the messages sent by Enigma were unbreakable, it was the human element that was fallible, and successes came from that. But it meant weeks, even months, of patient work to have any success in breaking further codes and some, indeed, remained unbreakable... it was a thrill when something I had worked on came out.

We both loved working at Bletchley Park.* Nothing would ever compare with it. It had been a wonderful place to work: a

---

* Joy met her husband at Bletchley Park.

classless society where brains, application and enthusiasm were criteria. The ethos of Bletchley meant that women were treated as equals – years ahead of any 'politically correct' dictates.

But codebreaking was not solely dependent on the specialist skills at Bletchley Park. When British destroyers sank a German U-Boat off Egypt, the German submariners abandoned ship. Lillian Henderson (née Brown):

> [My brother] Thomas Brown was the only one of three men who swam across to the U-Boat to survive. Before the U-Boat sank suddenly, the men recovered numerous documents that turned out to be Enigma codebooks that were invaluable to the codebreakers at Bletchley Park. The two men who were lost, Lt Anthony Fasson and Able Seaman Colin Grazier were both awarded the George Cross posthumously, while Thomas Brown was awarded the George Medal.

Helen Ouin's intelligence unit was housed at Wormwood Scrubs prison.

> In the first 24 hours several people managed to get themselves locked in their cell . . . our stay was abruptly interrupted when the building was bombed . . . so Churchill decided that our next residence should be Blenheim Palace . . . MI5 had a number of interesting people working for them, including Anthony Blunt, one of the Russian agents who was working with Burgess, Philby and Maclean . . . he used to take us round the palace giving us lectures on the contents, and was a most charming man.

Spying was not the exclusive province of the British. A young Canadian called 'Trixie' was an RAF plotter billeted with the Huddart family in Newcastle.

> I don't know how my mother became suspicious, but when she waited up for Trixie, the lady who let herself in was

unrecognisable to my mother, long hair, very well made-up features ... it was later revealed that the trunk in her bedroom contained a false bottom hidden therein were not only wigs, stage make-up and clothes, but the letters she had been receiving from her 'brother' in Canada, actually written in German and from her Controller in Germany, sent to Canada and reposted to England ... my sister and I were sent into the garden while her arrest was made.

Another spy was unmasked at Hinderwell, North Yorkshire.

An elderly lady took temporary lodgings but when the landlady, Hannah Jackson, hung out her washing, she noticed secret pockets sewn into the hem

The spy was found carrying maps and coastal charts and was arrested by the local bobby.

He also discovered, to general astonishment, that the old lady was actually a man.

Morton Bisset started a forgery unit for the Special Operations Executive (SOE).

My staff originally consisted of just three Polish civilians, only one of whom spoke any English, who had probably been doing similar work in Poland before the war; but with the recruitment of technicians from the Royal Engineers Survey companies; a handwriting expert from New Scotland Yard; an engraver from the De La Rue stamp and banknote printers, we were able to get into production.

We fully realised that agents' lives were at risk, so every effort was made to ensure the documents looked really authentic. To this end no expense was spared ... we faithfully reproduced all the imperfections on the original documents and had, at times, to age certain documents artificially to make them look genuinely old.

War opened opportunities for inventors that had not existed before. Ideas once seen as eccentric were suddenly funded. In Bedford, Major Cecil Clarke was in the forefront of inventiveness. His son:

> My father had been engaged in the design of a limpet mine, a new form of weapon for sinking ships. This had been dreamed up in conjunction with Stuart Macrae, the editor of *Science Armchair Magazine* and also a trailer and caravan magazine... both were brilliant at lateral thinking and the two men, within about a month, had evolved a practicable Mark-1 type of limpet mine.
>
> It was very much Bedford home-made. The two men visited Woolworths, and they got washing-up bowls made of spun aluminium to contain the explosives. They raided all the sweet shops in Bedford for aniseed balls that were used as a time delay for setting off the explosives... the aniseed balls were drilled with holes, and little detonator capsules put inside, and my father had these ranged around the house, setting them off at different times depending on the amount of aniseed ball that was used on each detonator.
>
> The local school swimming baths was used for tests. My father gallantly undertook these tests himself with a steel plate strapped to his tummy and the charge on the limpet mine attached to it.

Clarke's inventions were not confined to the swimming pool. Having moved on from aniseed balls to more sophisticated means of time delay, Clarke was involved in sabotaging an enemy-occupied power station.

> This consisted of saboteurs taking explosive charges, rather like miniature limpet mines; they were attached on a plate on the back of the saboteur, four charges could then be taken

into a power station, if you could evade the guard and plant them on the transformers to go off.

This was an extremely effective attack. It took place at a power station at Pessac, just south of Bordeaux... close by, controlled by this power station supply, were U-Boat pens for German submarine operations out in the Atlantic... the U-Boat pens were put out of action for several months.

My father at that time was also responsible, with another officer, for training the team of Czechs who carried out the assassination of Heydrich, the Nazi administrator of Czechoslovakia... dreadful aftermath, of course, with the death of all the saboteurs but also the blowing up of the village of Lidice and a great deal of misery as a result.*

Lance-Bombardier Walter Bowman, Inter Services Research Bureau (ISRB), would have been good with aniseed balls. Among the Walter's projects were:

A prototype of a small folding motorbike that could be dropped in a parachute container and to be used by paratroopers... the design and development of a miniature one-man submarine... an underwater canoe called The Sleeping Beauty... and a three-man submarine called The Welfreighter.

But the intelligence services also deployed low-technology solutions. Freddy Dyke, the National Pigeon Service:

Against the occupied countries of Europe, some 16,800 of our birds were parachuted to Allied SOE agents and only 1,280 returned with their message containers... [this] shows the very special duty that the birds were expected to perform

---

* Nazi reprisals wiped Lidice out, with about 340 men, women and children either shot or later gassed in concentration camps.

and the dangers that they faced in these operations under extremely hazardous conditions.

Pigeons also sometimes travelled with RAF crews.

> A pigeon called White Vision was responsible for saving 11 members of the crew of an RAF Flying Boat that had to ditch in the sea off the Hebrides . . . bad weather hindered rescue operations, and the search called off, the thick mist made location impossible. After some delay the bird was released by the Flying Boat Crew and the bird arrived at her loft with a message giving the position of the stricken plane. The search was now resumed, and the entire crew rescued . . . the bird was awarded an animal VC.

CHAPTER FORTY-ONE

The Yanks Are Coming, 1942–44

When thousands of US GIs arrived in Britain, the home troops just could not compete with American glamour. Like so many women, Land Girl Mitzi Edeson was stunned.

> They were like film stars and had badges for everything, 'Gee, honey, this one is for sharp shooting' and so on . . . they liked girls and were polite, it was 'Honey, you look like a million dollars in that dress' or 'Baby, when this war is over, I'm taking you back to the States.' . . . there were a few broken, or bent, hearts. Oh yes, you took it all with a pinch of salt, well you did if you had any sense.

Delphine Rowden from Bristol remembered the GIs dancing.

> No waltzes and quicksteps for them, it all became jitterbug and jive . . . girls that had shyly taken the floor for a foxtrot were now being thrown in the air and slung between legs . . . we now watched the swirl of legs, stocking tops, suspenders and knickers.
>
> The Yanks, being away from their wives, sweethearts and families, had quite a lot of spare cash and it became their habit to walk close behind any girl they fancied, jingling cash in their pockets. Lots of us young women, starved of luxuries, fell for this, coupled with the sweet talk, and soon became the proud possessors of nylon stockings, make-up and extra food for the family, then, later, not a few became the mothers of bonny bouncing babies.

With the cigarettes and stockings, sometimes came other offers, as young shop-girl Freda Hartley discovered.

> We danced together quite well, but he had been drinking and got carried away. After a couple of dances, he wouldn't release me but promised me nylon stockings and chocolate if I danced with him for the rest of the session and if I would go back to his hotel with him that night.

Sixteen-year-old Sylvia Merriman went to the Casino Dance Hall in Birmingham for a night out. Her friend arranged for an American soldier to take her home, and unwisely made the same arrangement with a British serviceman. Sylvia's friend sensibly decided not to turn up for either date.

> They found not my friend but each other instead; a fight broke out between them... If we had any sense, we would have left but we were 16 and naive. Almost immediately other British and American servicemen joined in. Corporation Street was just a noisy sea of fighting uniforms.

The United States War Department issued guidance for their GIs in Britain. The advice included, 'if you are invited to eat with a family don't eat too much. Otherwise, you may eat up their weekly rations.' They were also reminded that the British were 'reserved not unfriendly' and 'Don't make fun of British speech or accents.'

It was not just young women who were enthralled by the Americans, schoolboys were equally captivated by everything from their accents to their aircraft.

Seven-year-old Stanley Jones was standing outside his house in Staffordshire when he saw an American Mustang fighter in trouble.

> There it was, a silver-coloured fighter plane trailing black smoke... I could make out the pilot silhouetted in a

bubble-type cockpit. Seemingly composed, he was hunched within the canopy close to the front of the dome ... I wondered then, and to this day, whether he chanced to look down to see us standing there and what in the world he would have given in that desperate moment to have been there with us.

I could now see that orange flame laced the smoke. It belched out the right side of the fuselage, enveloping the cockpit before streaming back over the tail. The engine coughed and sputtered, cutting in and out ... my brother and I could do little but stand and stare, open-mouthed, our minds filled with a heady mixture of fear and fascination.

Minutes later it would crash and explode in a field of ripening wheat killing the pilot, Captain John Perrin of the United States Army Air Forces ... there was not much left of the plane ... the acrid smell of seared metal and burning aviation fuel permeated the smoke-hazed air. Shapeless pieces of material burned and smouldered; sinister blackened clumps scattered amid the jade-green wheat. Hushed groups of grown-ups stood about. Knots of grim faces turned toward one another, arms folded, speaking in hushed tones. And coming fast; ploughing through the waist-high wheat like a launch at sea, a bright red fire engine.*

At its peak, the number of GIs in the UK reached one million. Their arrival brought magic into the lives of British children. Terence Cartwright, aged 12, Leicestershire:

I had the unforgettable experience of tasting my first Wrigley's Spearmint Chewing Gum ... Trestle tables groaned under the weight of 'Camel' cigarettes, chewing gum, tins of exotic meat and foods we had never tasted before. These

---

* Capt. Perrin didn't bail out and kept flying long enough to avoid crashing into the local school and housing estate.

'Treasures' were dispensed by 'Gods' to the hordes of grubby, green-candled nosed, ragged trouser-bottomed 'Dennis the Menace' and 'Just William' lookalikes who descend on the camp like locusts. Yes – the Yanks had arrived.

Peter Stockton was a paperboy in Cheshire.

> I delivered papers to the troops in their barracks ... this was the first time I had ever seen anyone from another country, more so a coloured person ... my new friends gave me chewing gum, American comics, and fresh fruit ...

One morning Peter found his friends in one of dozens of trucks ready to head out.

> I found them sitting in the rear of one of the trucks, fully kitted out complete with rifles, etc. They lifted me into the truck, and I spent ten minutes there ... they all shook my hand and hugged me, then lowered me to the ground. As I stood there watching, orders went out and the vehicles fired up, and away they went down the road, out of my life for ever.

According to the BBC, around 3 million American servicemen passed through Britain between 1942 and 1945. Most of them were based in small towns stretching from Yorkshire to Cornwall, with a predominance in the south and west as D-Day preparations were made. John Ringham was a teenager in Cheltenham.

> The centre of Cheltenham was always full of US troops. Saturday night dances at the Town Hall became a Mecca for them picking up excited English girls. Delighted with gifts of silk stockings and chewing gum from young, homesick men with pockets full of money. On Sunday mornings, all around the town, there were impressive piles of used condoms.

Cheltenham itself changed in other ways, including the beautiful Imperial Gardens.

> The US Army took it over as a lorry park. Within a week or two it was a mud bath. The town was already beginning to look forlorn, like a dowager dame in need of more and more make-up. Imperial Gardens now emerged as a large wart on her chin. Sedate Cheltenham tightened its upper lip a notch or two.
>
> Every Cheltonian came to know an American on a personal level, there were so many of them . . . they had a generosity both of material things and spirit.

More than 100,000 of the Americans were black, far outnumbering the 7,000 or so non-whites already living in the country and largely confined to port towns. Very few Britons had ever seen an American, let alone an African American.

> Before the war it was rare to see a black man in Cheltenham. The only exoticism we could boast was a Chinese family running a laundry. Seeing black GIs daily as we came and went from school was exciting.

Black soldiers billeted next to John's school produced a concert, including an eight-piece jazz band.

> We'd never seen anything like it. The vitality was inspiring and the *joie de vivre* overwhelming . . . it was a wonderful, exciting afternoon.*

Thirteen-year-old Tommy Mac delivered bread to the US cookhouse on a Glasgow airbase.

> This was the first time I had ever met a black person . . . I was lifted bodily by a giant of a man. He simply lifted me and put me on the table like a doll. Then he shook my hand and gave me some chocolate with a big smile, and off he went.

---

* John Ringham became a well-known actor, appearing in *Dad's Army*, *Dr Who* and *Poldark*, among many other series. His second wife was German.

'Sonny,' one of them said, 'don't you recognise him? He is the Heavyweight Champion of the World, that's the great Joe Louis, the Brown Bomber.'

In the run up to D-Day, small British towns welcomed a growing flood of American soldiers preparing for the invasion, as Bernard Peters from Cornwall recalled. The GIs had been advised that the British were 'reserved, not unfriendly', but some young women soon forgot the reserved part.

> When they arrived, they were idolised, and the girls threw caution to the wind! They went overboard for them, and these young Americans were rewarded with what we could only dream about.
>
> One of the WRACS in a quickstep said to the [American] man, 'Do you mind taking that torch out of your pocket? And he said, 'Lady, that ain't no torch.' 'Well,' she said, 'if you've got the right paraphernalia, you can take the pants right off me.' Such was the freedom and attitude of wartime.
>
> At a Christmas party with the troops, balloons were blown up and let fly around the room. I thought they were strange-looking balloons until it was explained to me that they were 'Frenchies', i.e. Durex – my first encounter with such 'paraphernalia'. In wartime anything goes.

Bernard learnt about race as well as sex.

> There were black Americans and white. Segregation was a new word for us. Off duty they did not mix . . . the way the black GIs were kept apart from the whites – different camps, different off-duty nights – astounded our parents. It was puzzling and disappointing.

Ken Clark was a schoolboy in Talywain, Monmouthshire, Wales.

> He leaned down from his jeep and scooped me up into the passenger seat and I was dazzled. Gleaming-white smile,

flashing brown eyes, shining brown skin, and a beautiful uniform. He was the first American that I ever saw in real life... the first impression gained was of a bright, sparkling person... we loved those black American soldiers and did not think about colour.

The gossip group in our house was of the opinion that anyone who went out with an American soldier was a sex-crazed hussy. Later, this became more vitriolic if it was a black American soldier. I am sure the charge was imported by the white Americans, willingly adopted by our people because it gave more spice to the tale.

The perception about the sexual aspects of the relationship was well-founded. Around the time I saw my first real Americans I saw my first real condom, then always known as a 'French letter'.

When Ken and his friends followed a black GI and a girl into the woods, the girl was in a strange position.

The young lady hadn't been trained in the prone position [in case of air raids] for she was the wrong way round and had her legs in the air. I suppose the danger from broken glass and shrapnel was a bit remote, and anyway she was being protected by the man shielding her with his body.

Our next task after the couple were well rested, and gone on their way, was to insert a stick into the used condom and hold it up for examination. Not knowing what it was, it was perfectly natural to take it home and ask our mam what it was called and what was its function. This upset my mother, especially when she realised that it had been trailed through the streets waving on the end of a stick. What would the neighbours think!

Although my mother did not explain about condoms, we soon found out all about them... we used to collect them afterwards to hang on the gates, letter boxes and clothes lines of the people who were nasty to us when we played in the streets. There were plenty of chances to display our dislike because there were more condoms on Talywain Incline and Lasgam Wood than there were barrage balloons round London, and, according to our mam's gossip group, almost as big.

The US Army was strictly segregated, as was much of southern USA. When war began, African American troops were confined to support roles. In the UK they built scores of airfields for their airmen, but as the war progressed the need for replacement troops finally pushed black soldiers into the frontline, with 1,700 landing on D-Day.

British official attitudes to black GIs did not encourage integration either. But most ordinary British citizens did not understand this separation and saw black GIs as equal to whites. As George Orwell put it, 'The general consensus of opinion appears to be that the only American soldiers with decent manners are the Negroes.'

In Bristol those well-mannered black American soldiers were welcomed by the local girls but not by their white comrades. Delphine Rowden:

> We were confronted with hordes of white Americans, all arms and legs, and in an ugly, angry mood. A young woman with a Black American was intending to proceed down Castle Street. The white American soldiers surged forward and hit the Black American soldier on the head, and he fell to the ground with the girl screaming . . . what a sight! As far as we could see in the direction of West Street was American soldiers. The whole area was a seething mass . . . It looked as if the whole American Army was there, with no space between them, once again the mood seemed to be very angry . . . sitting or stretched out on the pavement we could see a line of wounded soldiers. Definitely time to go home!

As a result of wartime relationships, around 2,000 mixed-race babies were born to British women. Some married after the war and moved to America, but sometimes the children of these relationships did not know where their fathers were. There is one People's War archive testimony headed 'Trying to Find My American GI Father.' Sixty years after the end of the war, a woman is trying to find her father, William Dickinson or Dickinsen.

> I am trying to trace my African American GI Daddy stationed at Fauld, Burton-on-Trent, Staffordshire, England. As far as I know he was in the army or USAF. I was born 13th July 1945 at Chaddesden, Derby. My Daddy was there when I was born so he knows he has a daughter. I was named Margaret Christine Johnson. Mother's name was Christina Johnson . . . any help tracing him or any siblings he may have would be a dream come true.

Vivian Blake lied about his age when he signed up for the RAF at home in Jamaica, one of over 5,000 West Indian RAF personnel. He did not experience obvious racism in England.

> People were glad to see that everybody, regardless of colour or creed, were prepared to help the war effort.

It was different when he was sent to a large camp in Virginia, USA.

> The camp was in effect two camps; a white one and a black one . . . we were regarded as 'honorary' whites because we were British and billeted with the whites . . . a white American officer reminded his men, 'These ain't Uncle Sam's N****rs, these are King George's N****rs'.*

Allan Wilmot was also from Jamaica and served with both the Royal Navy and the RAF.

---

* Vivian worked in engineering after the war, living mainly in Gloucester.

Many of the white American GIs were from the southern states of America and, although they were in Europe (a very different social scene), they couldn't face the changes that took place. So, we had open wars, especially in dance halls and various places of entertainment, with the local whites as a back-up on our side.

The black American GIs were a different story. We got along very well indeed – the British black servicemen were their protectors. At times, they were attacked by groups of white GIs, especially if they were in the company of white girls.

In Allan's view, discrimination in the UK forces was subtler.

There was no official racial discrimination in the services, but seniority promotion for a black serviceman was rare, even though you were qualified for the job. Excuses for non-promotion were always there . . . they didn't want black personnel in charge of white servicemen.

We were well treated by white civilians because they were aware that you had left your safe country to help them in their time of need. And white British servicemen, in my case, were fine . . . but when I was on other duties and had to mix, there were some problems – mostly caused by stereotyping. People would say things like, 'Because you're black you don't need to wash' and 'where did you learn to speak English if you live in trees?'

At first, I took offence, but after deep consideration I came to the conclusion that it was best for me to try and re-educate my colleagues, which I did.*

---

* After the war, Allan was very active in West Indian ex-servicemen's organisations, as well as being a singer in the successful group The Southlanders.

The black GI experience helped sow tiny seeds for the birth of the American Civil Rights movement. Many GIs had seen that the world did not have to be segregated. They had shared food, dance floors, beds, workplaces, and fought on the same D-Day beaches as whites. They were not returning home to be discriminated against as before.

In London, Margaret Tapster saw black GIs as equal, as well as charming.

> A new element of magic had transformed our lives, with the sparkle and glamour of pink champagne. Over-paid, over-sexed and over-here, were those exotic creatures from another planet – the Yanks ... for the most part lonely and eager for the brief solace of warm human contact, they would hold a girl close, dancing cheek to cheek, smelling excitedly of expensive aftershave and French cigarettes, murmuring sweet inanities, 'You have the cutest little ears, honey, like pink seashells.'

Margaret Tapster enjoyed the attention of one particular American.

GIs dancing in London, 1943

The beguiling southern drawl of Sergeant Kurt Wagner Jr would pluck endearingly at my heart strings, as his long curling lashes fluttered against my cheek in playful butterfly kisses. 'Your hair smells like the jasmine flowers on our back porch. When we have won this little old war, I will take you home to see my Mom and Pop.'

Romance had to stop when another raid on London began, and Margaret grabbed her medical bag and dashed out on duty.

The stuff of dreams is a kind of self-defence against the stark brutality of real life, for inevitably the mythical song of the nightingale is bound to be drowned by the banshee wail of the siren – time to abandon the dancing shoes for the medical bag, as death drones overhead accompanied by the staccato tattoo of anti-aircraft fire. Dazzling searchlights swept the sky, dimming the brilliance of the stars and the serenely floating moon, trapping in their beams tiny toy aeroplanes engaged in vicious dogfights.

Soon the night is made hideous by the high-pitched scream of incendiary bombs, the crump of landmines, the crash of falling masonry, the crackling blue lightning of fractured powerlines. A cacophony of police whistles, clanging bells, frenzied motor horns, bellowed commands, heralds a scene of organised mayhem against a lurid background of leaping flames.

Towards daybreak an eerie peace prevails. In a merciful empty sky, pink and gold dawn clouds cluster over the blackened, smoking rubble and the naked, jagged ruins of what was, only yesterday, a gracious regency square.

We learn it has been a heavy night for casualties, among them Sergeant Kurt Wagner Jr was found with a shard of shrapnel in his heart, still protecting the live body of an injured ARP warden he had carried from a block of flats with blithe and fatal disregard for his own safety.

Oh, the mixed emotions and crazy values of those traumatic times; for even as we weep unrestrainedly for Kurt, we are childishly, disproportionately thankful for a small miracle – our canteen's gas and water supply are still working! Gratefully we clutch our steaming mugs of tea, while on the one surviving branch of a stricken plane tree, a thrush pours forth a glorious cascade of song. We watch the sun rise on a new day, and glad, as always, are vaguely surprised to be alive!

CHAPTER FORTY-TWO

Burma Advance 1944–45

In Europe, the Allies had pushed slowly north through Italy and were preparing for the D-Day landings in Normandy. But, in Burma, the Japanese were still in control. From the safety of India, General William Slim plotted the return of Burma to Allied control. He intensified jungle warfare training and demanded additional men and machines.

In March 1944 the Japanese, anticipating an Allied push and wanting to disrupt supply lines, launched an offensive in north-eastern India at Kohima and Imphal, a major British supply base. At Kohima the British–Indian troops held a tight defensive perimeter as the Japanese encircled the garrison. At one point fighting was at such close quarters the two sides were only separated by the width of the town's tennis court.

Rajinder Singh Dhatt was one of thousands of Indian troops at Kohima.

> I said that we Sikhs, we're not afraid of fighting . . . we came here to fight, and we will do that.

Despite being almost within touching distance, the Japanese underestimated the ability of the Allies to drop supplies and send in reinforcements.

At Imphal the RAF flew in nearly 19,000 tons of supplies and over 12,000 men. The brutal siege at Imphal lasted four months and was not lifted until 22 June, two weeks after D-Day. The continual supplies from the RAF had enabled the Allies to hold on until fresh forces arrived.

Imphal was one of the biggest defeats the Japanese Army suffered. They lost 54,879 men killed or wounded.

The exhausted Japanese, depleted by such heavy losses, were now on the defensive.

Henry Kirk survived Imphal, then followed the Japanese retreat south in monsoon weather.

> Nothing prepared us for what was to come in the seven weeks we spent going down this jungle valley, just a dirt road, littered with the wreckage of vehicles from our earlier retreat; Japanese bodies piled high and flame guns used to dispose of them to prevent the spread of disease ... we were never dry, and our clothing rotted on our backs.

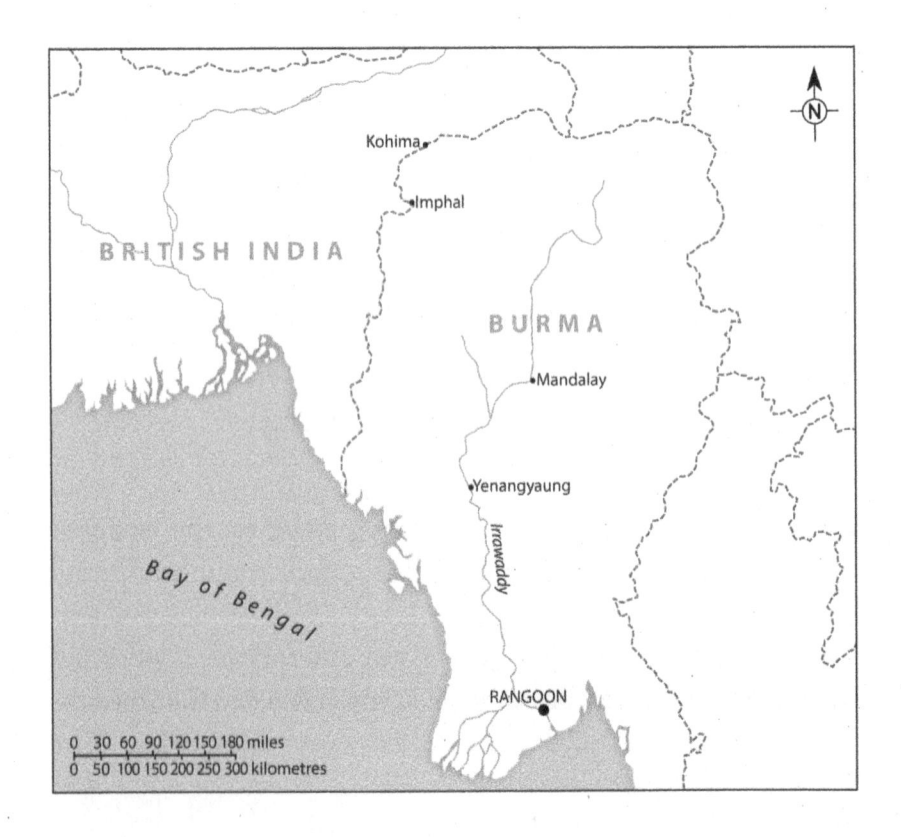

Nurse Kitty Calcutt from St Bartholomew's Hospital, London, served in India and Burma.

> Our forces were advancing and needed casualty-clearing stations up front. Normally these would have been staffed by male doctors and orderlies, but typhus was becoming a problem ... it was our first experience of Burma and fighting ... all around was jungle ... one large tent held diagnosed typhus patients ... rations and everything we needed were supplied by airdrop and had to be salvaged.

Extra Allied troops and weapons arrived, supply lines were secured, and the route for the jungle advance cleared, all helped by air supremacy from Indian bases. Sapper Dick Reynolds built roads, and de-mined land.

> I was given the task of taking my subsection forward to clear all the Jap corpses of booby traps ... they lay in various poses, their prominent yellow teeth grinning in the sun ... our job was to search the bodies for anything that might go bang ... the smell of death hung heavily in the air. Forty or fifty corpses were dealt with.
>
> A large attack on enemy positions was ordered ... the men waited, many knew they would not come back but they clung on to the chance of survival because life was very sweet for all of them, they had wives and mothers waiting for their return, but for the soldier there is no turning back ... some tanks were put out of the fight within the first few minutes and our boys were being carried in by the stretcher bearers, some had legs hanging off, others were shot in the stomach with their life's blood dripping from them onto stretchers.

It is hard to imagine there was time for entertainment in Burma amid the bloodshed. But Muriel Mason from Sheffield was a pianist with ENSA (Entertainment National Service Association) for six weeks in Burma.

My late brother was the entertainer and compere. We also had a comedian, conjuror and two girl acrobats.

We made a forced landing on a paddy field near an American camp ... the boys rubbed their eyes when they saw us, they hadn't seen a white girl for years! Things were rough and the loos were nobody's business – just a hole in the ground and pieces of canvas to hide us.

A second Chindit guerilla operation was also launched in March 1944, operating deep behind enemy lines again. This time the force was much larger, with improved air support. But Brigadier Wingate, the founding father of the Chindits, was killed in an air crash soon afterwards.

John Fone, Royal Engineers, built bridges for the advancing British and Indian troops.

We had a section of Bridge Building Elephants under command ... 14 elephants with their mahouts. The elephants had been trained by the Burma Forestry Commission before the war ... these had been sent for further training as bridge builders ... we had to build a road for 5,000 vehicles.

Stan Martin, Royal Welch Fusiliers, advanced south. The Allies might enjoy superior numbers and air cover, but the Japanese were dangerous opponents in retreat.

We crossed the Chindwin River. The Royal Engineers had built the longest Pontoon bailey bridge of the war, because of the width and the speed of the current it was regarded as an engineering feat ... the Japs were definitely on the run and all we had to put up with was their rearguard action, which were snipers in treetops and felled trees across the tracks to stop our transport ... when we did spot a sniper the top of the tree would be blown to bits, and we wouldn't have the pleasure of seeing him fall out of the tree because he was strapped in. After shooting all the leaves and small branches off, the sniper could be seen hanging there, riddled with bullet holes.

Eventually we got to the Irrawaddy River ... about halfway across they started firing mortar bombs at us. Two hundred yards from the other side we ran into barbed wire on a sandbank; a mortar bomb hit us dead centre and blew the bottom out of the boat. We were sitting ducks for the Japs. If they had stuck to their guns, they could have wiped us out but for some reason they pulled out ... I lost a young lad from my section. He was only a kid and had only left the UK six weeks before.

The next day we started our advance to Mandalay

Mandalay was captured on 20 March and, by 1 May 1945, just a week before war's end in Europe, General Slim's promise 'to kick the Japanese back to Rangoon' had been kept and Burma's capital liberated. The Allies had been fighting the Japanese in Burma for over three years, the longest land campaign fought by the British.

7th Rajput Regiment, Burma, 1944

They would not have prevailed without troops from India, Africa and China.

Indeed, the contribution of the British Indian Army has certainly been undervalued. They fought on many battlefronts including North Africa, Italy, Malaya, but most significantly in Burma. There were even 300 Indians at Dunkirk. By 1945 this was the biggest volunteer army in history and, of the 1 million men deployed to Burma during the long war there, 700,000 were Indians, drawn from all backgrounds and religions.

In the Second World War over 100,000 Indians were killed, wounded or missing. Field Marshal Auchinleck, Commander-in-Chief of the Indian Army from 1942, said that the British 'couldn't have come through both [world] wars if they hadn't had the Indian Army.'

CHAPTER FORTY-THREE

Prisoners of Japan 1944

As the Allies were attempting to push the Japanese back down through Burma in 1944, years of malnourishment and tropical diseases was taking a heavy toll on the women in Palembang Camp, Sumatra. Phyllis Briggs noted in her diary:

> Mackenzie ill with dysentery. Still no rainwater, ration reduced. Baby Darling died very suddenly. Grace Guer died. She had only been ill four days, a great shock to us all. She was young and pretty and had kept fairly fit . . . Sheila Brown is ill with malaria. All the missionaries ill – Mischa had diarrhoea and vomiting. I was on duty so a hectic time looking after all of them.

In August there was a temporary respite from the totally inadequate diet.

> Fresh fish arrived – they were still alive – it is several months since we had any – these must be river or mud fish as they have long feelers on their heads . . . Mrs Curran Sharp died . . . one teacup of water to wash in now – the wells have dried up and we long for rain . . . the women who were punished yesterday were made to work from 6.00 to 11.00 emptying the contents of the septic tank onto the plants – a nauseating job.

Letters from home were rare.

> Wild excitement! Letters from the outside world – the first time in over two and a half years of captivity . . .

But Phyllis was not one of the lucky ones. Her relatives wrote several letters, but Phyllis never received them. They had no idea if she was dead or alive.

For mothers of young boys, it was heart-breaking when the Japanese Camp Commandant made them drop their trousers. Those showing signs of puberty were immediately separated from their mothers and sent to the men's camp, not knowing if they would ever meet again.

On 20 October 1944, American troops landed on Leyte Island to recapture the Philippines. That same day Phyllis Briggs was shipped back to Muntok, Banka Island.

> The rest of the camp cheered us as we drove away, sitting on our bundles, with tin cans and other precious belongings tied to our backs. We took everything, not knowing what was in store for us. We drove down to the river and boarded the ship that was waiting for us. To my great surprise I discovered that it was one of the ferry boats which used to run between Penang and Butterworth. I thought of the times I had boarded the ferry in happier days, sometimes on the way to a dance or to play golf.

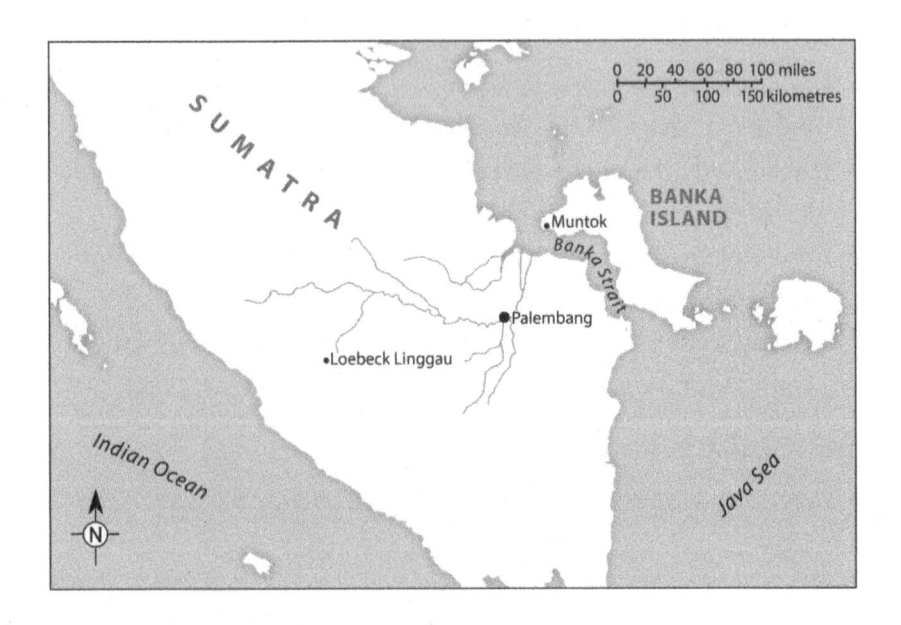

We were astonished to find that a lot more people were to join us. There were over one hundred women and children, nearly all Dutch. Many looked very ill and were unable to walk, including several nuns all suffering from malaria, malnutrition and beriberi.

We sailed down the river and there was a beautiful dawn, and the air was fresh. As we got nearer the sea, we hoped we had said goodbye to Sumatra for ever and that freedom was getting nearer . . . the sea was quite rough, and we were tossed around like corks . . . I felt terribly seasick and tried not to faint. By the time we reached the jetty I hardly had the strength to climb up the iron rungs of the ladder. Fortunately, two Japs at the top caught me just as I was about to fall backwards into the sea. They dragged me onto the jetty where I curled up in a heap for a few minutes.

Phyllis had been a prisoner for nearly three years now in several different camps. She continued nursing victims of beriberi, malaria, dysentery and tropical ulcers among the 700 prisoners in the camp.

I did regular hours of duty with other nursing sisters. We had to draw water from the well for all the patients. It was very tiring work and often the rope broke. The water smelt horrid, but we had to use it. Occasionally, we were allowed to go to a nearby stream for a bathe, but the only time I did so I became ill with fever and dysentery.

The latrines were in a disgusting state – there was no drainage – just a large tank that rapidly filled up to almost overflowing, with huge maggots crawling about. One had to crouch on bamboo slats, a foot on each side, with the foul tank below. Some of the women volunteered to clean out the tank, using buckets and emptying them out of the camp . . . years later I still had nightmares of this seething mass of maggots.

Unlike earlier years, carol singing at Christmas 1944 was non-existent.

> We could not sing even if we had tried, as most of us had lost our voices and were apathetic to what was going on around us even when our friends died ... most people developed fever, and the death rate rose rapidly.

In his camp on the River Kwai railway, Len Baynes, 1st Cambridgeshire Regiment, was also very ill. He suffered from a flesh-eating tropical ulcer, which often led to amputation or death. But in Len's case, his vicious ulcers were a piece of good fortune. A list of prisoners for transportation to Japan was posted. Len was keen to join the exodus but, because of his tropical ulcer, was only nominated as a reserve. Len never sailed and later discovered that his allocated hellship, as they were called, had been sunk by an Allied torpedo.

We don't know which hellship Len Baynes would have sailed on, but of the 30,000 Allied POWs transported on these rusty hulks, many, like Len, were survivors of building the Thai–Burma railway. In September 1944 over 900 already-skeletal men were stuffed into two stinking holds on the hellship *Kachidoki Maru* headed for forced labour in Japan. In the same convoy 1,318 British and Australian prisoners were crammed into the bowels of the *Rakuyo Maru*. As one railway survivor put it:

> I had spent two years of hell and thought that nothing could be worse than this, but how wrong I was – the worst was yet to come.

The *Rakuyo Maru* was the first to be hit by an American torpedo. The submariners believed they were sinking ships in a 13-vessel convoy carrying oil, rubber and other vital materials to Japan. They were unaware that hellships full of Allied prisoners were amongst the vessels. British Gunner Alfred Allbury, Lewisham, London:

There was a blinding, shuddering crash and a sheet of acrid flame, and the ship faltered, and then seemed to leap broken-backed out of the water. I tried to get to my knees, and a wall of green pounded me flat onto the deck. I lay there, flattened, helpless, as the giant seas boiled and hissed about me.

At 11 p.m. that same day, 12 September, it was the turn of the *Kachidoki Maru* when two torpedoes fired by American submarine *Pampanito* sliced into the ship. Gordon Highlander Alistair Urquhart was a River Kwai Railway survivor.

> The ship shuddered... it was sinking rapidly. I finished up in the water in a sea of oil.

Throughout the night survivors heard anguished cries for help and watched as dead bodies floated past in the moonlight.

> When dawn came, there was not another soul to be seen. My body was covered in oil, burning in the scorching heat. I was naked apart from a 'jap happy' (loin cloth).

Ernest Benford, Royal Artillery:

> I hoped that death would come swiftly. Dawn came and through the mist I could see there were rafts and wreckage in all directions. Clinging to half-submerged rafts were Jap soldiers, nurses, civilians and POWs, all shocked, cold and thirsty, covered in black oil.

After four days adrift on rafts, the survivors of both sinkings were desperate. Australian Sapper Harry Weigand:

> Men were begging for water... our mouths were burnt with oil, and my tongue was swollen.

Fellow Australian Jim Campbell:

> Horror filled the day. Six died before nightfall after what had seemed years of suffering. Most had gone mad.

Alistair Urquhart:

> Five days passed. My tongue was swollen, and I was unable to speak. All the way through I kept saying to myself, 'I'm going to beat this.'

Uruquhart was finally rescued by the Japanese.

> I cannot remember how it happened, but they took me off the raft.

For those survivors not picked up by the Japanese, their rescue was extraordinary. Four days after the sinkings, the USS *Pampanito,* the same submarine that had killed so many men, returned to the scene, hunting for fresh prey. The crew spotted a bobbing raft of men who they presumed were Japanese. The survivors screamed that they were British and Australian POWs. The Captain shouted cautiously back, 'Get the one who speaks English.' The reply was angry, 'You bloody bastards, we all speak English.'

American submarines believed they were attacking convoys of vital materials for the Japanese war machine, not ships transporting prisoners-of-war from their own side. But there is some evidence that US Intelligence knew from Ultra intercepts that these convoys included Allied POWs.*

The USS *Pampanito,* having torpedoed 400 men to their deaths, now rescued 73 survivors. Two other American submarines picked up another 32 between them.

The final survivor, British Gunner Alfred Allbury, was adrift for six days.

> The raft slid up and down steep-sided waves. It had been my home for nearly a week now. I could see nothing and, tiny

---

* In his book *Death on the Hellships*, Gregory Michno states that intelligence intercepts indicate that some ships were sunk 'with the full knowledge that there were Allied captives aboard.'

speck that I was, I knew nothing could see me. This was the end... I felt nothing, no emotion. I was past feeling anything at all. Mine I knew was the calmness from which I could slip only into unconsciousness and death.

This tiny speck was spotted by US submarine *Queenfish*. As Allbury was hauled aboard, all he could do was whisper, 'Yanks', before he slipped into unconsciousness. *Queenfish* commander Eugene Fluckey described the survivors, 'Most of them couldn't talk but would just cry... in their oil-soaked eyes you could see the expression of gratitude.'

Of the 1,318 prisoners on the *Rayoku Maru*, 1,159 died, with just 159 survivors, including Alfred Allbury. Of the 900 POWs crammed into the *Kachidoki Maru*, 400 died. He didn't know it, but Len Baynes had been very lucky to miss his hellship to Japan.

Rayoku Maru: two of the last Australian prisoners about to be rescued

PART SIX

I realised I had survived, and I was therefore not due to be killed that day after all. It was pretty much a toss of a coin that decided if we lived or died. On that day my coin landed the right way up.

Soldier in Europe, 1944

CHAPTER FORTY-FOUR

Arnhem, 1944

Neither Phyllis Briggs in Muntok, nor Len Baynes in his Thailand camp, could see an end to the war. They never learned that the Americans were slowly pushing their way up towards mainland Japan, fighting bloody battles on a string of Pacific Islands. On 15 June 1944, American soldiers landed in Saipan and, three months later, Peleliu. Nor did Phyllis and Len know the Allies were pushing the Germans back through Europe, and that in early September had captured the key port of Antwerp and finally breached the German Gothic Line in Northern Italy.

Progress since D-Day had been slow and painful, especially in Normandy, but the Allies now planned to drive straight into the industrial heartland of Nazi Germany. Rather than advancing on the broad front favoured by Eisenhower, Bernard Mongomery asserted that if Allied troops quickly secured the key bridges in Nazi-occupied Holland over the river Meuse at Grave, the Waal at Nijmegen and the Rhine at Arnhem, they would deliver an audacious knockout blow and have a good chance of ending the war by Christmas 1944.

But the ambitious Operation Market Garden plan was flawed from the start. Allied intelligence pinpointing the presence of two newly arrived German Panzer divisions was ignored, and enemy resistance was fiercer than expected. Equally, a shortage of transport aircraft meant the landings lasted three days, losing any element of surprise, and giving the Germans time to reinforce.

Glider Pilot Bernard Black headed for Holland and Operation Market Garden.

> We begin to roll forward and the towmaster waves his bat overhead and we are gathering speed along the runway; now we are airborne ... the early morning mist had not completely cleared ... we could see combinations from other bases joining the armada. We crossed the east coast, and our main impressions were of wonder and at awe at the sheer size of the operation.

Battle-hardened Sergeant Jock Walker had already served at Dunkirk, North Africa, Sicily and Normandy. He had retrained as a paratrooper and then as a cameraman. He was cheerful about the war's direction.

The Germans were in full-scale retreat, and they were moving towards the Fatherland faster than a suppository in a constipated behind.

Jock was embedded with the 1ˢᵗ Airborne to film Operation Market Garden with fellow cameramen Sgt Dennis Smith and Sgt Mike Lewis.

> I am not a happy person in a military glider, the continuous sight of those two tow ropes, stretching from glider wings to the tail of the tug, were our umbilical cords... the silence too, broken only by the swishing of air past the fuselage, was a bit unnerving, but it had a serenity of its own, a feeling of being detached from the rest of the fleet and just sailing along on a mat of fleecy cotton wool.

Jock filmed British and Polish paratroopers from the 1ˢᵗ Airborne landing, but their distant drop zones eight miles from Arnhem proved disastrous for lightly equipped troops facing Nazi tanks

1ˢᵗ Airborne, Arnhem

and heavy artillery. Many Paras did not reach the targeted bridge.

British forces that did make it through took up positions at the north end of the Arnhem bridge and others held landing zones in preparation for further drops. But handicapped by bad weather and lack of surprise, landings went badly for succeeding waves, as Jock Walker witnessed.

> The planes started to arrive bang into a hail of anti-aircraft fire and machine gun. The scene was horrible, at least two Dakotas were hit and set on fire, the Paras exiting in a hurry, into a hail of tracer and the planes themselves eventually crashing into flames. The heath was on fire, Paras were being killed and wounded as they descended, and many a glider hit the deck, out of control.

Tom Davies from Neath, South Wales, was a veteran of the Desert War and the Italian campaign. Now, as part of the 1st Airborne Division, Tom was gliding to Arnhem.

> The canals and rivers were like silver ribbons glistening from the sun which shone from a hard sky ... soon we were over the dropping zone ... the sky seemed to rain parachutists making a truly colourful spectacle, which, on reflection, I suspect from an aesthetic point of view was lost upon most of us ...
>
> Moving through the village of Oosterbeek in single file towards Arnhem, we were greeted by the people who came running out of their houses offering us apples and glasses of water as a token of their pleasure in welcoming us. Our role as conquering heroes or liberators had however, yet to be proven.

Tom was soon in action trying to hold a position near the planned bridgehead.

> Soon we ran into stiff resistance... the Germans fought with desperate fanaticism, putting up very strong opposition... a German staff car, obviously caught up while trying to escape back behind their own lines was slewed across the road, riddled with machine gun bullets. The doors were flung wide open with bodies hanging out on either side, cut down in their bid to save themselves... the driver, his lips kissing the dust from the road, his arms outstretched from his bullet-ridden body. In the back of the vehicle were two passengers, their bodies huddled closely together as if frozen in mortal terror of the fate that had befallen them. The shiny patent leather of the jackboots and the bright red gash on the side of the well-groomed head of the General, whose face was twisted in a devilish grin, gave a macabre feel to the whole scene.*

But Tom Davies could not dwell long on this disturbing scene.

> A German half-track vehicle crashed through the trees on our right, sweeping the wood with fire as it moved clumsily forward like some enraged prehistoric beast disturbed from its slumber... a pile of mortar bombs which we had stacked behind the gun we had been firing exploded, sending fragments of steel flying in all directions.
>   I felt a red-hot searing pain in the flesh of my calf muscle... I could manage to hobble along [despite] the discomfort from the blood that dripped down into my now-soggy boot.

As Tom hobbled from the planned bridgehead, the local population was in turmoil.

> Parts of the town were ablaze as the Germans brought their flamethrowers into action and Arnhem was fast becoming a burning holocaust as shells burst on our positions with

---

* Major-General Friedrich Kussin, Arnhem Garrison commander

searing impact. The merciless bombardment had no pattern, with red streaks of flying shrapnel sweeping across the sky and bursts of gunfire springing to life again and again.

Many civilians took to the cellars of their houses, others fled in utter confusion . . . many fell victims to the crossfire of machine guns and the steadily falling shells. Nobody knew quite for the best which direction to advise them to go.

One young lad ran round in a wild frenzy screaming as he clawed frantically at his face which was covered with pieces of warm flesh, clinging tenaciously to his skin. A shell had landed directly on one of his companions close by, scattering flesh in all directions.

The Germans, with their heavier weapons, were gaining the upper hand. Tom Davies was forced to dive into a nearby cellar.

Soon we heard the rumble of tanks moving in. The tank commanders called on us to surrender but we held on, knowing there was a slight possibility of being relieved . . . the tanks started to pepper the houses where we were sheltering with cannon fire, shaking the walls like canvas. Clouds of dust rose from the crumbling plaster, and broken masonry and glass flew everywhere.

Our position looked hopeless now with our ammunition just about gone and the men utterly exhausted . . . a stark shadow fell across the doorway and a young German soldier, closely followed by his two companions, appeared. They could not have been older than 17. Their guns jerking about in their hands expressed their nervous and excitable mood, their eyes darting quickly about the dimly lit room. I am certain that one careless move on our part would have been suicidal. They would surely have blasted us to ribbons.

They beckoned the three of us out of the dust-filled, battle-scarred room into the bright daylight where more of our captors stood, the flashes on their uniform indicating that they were soldiers from the SS Panzer Division. They were lined up in the garden, their fingers itching on the triggers of their guns.

We were bundled unceremoniously into waiting trucks to be taken back behind enemy lines . . . the noise of the battle in the distance like the faint thunder of a far-off storm as we travelled through the pretty Dutch countryside.

The locals Tom passed suppressed their emotions for fear of reprisal, except for one old lady waving sympathetically to the Allied prisoners.

She was given a short blast from a Mauser gun by a fair-haired German fanatic escorting us. She staggered back against the wall of the house . . . we could not tell whether she was mortally wounded . . . we eventually turned into a large, fenced enclosure . . . [we saw] Dutch civilians who, judged by their white, strained faces and anxious looks were obviously pleading for their lives. This was evident by the despairing gestures they were making to a couple of lean and hard-looking German officers, whom one might have guessed were accusing them of collaborating with the Allies. Despite our own plight we felt a great deal of pity for them.

Tom Davies was headed to Stalag IV B, Muhlberg-on-Elbe. The hostility of German civilians contrasted with the warm support from the Dutch.

At Dusseldorf station women spat and jeered at us as they were forced to move aside for us to pass along the platform. It was understandable that many people felt embittered having their homes bombed and razed to the ground, many suffering the loss of a loved one.*

---

* After the war Tom worked for most of his life at the Port Talbot steel works in Wales. He married and had two children but died aged 68, after a long illness caused by hepatitis contracted in the POW camp in Germany.

Tom Davies was already a war veteran, but Arnhem was Edmund Scrivener's first combat. Yet, sitting in his Horsa glider with 1st Battalion, Border Regiment, he felt surprisingly calm.

> At last, I went into action. The wicked Hun was to get his comeuppance... I wasn't really worried for we had been told that we would meet no opposition to speak of. All we had to do was secure the landing zones for the paras, and then belt off to Arnhem and the bridge and keep an eye on it... piece of cake. Better take a field dressing with you in case somebody scratched themselves on a bush. What a load of bullshit that was! In reality, we were flying into the biggest shambles of the war, for which 17,000 men would pay the price for the stupid incompetence of those in authority... I had no idea what to expect, and how I managed to avoid the consequences of my ignorance I'll never know.

Over the following days Edmund felt the full force of the enemy.

> Coming towards me were two Tiger tanks and the supporting infantry. My sergeant and I dashed behind a coal shed... unfortunately my sergeant made a run for it. They shot him down before he had gone five paces.
>
> Out of food, out of ammunition, we were getting desperate.

Like the young soldier, Edmund's luck could not last. He was hit while firing an anti-tank gun.

> The Medical Officer wrapped up my leg... we were surrounded, and it was only [a] matter of hours before we were captured. As dawn broke there was a hammering on the door, and when I opened it there were two Germans with guns at the ready. We straggled off to captivity.

It was also John Slatterly's first action.

A boy going to war for the first time, eager and afraid at the same time ... suddenly the landing zone at Oosterbeek, a small holocaust of fire and noise; tracer bullets were criss-crossing the sky and puffs of smoke erupted as shells exploded all around the silent descending gliders; there was no turning now. The plane had cast us off as we hissed our way to earth. Our glider was tree-high when the tracers found us. The glider pilot was hit first in his right shoulder, the same burst picked its way along the length of the glider and shattered my femur in an explosion of blood as the glider nosedived into the trees.

John Slatterly was hurried to a crowded hospital. He had not faced a minute of action before being gravely wounded.

I lay there with other casualties through the bitter days, hungry and afraid, with the daylight blocked out by the mattresses at the windows, night becoming day and each hour worse than the last ... my leg was now a mass of maggots, corrupted flesh and bad blood, the stench was overpowering.

But under the diligent care of Dutch medical staff, supervised by the Germans, John improved.

Back out on the battlefield the position of the Allied troops was grim. Twenty-year-old Leonard Moss, 11th Parachute Battalion, 4th Parachute Brigade:

It's carnage. British soldiers are cut down like corn before the scythe ... The dead lie in heaps, stacked by the side of the road like sacks of grain.

Frederick Hodges, The King's Own Royal Border Regiment, found four dead Germans in a field.

This soldier carried on him a photograph of his wife and two beautiful children and it was then that I realised that the man on the other side of the line was exactly the same as us. They had families they had left behind and somewhere a mother and her children were weeping for this lost man in battle.

Facing heavy losses, the British created a defensive perimeter around Divisional HQ, the Hartenstein Hotel in Oosterbeek, where 3,000 men dug in, including Sergeant Jock Walker.

> We had gone 24 hours over the time we were told we should be relieved, and hunger and thirst were beginning to bite very hard.

On the third day Jock joined up with the South Staffs when three German tanks attacked.

> Sergeant Baskerville* of the South Staffs won a VC (Victoria Cross), in view of many of us, by knocking out two of the tanks and then had his gun knocked out. Crawling to another gun which was working but whose crew was dead, he took on the third tank single-handed, which had withdrawn, but paid the penalty by being killed himself. A very brave man amongst many brave men.
>
> The German infantry was attacking meantime, but we gave them stick; the stupid bastards just ran into Vickers and sub-machine gun fire and wave after wave of them were sent to their particular Valhalla. They were massacred in their scores, the noise of the action was terrific, with the ripping sound of Spandau machine guns, the stutter of Sten guns and the steady thump of the 75's and the Mills bombs, all making their contribution to the massive Death March, but in 6/8 time.
>
> The noise to me that stood out above all else was the very reassuring heavy thump, thump of the Vickers, rising above the clash of the battle and the lads who played that particular instrument of death did it as if on the practice range;

---

* John Baskeyfield, 2nd Battalion, South Staffordshire Regiment, aged 20.

no panic, no wild burst, just a steady burst, then another and so on.

It was a wonder that any of us lived through it, but we did. It was a case of their life or yours.

Jock and his trapped colleagues depended on the RAF for supplies.

Captured Waffen SS snipers, Arnhem

The RAF supply planes and their dispatchers were giants among brave men; whenever they came over with supplies all the fury of the enemy was directed against them, but steadfastly they flew straight and low through the most fearful flak – the dispatchers at the doors throwing out the containers, even when repeatedly hit and set on fire, flying on, blazing torches in the sky, until they eventually crashed.

What devotion to duty and so sorrowful to watch. There wasn't a man on the ground that wasn't moved by this display of courage.

Alan Hartley flew with 271 Squadron resupplying the trapped troops.

> Our aircrew flew into a horrendous curtain of bursting anti-aircraft fire and small arms fire . . . my own pilot, Len Wilson, was hit after he had dropped his panniers [of supplies] and despite being badly damaged tried to crash his stricken Dakota into the gun which shot him down. According to eyewitnesses he must have died, slumped into the control column, veered to the port side, sliced a big tree in half with his wing and then crashed. Two dispatchers and the navigator bailed out, but the remainder of the crew are buried in the Airborne Cemetery . . .
>
> 175 RAF aircrews gave their lives on these suicidal re-supply missions, which, in my estimation, was the bravest flying of the war.

In the shrinking perimeter around Divisional HQ the siege continued. Jock Walker's fellow Army cameraman, Sergeant Dennis Smith, 23 September:

> The situation is serious. The shelling is hellish. We have been holding out for a week now. The men are tired, weary and food is scarce and, to make matters worse, we are having heavy rain. If we are not relieved soon then the men will just drop from sheer exhaustion.

Jock Walker was dug in alongside Dennis Smith.

> We were filthy, dirty, beyond tiredness, food and sleep were luxuries that belonged to another life, but we weren't broken, not by a long way, and we received the news with gladness that it would soon be over, and sadness with the loss of pals who wouldn't be coming back with us.

Late that night, 24 September, Jock headed to the river, trudging in single file holding the shirttails of the man in front.

ARNHEM, 1944

Arnhem, 1944

It was very overcast and pouring with rain and we had our feet muffled with sacking or other rags, and so we reached the riverbank.

The Second Army were banging in shell after shell into the German lines to cover our withdrawal and, as we lay in the mud, we hoped that they all found a target.

Jock crossed the river safely and trudged to Nijmegen carrying his camera, film and weapons.

Allied troops had expected to hold the Arnhem bridge for four days before the British XXX Corps arrived in strength to relieve them, but they were delayed by heavy opposition. After eight days the men on the bridge were so desperately short of food and ammunition they surrendered. Their message said, 'Out of ammo, God save the King.' Operation Market Garden had failed.

Over 2,500 others, like Jock Walker, retreated across the river. Laurence Scott:

> We didn't want to go; we didn't want to leave the Dutch people behind. We were resigned to fighting, to being killed.

> I felt so angry. It seemed such a waste. Nine days of fighting and all those people killed or wounded, and we had to leave the Dutch behind.

Canadian Engineers ferried escaping soldiers across the river to safety throughout the night. Leonard Moss:

> Hundreds of men are here. The enemy fire is intensifying... mortar shells continue to scream overhead splashing in the water... as soon as the boats unload on the far bank, they set off back to pick up more men.
>
> I saw tired faces everywhere, grimy, proud, undefeated faces and I wanted to cry... everywhere I looked I saw the eyes of men who had seen too much, given too much. Everywhere I looked I saw a hero. But for every man who escaped many more had died, been wounded, or captured, and they had no one to tell their story.

Given his humiliating retreat from Arnhem, what happened once Jock Walker had escaped across the river took even him by surprise.

> We flew back to England in a Dakota, as our picture record of part of the action was of paramount importance, and, as we were the first survivors home, we received a tremendous and most embarrassing welcome.

Jock's film and photographs were published worldwide, and he was told that the coverage had netted £156,000 for the Ministry of Information. It was a classic example of a propaganda victory masking a military defeat.

> We had each been recommended for a British Empire Medal, but with the inscrutable way the Army works, we were later told that... the award would not be possible. I felt very bitter about this, the second time I had been an 'almost'. It is not a question of gong-chasing, but a regular soldier's career will

often be influenced by what he wears on his chest, and soldiering was my life, and I had been cheated, not once but twice – so be it!

Jock Walker (centre), Dennis Smith (left), Mike Lewis (right) at Pinewood Studios on return from Arnhem

Soon after his photographic triumph, Jock Walker rejoined his parachute unit in Holland. The failure at Arnhem meant the war would go on longer but the Allies were still pushing towards Germany. As they slogged up through Holland, Jock filmed a sniper from the Marines slipping through enemy lines before daybreak.

> The cooks were starting to prepare their Teutonic breakfast, with many comings and goings but still we did nothing, until at last a figure sauntered over to a door, opened it, and went in. 'That's it,' he said 'there is always somebody [who] has an early morning crap. We will just give him time to get his trousers down and nicely settled on the seat. He deserves that as it will be his last one.'
> Then, taking very careful aim, he put a shot through the bog door, which banged open, as the presumably dead

German fell against it, and there he was laying halfway in and halfway out of the doorway in all his glory. I wonder what his last thoughts were. What a sordid way to go.

What an ingenious way of knocking off your enemy, catching him when least expected. After all, who expects to be shot when on the throne!

Tim Hardy, like Jock Walker, was now a fully trained paratrooper. He was still desperately in love with Doreen Fenner, across the other side of the country in Milford Haven. Tim was fully expecting to parachute into Arnhem but was first hauled in front of the Colonel on a charge of not carrying his personal weapon on active frontline service.*

He pronounced me 'Guilty' and in the next breath promoted me to Sergeant . . . so many Sergeants had turned their ankles, caught pneumonia, been captured, gone bonkers, or deserted that he was left severely short of them. He used his authority to confer a 'field promotion' on me.

Soon after Tim was promoted to Quartermaster Sergeant.

I'd helicoptered up four ranks in as many months; at that rate of promotion, I'd have entered Berlin carrying a Field-Marshal's baton.

Unconnected to his misdemeanours, Tim Hardy was never dropped into Arnhem. To his disappointment he was transferred to the 5th Independent Parachute Brigade, headed for Asia, not Arnhem. But he took a dim view of the military failure in Holland.

We could have told 1st Airborne a thing or two about Montgomery's intelligence, especially where bridges were concerned, and we weren't surprised to learn that German

---

* His real offence had been 'liberating' a duck board from a local farm to line his muddy trench. He couldn't carry the board and his gun at the same time.

forces had cut 1st Airborne to ribbons on the bridge and that bloodied survivors had to swim for their lives to the riverbank.

In any other walk of life errors of judgment on the Arnhem scale would swiftly have led to the wholesale sacking of the principals responsible, but this, being the walk of death, the generals weren't pressed even to say 'Sorry'.

Tim Hardy was a cynic, but one with good judgement. Market Garden might have freed much of Holland from occupation, but it was a failure. The objective of winning the war by Christmas would never be achieved and the human cost was huge. Over 13,000 Allies were killed or wounded, and 6,500 British and Polish troops captured in a badly conceived operation.

Wounded in his first wartime combat, Edmund Scrivener, Border Regiment, was imprisoned at Offlag 79, near Brunswick.

> One of the guards spoke to me in quite good English and after searching in his pocket, while I held his rifle (!!), he produced a photograph of his wife and children. I told him of my two girls and then looked him straight in the eyes and said, 'Why are we fighting each other?' He hesitated a long while as if he had never been asked the question before, then his eyes began to fill with tears, I touched his arm and walked away. To tell the truth I was damn near to tears myself. What utter stupidity. There we were, ordinary family men, whatever language we spoke, trying to kill each other. What madness had we come to?

Edmund might have been comforted to know that his captivity would be for less than a year. In early February 1945 Churchill, Roosevelt and Stalin met at Yalta in the Crimea to discuss the future of Germany and its empire in a European war they now knew they would win. Two days after Yalta, Bomber Command unleashed a firestorm over the German city of Dresden, killing between 40,000 and 100,000 citizens. While the Allied leaders in Yalta agreed the future, their generals were making final preparations to capture Germany itself.

CHAPTER FORTY-FIVE

Crossing the River Rhine, 1945

There was a final obstacle for the Allies before they drove into the industrial heartland of Germany – the mighty, and well defended, Rhine River, 766 miles long and 1,300 feet wide on average.

Montgomery, now a Field Marshal, had apparently learned lessons from the failure at Arnhem. Operation Plunder was a more considered, better resourced operation. A large-scale amphibious assault was planned across a 12-mile front near Wesel on 23 March, followed next morning by America's 18th Airborne landing two divisions behind enemy lines.

The Allied progress towards Germany after D-Day had been hard-won in Normandy, and at Arnhem. They had eventually repelled a surprise Nazi counterthrust which became known as the Battle of the Bulge, but not without sustaining heavy losses. Now the final conquest of the enemy was in the Allies' sights. Once again gliders,* a silent surprise for the enemy, were the chosen means of paratrooper transportation.

An anonymous contributor wrote:

> With 30-odd men to a glider, it was not unlike travelling by tube, but with a better view. And you did get a seat ... ahead of us was the biggest airborne crossing of the war, over the Rhine and into Germany, while on the ground the

---

* Mainly built by Airspeed in Christchurch, Hampshire, and Harris Lebus, furniture manufacturers in Tottenham, London. They could hold 30 fully equipped paratroopers.

Rhine would be crossed by thousands of other poor sods, on foot. Then we were off, a part of this awe-inspiring armada of aircraft towing their gliders, stretching as far as the eye could see.

We were released from our rope to start our long descent. And now we could hear the very realistic sound effects of rifles, machine guns, bigger guns... and the realisation came to me that this could be a bit dangerous... we could see the flaming and broken gliders on the ground below and other gliders milling around, apparently aimlessly... then in what seemed one continuous manoeuvre we suddenly flattened out our dive and seconds later there was an almighty thump, and a lot more bumping and grating, until I realised we were juddering along the ground. We had landed.

I recall a scene of utter confusion. Figures running, shouting, running, shooting; jeeps revving and skittering off on urgent missions; guns and trailers being hauled out of gliders and parts of gliders scattered about the landscape at crazy, impossible angles; gliders coming into land, or crash, from all directions... our safe arrival a testimony to the skill and cool bravery of our pilots.

Corporal John Cooper, 195th Field Ambulance, part of the 6th Airborne:

The glider that I was to travel in carried a jeep and 15 men. The jeep occupied the centre of the glider, with nine men at the front and six at the rear... a great deal of juggling was entailed so that eventually the contents of each glider were as near as possible to the maximum payload, without exceeding it... the 195 Field Ambulance occupied 13 gliders out of a total armada of 1,300, and in addition there was about 1,400 paratroopers. Gliders were made out of plywood and were very susceptible to light anti-aircraft, or even small-arms fire.

CROSSING THE RIVER RHINE, 1945

The work in the Main Dressing Station was hectic, and by midnight a 700-bed hospital was fully operative.

At 6 p.m. on 23 March, 5,500 artillery pieces bombarded the east bank of the Rhine and boats ferried 3,000 troops across the mighty river. A pontoon bridge was to be built to transport heavy machines. After the success of his Arnhem camerawork, Jock Walker was deployed to film the Rhine crossing.

> An airborne drop was laid on, a commando assault, plus an orchestra of death, namely every calibre gun imaginable lined up in rows by size.
>
> On the stroke the guns opened up and pounded the shit out of the other side of the Rhine . . . I crossed with the last batch and by the time I got there it was like Guy Fawkes Day, but, in the main, the fighting for the town was over, the Germans had mostly pulled back.
>
> Come dawn I returned across the Rhine to my secondary job (and return the film I had shot) which was picturing the building of the pontoon bridge . . . the airborne lift passed over under very heavy German flak and in fact one Dakota, carrying American Para troops, was hit and set on fire on our side of the river; the blokes in it had to make their jump at a very low altitude on our bank in order to escape the inevitable crash. I don't think the crew escaped. Shades of Sicily!
>
> On the other side [of the Rhine] it was sheer murder; aircraft were on fire, gliders with parts of their wings shot off were just falling out of the sky, and descending Paras were being shot up in the air. It was horrible to watch, especially the gliders, which were so vulnerable and, on hitting the deck, just smashed into matchwood.
>
> This disgusting episode over, I went down to the pontoon, which was well under way and busied myself doing my job and then Jerry started to stonk the damn thing. He didn't half give it stick, as they must have realised that, once the bridge

was secure, the weight of the 2nd Army would soon be rolling over the Fatherland.

The bridge was hit, repaired, hit again and again, repaired again and again, with the Royal Engineers buzzing in and out, towing the new sections to be added on. Very brave men.

The temporary bridge across the Rhine was built in record time, allowing the Allies to move tanks and military vehicles. Corporal Tony King, a veteran of the Falaise Gap and Arnhem:

> We eventually crossed the Rhine on a temporary pontoon bridge assembled under fire by the Royal Engineers. Driving a 30-ton tank on a floating bridge is a weird experience as the weight of the vehicle partly submerges the pontoon . . . after the crossing there was more fierce fighting to hold the narrow bridgehead, and when we broke out, we found that Jerry had liberally sown the roads with heavy Teller mines, quite capable of disabling a tank. Once again, the Royal Engineers mine-clearing quads were indispensable.

Ronald Levett also crossed the pontoon bridge across the Rhine in his tank.

> It was a lovely sunny day, so warm that many squaddies had removed their shirts and were sunbathing on the banks of the Rhine . . . as soon as it got dark the Luftwaffe attempted to bomb the bridge but were prevented from doing so by the streams of anti-aircraft fire. It was like Bonfire Night with streams of tracer filling the night sky, which was mild and cloudless.
>
> The following morning, we drove into the area where the airborne assault had taken place . . . at the end of the field was a German Flakvierling, a 4-barrelled 20 mm anti-aircraft gun. This had obviously been shooting up the gliders as they landed. Lying across the top of the gun was a Horsa glider, broken in half . . . the pilot had sacrificed his own chances

to put the Flakvierling out of action... Lying beside it were two members of the glider pilot's regiment, both of whom had been wounded. Their wounds had been dressed but afterwards they had both been shot in the head. I think this would have counted as a war crime.

Lying on his back was the body of a young German soldier who could not have been much older than 16. He had been shot in the back and the exit wound had ripped his ribs out through his chest. The thing I found most noticeable was the surprised expression on his face. In the trees parachutes were hanging, with a blanket-covered body under each chute. In a barn there were about half a dozen paratroopers, covered up, with just their boots showing. This was the day I realised I was becoming immune to the sight of death.

Cameraman Jock Walker had a near miss.

I had just sat down to put a new roll of film in my camera when I got hit in the eye socket. I saw ten million stars and thought my head had been blown off. Pulling my hands

15th Scottish Division crossing the Rhine

instinctively up to my face, it was a relief to find my head was still on my shoulders, and on inspecting my hands, found they were covered in blood, and I felt sure my eye and cheekbone were gone. However, one of the blokes washed the gore away with river water and there was revealed a tiny triangular slit just below my right eye.

Undeterred by his minor injury, Jock pressed on into Germany.

Over the Rhine poured the army, and forward through Germany; the tanks and infantry battled like Trojans each time they met a pocket of resistance. And, as we penetrate deeper and deeper into Germany, the French, Belgian and Dutch people who had been forced into slave labour found themselves free and started the long trek on foot back to their homelands.

We felt terribly sorry for them, trudging the roads with their meagre belongings on their backs. A very sad sight indeed, but it was our *raison d'etre* to free the enslaved peoples of Europe, and here was proof that all the hardships we had suffered this far were worth it, their weeping with joy whenever we appeared on the scene and the end to the hated Boche.

From now on it was a race for the Elbe, the river on which Hamburg was a port, but before getting there, there was the matter of the Concentration camps!

The final Nazi surrender was only six weeks away. Churchill could now write in Montgomery's autograph book, 'Forward on Wings of Flame to Final Victory.'

CHAPTER FORTY-SIX

Belsen, 1945

In the Far East the Americans had ended Japanese resistance in Manila and had launched a ferocious firestorm on Tokyo and other Japanese cities. In Europe Jim Palmer's thoughts were of his wife, Muriel, who he had married on a short leave in 1940 and had not seen since. As a reward for serving abroad almost continuously for over four years, Jim returned to Manchester from the Italian front. He had fought in France, the Western Desert, Burma, India, Syria, Palestine, Lebanon, Iraq and Italy. He was anxious that he might have been brutalised by so much death and destruction. And was Muriel a different woman to the one he had hurriedly left behind four years earlier?

> Deep down I was worried that the strain of our parting would make it difficult to take up where we had left off four years ago. My fears were groundless, and when Muriel met me at London Road Station, I knew all the aches and loneliness were over. There were tears but this time they were tears of happiness.

But Jim was quickly shaken out of his new domestic contentment.

> I got the bad news! I was to be posted to Germany ... I couldn't believe it – the war was nearly over, and I had to go away again. I was shattered.

Jim found himself in smashed cities and devastated countryside.

> Hamburg was a huge heap of rubble, and fires were still raging on the burnt-out shells... we had been part of a procession through a land that had been completely destroyed and laid to waste. Whole villages had been burnt to the ground, crops flattened, roads blocked by rubble, and civilians were sat on the side of the roads, with their few remaining belongings on carts and wheelbarrows.
>
> We were at the gate of a huge prison camp surrounded by high wire walls and watchtowers. Over the entrance was the name BELSEN.

Bergen-Belsen was liberated on 15 April 1945. Jock Walker's fellow cameraman, Sgt Mike Lewis, was the first man from the Army Film and Photographic Unit through the gates, followed later by Jock.

> Set in a really beautiful, wooded area, completely hidden, was this filthy blot on the countryside. As we approached [the camp] the smell, and taste in your mouth, was rank. At the entrance to the place was a huge banked-up pit, which was full of human excreta and urine, the place where the inmates emptied their buckets, and floating on this disgusting cesspool were many dead inmates. What a dreadful way to end your days.
>
> There was no rush of cheering inmates when we quickly took the camp, it took them all their efforts to breathe and just drag themselves about in an aimless, senseless fashion; for all they knew we were just another set of 'nasties' to belt and torture them. They were unnerving to watch.

Harry Langford, King's Shropshire Light Infantry:

> There were piles of dead bodies, some with their clothes on, others naked. The bodies showed every stage of complete starvation, bullet wounds, and lacerations. Some had their feet tied together, others showed evidence of cannibalism. The dead and the living were literally intermixed; in some huts the dead outnumbered the living... one had to walk

Cameraman Sgt Mike Lewis being sprayed against typhus with DTT at Belsen

through human excreta in the passage . . . it took the British ten days with a 'bulldozer' to bury the bodies.

Jim Palmer was ordered to burn the huts.

> We walked slowly through the gates and on our left was a hay cart with high trestle sides – it was full of dead, naked bodies, who all looked like children and babies. It was horrific and the stench was wicked. Some of us vomited. The bodies were like skeletons with the bones showing clearly; the stomachs bulging and the heads shaven and swollen like eggs. Their eyes had sunk into their sockets and their jaws were hanging loose. Bodies were lying around alongside the huts, and we couldn't tell if they were dead or alive; they were all motionless and looked like bundles of rubbish. Some wore striped trousers and others were naked; they were all filthy and grey-looking with flies covering their shrunken bodies.

> The wooden huts had no windows and, as we entered, we could see rows of wooden bunks almost up to the ceiling. On each of these bunks lay a body, naked and filthy . . . groups of young British soldiers started to tenderly move these bodies slowly onto stretchers made of planks of wood and carried them to lorries waiting outside . . . there was an incinerator choked with burnt human bones.
>
> Every day for over a week we reported to the camp, burning the huts, and sorting the living from the dead. There were hundreds of corpses a day put into mass graves, and I was sickened as I had never been before. This was Hell itself.

There were about 60,000 prisoners still alive from 20 countries, and over 13,000 bodies needed burial.

Joy Taverner (later Trindles) was a Queen's Alexandra Nurse in her early twenties. She had already survived the D-Day invasions and was now working at a hospital in Belgium.

> We were flown to this concentration camp . . . it was so terrible we cried ourselves to sleep for many nights in our tents two miles away . . . skeletons, naked, just standing about. Bodies everywhere. Some babies still just about alive. We erected a tent and the Sister collected the babies and put them in the tent. Our orderlies took stretchers and collected any bodies that showed signs of life. We sent our colonel and some soldiers out to get clothes, sheets and blankets. When our troops went by German women spat at them.
>
> One of our sergeants took over a building and put up a big notice that said 'Harrods'. Our sense of humour managed to survive.
>
> I was there for weeks. Bodies were collected by trucks every day. We had a board outside and we wrote the number of bodies to be collected. Huge burial pits were dug, and we

put hundreds of bodies in there . . . our padre would go along and pray over each truckload.

I had nightmares for many years after – my husband would wake me up and say I was crying again. I don't know how we survived – we all supported each other and cried every night with our arms round each other.

Beryl Andrews, a 19-year-old actress with ENSA (Entertainment National Service Association), could not have expected that her career would allow her to see inside Belsen.

Yes, I went into the Belsen Concentration camp before it was burnt to the ground and with my own eyes saw things I shall never forget . . . although we were spared the worst horrors, we saw what I can only describe as 'living corpses'; I would not have believed that the human body could be so thin and emaciated . . . a mile from the camp were healthy, well-fed German children.

Letter from Ronald Clark to his wife Pammie, dated 29 May 1945:

We have just finished five weeks at Belsen Camp and are at the moment enjoying a rest by the Baltic coast, in the Lubeck area. We were given the Belsen job a couple of days after the place was captured, and we stayed to burn the pestilential huts to the ground – about five weeks altogether.

I shall never forget the place . . . I shall make no excuse for saying something about our experiences there. I feel it is the duty of those who have actually witnessed these places to say out loud what they have seen – all the more necessary because the facts are almost incredible to those who have not witnessed them.

To describe the place as it was when we arrived is beyond my powers. How do you describe a stench? The figures are impressive but colourless. When we arrived, there were

40,000 living, half-living and near dead, and about 10,000–15,000 unburied corpses.

But figures do not describe. The corpses were nothing but skeletons covered with taut yellow skin, usually naked, for rags were taken by the living. These poor people were denied our last human privilege of looking beautiful in death. God knows they had been denied every other privilege of civilised man. These people were degraded to the level of beasts; every decency was denied. Imagine what happens when 40,000 people are herded together, all suffering from acute dysentery, without a decent latrine amongst them. They just relieved themselves where they lay or stood until the huts were one carpet of excreta. The smell from this, mixed with the reek of the dead, produced a stench which for me was the most horrible thing about this hell.

One of the female guards made a deep impression on Jock Walker.

The troops captured some of the guards, including the Commandant, and a young 18-year-old female guard whose parents were surely the Devil and the Harpies. She was evil! Strikingly beautiful and blonde, in looks, she epitomised Hitler's Master Race and in temperament she was complete 100 per cent Nazi. Totally unrepentant, she was eventually tried and hanged as a war criminal. Her name? Irina Gresser.*

But long before she was tried, she was put to work clearing up the camp, carrying the corpses to a huge pit that Royal Engineers had dug with bulldozers. They (the occupying force) treated the guards and her, except for the torture, just as they had treated the poor things in their charge. As each day's work finished, they weren't allowed to wash or change

---

* Irma Grese: executed for war crimes aged 22.

their clothes and, when I left, were getting one potato a day to eat.

It doesn't take much imagination to understand what sort of state they were in after a few days of this treatment, carrying rotting bodies with their bare hands, they smelt like the death they had brought to so many.

Jock admired the work of the liberators.

The troops did a noble job of sorting order out of chaos, delousing the people, erecting showers for them to wash, feeding them a baby-like food for a while, as ordinary food would have killed them, and housing them in sanitary conditions and providing clothes to wear. When it was all over and people evacuated and the dead buried (thousands and thousands of them), the whole stinking place was burned down to prevent the spread of disease, and to erase a sore on Europe's body.

Joseph Kiersz was one of the Belsen survivors. A Polish Jew, he had first been transported to the Death Camp at Auschwitz in 1943, aged 17.

I worked for IG Farben making the Zyklon B gas which was used to gas people. I was beaten and tortured at work, prayed to God not to wake up in the morning . . . conditions were so bad that inmates committed suicide daily by walking into the electric fences. There was continuous hanging of people.

In 1945, like Anne Frank and her sister Margot, he was transferred from Auschwitz to Belsen by train.

On the train we could not throw out the dead people, so I sat on a dead person all the way. Belsen – typhoid, cannibalism, people moaning – horrifying scenes. People were deranged and skeletons. I saw prisoners gunned down by the SS as they scrambled for a miserable raw potato – and all so close to liberation ... there were a lot of Jewish Kapos,* who became inhuman in the camps. People were tortured and died as a result of their treatment. Whichever Kapo we managed to find after the liberation was killed by inmates.†

After liberation, Joseph worked in the Allied army kitchens. He went with armed British troops to another camp, which now held Waffen SS prisoners. Joseph took his revenge.

They were told I was a camp survivor, and I was going to make sport with them as they made with us. I wore a British soldier's uniform but wasn't allowed to have a gun, otherwise I would have shot them all. I broke off a little tree as a weapon – the ground was wet and mucky – I made them run, fall down, up, run, down, hit them with the tree, trod on their heads and pushed their faces in the mud. For over an hour I did this to them. In the end the soldiers carried me shoulder high, and they were overcome with emotion and cried, realising what I had been through at a young age. I felt good.

Later, I found out that 103 members of my family had perished.‡

It was only witnessing Belsen's horrors that made some soldiers fully understand why war against the Nazis was necessary. At the same time, the Nazi obsession with the Final Solution had diverted human and financial resources from building the extra aircraft and tanks the Germans so desperately needed into creating hundreds of extermination camps.

At home, the horror of Belsen and other camps featured on

---

* Concentration camp prisoners who earned extra privileges by supervising slave labour, often brutally.

† Over 150 Kapos from different backgrounds were killed by the inmates on 15 April 1945.

‡ After the war Joseph worked as a butcher in Golders Green, London, for 39 years.

the newsreels and the radio, no doubt some images courtesy of Jock Walker. In Castleford, Yorkshire, nine-year-old Colin Pritchard saw a newsreel of Belsen's liberation.

> We saw naked bodies, piles of them, even their genitals. It was stark, harrowing, and was beyond rational description. But it was not the dead bodies that alarmed the nine-year-old boy, nor the first sight of adult genitalia; it was the reaction of the audience. I was sat amongst townspeople I had known all my life... now men and women (the latter was even more extraordinary), stood up and yelled and screamed obscenities, 'Do it to them... bastards... bastards... bastards... fucking bastards... kill them, kill them!' People screamed and keened with grief and rage, with tears and spittle running down their cheeks.

CHAPTER FORTY-SEVEN

Germany, 1945

The war was now very close to the end. Six days after Belsen's liberation, Bologna, the last German-held Italian city, fell to the Polish 8th Army. Across the world the Allies had entered Rangoon in Burma, and the Americans were engaged in a brutal fight for the Pacific Island of Okinawa, which could provide a vital airbase and anchorage for the final Allied assault on Japan.

This progress might have comforted Jock Walker, but he was profoundly uneasy. He had survived Dunkirk, the Desert War, Sicily, Normandy, Arnhem and the Rhine Crossing, and now he had witnessed the horrors of Belsen. But, like other survivors of a long, brutal, conflict, he was convinced his luck would run out in the chaotic fag-end of war.

> I started to get a fear of being killed or maimed; it is difficult to reason it out, it was not that I was a heroic figure, far from it. I've been terrified more often than I care to think about, but the thought of being killed had just not occurred to me. I took my chances with the rest of the blokes without undue thought, but this was different. I was starting to look over my shoulder, wondering if there was a mine in the ground where I walked or if the next mortar bomb would blow me apart!
>
> In short, my nerve started to go, and this horrified me as I wasn't sure I wouldn't break under pressure, but as luck would have it, it never came to a showdown as the war was set on finishing.

In Italy Ron Goldstein, now with the 4th Queen's Own Hussars, shared Jock Walker's gloomy feelings of mortality in the raggedness of war's end, as he fought yet another battle.

> I realised I had survived, and I was therefore not due to be killed that day after all. It was pretty much a toss of a coin that decided whether we lived or died. On that day, my coin landed the right way up.

But Jock Walker still had work to do. His next stop, on 29 April, was Sandbostel, 20 miles downriver from Hamburg. On one side of the narrow road was a neat POW camp, but, in the concentration camp on the other, the picture was completely different.

> Although not in the same league as Belsen (what squalor could ever equal that?), it assailed the nose with the usual stink of urine and excreta one had come to associate with concentration camps and the half-mad listlessly dragging the rags, skin and bone that passed for their bodies, around and around the compound.

Ordinary food was not provided because it would be lethal to starving prisoners.

> Some bloody fool, no doubt inspired by compassion, threw a couple of unopened tins of corned beef to them, and the ensuing fight was utterly sickening; ears, eyes were torn off in the struggle for possession, and by the time the troops separated them, there were seven dead and about 20 more or less badly injured men on the ground.
>
> To such depths can people descend when the veneer of civilisation is removed by hunger and degradation. I was very glad to get away from that place, but the spectacle that had taken place haunted me.

In this final thrust into Germany, rules were much less clear cut than before. Who was telling the truth? Who was just out for revenge? In one village Jock arrested a baker, who was apparently a Gestapo informant.

> He was absolutely terrified . . . he kept on saying he wasn't really a Nazi but was forced to act as the village spy (we never met a self-confessed Nazi!) . . . the officer we saw quite definitely didn't want to be lumbered with a civilian . . . 'What the devil do we do with him?' said we. 'Take the evil bastard into the yard and shoot him,' said he. Stalemate! He was quite a senior officer but to execute someone is very different to an impersonal shooting in action, and we weren't very happy, but took him into the yard just the same.

Jock Walker and his fellow cameraman, Sgt Dennis Smith, moved very slowly. The baker gibbered with fear and revealed where the local Gauleiter* was. As a reward the baker escaped execution. A relieved Jock handed the baker and the Gauleiter to the Field Security Police, who locked them up in the POW cage.

> When they were behind the wire the Field Security Sergeant called the other prisoners to order and said something to them. I asked him what he had said to the other German POWs. 'Oh,' he said, 'I told them these two were Gestapo.' The next morning their dead bodies were found in the compound.

The final stand of the German Army was in the port city of Hamburg. The remnants of the Wehrmacht did not give up, but superior British firepower soon told, and any remaining resistance was squashed. On 30 April Hitler committed suicide in Berlin and, on 3 May, the German Army in Hamburg formally surrendered.

Jock Walker and Dennis Smith arrived to film in Hamburg soon after as the 7th Armoured Division swept through the city.

---

* Provincial governor in Nazi Germany and the third highest rank in the Nazi political leadership.

We drove up the road past shipyard after shipyard wrecked by Allied bombings, without seeing any sign of activity; there was about 20 miles of this utter destruction and it was very eerie, no sign of life at all. Then we saw two German officers.

We got out of the jeep and approached them, hands on holsters, when one of them said in impeccable English, 'You won't need that, sergeant, we aren't armed, and the war is over.' I am not the type to be rendered speechless but, on this occasion, I was, a day or so ago we would have tried to kill or maim each other, and now we were meeting face to face, and they were eager to chat.

The officers had stayed behind to hand Hamburg over while surviving German troops headed towards the Danish border.

Out came the Primus stove and in no time at all a good old British 'cuppa' liberally laced with Scotch whisky was being drunk by the four of us, all chatting like old pals who had met up after a long absence.

They invited us to their HQ, which was a large hotel just down the road, and the four of us got well and truly sloshed with schnapps and whisky.

Paula Kuhl (later Alexander) survived the Hamburg bombings, having miraculously found her mother alive a week later. Paula never forgot the British army's arrival in Hamburg.

I find it impossible to describe my emotions when I saw the first British tanks roll into my battered town . . . through the trees I saw the tanks, rolling slowly and peacefully by, about 150 feet from me and the sun gleaming on them. I sighted the first English soldiers, looking out of the turrets, enemies no more, and soon to become my friends.

I hardly realised that tears were streaming down my face. Even now after all these years tears still spring to my eyes when I talk about it, in fact my eyes are wet while I am writing this down.

After Hamburg, Jock Walker was in Kiel when the unconditional surrender was signed at Luneberg Heath, 80 miles south at 6.30 p.m. on 4 May.

> The marshalling yards at Kiel were just like a plate of spaghetti . . . what a shambles! Proof, once more, that the RAF and the Americans had done a good job . . . still there was one more place to be freed, Denmark.

Jock was uneasy about entering a country full of retreating Nazis, particularly as he was not permitted to carry a weapon now the war was over.

> It was very eerie to be in a city full of armed Germans and us with nothing . . . thank goodness they didn't turn stroppy. The wounded, who were many, were put into Red Cross trains and were returned to their homeland by rail.
>
> All this was done, without any fuss, no fights at all. We all heaved a sigh of relief, went back to Copenhagen where to our total amazement, we were feted like heroes!

In every country liberated from the Nazis, locals reserved the same treatment for women accused of fraternising with the enemy. In Denmark Jock was invited to attend a special parade.

> This turned out to be a parade of all the girls who had fraternised with the Germans; it consisted of females without a stitch on, all their hair cut off, and with placards hung round their necks proclaiming that they were whores, professional and amateur, who had consorted with the detestable Boche, being marched all through the town being jeered at and pelted with rubbish all the way.
>
> A degrading spectacle to us, but to the people of the liberated countries, a soft punishment for making life a bit easier

for the enemy, and knowing what these people of many different nations had suffered, who could blame them?

Whatever he thought of this parade of shaven female heads, and however fatalistic he had been during the fag-end of war, Jock Walker had survived.

> I was in Denmark for six weeks of a lovely sloth-like existence, which enabled me to get the shakes and fears out of my system and thank the Lord that I had managed to survive, more or less whole, the six years of war we had been through, although very, very few of my old boozing school and subsequent mates had.

From Denmark, Jock was dispatched to the destroyed industrial cities of the Ruhr and then to Berlin.

> Berlin was a city in utter ruin except for a few streets here and there... my job was to accompany any notables visiting there, as a photographer... such as Foreign Secretary Ernest Bevin.

Cecil Robinson was a Drapery Manager from Sheffield but became one of Winston Churchill's wartime drivers. He kept a journal. He drove Churchill at the Victory Parade in Berlin in July 1945. His wife, Edna:

> He got a chance to see Hitler's bunker... he got a small piece of brown marble. It was part of Hitler's desk. Other articles he collected included Heinrich Himmler's visiting card.

War's end left Jock Walker with deep contempt for politicians.

> The politician's cock it all up, then call the Armed Services in to restore the status quo, who do their job excellently, sort it all out, and hand it back to the politicians in a nice, neat, bundle, who then proceed to cock it up again.
>
> Is that what my mates were killed and maimed for?
>
> War is a stupid, stinking, filthy business... but as a regular soldier war was my business and, perversely enough for all my

distaste for those who try to glorify it, I enjoyed it. But then again, how much was this revenge for what had happened to my pals and the civilians at home? In seeing those evil bastards decimated, and make no mistake, evil they were, arrogant, jack-booted murderers and I am very pleased with the part I played in helping destroy them.

After the war Jock ran his own camera shop before rejoining the army. He died in 1992.

In 1939, when the Nazis invaded Poland, Zygmunt Skarbek-Krusewski and his Lithuanian wife, Marushka, thought they had lost each other in the chaos of evacuating Warsaw, but were reunited by chance in the endless telephone queue at Warsaw station. They vowed never to be parted and spent the war together, mainly in Lithuania.

They returned to their home city in 1944, just in time to see the Germans fleeing.

> In cars, Germans in [Nazi] Party uniforms were sitting on furniture, crates and suitcases . . . most of the females hugged their fur coats. They were leaving with a rich booty taken from the Jews. The rich heirs of the slain were reluctantly returning to their Fatherland. Here, they had spent their fat years.

But the Nazis hesitated about leaving and the Warsaw Uprising began.

> Warsaw's time had arrived. The army of insurgents had come out from the underground. Gates were being locked, shutters let down, no trams were moving . . . houses became fortresses, streets and squares battlegrounds.

The Nazis were as dangerous in retreat as when advancing. They could not let the uprising succeed. They took control of Zygmunt and Marushka's block of flats, where over one hundred families lived, including some partisans.

> They were the masters of life and death ... holding their automatic guns at the ready. They covered all the exits and ordered all the men to come down to the yard. There was no way out. Slowly, and full of distrust, we assembled in the yard. We were surrounded by SS men. Behind them stood our women, weeping. Their sons, husbands and brothers were here. The Germans ordered us to line up against the wall with our hands up.

Zygmunt waited, filled with fear. Marushka looked on, equally fearful. The SS meticulously searched the flats. No weapons were found. Zygmunt lived on.

The couple went on the run again but evading the Nazis only brought them closer to advancing Soviet troops. By 1945 the threat of Zygmunt being dragooned into the Soviet Army was very close. So, using fake documents, and their Lithuanian passports, the couple escaped into a quiet corner of Germany close to the Swiss border. As a hiding place, Nazi Germany itself was counter-intuitive, crazy even, but to Zygmunt it was safer than being forced into the Red Army.

But at Isny in the Alfauer Alps, they learned that accommodation and ration cards were only given to working men and women. So, Zygmunt was allocated to a factory building aircraft wings and V1 doodlebug rockets to be fired on London. He had spent six years evading the Nazis. Now he was making weapons for them.

> I stopped being an individual and became a cog in the huge working force of the Third Reich ... I became one of the 15 million labourers who were employed in the production of tools for murder, direct or indirect.

But in 1945 their war juddered to an end.

> The first tank rumbled into the marketplace ... behind the tank came an armoured military car, on top of which were

lying soldiers, pointing their machine guns, ready for instant action. From the armoured car came a French officer . . . we only realised that the war was truly finished for us when we saw the first group of German prisoners, guarded by the French.

This was the 62nd Regiment of African Artillery, soldiers mainly from Senegal. The irony of guards from Africa, descendants of slaves, escorting those men wanting to become the Aryan masters of Europe and enslave millions was not lost on Zygmunt.

These men from Africa walked now, smiling, and proud. They were pushing ahead the whites, the whitest of the white masters. They who were once slaves were ordering about a white nation in their own land.

After six years in hiding, Zygmunt and Marushka's war was finally over.

Zygmunt and Marushka, a married couple.

CHAPTER FORTY-EIGHT

VE Day, 1945

The end of the war in May 1945 was marked by the renewal of simple pleasures. Mary Burgess and her nephew enjoyed a carefree walk.

> The striking aspect of it all was the banks of daffodils everywhere. It was though the whole world was new, was young again – and clean.

They joined a queue for ice cream.

> Never have I tasted ice cream so creamy, so sweet and so cold. And the texture was just right – perfect! So, there we were: Mary and I walking along in the spring sunshine, licking ice creams down to the last milky drops which we sucked noisily out of the cardboard corners and happier than we had been in years. That was when the war ended for me, and that was when there seemed to be a future.

Barbara Vanderstock's father had still not returned from the war by VE Day.

> Never mind, we were going to celebrate. Mum organised a massive bonfire in the garden and all our friends came. The flames were as high as the house. We all sang songs of victory – 'Roll out the Barrel', 'It's a Long Way to Tipperary' and 'We'll Meet Again' – a song I later learnt from Dad made soldiers in the western desert weep.

> Next, we went round to the street bonfire party where older boys carried lighted flames and marched in procession, ironically a sight reminiscent of the pre-war Nazi rallies . . . there were flags, trestle tables, home-made paper hats, orange juice, jellies and cakes and we sat there surrounded by laughing grown-ups who would give us anything we wanted. All we children wanted was more cakes, more jelly, and to laugh with everyone else.

The 16-year-old Frank Mee celebrated VE Day in Stockton-on-Tees.

> I went off to a dance and it was riotous, flags draped around the hall and lights full on, everyone kissing everyone else. I drew the line at the hairy-faced sailors and stuck to the girls, making sure I went round several times. We sang, we danced, and we all held hands singing every song we could think of . . . we walked home in groups feeling as if a huge cloud had lifted off our shoulders and I must admit I never once thought of the war in the Far East still going on, as we sang and danced in the streets. Each time we met a group going the other way we shared bottles and kissed all the girls, to a 16-year-old with raging hormones it was seventh heaven.

The scene was similar in Glasgow. Tommy Mac was 14.

> She was an older girl, perhaps 16 or so. Still, she was to be my companion for the rest of the day. We made our way hand in hand from where we lived to find the main celebration in George Square . . . I didn't see many drunks, now I think on it. There was no need. The spirits were lifted high enough as it was. It was quite wonderful to see all the men and women in uniform hugging, kissing, and generally flirting with the civilian population.
>
> During all this time I never once let go of my companion's hand. I danced with her, hugged her, kissed her too. I don't know how many times. I never did find out what her second

name was. All I knew was her name was Norah, my lovely
Norah. In all my life I have never forgotten her, and although
we were as close to being intimate as possible, there was
never any impropriety. We stayed together until 4 a.m. when
we finally kissed and said goodbye, each hugging the other.
I never saw her again, and to this day I sometimes wonder
whether or not Norah remembers as well. My lovely Norah,
with you I shared the most memorable day of my life.*

George Grant was busy on VE Day flying POWs back to England from Germany.

We had the privilege of flying back over England on the
evening of VE Day when all the bonfires were lit. It was a
magnificent sight! . . . I did get a drink sometime early on
the morning of the 9th as the girls in the telephone exchange
found a bottle of gin that had something left in the bottom. I
had a very tiny tot of gin. That was my VE Day!

Ron Goldstein spent VE Day near Venice.

There we were in this field in the middle of nowhere, when
someone on another tank called out, 'They're going mad back
home, get the BBC on your set or you'll miss all the fun.' I
turned my set to the Home Forces station and, for the benefit
of those outside the tank, hung all the earphones over the side
of the hull. The crackle of the headphones soon drew a small
crowd around the tank, and we all listened in amazement to
an unknown announcer describing the scenes in Trafalgar
Square.

    I remember quite clearly that my emotions at the time
were mixed. On one hand it was good to feel that perhaps

---

* After the war Tommy was posted as a peacekeeper to Trieste. He was blown up by a mine and had a leg amputated below the knee. He was happily married to Jean, and they had two children.

some of my loved ones back home were taking part in these scenes. On the other hand, I, and in hindsight, I'm sure most of my comrades, felt somehow cheated that we, who had risked life and limb and had been away from home for so many years, were not there in England to share in the triumph.

A few days later Ron had bad news.

> I received a letter to say that my brother Jack had been shot down over Germany and had been posted as missing. It reached me within a week of the war ending in Europe...

Ulric Cross, a Bomber Command navigator from Trinidad, was the most decorated West Indian in the RAF. He was nicknamed The Black Hornet. Ulric travelled into Central London to join in the celebrations around the blazing bonfires, but immediately headed home.

> Everybody was overjoyed and I just didn't feel like taking any part in it. I just felt a lot of people had been killed. This was not a cause for celebration... a lot of my friends were killed... I was extremely glad the war was over.

Polish teenager Maria Hay had been snatched by the SS in Poland and transported to Germany as forced labour. She had received no news of her parents for five years.

> Bells were ringing, we looked out and saw the Americans, the German were hanging white pillowcases out of the windows... there was a young Englishman from Sunderland who delivered medication. I got to know him. He said he would take me to England, and 'you can stay with my family' and I will try to trace your family.
>
> The paperwork was dauntingly complex, so the man's officer suggested it would be simpler to get married, which

we did . . . I was fond of him, and I knew he loved me. I found at that point in time difficulty in loving anyone.*

Not everyone had the chance to start a peacetime life. Thirteen-year-old Terence Cartwright was cycling near Leicester a month before VE Day.

> Newly cut grass, blossoms and farmyard manure produced a cocktail of sensations, which could only portray a typical, peaceful English summer Sunday. The war was coming to an end, rations were easing, and it felt good to be alive . . . there was a simmering haze covering the rolling green fields and, in the distance, we heard, and then saw, a Lancaster bomber with an accompanying Spitfire tagging behind, droning majestically towards us.
>
> A minute or so after the drone of the engines changed abruptly to a high-pitched scream. We looked up in alarm and to our horror we saw the Lancaster in a vertical dive, descending at a terrifying speed towards the ground, only a few yards from where we stood. We tried to run but could not move. Our legs were rooted to the spot. Just when we thought our end had come, a miracle happened, with engines howling, the plane suddenly began to pull out of the dive, as if trapped inside the invisible U-bend of a waste pipe . . .
>
> [Then] we witnessed the plane turn on its back and plunge earthwards once more. We saw its black silhouette disappear below the horizon of the railway embankment and a split second later a tremendous orange/red/black mushroom of fire clawed its way into the blue sky . . .
>
> The site of the crash was covered in a layer of smoke . . . there in the meadow, as if stamped by a giant's hand, was a scarred outline of the Lancaster . . . ammunition was

---

*The marriage worked, and the Red Cross found Maria's family.

exploding, sending puffs of ash into the air like a volcano ready to erupt... with a numbing sense of shock I realised I was looking at what appeared to be a human shoulder blade. I then saw a sock... inside was half a foot.

The smells of the countryside had dissolved into an unforgettable stench of burnt fuel and flesh. The summer haze now acrid smoke... I don't remember the journey home.*

Arthur Kenvin from Merthyr Tydfil, Wales, was a navigator with RAF 625 squadron. He was killed just seven weeks before VE Day. Nine days before he died, he wrote a letter to be read in the event of his death.

Dear Mam and Dad, Mary, Marg and Dave,

As you read this your hearts will be heavy, and your sorrow will be great. The future and the past are blacked out by this tragedy of war, and the burden of personal loss will feel too heavy to be borne on your shoulders... if all hopes of my return are gone, then, Mam and Dad, Mary and Margaret, please accept the facts without bitterness in your heart. Find great comfort that I found great happiness in our home.

All around us is unhappiness, but in our four walls enclose a real family love I set out in the world knowing that I had the love and understanding of you all behind me. I learned the good things in life, how to appreciate the beautiful, simple things around me, and I thank you for all the happiness I have enjoyed. I have no regrets, and you can have none too because you have all done so much to make our home life a happy one...

Until we meet again, May God Bless You and Sustain You,
All my love to all I know from your loving son,
Arthur.

---

* All six men died. Norman Cook, the pilot, was 23. The Lancaster was from the 1653 Conversion Unit. A memorial was erected on the site at Thurnby Lodge.

CHAPTER FORTY-NINE

The Far East, 1945

There might be joy in Europe, but fighting was still fierce in the Far East where prisoners-of-war knew nothing of VE Day. In his camp on the River Kwai Railway Len Baynes's only focus was on staying alive. He was a natural survivor, adept at every task. He performed burials, killed and butchered animals, and created mugs for sale out of discarded metal. But years of malnutrition and illness threatened to bring even Len down.

> Seeing neighbours die every day, I became very depressed... I was determined to get away from this camp of sick men, lest I also lost the will to live... [but] no matter how many friends I saw carried out feet first, I never seriously considered joining them. A confidence from outside myself seemed somehow to make me feel that I was different from the others who were dying.

Len led working parties repairing bridges on the River Kwai after the Allies bombed the railway line so many thousands of POWs had died building. He was shocked when he saw trains transporting sick and wounded Japanese soldiers arrive at the station. Their conditions were as brutal as those endured by the POWs transported from Singapore to the River Kwai.

> A train of closed-steel cattle trucks pulled into the siding 25 yards from where we were sitting. A party of Japs appeared from the station hut carrying buckets of rice which they

placed beside the train, one to every third truck. They went back and appeared with buckets of water which they set down beside the rice. Then, they slid open all the doors.

As we watched, thin legs pushed out of the door openings and weakly reached for the ground. One emaciated creature fell out and remained in a crumpled heap where he had fallen, quite still.

A Japanese guard told Len they would not help their dying comrades because it was dishonourable, and that the wounded men should have killed themselves. As one, Allied prisoners rose to help.

We were greeted by a terrible stench as we approached the trucks. These poor chaps must have been shut in without food or water, and no toilet facilities, for several days. Some were only boys, most under 22 years. Nearly every truck contained several dead; many had terrible wounds, undressed, and covered in flies.

Others had amputations only covered in field dressings... our men, their prisoners, walked the length of the train lifting those out who were able to stand, and filling mess tins and water bottles for the others. When we had done all we could, we returned, nauseated, to our guards.

About ten minutes later a Jap drove up in a lorry. Tamils piled out and commenced loading the dead from the train into the back of the lorry. As it drove off into the jungle, we could see that the bodies were piled up higher than the sides, and the Tamils were sitting on top of the load. We soon saw smoke rising from the jungle as the bodies were burned.

In her prison camp on Banka Island, Phyllis Briggs's close friendship with Mary Jenkin had survived three years of grim captivity.

Mary was still weak when one day the ration lorry arrived. It had come from the men's camp and beside the rations came bundles belonging to the men who had died and whose wives were with us. Mary was handed a pair of boots and a small case – evidently her husband had died a few weeks earlier. Mary was very brave – quiet and unable to cry, she was determined to keep going for the sake of her son, Robert, who was 21 and in England the last time she had seen him.

In early March 1945, Phyllis and Mary endured another miserable, long journey from Muntok to their next camp, Loeboek Linggau, deep in Sumatra's malarial interior. Two prisoners died on the sea journey before the women were transferred onto trains.

> Mary was feeling ill and could hardly stagger along . . . [we] were in a closed train truck which had previously been used for coal. It was filthy and very hot because the Japs made us keep the steel doors shut. There was a large pot of water in the truck, and it slopped over and mixed with the coal dust on the floor where the patients were lying.
> The patients were mostly Dutch nuns suffering from fever and diarrhoea and asking for bed pans all the time. These we had to empty through a small opening in the door . . . the smell and the heat were almost beyond endurance.
> At the end of our second night, we were bundled out before dawn into torrential rain. We had to carry the sick who were unable to walk, and everyone got soaked to the skin. We had to lift the stretcher cases along a road and up a steep slippery bank to a warehouse. We were exhausted and shivering by the time we had finished.
> I looked round our new camp and was not impressed. The camp was in the middle of a large rubber estate, surrounded by jungle . . . huts were badly built, the roofs leaked, and the floors were of mud. There were puddles of rain, and grass grew inside.

Phyllis's only case arrived two days later.

> Many people had had clothes and other things stolen. My precious sewing needles had gone and other things of real value.

I could have wept because I only had a few cents left and just did not know how I was going to manage. Later I sold my last piece of jewellery – Mother's gold bracelet. I should have had five times as much, but not being in with the black-market people, I had to get someone to sell it for me and she got a good rake-off.

Phyllis nursed the sick without any medicines in appalling conditions in the 'hospital' huts.

The wood was rotten, and the roof leaked. Both buildings were rat-infested. The rats squeaked and ran about all night . . .

Mary Jenkin showed signs of improvement but couldn't undertake hospital work.

I used to go up to see her every day and was glad to see her getting stronger . . . the best place in the hut was bagged by Mrs Rover – a German married to a Dutchman who was somewhere in Java . . . she evidently got on quite well with the Japs, for when she was sent to join us 18 months after we had been captured, she arrived looking as fit and fat as if she had been through no hardships . . . she loved her coffee and her cigarette and always had plenty of both as she was well in with the black-market people.

Mary improved but food was still a problem.

We sometimes got carrots, which were welcome, but there was never enough of anything. The only thing we got more of was coffee and palm oil. Although we had to buy the coffee, it was really good quality – very coarse and grown locally . . . many times when I was on the verge of fainting, a cup of coffee and a spoonful of sugar would bring me round – Mary generally came to my rescue . . . once the Japanese sent us black bear – this meat was good but we had such a small portion that it made us hungry for more. Once we had monkey, the grey long-haired variety and, although we only had about a dessert spoon of stew each, it tasted very stringy. Once we had some stew sent to us that the kitchen staff said was jungle meat. It did not taste as strong as the monkey – later we discovered it was panther!

In normal times the estate must have been a rather lovely place – ferns large and small grew all along the riverbanks ... some were pink tipped, almost coral colour – others were blue and green like shot silk ... latterly I picked them for funerals – and I shall always connect ferns with dear friends who had gone.

The coffins were very rough boxes made of boards that did not even join together properly. We used to cover the coffin tops with ferns to make them look more decent and fill the gaps.

Phyllis had no idea the European war was over. At home, men and women were pulling the threads of normal life together again, working, loving, reconnecting. In Phyllis's world the casualties of war only grew.

Miss Dryburgh, Nan Wier, Miss Livingstone, Mary Cooper, Macfle – all real friends dying one after another – several Dutch nuns and Australian sisters died – always one or two deaths every day.

The gravediggers found it difficult to dig deep enough, it took so much strength. In the end it was the children who were the strongest and it was they who did the digging.

It was Margaret Dryburgh's death that was most disturbing. She had been co-founder of the vocal orchestra,* writer of poems and hymns, and an inspirational fighter for survival. A little cross with her name and date burnt into it was placed by her jungle grave. Margaret was one of 89 women who died at the camp in just a few months.

---

* Margaret Dryburgh wrote down music from memory and hummed Beethoven and Brahms. She died of dysentery on 21 April 1945.

CHAPTER FIFTY

Japan, 1945

In 1945 the Allies prepared for a final assault on Japan. The Americans had successfully fought their way up towards the Japanese homeland, island by island, encountering fierce resistance from the enemy, with huge loss of lives on both sides. In Okinawa alone, 240,000 troops and civilians died, including nearly 50,000 Americans killed, wounded or missing.

A final invasion of mainland Japan would cost even more lives. One British priority, however, was to capture a Japanese-held airfield in Malaya, as a springboard for the recapturing of Singapore. Tim Hardy, 5th Independent Parachute Brigade, sailed to Mumbai for this final assault on Japan's empire.

> We weren't in India simply to marvel at the marbled palaces, sublime temples, beautiful people and the grossest possible abominations, but to mug up on ways of slaughtering the Japanese. Long reconciled to expect little better than idiocy from our generals, we raised scarcely an eyebrow when they told us we were about to storm Japanese-held beaches from the sea. We, who'd been trained for years with one thing in mind; to drop on the enemy from the skies, we, who'd never set eyes on a landing craft let alone been aboard one, were nonetheless scheduled to sail into battle by sea.
>
> To a cynical old soldier like me, the plan sounded familiarly hair-brained ... we were all told to trust the

intelligence-wallahs who knew what they were about. Given our past experiences, it was advice that made our hearts sink.

While Hardy's heart was sinking, Len Baynes was repairing the Thai–Burma railway, and Phyllis Briggs was burying her friends. One hundred and forty thousand other men and women, British, Australian, Dutch, and American, were prisoners of the Japanese in all corners of its fading empire. In Japan itself there was scarcely a coal mine, shipyard or munitions factory that did not function without the forced labour of POWs. In the port city of Nagasaki, home to Mitsubishi, builders of warships, fighter aircraft and torpedoes, nearly 2,000 men were imprisoned in two camps. The POWs were certain an Allied invasion of the Japanese mainland would result in them all being executed.

News of Hiroshima's bombing on 6 August 1945 never reached the prisoners in these Nagasaki camps, but three days later it was their turn.

New York Times writer William Laurence flew in an observer aircraft alongside Bock's Car, the B-29 bomber carrying an atomic bomb. Laurence described the explosion 45 seconds after detonation over Nagasaki.

> It was no longer smoke or dust, or even a cloud of fire. It was a living thing, a new species, born right before our incredulous eyes. At one stage in its evolution, covering millions of years in terms of seconds, the entity assumed the identity of a giant square totem pole, with its base about three miles long... its bottom was brown, its centre amber, its top white. But it was a living totem pole, carved with many grotesque masks grimacing at the earth... there came shooting out of the top a mushroom that increased the height of the pillar to a total of 45,000 feet. The mushroom top was even more alive than the pillar. Seething and boiling in a white fury of creamy foam

Bomb over Nagasaki, 9 August 1945

Yorkshireman Ron Bryer from the RAF was repairing a small bomb shelter in Camp 14b, just over a mile from the detonation point.

> There was this tremendous violet, white flash, almost liquid in intensity. Not a momentary thing. It seemed to last for several seconds . . . there was a tremendous vibration along with it, not an explosion at all. And then, as the vibration continued, the wall of the factory came down. I remember bricks pouring through the hole and thundering on top of the shelter and the shelter gave way and a weight came onto my back. I think I must have been struck on the head by one of the bricks because, when I came out, I had a mark on my head. Momentarily everything went black. When I came to there was nothing to identify with at all. I thought I was dead.

The prison camp was wiped out. As he came round, Ron Bryer saw Japanese workmen running wildly through the haze.

Possibly a hundred in number. Leaping and scrambling with desperation over the fallen fences and rubble. None looked either left or right as they passed me on both sides. I heard no sound except the noise of their panting. The desperate noise of animals cornered after the hunt. Deep sobbing gasps of despair from lungs tortured by the demands of a flight from death. Many wore clothing still on fire. It smouldered and sparked as they ran. But others cared not. Others, almost naked, bore huge blisters as big as party balloons on arms and legs and torn remnants of scorched cloth burned into other body areas exposed to the blast. Blisters collapsed as I watched, and streamers of ragged skin fluttered like wind-torn pennants as the men fled in terror towards the imagined safety of the open countryside.

The exact number of dead at Nagasaki from the bomb and its aftermath is contested, but 70,000 is the most common estimate. Of the 195 POWs in Camp 14b that day, miraculously only eight died despite being just 1.1 miles from the bomb's epicentre. Nagasaki's citizens lived in flimsy wooden structures and the brick buildings of the camp offered much better protection.

In Camp 14b, Claude Belloni, Royal Dutch East Indies Army, wrote a diary.

Little is left of Nagasaki. No flowers, no trees, no more grass. Only boiling concrete and molten iron and steel. Within a minute thousands of houses were on fire. There were only flames... smoke... and the weeping of the dying... and then the stench, the pungent stench, in particular, was indescribable, a greasy odour of burnt flesh of thousands and thousands of people. Many dissolved into nothing, some of them have only their shadow left, their bodies printed on cement or on a wall.

Tim Hardy was also liberated by Hiroshima and Nagasaki. Now he would not be killed the minute he landed on a Malayan beach.

> We were as cheerful as men on death row hearing of their reprieve... we danced on the decks.

But the reprieve was only temporary.

> We danced on the decks too soon. As we might have guessed, our generals had other ideas. Disappointed at being cheated out of a bloodletting, they still wanted to play their war games. Operation Zipper, they declared, would go ahead regardless. What followed, even without an enemy to fight on the beaches, turned out to be one of the greatest military cock-ups in history.

The paras, more used to airborne than seaborne landings, were so overloaded with equipment they swiftly sank into the water.

> I paddled my feet like a duck and managed to inch my way towards land without having to jettison anything more than a grenade or two but most of the others, panicking, threw away guns, boots, packs, helmets, everything. Then, just as were about to touch down on what we thought would be firm sand (we had been assured it was 'just like concrete'), we felt ourselves being sucked into the gooey black paste of mangrove swamp across whose odious surface we flopped like beached whales.

Ken Cragg was also part of Operation Zipper.

> Our backpacks weighed 40 pounds... [plus] our rifle and 150 rounds of ammo... the ramp was lowered, and I jumped only to find myself up to my neck in water.

Tim Hardy:

> Having slithered our way across the ooze on our bellies like mudfish, there fell upon us another terrible misfortune... an electric storm crashed through the heavens, pitilessly, for

> hour after hour... there we stood, hundreds of us, stock-still in the pitch dark, deluged jungle, our bare feet sunk, letting our blood to mosquitos and leeches, cursing all officers, and praying for daybreak.

The wretched shape of their sodden troops forced the generals to call the pointless operation off.

> What would have happened if the war had not been called off a day or two earlier? What would have happened is that the blood of their soldiers would have stained the sea crimson all the way back to the motherships.

On 15 August an extraordinary event took place in Japan. For the first time, the Japanese heard the god-like figure of their Emperor, Hirohito, on the radio. He announced that the war was over.

In Len Baynes's Thai jungle camp, the prisoners heard the news.

> We responded spontaneously with a deafening cheer, and then gathered in little groups to discuss the news. How can I explain what it felt like to be told that a bad dream of nearly four years was at last ended? It was a most complex reaction. Why was my soul not soaring with rapture at the thought of the fast-approaching freedom? My tummy turned over with an unidentifiable fear... I had left home a lad, but to use my sister's words after I had returned home, I came back looking like a queer old man.
>
> Just outside our camp was a large cemetery, containing the remains of all the POWs who had died... we held a memorial service there, attended by all the fit prisoners, plus the Jap camp commandant and his staff.

Two weeks after war's end, Sergeant Len Baynes was packed into a US Air Force Dakota and flown out on the bumpy runway the prisoners had built themselves.

> Had there been a window in the floor I might have taken a farewell look at the railway line, every sleeper of which represented a man's life.

American bombers dropped desperately needed food supplies into camps where skeletal survivors waited to be shipped out. Neil Reid was in a POW camp not far from Nagasaki.

> The bomb doors opened, and a large pallet stacked with 60-gallon steel drums welded together in two's were dropped. The parachutes attached to the drums broke away almost immediately and the drums dropped like bombs. Two Koreans in the next camp were killed ... two days later the planes returned, this time with smaller cardboard cartons filled with tins of peaches, salmon, soup and Spam.

In Nagasaki, A-Bomb survivor Ron Bryer almost died when a consignment of chewing gum dropped from the sky missed him by inches.

> Having survived the atomic bomb, I don't think it was written that I should be killed by a ton of American chewing gum.

Alistair Urquhart:

> After three and a half years as a POW, I was a dirty, stinking, demoralised and degraded human being. I weighed 5 stones 12lbs (I was nine and a half stones when I joined up). I was bald, my hair having fallen out at the shock of being sunk. The oil I swallowed had burned my vocal cords ... the luxury after all that time was a shower with soap!

At Loebeok Linggau, Phyllis Briggs heard nothing of the atomic bombing or the Japanese surrender, and her friend Mary Jenkin grew weaker. Phyllis made soup for Mary, but she could not swallow.

> I realised that she could not live much longer, in fact her emaciated body was in such a state we hoped it would not be

JAPAN, 1945

> long. Helen MacKenzie was very good and helped me every morning to bathe her and make her as comfortable as possible and at night I used to go over to the hospital and tuck her up.
>
> On 16 August Mary was much worse. She dozed most of the day, she had very little pain and about 7 p.m. the last thing she said was, 'I can't do anymore – I'm going to join Charlie.'*
> I spoke to her and said I would see Robert, her son, when I got home to give him her love and to say how brave she had been – she gave a little smile – then soon after became unconscious and died within an hour.

Mary died one day after Japan's capitulation. She was the tenth woman out of Phyllis's original group of fifteen from Garage 9 to die.

On 24 August Phyllis and the others were summoned and a Japanese captain† announced that the war was over and that 'we are now all friends'.

> I think most of us were so stunned we would not let ourselves believe it at first. Later we found that the war had been over since 15 August. The next day we were all given cholera injections! Rations increased and included things we had not seen for years – Milo, Klim milk, tinned butter – even lipsticks! The Japs obviously wanted us to look in better shape by the time we were freed.

The officer in charge of their liberation, Major Gideon Jacobs, Royal Marines, was shocked by the appalling state of the camp and the emaciated women and children inside it. The Japanese had held back significant amounts of life-saving medicines, like quinine. He requested an air drop of supplies.

---

* Charlie Jenkins, her husband.

† Capt Saiki Kazue: a War Crimes Tribunal in 1948 sentenced him to 15 years imprisonment for harsh treatment of internees.

> An Allied plane flew low over the camp and dropped bread and newspapers by parachute – the first bread we had tasted for three and a half years. Unfortunately, the extra rations arrived too late to save a number of people. Molly Watts-Carter was among those who were dying, but she was fully conscious and calmly whispered to me that she was happy to have lived long enough to know that soon we would all be free.

The women in Phyllis's camp were the last Allied prisoners to be liberated in Sumatra, because finding the women in such a remote camp had been so difficult. It was not until 16 September 1945, five weeks after the atomic bombs were dropped, that Phyllis left Loeboek Linggau. She weighed less than six stone.

Phyllis was shipped to the Queen Alexandra Hospital, Singapore, where the Japanese had massacred hundreds of patients and staff in early 1942.

> It was wonderful to be in a real bed between white sheets. The Sister came over to see me the next morning and I felt ashamed as I saw her staring with horror – a bed bug had crawled out of my little bag and was crawling across the snow-white sheet!
>
> We had tried to keep ourselves free of vermin. I weighed six stone and had scabies but was thankful not to have swollen legs and a rice tummy like so many others. The hospital staff looked funny to us, they all seemed to have such large busts and behinds until I realised that we had gotten used to only seeing emaciated people.

Freedom for Phyllis Briggs was bittersweet. In her nearly four years of imprisonment over 500 men and women had died in her camps.*

---

* Judy Balcombe, Muntok Peace Museum.

JAPAN, 1945

Several husbands from POW camps came looking for their wives. We had to tell them that they had died, and others had been drowned leaving Singapore three and a half years before.

When Phyllis was fit enough, she searched for her fiancé, Tony Cochrane, who had proposed to her before the Allied surrender of Singapore. She located an office for missing people.

I was told that Tony had never been a POW in Singapore and that he was listed as missing presumed dead. He must have been one of the many who perished at sea in February 1942. It was a bitter blow.

CHAPTER FIFTY-ONE

Homecoming, 1945

Both British civilians and troops were excited about homecomings, but joy was intermingled with anxiety because many men had not been home for years. Would their children recognise them? Were their parents and siblings still alive? Would their wife or girlfriend have found another man? And, for women, would her husband or boyfriend be the same person after witnessing so much horror on the battlefield or in a POW camp?

Eunice Edwards (later Jones), a Birmingham typist, wrote well about her daily experiences. Hers was an undramatic war, but she understood how deeply the world had changed for many.

> Everybody longed for the end of the war – to come home and get back to normal. Alas, no one could go back to 1939. Everything had changed. Some people had married and wanted new houses; some had lost loved ones and couldn't rejoice. Some people didn't want their old jobs back. Some people got married after long separations and others got divorced as soon as they could. Some girls had married soldiers from America and Canada and went away to start new lives. It was a case of new beginnings for all of us.

Sergeant Len Scott, Royal Army Pay Corps, and his Danish-born wife Minna enjoyed a passionate marriage, but three years apart heralded deep anxieties. Minna wrote to Len:

HOMECOMING, 1945

> I seem to be very keyed up about your return and so, it would appear, are you. Shall we find each other changed... so many things have happened in three years with such large proportion of grief, loneliness, and suffering... oh, my dear, I sometimes wish you did love me less. I just cannot live up to it and cannot bear to hurt you.

Len Scott:

> There are nearly a hundred steps from this road to our hilltop house. It is winter and the garden has that half-dead look which makes one disbelieve in a coming spring... there is a light in our sitting-room window. I reach our front door. I had shut it behind me more than three years ago. It will be a doorway to a new life. I press the bell.

Kenneth Hulbert had been away over four years.

> It was 9 p.m., pitch dark and I had difficulty finding the house. I rang the bell and Violet answered. She was totally aghast and said 'Oh, Ken', and went for Mother. She was excited and her immediate reaction was to get a meal, which was my first taste of Spam.*

Henry Lund, captured at St Valery-en-Caux, the 'Other' Dunkirk, in June 1940, had been a prisoner for five years and now weighed just seven stone.

> I knocked on the back door and opened it and saw a very small boy hiding behind a cupboard. He looked at me with two very wide brown eyes and fled upstairs shouting: 'My Daddy's home.' He was five years old, and this was the first time I had seen him.

---

* Kenneth died aged 90 in 2003.

Bert Ruffle from Birmingham had been a POW since Dunkirk, May 1940.

> I stood on the corner of Ludstone Road and looked at number 5. It was so silent and peaceful. I crossed the road and sat on the fence and lit a fag... I threw some bits of grit up at Edna's window. Then a voice I had not heard in five years came from the other bedroom, 'I'm coming.' I heard a shout, 'He's here.' I was home... at last!

Eight-year-old Barbara Vanderstock's father did not return home until September 1945.

> We went to town on the decorations, crowning our efforts with a large poster 'Welcome Home Dad.' We didn't know when he was coming so the decorations were up for some days... one night we went to sleep and we were woken up by Dad, who was in his army uniform standing at the door, he said 'Hello Erbs', and we said 'Hello Dad.' It was a strangely ordinary moment.

In November 1945, Ron Goldstein was given his first home leave, having been fighting abroad since April 1943.

> As I got off the bus in Manor Road, I could see the front door some 200 yards away. Over the doorway I could see some decorations had been placed in position in patriotic red, white and blue. It was obviously one of those many 'welcome home' signs that I had been seeing all the way from Dover, and I must confess to being quite touched.
>
> It was only when I got right outside the door that I could read the sign itself. It said, 'WELCOME HOME JACK'. My name is Ron! My brother-in-law had beaten me to it and had taken all the wind out of my sails!

For Tim Hardy peacetime was a chance to finally cement his smouldering relationship with Doreen Fenner. On 8 June 1945, they were married before he was dispatched to the Far East.

> Maybe she was turned on by imagining me in tropical shorts; whatever sparked her off, it was Doreen herself who put forward the idea that we might share a bed before I sailed. The proviso, standard in those days, was that bedding came only after the ritual of holy wedlock.
>
> It was a daft, brave thing to have done. But we did it. We parted, neither for the first or the last time, to go our separate ways, not just across county borders, not even to put only a country between us, but to be separated by whole continents. Always though, to come back, happily, to each other.

Having escaped H and C. H. Blinkhorn, the Nottinghamshire hosiery manufacturer, to join up in 1939, the acute need for wages led him back there. To Tim, Blinckhorns had not improved in the six intervening years.

> The old sickly-green sign was still there, the dreadful driveway still pitted and sludgy, the surroundings still befouled with factory waste and chicken shit (Harold kept a run of fowls)... No ruling family outside a Zola novel ever exploited its workers so calculatedly or callously.

In 1950 Tim Hardy escaped Blinckhorns for a second time and, in a surprising turn for an anti-establishment man, joined the Colonial Police in Malaya. He specialised in counterterrorism, and also served in Tanzania, Fiji and Hong Kong. He was happily married to Doreen, and they had two children. He died aged 91.

Homecoming was even more difficult for survivors of Japanese imprisonment. By the time they straggled home, VE Day was long past, and a new chapter in everyone's life had opened. These skeletal survivors were almost an embarrassment. Friends and relatives did not know how to deal with men who had been malnourished and tortured. For the children who had not seen their dad for four years, it was a strange day when a gaunt man calling himself 'father' turned up. Mike Nellis met his dad on Scarborough Railway Station.

> It was a dank sort of night and the train came into the station with all the steam and hissing and what have you, and we looked down the platform and the doors opened and this figure came out and my mother stiffened up a little bit and my sister grabbed her hand . . . then this figure with his cap dropped his kitbag on the platform and they just rushed into each other's arms . . . and my father huddled up to me – and that's the last time he ever cuddled me. I can remember it like yesterday! He was shaking and there were tears in his eyes.

After a long journey from Thailand, Len Baynes finally arrived home in Cambridgeshire.*

> My sister told me afterwards they hardly knew me. I had left home a fresh-faced young man and now I looked (to them) like an old man.

Three years after the war, Len had a leg amputated after a terrible car accident. He married, had three children and was a successful builder. He never harboured anger with the Japanese and died at the age of 91.

With her fiancé Tony Cochrane dead, Phyllis Briggs did not know what to do next until her brother suggested Phyllis joined him in New Zealand.

> We disembarked and were then seen by a doctor – finally we were able to join our friends and relatives. Dear Tom and Mabel had been waiting a long time. I do not remember anything about the first evening with them. I only knew they

---

* Seven hundred and eighty-four Fen Tigers were killed or died in Japanese captivity.

were most understanding and it was wonderful to be free and in a real home once more.

Adjustment to life outside the camps was difficult.

> It was frightening to be alone – even to be in a bedroom alone...
> I was afraid to even cross the road alone, to go into a shop or on a bus. It took a lot of courage to do any of those things.

Phyllis was yellow, with scabies on her skin, and hair that came out in lumps. She craved normality. Once she was healthier, Phyllis wanted to return to nursing in Malaya but was overwhelmed by anxiety when she returned from New Zealand.

> I really am alone. I've left my brother; my fiancé is lost; I have to start a job again. I couldn't face it. I walked up and down the bedroom three or four times and when I got near to the window, I felt I wanted to jump. It was a terrible struggle to resist the feeling.

Phyllis returned to Malaya with the Colonial Nursing Service in 1947, where she met and married Robert Thom, a senior colonial policeman who shared her POW experience. He was captured at the 'Other' Dunkirk at St Valery-en-Caux and was a POW of the Germans for five years. Phyllis had only been married for 19 years when Robert died, leaving her with two young daughters. Phyllis stayed strong, and died in Bournemouth in 2008 aged 100. She didn't talk about her Japanese prisoner experience for over 40 years.

Phyllis in 1947 and later

Unlike Phyllis Briggs, some former POWs of Japan were lucky enough to be reunited with their loved ones. Gus Anckhorn:

> Just touching hands was the most incredible experience you could imagine. I had known only harsh, sun-parched hands and calloused skin for so long and now, suddenly, the softness and wholesomeness of Lucille was like an electric shock awakening me.

Ambulance driver Monica Littleboy had no idea that her handsome boyfriend was still alive in a Japanese camp until he returned home. In the meantime she had found a new man, who she now decided to let go.

> It was as if a life had suddenly come back from the dead ... he stood there, and I couldn't believe my eyes. This was not the young man I had known. I was stunned. Misshapen. Pitted, scarred. Only the eyes were the same. I could have wept ... I looked at this hulk of humanity and my heart bled ... could I keep this man alive and help him get back into life again? I loved the spirit of the man but could love nothing else. I had to do it.

Sapper Lionel Morris's family had been told he was missing, believed dead.

> My heart beat like a hammer. I rang the bell a third time ... a window opened above my head and my father's voice enquired, 'Who is it?' I answered, 'It's Lionel.' He, somewhat bewildered, asked, 'Lionel who?' 'It's Lionel, your son, who else should it be?' He came down the stairs two at a time, the door flung open, and he stood there gaping, unbelieving. I though he was going to fall, but at last he got the message. 'I'm all right,' I said, 'I've come home.'

EPILOGUE

Remembrance, 1945

Since the end of the war there have been thousands of acts of remembrance, both individual and collective. RAF and Luftwaffe pilots shake hands years after shooting at each other in the Battle of Britain. The children of men and women murdered in the Nazi concentration camps weep beside graves full of impersonal ashes. Former prisoners of war return to Nagasaki, where they were incarcerated, invited back in a spirit of reconciliation; both prisoners and their former enemy struggling to make sense of atomic horror.

We live in the present and dream of the future. It is all too easy to forget the past. So, I have chosen a handful of these memories to represent much more than an individual act of remembrance; they stand for all; their voices are the voices of everyone who lost loved ones; their tears are shed for all who died in the bloody conflict that was The People's War.

Prince Hill, Cheshire, England: in 1944 a Wellington bomber crashed in a peaceful farmer's field here. Six young men were killed on their final training flight before their first bombing mission over Europe. One man survived. An 80-year-old widow, despite a new life in Canada and another husband and family is still grieving; over 50 years later she wants answers to what happened when her young husband died.

The widow had to see the site; was determined to know every detail. Somehow it might assuage the grief. Fifty-six years after the crash, she flew to Cheshire, England. She found it to be just a farmer's field. But spirits haunted the hedgerow, where the holly bushes had been roughly pruned by the plummeting aircraft. No scars remained in the earth now, no hint of the wind and the ice and the screaming impact. Now, only memories lingered. And a bit of the aircraft presented by the farm boy to the grieving widow.

The farm boy was no longer a boy, but was now in his sixties. The farmer himself, now aged 97, still farmed the field. Aircraft remnants were occasionally turned up by his plough. They were pleased to meet the widow.

She laid flowers. She wept bitter tears. The local people observed in respect and wonder; that their field could stir such memories; that someone could come 'all this way' to weep at the site. They thought it a touching and final goodbye.

But they also thought too many widows were passing on, taking their memories with them. The next generation needed to be reminded. And they did something about it.

And so, in October 2023, it came to be – an elegantly simple blue-brick memorial built by local volunteers using donated materials . . . the names are touched with silver – six souls and one lone survivor. The dedication ceremony was attended by a lone bugler, standard bearers, an honour guard. Local residents streamed into the field to observe the event. The families came to lay wreaths in respect, to honour their fallen relatives. Representatives from the Royal British Legion and the Royal Air Force saluted and spoke their words. The mayor carefully folded a flag. Heads were bowed in prayer. Voices were lifted in praise.

EPILOGUE

Six lives were lost that day, in training for battle they never fought, yet as dead as any who died on the cruel battlefields in Europe. Gone, but remembered still.*

The widow was Marjorie Harrison. She had been married for just four months when her husband, Laurence, was killed.

Roy Weaver lived as a child in the small village of Parham near Framlingham, Suffolk, close to the home of the US Air Force 390th Bomb Group, 570th Squadron. When he first visited America as an adult, Roy felt a strange connection.

> I felt as if I had fallen out of the sky and landed where I was supposed to be. It was one of the strangest feelings I had ever experienced.

Fifty years after the war, his sister told Roy that his father was not who he thought he was but an American GI who had returned home four months after Roy's birth.

> If anybody had touched me at that moment, even very lightly, I think I would have fallen over.

For months Roy searched desperately for his father, Kenneth Weaver from Pennsylvania. He eventually tracked down a likely candidate to a trailer park in the California desert.

> I looked at the California number that was straight in front of me and I swear to God that my blood reached boiling point. At least I had it, the closest I had ever been. This must be him, it had to be him.
>
> I heard an older man's voice, 'Hello, this is Ken Weaver.' ... I began by asking if he was based in Parham, Suffolk, during the war. 'Yeah, sure I was,' he said ... 'Do you remember a lady, her name was Lou, Lou Ellis?' 'I remember her very

---

* Words by her daughter, Anne Shelton.

well,' came his reply... 'From what my sister tells me, I think there is a strong possibility that we could be father and son.' I stopped talking just as if I had dried up. I waited with my heart thumping like a sledgehammer.

After just a few seconds, Ken slowly replied, 'It's more than a strong possibility. I don't know how long you have been searching, partner, but it's over now. You've found the man you are looking for.'

Roy met his father in California. Ken died three years later but Roy formed a long-lasting relationship with his half-siblings.

Like Roy Weaver, Michael Skeet spent a lifetime excavating family secrets buried by war. His father, Maurice, was a Bomber Command Squadron Leader on the 1,000-bomber raids to Germany. Michael was told that his father had been killed in action, but the family's evasiveness around his father's death made him suspicious. At 13 Michael secretly searched through his mother's personal papers.

'Haemorrhage and lacerations of the brain from a gunshot wound. Took his own life while the balance of his mind was disturbed.' It took some moments for the words I had just read to penetrate my brain. I read it again. This was my father's death certificate. Suicide. It couldn't be. It was. His name was there. His address. His rank. Please. No! No! In disbelief, my childhood pride screamed out for it not to be true. The horror and anguish tore at my very existence.

Michael Skeet spent years trying to solve the mystery of his father's death. It was clear that his father was a respected pilot but was troubled by dropping bombs on German civilians.

My father had been unable to reconcile his conscience with his duties... a victim of conflict of conscience... I am convinced that my father acted with great courage and the best of intentions and was just as much a casualty as all the other

EPILOGUE

brave and valiant fighting men who gave their lives in the service of this country.

Michael found his father buried in an RAF grave in Yorkshire.

> With a sob of long-supressed and unresolved grief, I choked on the words 'Hi Dad, it's me, I'm here.' I found myself announcing my presence with the respect and homage of a long-separated son, oblivious to the rivulets of tears dripping from my cheeks. Time stood still . . . my mind was consumed in a maelstrom of emotions . . . an overwhelming feeling of warmth and dignity came over me . . . the releases of my long-repressed grief began to sweep away the disappointment and shame that had plagued me . . . I wiped the now drying tears from my face . . . I was alone in silence except the chirping of the birds and the rustling of leaves.

Utrecht, the Netherlands. The daughter of Robert Halberstadt is sorting out her mother's possessions before she moves into a care home. Her father was a Sergeant-Pilot, shot down and killed by the Japanese in Java in 1942. She was born after his death and never knew him.

> Right at the back of the drawer is a small old battered brown wallet . . . it contains some treasures; small, folded scraps of paper describing his love to my mother, lovingly kept and which surprisingly survived her prisoner-of-war camp years. I start to feel I am intruding, and I decide not to look any further. I am moved and excited at the same time . . . I take it to Mum, who stares at it for a long time. Memories must be chasing each other inside her head.
>
> I am holding his identity tag now. I had never known of its existence before . . . his posthumous daughter, I am holding this tag and chain in my hands and at this very moment I feel very close to a father I have never known. The last time he had held this tag was just prior to his death. Now I am holding it

Stan Scislowski, during the war and later on

in my hands. I have a very strange sensation that our hands are touching, and I feel choked. We have met . . . finally.*

Monte Cassino, Italy. Here, nearly 8,000 men are commemorated, British and Polish, Gurkhas and French, Canadians and New Zealanders. This is just one of thousands of meticulously maintained Commonwealth War Graves Commission cemeteries – some vast solemn lines of white crosses, others merely a handful of tombs. Canadian Private Stan Scislowski from the Perth Regiment, returned to Cassino in 1975.

> If I had not been here as a young Canadian soldier, it would have been impossible to believe that the hot rake of war had been dragged across this pleasant countryside. But I knew different. I had seen this place when the fields were red with poppies, and red where our boys lay in the awkward postures of sudden death. I knew this valley when it was crowded with smoke, and foul with the stink of long-dead bodies.
> Where there's now tranquillity, there was once a terrible bloodletting, a monstrous raging of man-made forces that

---

* Her father threw the identity tag out of his aircraft before he crashed into a rice paddy. He must have worried that it would disappear in the muddy depths of the paddy. Maybe a last goodbye to his wife?

EPILOGUE

seared and ravaged the towns and laid waste the valleys and the mountain slopes. Four long and agonizing months it was that the killing, the maiming, and the destruction went on. Nowhere could a soldier hide without tasting, hearing, and smelling the hot fetid breath of bursting shells and mortars... everywhere around him Death was present in the bloated remains of the long dead men and mules.

On this May day, 31 years later, as we walk in the bright sunshine down the gravel roadway leading to the cemetery the air is clean and refreshing and the flowers are in full bloom... the land is serene, and in every sense beautiful again. On entering the cemetery our eyes at once take in the wide spread of grave markers. A tightness comes to my throat. A sigh – almost a sob – escapes me, and I find it hard to hold back the tears.

Each of us, men and women alike, walk slowly along the rows of grave markers, pausing to read the descriptions thereon, looking for those we knew, buddies we had left behind in the tortured valley below Cassino town. There were widows and mothers amongst us who came to honour the memory of their loved one. As I paused to read the name on a stone bearing the Maple Leaf design I looked to the grave on my right and saw a woman, a touch of grey in her hair, kneeling beside the stone. A widow, a sweetheart, a sister? I don't know which. Her right hand rested on top of the of the stone where she had placed a short-stemmed rose. Her head was bent in prayer. She knelt there for perhaps five minutes and then, as she braced herself to stand, I saw teardrops kiss the flowers on his grave. Tears well upped in my eyes and I turned away...

Only my memory speaks. It brings me to that awful moment when Pete and Bob* died and how close I came to

---

* Sgt Pete McRorie and Cpl Bob Adair.

being killed along with them. Only a few seconds and a few scant feet, the difference between life and death . . . I think for a moment what their lives might have been if there had been no war – the years of love they missed and the families they would have raised. I walk slowly away, tears running down my cheeks.

For some dead in unknown Italian resting places there are no crosses.

They have no stone where wreaths of remembrance many be laid; yet their graves are everywhere. They are there on the mountain terraces and down in the gullies and ravines. Along rich fields of grain their graves might be, or where the grapes are grown. They are there by rush-choked streams and in the mud of riverbanks. The streets of towns and villages are their graves. The whole of Italy is their grave.*

---

* Stan Scislowski died in 2014 aged 90. Estimates of war dead vary, but at least 60 million died worldwide.

Bibliography

No doubt inspired by the BBC People's War, several contributors to that archive wrote books after The People's War project, some of them self-published. On the rare occasion that there was any difference between the two accounts, I have stuck to the testimonies published by the BBC. But all these memoirs provided a helpful reference point and may be of interest to readers.

Baynes, Len, *The Will to Live*, Pen and Sword, Barnsley, 2013
Hardy, Tim, *The Reluctant Imperialist*, Marshall Cavendish, Singapore, 2009
Hershel Nelson, William, *The Untold Story*, Athena Press, London, 2009
Palmer, James, *The Militia Boy*, Austin Macauley, London, 2018
Scislowski, Stanley, *Not All of Us Were Brave*, Dundurn Press, Toronto, 1997
Skarbek-Kruszewski, Zygmunt, *Bellum Nobiscum*, Skarbek Consulting, Australia

Several authors have written excellent books about multiple theatres in this war, an invaluable resource to anyone writing about this period. They include Anthony Beevor, Max Hastings, Jonathan Dimbleby, Saul David, Martin Middlebrook and James Holland.

Other helpful background guides included:
Gardiner, Juliet, *Wartime Britain*, Headline, London, 2004
Holmes, Richard, *Battlefields of the Second World War*, BBC Books, London, 2001
Parkes, Meg and Gill, Geoff, *Captive Memories*, Palatine Books, Lancashire, 2015
Michno, Gregory, *Death on the Hellships*, Pen and Sword, Yorkshire, 2001
Nicholson, Virginia, *Millions Like Us*, Viking, 2011
Parker, Matthew, *Monte Cassino*, Headline, London, 2003
Warner, Lavina and Sandilands, John, *Women Beyond the Wire*, Michael Joseph, London, 1982

Wynn, Neil A., *The African American and the Second World War*, Elek Books, London, 1976

I was also lucky to be able to draw on my earlier books, in particular:
Nagasaki: The Forgotten Prisoners, Mensch Publishing, London, 2022
Secret Letters: A Battle of Britain Love Story, Mensch Publishing, London, 2020

The Imperial War Museum, London and the Muntok Memorial Peace Museum, Banka Island, Indonesia were invaluable sources of information.

References

The overwhelming majority of the testimonies in this book are directly from the BBC People's War archive. Even if a contributor subsequently published their memoirs as a book, I have relied on their earlier contribution to the BBC because that is the framework for this book. However, I have included some short contributions from other sources for reasons of clarification or completeness:

CHAPTER TWO

Trudy and Curt Feige – BBC News, 28 January 2024

CHAPTER THREE

Ron Jervis – author interview, November 2024

CHAPTER FOUR

Geoff Myers – John Willis, *Secret Letters: A Battle of Britain Love Story*, Mensch Publishing, London 2020

Air Chief Marshal Hugh Dowding, Letter to the Secretary of State for Air, 16 May 1940

CHAPTER SIX

Tony Bartley letter to his father, *Smoke Trails in the Sky*, William Kimber, London, 1984

CHAPTER SEVEN

Derek Lang, *Return to St Valery*, Leo Cooper, London 1974

THE PEOPLE'S WAR

CHAPTER EIGHT

Alan Henderson – Interview with author, 1981
David Hunt – Esther Terry Wright, *Pilot's Wife's Tale*, Bodley Head, London, 1942
Geoff Myers – John Willis, *Secret Letters: A Battle of Britain Love Story*, Mensch Publishing, London 2020

CHAPTER FOURTEEN

Tom Conti – BBC News, 27 April 2013

CHAPTER SIXTEEN

Cedric Brown, *Suez to Singapore*, Random House, New York, 1942

CHAPTER TWENTY-ONE

Nini Rambonnet, *Stand to Attention, Bow, Stand Up*, Batavia Publishing, the Netherlands
Ron Bryer, *The White Ghosts of Nagasaki*, self-published, Yorkshire, 1997

CHAPTER TWENTY-EIGHT

Louis Baume, Imperial War Museum, London
Harry Silman/Imperial War Museum, quoted in Rosalind Hearder, *Keep the Men Alive*, Allen and Unwin, Australia, 2009

CHAPTER TWENTY-NINE

Douglas Capes and Jean Clarkson (edited by Ruth Marlee), *Thank You Darling*, unpublished manuscript

CHAPTER THIRTY-TWO

Richard Holmes, *Battlefields of the Second World War*, BBC Books, London, 2001

REFERENCES

CHAPTER THIRTY-EIGHT

Dwight Eisenhower, *Crusade in Europe*, Doubleday, New York, 1948
Anthony Beevor, 'An ugly carnival', the *Guardian*, London, 5 June 2009

CHAPTER FORTY

Hinderwell, North Yorkshire – Grant McKee, *Staithes: A Life Story*, 2QT, Yorkshire, 2023

CHAPTER FORTY-THREE

A.G. Allbury, *Bamboo and Bushido*, Robert Hale, London, 1955
E.S. Benford, *The Rising Sun on My Back*, Lane Publishers, 1997

CHAPTER FORTY-EIGHT

Ulric Cross – Stephen Bourne, *The Motherland Calls*, The History Press, London, 2012

CHAPTER FIFTY

William Laurence, *New York Times*, New York, 9 September 1945
Ron Bryer, *White Ghosts of Nagasaki*, self-published, Yorkshire, 1997
Claude Belloni – www.fukuoka14b.org

CHAPTER FIFTY-ONE

Mike Nellis – Louise Cordingley, *Echoes of Captivity*, High Winds Publishing, London, 2020
Gus Anckhorn – Peter Fyans, *Conjuror on the Kwai*, Pen and Sword, Yorkshire, 2016
Monica Littleboy – Felicity Goodall, *Voices from the Homefront*, David and Charles, Devon, 2006
Lionel Morris – Brian MacArthur, *Surviving the Sword*, Time Warner, London, 2005

Acknowledgements

First and foremost, many thanks to every single person involved in collecting this huge volume of remarkable testimonies. Not only those inside the BBC, led by Chris Warren, the founding-father of the BBC People's War project, but also the thousands of volunteers and supporters up and down the country who gave up their time to collect so many remarkable stories.

Of course, none of this would have been possible without the thousands of ordinary men and women who shared their wartime memories, often with candour and humour. I have spent so long with Jock, Phyllis, Len, Tim, Ron, Jim, Stan, John, William, Ronald, Douglas and Jean, Zygmunt and Marushka and hundreds of others, they have become like friends rather than distant names in a project that closed twenty years ago. Their courage, always expressed modestly, is remarkable. Britain is lucky to possess such a wonderful archive.

Thank you also to the relatives of these contributors for their help. Despite best efforts I could not find the families of all the leading participants, but I appreciated the support of Christine Buckley (daughter of Phyllis Briggs), Lisa Hudson (daughter of Len Baynes), Jerry Scislowski, Ruth Marlee (daughter of Douglas and Jean Capes) and George Skarbek (son of Zygmunt and Marushka) Thanks to Ron Jervis, still sprightly aged 98, and to Francois de Bourgoing and Carol Mallet for help in Normandy when researching D-Day.

Thanks to the excellent team at BBC Books/Ebury Publishing: Molly Maynard, Jessica Anderson, Anna Hervé, Antony Heller, Aslan Byrne, Ben Green and Bethany Stuart. But special

ACKNOWLEDGEMENTS

gratitude to Shammah Banerjee, my talented and thoughtful editor.

A book this ambitious does not spring out of nowhere. My previous four books, all published since 2020, have provided a strong platform for my biggest book yet. So, thanks to those who supported me on this journey, especially Christine Kavanagh, Patrick Kidd, Josette Bushell-Mingo, Robin Ellis, Meredith Wheeler, Lesley Clark, Louise Reynolds, Meg Parkes, the late Robert Myers, David Grossman, and The Blackheath Halls. But no one deserves greater thanks than my regular publisher, Richard Charkin at Mensch, who not only published my first four books but also helped get this one into print, even though it was for another publisher.

Last, but certainly not least, this was such a gargantuan task – 47,000 testimonies to be shaped into a narrative covering six years of war – that many readers will imagine an army of researchers beavering away on the People's War archive. In fact, the only other researcher on the book was Janet Willis, who I must thank not just for her painstaking research but for her shrewd and thoughtful observations as the manuscript evolved through different drafts. I was lucky to have Janet by my side.

John Willis, December 2024

Image Credits

All photos are from the BBC The People's War archive, except for the following:

CHAPTER TWO

Sgt Gordon 'Jock' Walker: Imperial War Museum

CHAPTER FOUR

Geoff Myers: courtesy of the Myers family

CHAPTER EIGHT

Sgt Denis Robinson: Battle of Britain Monument
Plane crash: Battle of Britain Monument
Commonwealth War Graves: photo taken by the author

CHAPTER TEN

Churchill tanks in the desert: Imperial War Museum

CHAPTER SIXTEEN

Phyllis Briggs: courtesy of her daughter, Christine Buckley

CHAPTER TWENTY-TWO

Stan Scislowski: courtesy of the Scislowski family

IMAGE CREDITS

CHAPTER TWENTY-NINE

Photos of Jean Clarkson: courtesy of her daughter Ruth Marlee

CHAPTER THIRTY-FOUR

1st Infantry Division in Anzio: Imperial War Museum

CHAPTER THIRTY-EIGHT

Head-shaving in Marseilles: Photo by Carl Mydans for Time Life/Getty Images

CHAPTER THIRTY-NINE

Ron Homes images and artwork: courtesy of Molycullen Central School/Leon Conroy

CHAPTER FORTY-ONE

GIs dancing: Photo by Hulton Deutsch/Getty Images

CHAPTER FORTY-TWO

7th Rajput Regiment in Burma 1943: Imperial War Museum

CHAPTER FORTY-THREE

Rayoku-Maru: Australian War Memorial, Canberra

CHAPTER FORTY-FOUR

Gliders and paratroopers landing: Photo by Sgt Dennis Smith/Imperial War Museum
Captured Waffen SS snipers: Photo by Sgt Dennis Smith/Imperial War Museum
Arnhem, 1944: Photo by Sgt Dennis Smith/Imperial War Museum
At Pinewood Studios after Arnhem: Photo by Jack Barker/Imperial War Museum

THE PEOPLE'S WAR

CHAPTER FORTY-FIVE

Crossing the Rhine: Photo by Sgt Dennis Smith/Imperial War Museum

CHAPTER FORTY-SIX

Typhus spraying: Photo by Sgt H Oakes/Imperial War Museum

CHAPTER FIFTY

Nagasaki bomb: Getty Images

CHAPTER FIFTY-ONE

Phyllis Briggs: courtesy of her daughter, Christine Buckley

EPILOGUE

Stan Scislowski: courtesy of the Scislowski family